0

A⊦

THE COMPLETE HANDLOADER

by John Wootters

Photos by the author unless otherwise indicated
Drawings by Lloyd P. Birmingham

OUTDOOR LIFE BOOKS, Danbury, Connecticut
Stackpole Books, Harrisburg, Pennsylvania

Published by

Outdoor Life Books
Grolier Book Clubs Inc.
Sherman Turnpike
Danbury, CT 06816

Distributed to the trade by

Stackpole Books
Cameron and Kelker Streets
Harrisburg, PA 17105

Produced by Soderstrom Publishing Group Inc.
Designed by Jeff Fitschen

Library of Congress Cataloging-in-Publication Data

Wootters, John.
    [Complete book of practical handloading]
    The complete handloader/by John Wootters; drawings by Lloyd P. Birmingham; photos by the author.
      p.   cm.
    Previously published as: The complete book of practical handloading. c1976.
    Includes index.
    ISBN 1–556–54036–1
    1. Handloading of ammunition.   I. Title.
TS538.3.W66 1988
   683.4'06—   88-12455
dc19   CIP

This book is lovingly dedicated to
JEANNIE
without whom it would never have been.

Contents

Preface to the Second Edition

Handloading ammunition is as distinctively American as baseball. Although common in this nation since the invention of self-contained cartridges, handloading has only recently begun to be an important pastime for shooters elsewhere. Even now, only a tiny minority of gunners reload their own ammunition in Canada, Australia, South Africa, Great Britain, and a few of the western European nations.

One reason that handloading didn't catch on elsewhere is that relatively few governments are comfortable with the knowledge that their citizens have free access to gunpowder, primers, and bullets and the tools and technology with which to assemble them into functional ammunition. Such freedom is of course unthinkable for the majority of the world's people, who may not even possess firearms.

Against that background, I'm proud that we Americans have the Bill of Rights Second Amendment, which guarantees our right to keep and bear firearms, and I'm proud of the shooting heritage that resulted. Since handloading is an integral part of that heritage, it can be regarded as one symbol of American liberty, and that is one of the reasons I've created this book. As I write this, the forces that would deprive us of our right to own and lawfully use guns are gathering strength for a fresh assault upon that right, via the public media, in the schools, and on Capitol Hill. Perhaps this book is a gesture of defiance to that movement. But I'd prefer to believe that it is an affirmation of my faith that the anti-gun movement will fail once more, and that Americans will forever enjoy the shooting sports, including handloading, as they have in the past.

I've been reloading my ammo for all purposes for so long that it's difficult to remember all those who helped me get started, and thus helped me write this book. Two of them were my mother and father, who encouraged my interests in shooting, firearms, and hunting almost from birth. Others, whom I never had the pleasure of knowing personally, were Col. Townsend Whelen, Phil Sharpe, and Earl Narramore, all authors who pioneered handloading literature and whose works are classics in the field today. A very important guy is Warrant Officer Frank W. Washam, U.S.M.C., with whom I jointly owned my first set of reloading tools, and who patiently endured my earliest efforts at writing about guns. Editor Neal Knox and publisher Dave Wolfe of *Handloader* magazine deserve special gratitude, as do the editors Alex Bartimo of *Shooting Times* and George Martin then of *Guns and Ammo*. These and many others helped to write this book without knowing it.

Most of all, my wife Jeannie must bear a part of the credit (or blame, as the case may be); she really wanted me to write the book, and cheerfully made sacrifices over the course of my career that made this book possible. In the final analysis, the publication of a book is an event of much greater importance to the author and those who suffered through its creation with him than to any reader. These acknowledgments are, therefore, superfluous to all whose names do not appear in them, and I know it well. Still, every author has emotional debts, and I'm relieved to get them off my chest. For the rest of the shooting world, I can only contribute what follows in the hope that it may prove useful.

John Wootters
Houston, Texas

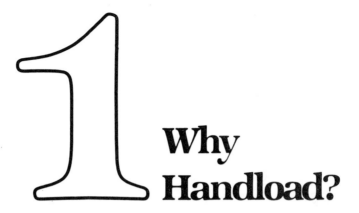

1 Why Handload?

andloading is the fastest-growing aspect of the shooting sports today. There was a time, not too many years ago, when a reloader was regarded as a practitioner of the occult, a dabbler in dangerous mysteries, and perhaps a bit of a nut, but the shooting public's attitude has changed. Today, to be a handloader is the "in" thing. A handloader should be respected as a knowledgeable shooter with something of an edge over his non-reloading brethren. Perhaps a faint aura of mystery still clings to the handloading hobby (which this book may help dispel), but shooters are joining up literally by the millions.

Estimates place the number of active reloaders today at more than three million, with an annual growth rate of about 10 percent. These people assemble and presumably fire more than one *billion* rounds of ammunition each year and spend about $50 million per year on their hobby. Handloading has come out of the dark ages!

ECONOMY

There must be reasons for this wholesale enlistment into the ranks of reloading, and there are—about as many different reasons as there are shooters. The one most commonly cited is economy, especially in this day of ever-increasing costs of everything, including ammunition. There's no doubt the reloader shoots more cheaply than his buddy who limits himself to factory-loaded ammo; a rifleman can assemble full-power hunting or target loads for about one-third the price of factory cartridges, and a gunner can save about two-thirds on shotshells as well. Pistoleros do even better; by purchasing components in volume and casting their own bullets, they can fire their

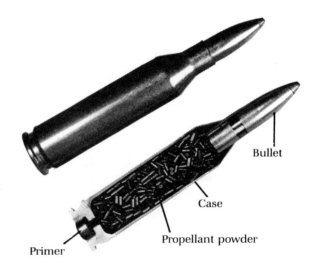

This cutaway view shows the four standard components of a metallic cartridge—casing, primer, propellant powder, and bullet. Of the four, only the casing is not expended or consumed. Reuse of this expensive brass is the foundation handloading.

big-bore revolvers and autoloaders for about the same cost as shooting factory loads in a .22 rimfire handgun.

Depending on the price of their reloading setup and the quantity of ammunition they shoot, reloaders can figure on amortizing the investment in tooling in anywhere from a few months to a year or two. This process can be hastened by joint ownership of the tools between two or more shooters. Several years ago, I helped five friends of mine set up a shotshell

A well-equipped reloading bench is a small ammunition factory. Here you can assemble the specialized cartridges for any kind, caliber, or gauge of firearm.

Nearly all calibers and kinds of sporting small-arms ammunition can be handloaded. Rimfire cartridges are not reloaded in the United States but are in some parts of Russia. Reloading dies are readily available for virtually every standard cartridge in history, as well as for most wildcats.

handload shoot more, and thus it's probably more realistic to say that a novice handloader will get to shoot perhaps three times as much for the *same* cost, rather than to say he'll save two-thirds on costs for factory-loaded cartridges.

REDUCED LOADS
FOR PRACTICE AND SMALL GAME

There are other reasons for entering the reloading game. One of the best is that a loading tool can be used like the accelerator pedal on a car, to speed up (at least to some degree) or slow down the machine according to the need of the moment. At one time, a shooter could purchase reduced-power loads in some calibers in factory ammo, but those days are gone forever. Nowadays, the shooter who confines himself to commercial ammunition has no choice but to run flat out, full throttle. Only by reloading can he adjust downward the power of his firearms.

So who wants to do a thing like that? Well, a man who has a young son or daughter coming along is wise to introduce the youngster to centerfire rifles or shotguns via light-kicking, quiet, reduced loads. They're more fun and less intimidating to shoot. The youngster is more likely to hit something (and thus enjoy himself earlier and more) and less likely to develop the dreaded flinch.

For that matter, there's no particular reason why a veteran shooter should have to use a full-power ammunition for paper-punching, plinking, and off-season practice. Such shooting is hardly ever at long range or at living targets that require a great deal of killing power. Why use more power than needed, especially when to do so is so much more expensive?

Certain kinds of wild game, in fact, are best shot with reduced loadings. In my home state of Texas,

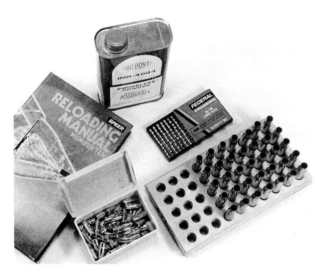

The essential components for metallic ammunition include bullets, cases, primers, powder and—perhaps most important—knowledge, as represented by the reloading manual at left.

reloading press. They agreed on a single loading that would serve for informal clay-bird busting and upland bird hunting, and purchased shot by the hundreds of pounds, plastic wads by the thousands, and powder 8 pounds at a whack. The press was mounted on a plywood base so that it could be moved from house to house and C-clamped to a kitchen table for use. The ammunition worked well, and these fellows ground out 20-gauge cartridges by the tens of thousands at a cost of about a dollar per box, plus an evening's time every few weeks.

I should add, however, that most shooters really don't save much money by reloading, for the simple reason that they shoot up their savings. People who

Acquisition and retention of competitive skill with the handgun requires so much practice that even a wealthy shooter usually finds the economy of handloads quite attractive.

Serious clay-target shooters usually reload for economy. Another reason is the ability make up light-kicking loads with which to introduce women or youngsters to shooting.

whitetail deer and wild turkey seasons run concurrently, and it's common to encounter turkeys while carrying a powerful centerfire rifle. With normal big-game loads, the hunter has his choice of passing up a turkey dinner or trying for a neck shot. Not even an expert can consistently bring off the neck shot on a gobbler at anything more than point-blank range, and if the bullet strays into the body the result is most depressing: the turkey looks as if it had been assaulted with a hand grenade.

The obvious and easy alternative for a reloader is a pocketful of specially prepared turkey loads with nonexpanding bullets moving at very modest velocities. These loads can be made up for any deer rifle and can usually be adjusted to conform with the same sight setting used for the full-power load. Such special loads in my shirt pocket have produced tasty turkey dinners for me innumerable times.

The reloader can take this process even further by loading down a deer-powered rifle for squirrel shooting. Such home-cast bullets destroy no more meat than a .22 rimfire. A chapter in this book is devoted to such loads.

That same deer rifle can, by handloading, be made even more versatile. A load adjustment may not make the rifle an ideal long-range varminter for shooting such pests as jackrabbits and woodchucks, but it may make it a surprisingly good one. And the souped up ammo lets you dust off the deer rifle between seasons. A set of reloading tools is a lot cheaper than a second, special-purpose rifle, too, although I'd never deny a shooter his excuse to buy a new gun. Handloading

can thus extend the versatility of a single rifle so that a hunter can enjoy it year-round. And this can improve instinctive handling skills when that big white-tail begins busting brush in November. There is simply no substitute for *shooting* as a means of developing and maintaining shooting skills. Reloading makes it easy, fun, and cheap.

HARD-TO-GET AND WILDCAT CALIBERS

Some people get into reloading because Uncle Bill willed them a rifle for which commercial ammunition is not available, or perhaps because the gun is chambered to some foreign, rare, or obsolete caliber. Handloading is the only way to provide safe, efficient ammo for such a rifle, and almost any cartridge that ever achieved any degree of popularity anywhere in the world can be made up by a skilled reloader. Dies for making the cases and assembling the ammo are available, and suitable components can be bought or made. In many cases, if one wants to shoot a war trophy rifle or an old buffalo gun, he *must* handload.

The same is true of what are called "wildcat" cartridges for rifles or handguns. These are nonstandard rounds that cannot be purchased in commercial form, a sort of design-it-yourself project for handloaders who have a ballistic itch they cannot scratch with anything offered by the major ammunition manufacturers. I'll have a lot more to say about wildcats in later chapters, but for now they must be added to the list of reasons for handloading.

Fresh factory ammuniton is not available for many obsolete calibers such as this Winchester 1886 chambered to .40/65 WCF. And old live ammo sometimes sells at collectors' prices. Here reloading is the answer.

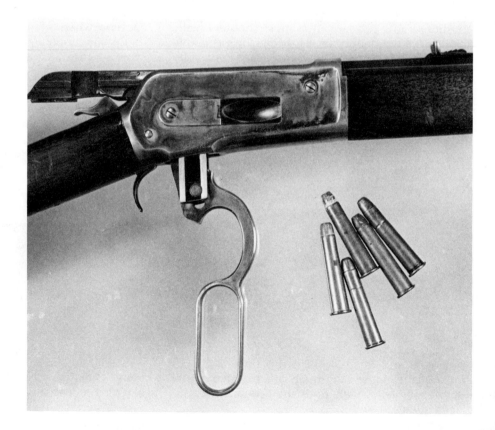

THE RIGHT BULLET FOR THE JOB

I think one of the biggest—and most overlooked—advantages in handloading, at least for big-game hunters, is the ability to select precisely the correct round for the game and hunting conditions expected. Not that the commercial ammo makers don't load reliable cartridges; they do, but their bullets must be compromises to cover shots on small whitetails in the thickets, on pronghorns at 400 yards, and on bull elk across a mountain meadow. The factory loads do a surprisingly good job, but the conscientious handloader can do better.

MORE POWER—SOMETIMES!

Many new reloaders tell me they became involved in handloading to increase the range, power, and accuracy of their rifles and shotguns. Unfortunately, their expectations are often exaggerated. With patience and much experimenting, they may improve a shotgun's patterning, which translates to more game in the bag, but they will not substantially increase velocity or "power." The same is true of most modern rifle cartridges; accuracy can almost always be improved, often dramatically, but it may not be possible to safely soup up velocities. On the other

Perhaps the biggest single advantage to reloading metallic ammo is the ability to select exactly the right bullet for the specific job at hand. These three premium-quality 7mm big-game hunting bullets, shown sectioned and recovered from game, illustrate major differences in interior construction. At left, the Bitterroot Bonded Core bullet has a pure lead core soldered to a thick jacket of pure copper tubing. The Nosler Partition at center has two cores separated by a jacket-material wall that retains the rear core under any circumstances. At right, the Speer Grand Slam has two cores of different hardnesses, plus several other features to ensure expansion with weight retention after impact.

Cartridges like these, for classic British double-barreled rifles, often cost more than $50 each, making plinking a bit expensive. From left, the cartridges are the .416 Rigby and the .476, .577, and .600 Nitro Expresses.

Competitive rifle games like Metallic Silhouettes, which require a combination of target accuracy and hunting power, are shot with handloaded ammo.

hand, with some of the older cartridges such as the .257 Roberts, 7 × 57mm Mauser, or .30/06, very significant increases in velocity, trajectory flatness, and terminal energies are possible in perfect safety, provided a sound, modern rifle is used.

ACCURACY

Serious accuracy fans, epitomized by the benchrest clan, are reloaders to a man, as are most varmint shooters. Again, the ammo factories make remarkably reliable and accurate ammunition, considering that they turn out cartridges by the millions that must function correctly in any rifle. The handloader, however, can determine the exact combinations of bullet, powder, and primer for his individual rifle and then take all evening if need be to assemble 20 rounds to approximately *zero* tolerances. Since uniformity is the name of the accuracy game, it's not surprising that rifle accuracy is so amenable to improvement through reloading.

BECAUSE IT'S FUN!

Most people who get into handloading discover that it is an absorbing and relaxing hobby in and of itself, rather than merely a means of feeding a rifle, pistol, or shotgun. It's a hobby without limits; a handloader can simply pick a suitable load out of a loading manual and assemble quantities of it without further ado, or he can pursue handloading into the most rarefied

realms of theoretical ballistics, concerning himself with J-factors, ballistic coefficients, expansion ratios, and other esoterica. And it's a satisfying game on every level. No engineering degree or grasp of differential calculus is required, but I've noticed that handloading appeals to many professionals who have such credentials.

A glance around the shooting club range will reveal that handloaders come from every walk of life. At one shooting bench, a Ph.D. may be taking lessons in reloading from a pipefitter, while a farmer, a doctor, and a ditchdigger look on and comment. Handloading is, by the way, historically a distinctively American pastime. In recent years, though, it's been spreading to a few other nations where people still have the freedom to own sporting firearms and purchase components.

Most serious handloaders are not only knowledgeable amateur ballisticians but also better-than-average marksmen, simply because they fire so many more rounds in a year than the fellows who buy commercial ammunition. They come to know their guns intimately and to understand their capabilities—and limitations—through extensive use. All this makes them deadlier in the hunting field or on the target range, which is not a bad reason in itself for handloading.

You may have other reasons not mentioned here; as I said, there are as many excuses for buying that first reloading tool as there are reloaders. But the first, last, and best reason I know is simply that handloading, in all its varied aspects, is great recreation.

Basic Ballistics

Handloaders are amateur ballisticians. The process of assembling your own ammunition either starts with a basic understanding of ballistics, or it eventually imparts that understanding through experience. Obviously, progress will be faster and satisfaction with your home-brewed loads will be greater if the grasp of ballistics comes first. Before going any further, then, let's take a look at the science of ballistics, which is the study of projectiles in motion.

The movement of a projectile is divided into three parts: *internal ballistics*, which takes place before the bullet or shot charge leaves the muzzle of the gun;

external ballistics, which describes the projectile's flight from muzzle to target; and *terminal ballistics*, which involves the stopping of the bullet.

I'll use terms dealing with the rifle here and assume that you'll infer the parallels with shotgun ballistics.

INTERNAL BALLISTICS

When the firing pin of a breechloading rifle falls, it strikes the face of the primer cup, indenting it enough to crush the primer pellet against its anvil and det-

The three stages of "ballistics"—interior, exterior, and terminal—can be thought of as beginning at the rear of a cartridge and moving forward. *Interior* ballistics begins with the detonation of the primer, which ignites the powder, building pressure to drive the bullet out of the barrel with a given velocity and energy. The *exterior* phase concerns the projectile in free flight as it overcomes air resistance and gravity. *Terminal* ballistics involves the dynamics of the bullet at the target.

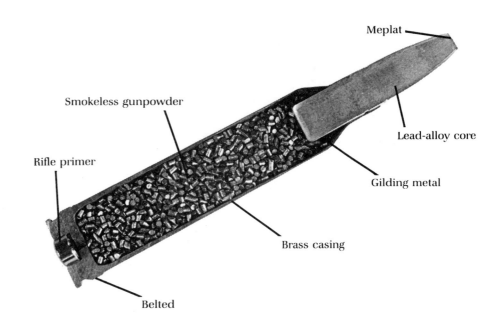

onate the mixture. Flame from this detonation passes through the flash hole in the bottom of the case's primer pocket and ignites the powder charge. Smokeless powder does not actually detonate, but burns very rapidly at a controlled rate, evolving large quantities of gas. This gas exerts pressure in all directions, but only the base of the bullet can be moved. Actually, the brass walls of the cartridge case also expand slightly, until stopped by contact with the steel firing chamber walls. Evolving powder gases also relax the tight grip by which the bullet is held in place in the neck of the cartridge.

Some few nanoseconds—as billionths of a second are called—are required to overcome the inertia of the bullet and to start it on its journey down the barrel. For the first few fractions of an inch this movement is free, but the bullet then strikes the inner barrel's spiral lands and grooves that make up the rifling. The rifling imparts a rotation to the bullet as it continues to accelerate up the bore, propelled by the still-increasing pressure of the gases now sealed behind it.

In most cartridges, this chamber pressure peaks by the time the bullet has moved a very few inches, and it then drops fairly rapidly as the bullet continues to move, increasing the volume of the sealed system behind it. In modern, high-intensity rifles, peak pressures routinely run as high as 65,000 pounds per square inch absolute (PSIA). However, in most reloading references, another system of measurement is more common than pounds per square inch absolute, and this is called "crusher pressure." I'll cover the technique for determining crusher pressure later,

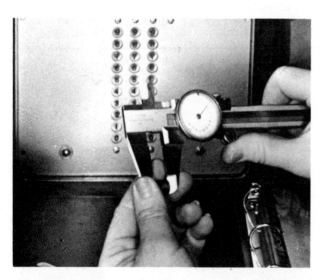

Shotshell pressures are determined in factories by firing in a special gun that permits the powder gases to drive a piston that compresses a precision lead slug. Measurement of the shortened slug, here with a dial caliper, indicates pressure in LUP (lead units of pressure). LUP and pounds per square inch absolute (PSIA) are not the same thing. Copper slugs are used for higher pressures in rifles and some handguns, yielding CUP (copper units of pressure).

but the units used are *copper units of pressure* (CUP) for rifles and handguns and *lead units of pressure* (LUP) for shotguns, in which normal peak pressures never exceed about 12,000 PSIA.

Although chamber pressures decline as the bullet moves along the bore of the gun, they remain high enough to impart continued acceleration to the projectile, and within certain limits, the longer the barrel, the higher the muzzle velocity will be.

EXTERNAL BALLISTICS

When the bullet departs the barrel, interior ballistics has ended. The bullet has been given a velocity, a kinetic energy, and it has been spun on its axis at a startling speed often exceeding 100,000 RPM with ordinary hunting bullets. At this point it becomes an unguided missile, and must contend with a whole new set of forces that conspire to slow it down, drive it off course, and pull it to earth. From here on, the bullet is on the exterior-ballistics leg of its journey.

A projectile has a couple of physical properties the handloader must know about to understand exterior ballistics. The most basic of these is called *sectional density* (SD), which is a mathematical description of bullet weight as related to its cross-sectional area. Of two bullets with identical diameter and nose shape and composed of the same materials, the longer one has the higher sectional density. The numerical expression of SD is derived by dividing the bullet's weight in pounds by the square of its diameter, in inches. Handloaders need not do the arithmetic often, however, since most bullet manufacturers publish the sectional densities of their products.

The importance of the SD concept is that the higher the sectional density, the harder the bullet is to stop and the more penetration it will achieve in any medium, if all else is equal, including air resistance.

The second property of importance is called the bullet's *ballistic coefficient* (BC), and this is related to the sectional density. Essentially, the BC is a mathematical expression of the shape of the projectile that expresses streamlining. A bullet of high BC slips through the atmosphere more readily than one with a lower BC and thus has a flatter trajectory and more retained velocity and energy at any range, if initial velocities were the same.

Actually, the ballistic coefficient of a bullet describes its ability to overcome resistance relative to a standard, experimental projectile, and the numbers are derived by multiplying the sectional density by a form factor which describes the shape of its nose (and heel, in the case of boat-tailed bullets). A long, sharp point on a bullet gives it a higher BC than a blunt profile. A round ball, such as a shotgun pellet or a ball from a muzzleloading rifle, has the poorest possible ballistic shape, as well as the lowest possible sectional density.

Thus SD and BC are critical to the handloader of rifle and pistol ammo because they determine the performance of a bullet in flight.

Bullets of similar shapes and made of the same materials always have similar sectional densities, regardless of caliber. At near left are .45 and .38 bullets whose sectional densities are identical: .140. At right are .30 190-grain and 7mm 160-grain boat-tailed bullets of similar shapes and closely similar sectional densities—.286 and .284, respectively.

These five bullets, despite their varied appearance and diameters, all possess similar ballistic coefficients (BC's). From left they are: 100-grain 6.5mm (BC .294), 100-grain .270 (BC .291), 500-grain .458 (BC .297), 170-grain .321 (BC .291), and 220-grain .358 (BC .299).

"Ballistic coefficient" means streamlining. All 180-grain .30s, these four bullets have identical sectional density but radically different ballistic coefficients due to different shapes. From left, the round-nose's BC is .312, that of the flat-point is .361, the flat-based spitzer's is .474, the boattail's BC is .535. The higher the number, the more efficiently the projectile overcomes air resistance, resulting in flatter trajectory and higher retained energy.

Despite differing shapes, weights, and calibers, these projectiles exhibit almost the same sectional density. They are (from left) a 250-grain .358 (SD .279), a 270-grain .375 (SD .275), a 400-grain .457 (SD .272), a 154-grain .284 (SD .273), a 180-grain .308 (SD .277).

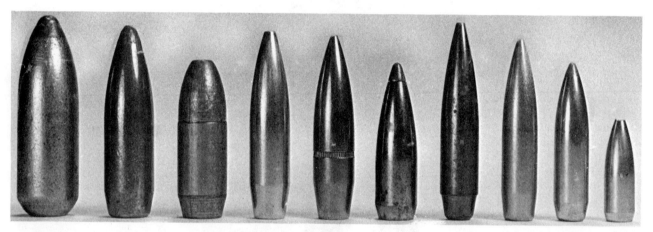

A tapered heel, or "boat tail," is sometimes used to improve the ballistic coefficient of spitzer bullets for target-shooting and hunting across the full range of calibers, as shown here. The third bullet from left is actually a boat-tailed cast bullet, poured into a copper-tubing jacket, and the fourth from right is called a "rebated boat tail." From left, calibers are .45, .375, .375, .30, .30, .30, 7mm (.28), .264, .25, and .22.

As the projectile is launched from the muzzle, two things happen to it immediately. It begins to lose velocity as it encounters air resistance, and it begins to fall toward earth as the force of gravity is applied. The greater the initial velocity and the higher its ballistic coefficient, the farther from the muzzle the projectile will get before these two factors bring it to earth. The rate of loss of velocity is quite rapid, but the bullet always falls downward at exactly the same rate, with or without forward motion.

Although the loss of *velocity* is quite rapid, the loss of the bullet's rotational speed is negligible, and it strikes the target at any ordinary range with about the same RPM it had on leaving the muzzle. In fact, if fired straight up, the bullet will come to a dead stop and fall back to earth, still spinning. This factor has little effect on exterior ballistics, but it does have an effect on the bullet's performance upon impact, which I will describe later.

As a bullet flies toward the target, it is subject to a lateral force from wind and will drift away from its line of departure from the bore. The amount of lateral displacement of the point of impact depends upon the velocity and angle of the wind, of course, and upon the difference in *time-of-flight* (TOF) of the actual bullet under the actual atmospheric conditions fired and the theoretical time-of-flight of the same bullet when fired in a vacuum.

A .22 rimfire high-speed bullet fired in a crosswind may actually drift more than an identical bullet at standard velocity, because the faster slug happens to be supersonic while the standard-speed one is traveling below the speed of sound. The "lag time" (difference between actual TOF and TOF in a vacuum) is greater for the supersonic projectile; so the wind-drift is greater. Although this all sounds very complicated, and indeed is, the effect on the handloader is rather simple; just pick a bullet with the highest practical ballistic coefficient. Just as it will show less drop over a given range, so will it be less subject to wind-drift.

Gyroscopic stability of a bullet in flight is another aspect of exterior ballistics. The spin imparted to the bullet by the rifling tends to keep it flying point forward. Proper stability depends upon the rate of rifling twist, muzzle velocity, and the length of the bullet itself. In general terms, a given rifling twist can be exactly right for only one style of bullet at one velocity, but from a practical viewpoint, a compromise twist can usually be made to stabilize a fairly wide range of bullet weights (lengths) at least adequately. A heavier (longer) slug requires a quicker twist than a lighter (shorter) bullet and, if bullet weight remains the same, a lower velocity requires a quicker twist. Since overstabilization is a lesser sin than understabilization, most compromise twists tend toward the quicker side, at least in calibers where relatively heavy bullets are commonly used.

An example of this matter of rifling twist rate is found in the early results with two competitive cartridges, the .243 Winchester Center Fire (WCF) and the .244 Remington. Bullet diameter in the two calibers was the same. But the .243 rifles had a 1-turn-in-10-inch rifling rate because Winchester envisioned the round as a combination deer-and-varmint number and wished to stabilize the heavier bullets that might be employed on whitetails. Remington saw the .244 as a pure varminter, and produced rifles with a 1-turn-in-12-inch twist for best accuracy with the lighter slugs. Winchester's concept proved to be in agreement with that of the general public, and the .244 soon fell by the wayside in the marketplace. Remington discontinued chambering rifles for the .244 and reintroduced the identical cartridge under the designation 6mm Remington, in rifles with a 1-turn-in-9-inch rifling.

A custom-barreled 7mm Mauser rifle of mine illustrates the relationship of twist rate, velocity, and bullet length in another and unique way. The rifling is exceptionally slow for the caliber, only 1 turn in 12 inches. Hornady happens to make two different 7mm bullets weighing 154 grains but having different shapes: one is round-nose while the other is a spitzer and, therefore, considerably longer. The round-nose consistently shoots the smaller group average from this rifle of any bullet I've yet tried, whereas the pointed slug scatters holes all over the paper.

In this case, the weight of the two bullets is identical, as is velocity. Only the lengths of the two projectiles differ, but it is a decisive difference. I can, in fact, select bullet designs for this particular rifle with a caliper. Any that do not exceed that 154-grain Hornady round-nose in length will be accurate, but any longer projectiles will be a waste of powder and time.

I once tried to develop a low-velocity turkey load in a certain wildcat rifle of 6.5mm caliber, using the Norma 139-grain full-jacketed target bullet. This is a long, sharp, boattailed slug, and there was a low-end velocity that opened shot groups badly and produced oval-shaped bullet holes in the target paper, a sure sign that the bullets were wobbling or yawing upon impact. Accuracy was excellent at velocities of 2,600 feet per second (FPS) or better, but when I reduced the powder charge to produce speeds below that figure, results quickly went to hell. If I could have magically changed the twist rate in that barrel to a quicker

one, no doubt I could have achieved the 2,000-FPS turkey load I wanted.

I hope the above experiences clarify the relationships between rifling twist rate, velocity, and bullet length, for they are important.

An interesting sidelight on this matter of stability is that a bullet usually does not "go to sleep" or stabilize perfectly for quite a few yards after it has left the muzzle. This phenomenon is commonly seen when measuring muzzle velocities by firing through paper chronograph screens. The screens will show slightly oval holes, indicating the bullet was still yawing, yet the same bullet at 50 yards will print a perfectly round hole. Occasionally, this tendency will produce a handload that delivers better groups, in terms of minutes of angle (MOA), at 100 yards than at 25 yards. The tendency is most pronounced with fairly long, heavy bullets at moderate velocities.

TERMINAL BALLISTICS

The last stage in the bullet's journey, terminal ballistics, occurs after impact with the target. This area is of interest principally to hunters, since target shooters could care less how hard their bullets strike the backstop after passing through the paper.

A hunting bullet still has most of its work to do once it hits a game animal. If the target is a groundhog, the bullet must expand explosively and minimize ricochets. If it's a deer, both expansion and penetration are important, and if it's an African elephant, penetration is the supreme criterion of success. Much of this performance is built into the bullet itself, which I will deal with later, but what makes the bullet work is the velocity, and resulting kinetic energy, when it strikes. Kinetic energy (essentially the weight of the bullet multiplied by the square of its velocity) may or may not be a direct measurement of killing power; that has been the subject of argument since the late 19th century. But it does give us an adequate *comparative* measurement of various bullets at various velocities. Note the importance of velocity in that formula above; its *square* is used, which means that the faster the bullet is traveling, the harder it hits. And that means a slug with a high ballistic coefficient hits harder than one with a lower BC at the same range.

The instant an expanding bullet strikes the body of an animal, its nose shape changes very rapidly, and with it the ballistic coefficient, since that number depends upon the bullet's form. Note now, though, that the sectional density changes only as the cross-sectional area of the nose becomes larger. Assuming for the moment that all expanding bullets expand at about the same rate and to the same degree upon impact with similar targets, you can see the importance of the basic sectional density characteristic. If all else is equal, the bullet with the highest sectional density will penetrate most deeply. In the case of non-expanding, steel-jacketed bullets for use on the heaviest African game, sectional density is almost a direct linear measurement of lethality, that is, assuming velocities are similar.

ENERGY AND TRAJECTORY

Kinetic energy is usually expressed in terms of footpounds (FP), and that terminology will be used throughout this book. A bullet is carrying a certain number of foot-pounds of energy when it strikes, but it is also spinning, remember. A good deal of controversy has arisen over whether this rotational energy has a significant effect on penetration of a game animal, and some fairly hairy special rifles and cartridges have been put together to test the matter. But simple calculations can show that a bullet's spin, even if it stopped in the animal's body, could not apply more than 4 or 5 foot-pounds of energy, as contrasted to from 1,500 to 3,000 or more FP delivered by the forward motion of the same bullet.

However, an often overlooked factor is that the spin of the bullet, which is practically undiminished at impact, represents very great centrifugal forces acting to help expand the bullet as its physical integrity is disrupted. For this reason, experiments in bullet expansion conducted by firing them into recovery media at reduced velocities to simulate long-range impacts must be regarded with suspicion, since slowing down the bullet also greatly reduces its RPM.

This has been a very simplified—some may say "oversimplified"—discussion of ballistics, but it may serve to relate certain important concepts if you are a beginning handloader and help you visualize all that takes place between the fall of the firing pin and the impact of the bullet.

Here, now, is the great secret to becoming a ballistician without benefit of computers, slide rules, or laboratory equipment. All you really need is a cheap plastic ruler, a rifle, and a batch of handloaded cartridges. You take all three out to the range and fire a group, holding dead center on the bull's-eye (with a properly zeroed rifle) at 100, 200, and 300 yards, and farther if possible. Then you walk up to each target and with the ruler, measure the distance between the group center and the center of the bull. Presto—you have determined the trajectory of your handload at least as accurately as any computer could have done it. If there was a wind blowing and you can make a fair estimate of its speed and angle, you will also have determined the "wind-bucking" qualities of the load, at least to the ranges fired.

If you wish, you can use the drop data you have accumulated to make a graphic plot of the trajectory on regular (not logarithmic) graph paper, compressing the scales for convenience by using one small square for 5 or 10 yards horizontally and 1 inch vertically. Select a line-of-bore (sometimes called "line-of-departure") and plot the measured drops at the various ranges below it. Now you can sketch in the actual path of the bullet, either using a French curve or roughly freehand, and extrapolate it at least another 100 or so yards.

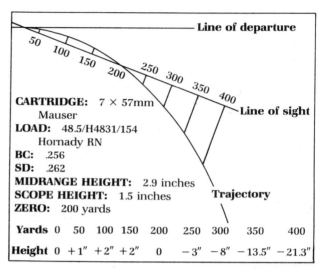

CARTRIDGE:	7 × 57mm Mauser							
LOAD:	48.5/H4831/154 Hornady RN							
BC:	.256							
SD:	.262							
MIDRANGE HEIGHT:	2.9 inches							
SCOPE HEIGHT:	1.5 inches							
ZERO:	200 yards							
Yards	0	50	100	150	200	250	300	350	400
Height	0	+1″	+2″	+2″	0	−3″	−8″	−13.5″	−21.3″

As discussed in text below, slide rule ballistic calculators can help you develop trajectory graphs like this one. This diddling can substitute for some preliminary test firing.

Next, draw a line-of-sight, beginning about 1½ inches above the origin of the line-of-bore, to represent the difference between the mounted scope and the axis of the bore, to cross your trajectory at whatever distance at which you intend to zero the rifle with at load. Now, you can actually measure the path of the bullet above or below the line-of-sight at any distance, remembering to measure perpendicular to the line-of-sight.

Since most popular reloading manuals include very comprehensive ballistics tables today, the above exercise may not be as valuable as it once was. But I still recommend it, especially to the beginning reloader, if only because it gives him such a clear mental image of a bullet's trajectory. He may be startled at just how rapidly even the flattest-shooting cartridge actually drops at hunting ranges, and he can use his ruler to play with various possible zero points to see how the trajectory can apparently be flattened by proper sighting-in, and by the use of a telescopic sight. And if he goes to the trouble of constructing similar trajectory charts for blunt- and sharp-snouted bullets of the same caliber and velocity, he will see very graphically the value of a good ballistic coefficient.

Such charting can be done without actually firing a shot, through the use of a cardboard device called the Speer Ballistics Calculator, which resembles a slide rule. By following the simple directions with care, very accurate trajectory graphs can be drawn for bullets of various weights, BCs, and velocities. For example, you might determine that, in a given cartridge, a heavier bullet might be flatter-shooting at long ranges, due to its better BC, than a lighter slug even though the latter could be launched at much higher velocity. Such theoretical diddling can be fascinating, and, better than that, it can save a lot of money for components, as well as time on the target range and at the loading bench.

3

Planning The Load

There is no such thing as the perfect rifle, spouse, automobile, or dog. And neither is there a perfect handload. Every combination of components that goes into a round of handloaded ammunition is necessarily a set of compromises. For example, maximum power and maximum accuracy in a rifle or pistol load usually work against each other, just as top velocities and optimum patterning do in a handloaded shotshell. The cheapest load is never the most efficient hunting load. The lowest-recoiling practice, plinking, and small-game load very rarely delivers at point of impact relative to the full-power big-game load, which will permit the identical sight-setting. And so it goes; any handload represents a series of trade-offs, ideally approaching the handloader's goals.

COMPROMISES, COMPROMISES

There are several characteristics that must be juggled to achieve the goal. In metallic (rifle and handgun ammunition) cases, some of them are: high velocity, which contributes to flatness of trajectory and high-impact energies; bullet selection, which contributes to the same things, plus accuracy and expansion on game; high accuracy; low cost; low-recoil and noise levels; and compatibility with a particular firearm. Or perhaps the reloader has acquired a large quantity of cases, bullets, or powder that he wishes to use up. Then of course, his purpose may be the opposite of *high* velocity; he may be seeking a *specific* velocity level of, say, 2,000 FPS for turkeys.

In shotshells, you have to try to balance velocity and patterning percentages in a given gun's choke against costs and another factor not encountered much in loading metallic ammo: production speed and ease. Rifle cartridges for hunting or target are rarely assembled in batches of more than 20 to 60 rounds at a sitting, so varying components doesn't alter the rate at which the batch can be completed. But shotgun shells are expended in much greater numbers, whether on clay targets or gamebirds, and most handloaders of shotshells measure their production rates in terms of boxes per hour. Some loading tools are capable of producing many hundreds of cartridges per hour.

High output demands standardization of components, especially wads, and most tools are set up strictly for the one-piece plastic wad columns, which incorporate an over-powder sealing cup, a spacing and cushioning element, and a shot-protector cup, all in the same unit. A reloader with a specific purpose in mind for a given load may very well discover that these plastic wads, while convenient and fast, do not deliver the exact performance he is seeking. Instead, he'll choose to put together a "built-up" wad column composed of several separate pieces. This means making many more hand motions in loading a single cartridge, and cutting his production rate to half or less of the rounds per hour his tool is capable of producing. Again, he has to decide upon his priorities: Is the gain in performance worth an extra evening or two at the loading bench?

Although experienced reloaders know of these necessary compromises, it's amazing how few of them take the trouble to solve the problem in the quickest and most satisfactory manner—unless they happen to be professional engineers and thus are accustomed to the process of sitting down and writing out a set of specifications!

Planning a pronghorn load begins, as it does for any hunting round, with bullet selection. The load must be flat-shooting and accurate.

This should be the first step in developing any sort of handload for any kind of gun. The idea is that you can't know when you've arrived if you don't know exactly where you wanted to go in the first place.

For illustration, let's examine the case of a hunter who plans his first hunt for pronghorn in Wyoming and intends to use his own handloads (naturally!). He figures that he has to be prepared for a very long shot at a target no bigger than the average whitetail deer. Furthermore, since that target is a living creature, it's crucial that the bullet be capable of a quick kill. His rifle is chambered for the .270 WCF (Winchester Center Fire) cartridge, one of the best for such shooting.

This fellow (let's call him Joe) can nose around in the reloading manuals and pick a load formula at random, hoping it'll work on pronghorn, or he can go about it in a bit more organized fashion, selecting his performance criteria in advance and deciding on the compromises he's willing to make to achieve his goals.

First comes bullet selection, as it nearly always does regardless of the purpose of the load. This must be a bullet designed for big game; obviously, a non-expanding target bullet or one intended to explode on a jackrabbit is unsuitable. Second, it must be a bullet with a high ballistic coefficient, to flatten the trajectory and retain high terminal energy at long range. Third, it must be accurate in his particular rifle at more or less maximum velocities, and, fourth, its weight must allow adequate velocity. A tall order? You bet, but that's one of the virtues of this handloading business; such bullets exist, and can be found by the reloader for almost any set of specifications. The beginner may be bewildered by the vast array of .270 slugs on the market today, but the chances are the reloader with a little experience already has some "book" on bullets of various makes in his own rifles.

In any case, let's say Joe decides on the 130-grain Hornady Spire Point bullet for his pronghorn load. This one meets all his requirements, plus it has a reputation for slightly better than average expansion at long ranges where velocities have dropped below normal. Whether it will be accurate in his particular .270 cannot be predicted. All rifles are individuals, and only testing can determine their tastes in bullets. Assuming the Hornady passes that test, the load planning can proceed. The bullet/rifle combination must be capable of hitting a pronghorn in the vital chest area with every shot at, say, 300 yards with a perfect hold, and that means grouping within about a 12-inch circle at that particular range.

That's really not a very demanding standard. In fact, most combinations should do twice that well, but it gives Joe a specific way of knowing when his handload has achieved the accuracy necessary for his upcoming hunt in Wyoming.

With the bullet selection finished, Joe interests himself in velocity, since this will be his only other key to flatness of trajectory and terminal energy. In this instance, the more the better. He can peek into the Hornady *Handbook of Cartridge Reloading*, Vol. III, and discover that the 130-grain slug can be launched at about 3,200 FPS from a 24-inch barrel. He can then turn to the ballistic tables and read off the flight characteristics of this bullet at this velocity. The drop figures presented here are drop below *line-of-sight*, and therefore represent actual bullet path. He will see that if he zeroes the load at 200 yards, his bullet will be 1.3 inches high at 100 yards and 6.1 inches low at 300. If he zeroes at 300 yards, his slug will be 3.4 inches high at 100 yards and 4.1 inches high at 200, dropping 9.9 inches at 400 yards. If he intends to limit his shooting at a pronghorn buck to about 300, it's obvious that this bullet at this velocity has plenty of trajectory for a clean kill without much, if any, holdover at any range.

Since these same figures are given for the same bullet at all feasible velocities, he can also determine the trajectories that will result if he fails to achieve the full 3,200 FPS suggested by the loading data.

At this point, the load is taking final shape on paper. Joe has the right bullet in mind, and knows the velocity range within which it will deliver the desired performance if he does his part in aiming and squeezing.

Now for the compromises. Cost, recoil, and muzzle blast will be traded off in a serious big-game hunting load for the necessary trajectory, power, and accuracy.

The criteria for this particular load are fairly simple. Joe must achieve at least a 12-inches-at-300-yards grouping with the Hornady bullet, and he wants a velocity as close to 3,200 FPS as is practical and safe in his rifle. If he can beat that accuracy figure, so much the better, because it will allow for a little more aiming error in the excitement of the hunt. But he has avoided adoption of some such vague description as "good enough" by writing down his specs before sitting down at the loading bench.

I will explain the actual development and testing of the load in Chapter 10. In the meantime, let's take a look at the problems of Joe's buddy, Jack, whose ship has come in and who is therefore planning an African safari.

PLANNING A LOAD FOR AFRICA

Jack wants to bust a couple of Cape buffalo, an elephant, and maybe a lion, and he has bought a rifle chambered for the .458 Winchester Magnum cartridge. Obviously, Jack's concerns are wholly different from Joe's since the heavy, dangerous game is always shot at the closest possible range, and since these beasts are not easy to drop even with the mighty .458. Jack's accuracy standards will not be high—say, minute-of-buffalo, instead of minute-of-angle—but he is preoccupied with delivering the very maximum of smashing power possible, and is prepared to sacrifice everything else for it, including cost, pleasant recoil sensation, and muzzle blast. Since he will probably wish to use soft-point bullets on the lion and will surely choose the so-called "solid" full-metal-cased ones for elephant, he will write into his specifications that both types of bullets have the same point of impact with the same sight setting.

Jack might go again to Hornady, which makes 500-grain .458 bullets of both types (I am aware of no other custom bulletmaker, except Barnes Bullets, that does). His main interest in testing will be development of maximum short-range energies, and a similar point of impact of both bullet styles. As always, the more accuracy, the better, but Jack will not trade off 1,000 foot-pounds of energy for an inch better grouping at 100 yards. A Cape buffalo is a big target, compared to Joe's pronghorn, and the buff is quite likely to shoot back if not walloped properly with the first round.

Criteria for success with a .458 Winchester Magnum handload for the African "Big Five" are totally different from those for the pronghorn load. Here the emphasis is on power and penetration.

VARMINT LOADS ARE DIFFERENT

Another reloader, John, couldn't care less about Cape buffalo, but gets his kicks from clobbering groundhogs at extended ranges. For this purpose, he has acquired a new, heavy-barreled .22/250 Remington rifle with a 24-power scope. Let's see how he writes his load specs.

First, last, and always, the varminter is after accuracy. He may write down a minimum requirement of 1-inch groups at 100 yards, or perhaps even smaller since he'll be shooting at such small targets. John will sacrifice all else (except safety) for accuracy.

Other characteristics are also very important to the varmint shooter. He needs the flattest possible trajectory and also the smallest possible wind-drift characteristics in order to score consistently. He also prefers minimum recoil because he knows that any rifleman can do better precision shooting when he isn't being belted every time he pulls the trigger. Minimum muzzle blast counts too because loud reports make farmers nervous, and the woodchucks John likes to shoot live on the farmer's property. For the same reason, John is concerned about ricochets; bouncing bullets, whining across the landscape, make farmers extremely nervous.

Again, bullet selection comes first. John may discover that his new rifle does best with Speer's 52-grain hollow-point bullet, or perhaps Nosler's Solid Base slug of the same weight. These are famed for accuracy and reliable blow-up upon impact, although others on the market also have a good reputation.

John Varminter must now begin to compromise. If he knows his business, he will not be surprised to discover that he receives the very finest of gilt-edged accuracy with the bullet moving at something less than maximum muzzle velocity. He trades off a bit of trajectory for an increment of accuracy, getting a slightly lighter recoil sensation and a bit less blast into the bargain. Power is of no importance to John, whereas it was of supreme importance to Jack, the African safarist.

OTHER LOADS

Another reloader may want a turkey load for his deer rifle. He'll need a bullet that will not expand and a low muzzle velocity of about 1,800 to 2,000 feet per second, plus a point of impact that is at least usable with the standard zero of his rifle for the big-game load.

Another man who has a boy coming along and wants to do a lot of off-season practice shooting is likely to put economy at the top of his specification list. He'll pick a cast bullet, which he will mold himself, and will choose a powder charge that not only delivers moderate velocity (and kick and blast) but will also allow him to extract more rounds of ammunition from a pound of powder. He'll have to give up a bit of accuracy, more than likely, and will surely have to change his sight setting, but that's an easy

Accuracy, flatness, and wind resistance are the keys to a good long-range varmint load. Intelligent load planning ensures success with the minimum of components, time, and money.

compromise. He'll get to shoot maybe 100 rounds for the price of a box of 20 factory cartridges, plus a little more work in making his own bullets.

SHOTGUNNERS HAVE OPTIONS TOO

A shotgunner will, of course, have an entirely different set of criteria for his proposed handload, and a somewhat different set of compromises to make. Velocity is not so critical in shotshells, within broad limits, but patterning is of supreme importance. With most shotshell reloads, this is where the written specifications list will start.

A goose hunter wants 80 percent or better patterns for killing effectiveness at long range, whereas the quail hunter looks for wide, uniform patterns with small shot at 30 yards. The target shooter loads his practice ammo for maximum density and uniformity to break his clays at target ranges. But he'll shoot so many of these loads that the price per shell and production rate can become important to him.

A father who wants to introduce his offspring (male or female; girls love to shoot, too!) to the joys of scattergunning will be wise to load light shot charges at very moderate velocities to reduce recoil to a minimum for early training. He always wants the best possible patterns, just as any rifleman likes to see smaller groups than his specs called for, but Dad will gladly trade pattern efficiency in this case for soft re-

coil and an enthusiastic young shotgunner.

The important lesson is that any handload should be carefully thought out in advance, regardless of its purpose or the type of firearm used. This need not necessarily be done on paper, but I often find that forethought helps clarify my thinking, especially with loads in which two or more characteristics are almost equally important and a balance of performance levels must be struck. Otherwise, the process of developing and testing a new load has a way of wandering off into irrelevant channels or focusing upon features of the load that do not really count in its overall efficiency.

This results, usually, in a great deal of wasted time both at the bench and on the range, not to mention the cost of components expended to no particular purpose. Furthermore, launching a load-development project without specific criteria can lead to a futile effort to maximize *all* performance characteristics, and it can becloud the necessity of making intelligent compromises.

Worst of all, failing to plan a load in specific terms deprives the handloader of the sense of accomplishment that comes with realizing the goal has been achieved. As I said before, you can't know you've arrived if you don't know where you are supposed to go. Planning a handload is like marking off a road map, detailing not only the destination but the route by which you expect to get there. In the long haul, "planning your load and loading your plan" is sure to add greatly to your reloading pleasure.

4 Brass

When you hear a reloader use the word "brass," he's usually referring to the cartridge cases in which he assembles his handloads. These cases are made of brass as a matter of course, although various other metals such as steel and aluminum have been employed experimentally or in wartime when brass supplies were limited.

Because rifle and pistol cases are entirely of brass, they are called "metallic" cases. Actually, shotshell cases were once made of brass too, but brass shotshells are rarely reloaded today. Modern shotshells are of paper or plastic, with or without some metal portions, and they are not considered metallic cases. At this point it's best to separate metallic and shotshell reloading, so I'll devote the next several chapters to the metallics. In general, what is said of rifle cases also applies to those used in revolvers and pistols.

I'll cover those differences in the chapters on handgun reloading.

Cartridge brass is an alloy composed of about 70 percent copper and 30 percent zinc. Some common American brands may reveal a trace of silver, and alloy proportions may vary by a few tenths of a percent. The reloader may encounter many handgun cases and a few rifle cases with a plating of nickel, but they're still brass and are treated as such in all reloading procedures.

A brass case has two fundamental jobs. It provides a durable and convenient package to contain the other components of a cartridge for safe and easy handling, and it seals the breech of the firearm against the rearward escape of powder gases during firing. It performs the latter task by expanding as the chamber pressure mounts and clinging to the walls of the

The anatomy of a metallic cartridge.

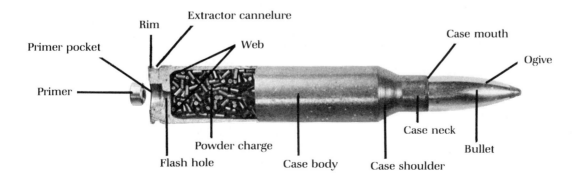

chamber tightly enough to prevent gases from flowing backward around the case.

It was the discovery of the ability of brass to do these jobs that made practical the first successful breechloading firearms and, of course, the earliest repeaters other than muzzleloading revolvers. Although metals technology has made fantastic strides during the century or so in which brass has been used for centerfire cartridge cases, brass has yet to be improved upon. The general characteristics of the brass case have changed little since the universal adoption of Boxer primers in this country.

Speer-Omark, a company well-known among reloaders for Speer bullets and CCI primers, introduced a line of loaded ammunition, both rimfire and centerfire. Subsequently, the line was expanded to include several common handgun cartridges in all-*aluminum* casings. Aluminum cases are considerably cheaper than brass ones, making it possible to sell them for less. However, although perfectly safe and satisfactory for one-time use in low-pressure cartridges, they cannot be reloaded.

Besides the dull silvery appearance, these CCI "Blazer" cases are headstamped with an "N" and an "R" on opposite sides of the primer, meaning "Not Reloadable." Don't reload them!

It's possible that a reader might come across a few rifle cases with what appear to be stainless-steel heads and brass bodies—which is exactly what they are. These are called "Steelheads" by the firm that makes them, O'Connor Rifle Products, and they're two-piece cases that actually screw together. The manufacturer claims Steelheads will stand firing pressures that sound more than a little hairy to me, but I'm sure the manufacturer has run tests that substantiate the claims. However, whether this idea represents the handloading revolution claimed and/or the thrust of future technology, it is at this writing too new for thorough evaluation. In any event, there are more consequences associated with high pressures than just high velocities, and most of them are considered negative in the light of *today's* technology.

Steelheads are quite expensive, so it's unlikely you'll acquire any great quantity of them secondhand. Should you do so, I recommend that you contact the maker for more information; certainly, remarks and instructions that follow do not necessarily apply to them in any way.

I should add that brass cases made handloading possible, since the case is changed very little in the process of firing. It is the only one of the components of a cartridge that is not consumed or expended when the cartridge is fired, and this is fortunate, since the case is by far the most costly of those components. The ability to reuse the case five, ten, or fifty times is the principal source of the savings on ammunition possible through handloading. When a shooter of factory ammunition ejects an empty case and leaves it lying on the ground, it is as though he took 25 to 50 cents (depending on the cartridge) out of his pocket and pitched it into the grass. That's why chronic reloaders get sore backs from sniping discarded cases on a public range. Professional hunters in Africa tell me that they have trouble with American clients who reload. Reloaders fail to deliver the quick follow-up shots so necessary on dangerous game because of their habit of opening a rifle bolt slowly enough to catch the case as it's extracted. I have developed the same habit, and it's a hard one for a handloader to break.

PROPERTIES OF BRASS

Brass as an alloy has several characteristics that make it well suited to use in cartridge cases. Its tensile strength is high enough to withstand the gas pressures generated in rifle cases when properly supported by the chamber and bolt, and yet it can be formed by extrusion, milling, and stamping for economical fabrication. It is elastic enough to expand and seal the breech of a gun, and still springy enough to break that seal so that it can be extracted. To put that another way, brass is elastic enough to firmly hold a bullet forced into a cartridge case neck, and yet soft enough to be expanded by gas pressure to release that bullet at the correct instant. It is easily worked in simple reloaders' dies, not only to prepare it for its next loading but also to change it into a completely different configuration.

Like all metals, brass has a grain structure that can be made visible under high magnification (about $150\times$) with proper polishing and etching. This microstructure can be changed by either cold-working or annealing (heat-treating), and indeed is changed with every reloading operation on the case. When the microstructure changes, so do the physical properties, especially those of hardness and elasticity

"Steelhead" cases (a trademarked name) are of two pieces, a brass body and stainless steel head which screw together. Some claim these assemblies markedly improve rifle performance.

(springiness). A cartridge case must have three different degrees of hardness and springiness in various portions of its anatomy, in fact, to perform as it should. The head portion, the first half-inch or so forward from the primer end, must be very hard, while the neck must be considerably softer. The crystalline structure of the alloy is much larger in the head and relatively smaller in the neck. The body of the case falls between the two extremes, not as hard as the head section and much harder than the neck.

The reason for differences in structure is that these segments of the case have different jobs to do. The head must be strong enough to support the tremendous pressures generated by powder gases without rupturing. The neck must be soft enough to grip the bullet and to expand upon firing, while the midsection of the case needs an intermediate hardness.

Cold-working the brass, which happens when it is resized after firing, tends to enlarge the crystalline structure of the metal and make it harder. When it becomes too hard, the neck of the case, which receives the most severe cold-working, will crack or split, and this is probably the greatest cause of lost cases for most reloaders. This can be avoided by re-heat-treating the case necks, as described in the following chapter.

The more a cartridge case is used, the more brittle the thin brass sections tend to become, especially in neck and shoulder areas. This tendency can be reversed by annealing, but application of heat to any cartridge case must be carefully controlled, lest those sections that must be hard and tough become soft.

If the annealing process is carried too far and the head area of the case is allowed to become too hot, the head area will be softened enough to ruin it, since its ability to withstand high pressures will have been destroyed. Once in a very long while a batch of factory cases with soft heads may get into commercial distribution, or even one or two cases in a batch can exhibit this defect. I haven't encountered the problem in commercial brass for more than 10 years, and then it was under a European label. Actually, the reloader doesn't have to deal with brass hardness very often, and it isn't as complicated as it may sound, but it's essential that you understand the basic physics in order to understand certain other matters.

The strength of a firearm is to some degree the strength of the cases fired in it, since the brass case is the weakest link in the mechanical structure of a gun. At the moment of firing, the case actually becomes an integral element in the gun itself, and if it fails, the gun fails. Since brass is weaker than steel, how is it that the case withstands pressures of firing? The answer is that those pressures are applied over so short a time that the brass literally hasn't time to yield before the stress drops back within tolerances. If this sounds strange, note that the temperatures developed within a rifle chamber at the instant of firing are not only far in excess of the melting point of brass but also higher than the melting point of steel, yet neither brass nor steel in a gun melts because these temperatures are applied so briefly.

THE CONSEQUENCES OF IMPRUDENCE

We're talking about *normal* temperatures and *normal* pressures now; if chamber pressures rise far above normal limits, the brass case will be permanently deformed and ruined. The diameter of the case head, rim, or belt may be enlarged, and the primer pocket may be so expanded that a primer will drop out of it. In extreme cases, the brass may be so swollen within its chamber that it cannot be extracted by the rifle's mechanisms, but in such cases some damage is usually done to the weapon itself.

If all this suggests to you that case life upon repeated loadings and firings is an indication of the pressures developed, you're a most perceptive reader. If dies and chamber are normal and cases begin to fail at the second or third firing, chances are pressures are much too high for continued use even though the gun is not damaged. Cartridge brass, then, serves as a sort of early warning system for reloaders who tend to bite off more than their rifles can chew.

If the warnings are ignored and pressures pushed even higher, you will eventually see the results of a case failure, and I guarantee that you'll be impressed. The damage done depends upon the type of arm, but typically a tremendous quantity of high-temperature, high-pressure gas rushes back through the rifle's action, often wrecking it. Locking lugs will be set back, the extractor blown off, the magazine blown out, the stock demolished, and quite often the person shooting the rifle will be injured. The fact that I've never heard of a bolt being blown completely out of the receiver or a handloader killed is a tremendous compliment to the design and strength of modern rifles. I know of instances in which shooters lost the sight in one or both eyes and suffered serious injury to the hand and arm supporting the gun's forearm. And potential personal injury is reason enough to understand the capabilities—and limitations—of the brass cartridge case. Reloading safety begins with a due respect for those limitations. Forget the case limitations and you're walking the razor's edge between pleasure and disaster.

HEADSPACE: MARK IT WELL

An important mechanical aspect of a cartridge case is its system of headspacing. Remember that word, *headspace;* you'll hear it and read it a lot in discussions of handloading.

Headspace may be defined as the amount of possible forward and backward movement of a chambered case when the breech is closed and locked. Ideally, this end play should be zero, but this is impractical in factory ammunition because of manufacturing tolerances in both cartridges and chambers. Therefore, industry standards set allowable headspace at .006 inch *maximum*. Four one-thousandths of one inch is not a great deal of space, but more headspace than this in a chambered cartridge is considered excessive and potentially dangerous.

The gap between the jaws of this dial caliper represents the maximum allowable headspace of .006 inch in centerfire metallic cartridges. More headspace than this may create a hazardous situation, while less can cause difficult chambering.

HEADSPACE

RIMMED CARTRIDGE

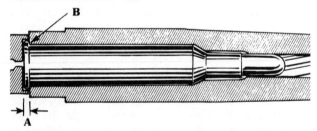

Headspace (**A**) is measured from boltface to front edge of rim. Rim (**B**) holds cartridge in place and stops the travel of the case into the chamber.

BELTED CARTRIDGE

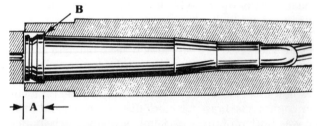

Headspace (**A**) is measured from boltface to front edge of belt. The belt on the case (**B**) seats against a shoulder in the chamber and stops travel of the cartridge into the chamber.

RIMLESS CARTRIDGE

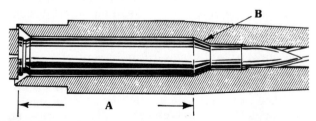

Headspace (**A**), the distance between the boltface and case head, is determined by the case shoulder. On rimless cartridges, the shoulder of the case (**B**) stops travel of the cartridge into the chamber. (Ray Pioch drawings from *Complete Outdoors Encyclopedia*)

RIMLESS PISTOL CARTRIDGE

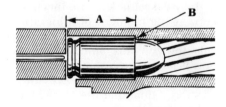

Headspace (**A**) for rimless pistol cartridges is measured from boltface to edge of case mouth (**B**), which seats against shoulder in the chamber and stops travel of the cartridge into the chamber.

Headspace is controlled by some part of the cartridge case being contacted and stopped by a corresponding surface within the chamber as the round enters. Four systems of headspacing are in common use in sporting arms today. The most common, at least in rifle cartridges, is the *rimless* case, typified by such rounds as the .30/06, .270, .243, and a host of others, which are said to headspace on the shoulder. These are stopped as they enter the chamber by contact with the shoulder at a point at which the case shoulder has a certain specified diameter, and the headspace is measured from a plane through the shoulder at this point to the face of the base head.

Another popular system involves the *belted* magnum cases, which headspace on the belt around the case head just forward of the extractor cannelure. Theoretically, this is supposed to be a very precise method of controlling headspace, since the distance from the case-head face to the front face of the belt is quite small. In practice, however, it ain't so.

The third system involves *rimmed* cases, and is used with most of the old black-powder cases in rifles, the .30/30 and .45/70, many revolver rounds including the .38 Special, .357 Magnum, .41 Magnum, and .44 Magnum. It is also the only system used in headspacing shotshells, although headspace is much less critical in shotguns because of the lower pressures involved. In rimmed cases, the forward movement of the case in chambering is stopped by contact between the front face of the rim and a recess cut in the chamber for the purpose. The headspace measurement on rimmed cases is, therefore, the thickness of the rim itself. This is probably the most precise

method of headspacing in use today, although it's also the oldest.

The fourth system is used for rimless, *straight* cases, which have no shoulder, and these are said to headspace on the mouth of the case. The only rifle cartridge using this method is the .30 M-1 Carbine round. A few semiautomatic pistol cartridges such as the .45 ACP, 9mm Luger, and .380 also headspace on the mouth. With these, the depth the cartridge can enter the chamber is controlled by a recess in the chamber which contacts the casemouth, and the headspace measurement is the full length of the case itself. Such cartridges can't be crimped onto their bullets, since this will change the headspace.

Two modern cartridges, the .220 Swift and .225 WCF, are called *semi-rimmed* rounds. They have a kind of rim, but happen to headspace on the shoulder the way rimless cases do.

The handloader is wise to get into the habit of thinking of headspace as relative to both the specific firearm in question and the cartridge. The cartridge can be of normal dimensions, but if the chamber itself is too long, the combination has excess headspace. Similarly, the chamber can be normal and still exhibit excess headspace with an individual cartridge that happens to be too short in the headspace measurement. In working with one rifle, the handloader can adjust his dies to produce cases that approach zero headspace in that rifle. He can also adjust belted magnum cases to headspace on the shoulder, as do rimless ones, rather than on the belt, and reap certain benefits. All these adjustments will be more fully explained in Chapter 11, ''Perfecting the Handload.''

The four common methods of headspacing cartridges are represented here. From left, the .30 M-1 Carbine (headspaces on the *mouth*), the .243 WCF (on the *shoulder*), the .224 Weatherby Magnum (on the *belt*), and the .30/30 Win. (on the *rim*).

CASE SHAPE AND PROPORTION

Another mechanical characteristic of brass cases is the shape of their combustion chambers. A good deal of controversy has raged around the gunshop hot stoves about the importance of this shape in internal ballistics. The whole line of Weatherby magnum cartridges has what are called venturified shoulders, with distinct radii where neck and body meet the shoulder proper. This was claimed as an advantage in the earliest days of Weatherby promotion, but I've heard no such claims in recent years. Many ballisticians have long felt that a very sharp, abrupt shoulder contributed to better burning, especially of the slower powders, and it has finally been demonstrated scientifically that this is really true, although the advantage is quite small.

It has also been proved that cases with extreme body taper transfer more thrust from powder gases to the bolt face, stressing the locking system more heavily than do relatively straight-sided cases. Some taper is necessary, however, for proper feeding from magazine to chamber and for extraction.

Neck length of cases plays its role, too. Many modern magnum (and some nonmagnum) rounds have been designed with very short necks, or, rather, very long bodies relative to overall length, in order to get more powder into a cartridge that will work through standard, .30/06-length actions. The 7mm, 6.5mm, and .350 Remington Magnums and .300 Winchester Magnum are classic, horrible examples. For short-action rifles, the .300 Savage, .243 WCF, and .308 WCF are just as bad. Short necks are one of the banes of the reloader. One reason is that it's difficult to make them grip a bullet firmly enough to resist displacement under recoil. Factory cartridges can be stab-crimped to hold the bullet in place for the single firing for which they're made, but reloaders are limited to the roll or taper crimp methods, and short necks create problems. The custom bullet-making firm of Nosler once offered a series of bullets especially cannelured for use in the .300 Winchester Magnum cartridge, since the Nosler design in use at that time simply couldn't be made to work with this short-necked case. Another problem with short necks arises when the handloader tries to seat a very long, heavy bullet. If the magazine is short, limiting overall loaded-cartridge length, the base of the bullet may protrude so deeply into the powder space inside the case that full ballistics cannot be realized. This was a particular problem with the .350 Remington Magnum in the short-actioned Model 600M carbine.

There is also some evidence that short necks detract from accuracy unless special handloading procedures—procedures few hunters employ—are used. In summary, short necks on cartridge cases are bad news for handloaders. Unfortunately, many very popular cartridges were so designed and you simply have to live with them. But any reloader who gets used to working with such rounds as the .257 Roberts, 7 × 57mm Mauser, .25/06 Remington, .270 WCF, or .30/06 will learn to curse the geniuses who designed such neckless wonders as the .223 Remington, .243 WCF, 7mm Remington Magnum, and others mentioned above.

The final mechanical element of the case the handloader must consider is design of the web, which is the solid section of brass in and just in front of the

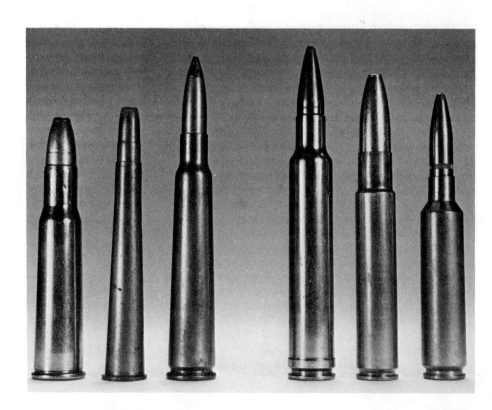

Excessive body taper in a cartridge case facilitates feeding and extraction but reduces powder capacity and increases stress on the gun's locking system. At left are three such cartridges, the .348 WCF, 6.5×58r, and .280 Ross. At right, three very straight-sided cases: .300 Weatherby Magnum, .35 Whelen Improved (wildcat), and the .284 WCF.

From a reloader's point of view, case necks that are too short are design faults in cartridges. The two at left, .300 Savage and .300 Winchester Magnum, exhibit this fault in spades. The two at right, the .30/06 and .30/30 Win., have more than ample neck length.

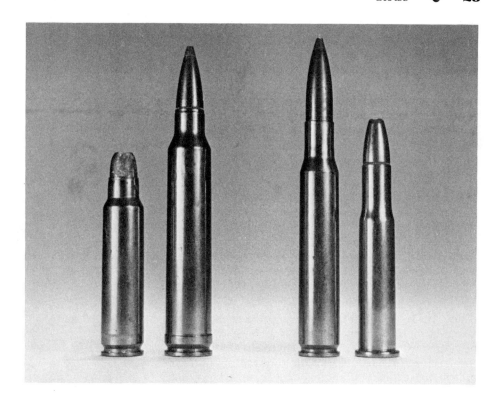

Left: The cutaway case at left reveals how much of the powder capacity of a short-necked case can be occupied by the rear of a long, heavy bullet seated to standard factory length. *Right:* Body taper and shoulder angle control powder capacity and the shape of the combustion chamber. The .30/30 (left) exemplifies considerable taper and a very gentle shoulder, while the .284 WCF (right) illustrates minimum taper and the sharpest factory-cartridge shoulder of all.

These case cross sections show all major metallic case-head types. From left: belted, rimmed (without cannelure), rebated rimless, semi-rimmed, rimmed (with cannelure), and rimless. Note differences in the distribution of metal in the case heads, which affect the strength of the various types.

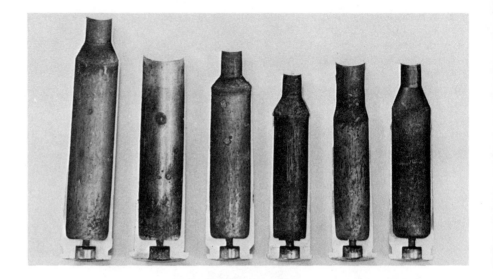

head. This is shown in the photograph above, which also make it obvious that certain web designs are inherently stronger than others. The web, along with the temper, or hardness, of the brass alloy, determines the ultimate strength of the case, which, in turn, represents the ultimate strength of the firearm itself. For the most part, cases of recent manufacture are well designed, more than adequate to contain the maximum pressures that reasonable handloaders demand of them. An occasional batch of old cases, in .44 Special, .45 Long Colt, and others, does not have a solid web at all, being of the folded-head or balloon-head style used decades ago. With good, virgin brass available today in these calibers, there's no point in using the old cases. Retire them; they're relics of the past and have no place in the practical handloading scene. If in doubt, simply section them lengthwise with a hacksaw.

A case is designed to work at a certain pressure level, and use of recommended charges of the proper powders will achieve these pressures without exceeding built-in safety margins. However, now and then a wildcatter gets a brainstorm about necking this or that up or down to produce his personal dream round. There's nothing wrong with this, except that he should make certain *before* he spends his dough for a custom barrel and loading dies that the webbing in his chosen case is designed for the pressures he anticipates in the final, wildcat version. A parent case designed to work at 45,000 PSIA (Pounds per Square Inch Absolute) will still be a 45,000-PSIA case even when altered in a wildcatter's dies to some new, exotic shape, and will surely give trouble if he tries to operate it at 60,000 PSIA. Wildcatting almost never changes the *head* of the case, and that's where the basic strength of the brass case is.

BASIC STRENGTH

And, by the way, research has pretty well demonstrated that there is no fundamental difference in the

At left is a Berdan-primed case, marked by the integral primer anvil and dual flash holes, compared to the standard American Boxer style at right.

ultimate strengths of the modern rimless and belted cases. Due to differences in hardness and web thickness, it's possible to find a lot of rimless stuff that will stand more pressure than a given lot of belted brass, or vice versa. But, overall, the two types of cases are equal in ultimate strength, regardless of rumors to the contrary. Perhaps it's academic from the handloader's point of view, but the strongest case in manufacture today is probably a semi-rimmed number, the semi-obsolete .220 Swift.

Brass is the starting point for all reloading operations. Everything depends upon it—safety, mechanical functioning, and, as you will see, much of the accuracy and power you can crank out of your rifle through reloading. Now, having examined the various metallurgical and physical characteristics of brass (in both handloading senses of the word), let's proceed to the actual operations involved in converting empty cases into live rounds of ammunition.

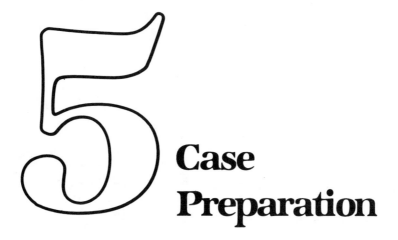

Case
Preparation

Many shooters think of a cartridge case as little more than a package, a sort of little brass bottle whose principal function is to hold all the "working" components of the load in proper relationship to each other prior to firing, and to be discarded afterwards. As seen in the previous chapter, there's quite a bit more to a cartridge case than that, and I will show in this chapter that the case is important, even crucial, to correct and safe functioning of the ammunition.

All cases manufactured anywhere in the world for a given caliber conform to precise specifications in external dimensions. This is assured by an organization known as the Sporting Arms and Ammunition Manufacturers Institute, usually referred to as SAAMI. When a manufacturer introduces a new cartridge, engineering drawings and specifications are placed on file with SAAMI, detailing cartridge and chamber dimensions, working pressures, and other data. This information is available to all members of the Institute. By this means, .30/06 ammunition manufactured by, say, Norma of Sweden, C-I-L of Canada, or Federal of the U.S. will chamber and function safely in rifles made by Remington, Winchester, Sako, or any other SAAMI subscriber. This is remarkable, considering the extremely small tolerances to which ammunition must be fabricated, and shooters and handloaders benefit greatly from this system of standardization.

We take it for granted that any cartridge that comes out of a box marked ".30/06 Springfield" will work in any rifle whose barrel is similarly marked, regardless of brand name or even the nationality of the maker.

As a sidelight, this is the reason that certain cartridges' performances can be materially improved through reloading, while others cannot. Once standardized, pressure and velocity specifications are never changed. Therefore, cartridges such as the .257 Roberts, .30/06, 7 × 57mm Mauser and others (developed and standardized in an earlier era when modern progressive powders were not available and rifle actions may not have been as strong) are forever limited to pressures and velocities that may be safely exceeded in today's arms. Manufacturers do not choose to exceed those specs in factory-loaded ammo out of concern for liability, but handloaders working with sound modern weapons are free to maximize the ballistic potential of those cases in perfect safety.

On the other hand, cartridge designs that have been standardized since World War II, including the very popular .243 WCF, 7mm Remington Magnum, and others already take advantage of the best of today's components and firearms. In fact, since ammunition makers may use special propellants not available over the counter to handloaders, it's sometimes difficult to even equal the performance (in terms of velocities) of modern factory rounds without exceeding sensible pressure maximums.

Although *external* brass dimensions are standard throughout the industry, *internal* dimensions and certain other characteristics, such as the hardness of the case heads, are up to the engineers of each individual manufacturer and may vary quite widely among brands or even among lots of the same brand. Obviously, if case walls are made thicker and external dimensions are standard, internal volume of the cases will be reduced, and this has its effect on powders, charges, and pressures. Similarly, up to a point, if case heads are made harder and thus able to withstand higher pressures, charges can be safely increased in a given case brand beyond a point that might be safe in another brand of equal quality.

The handloader is likely to encounter cases from

many modern makers, including Winchester-Western, Remington-Peters, Federal, DWM, RWS, Sako, Norma, Browning, various U.S. military arsenals, and a host of others. To complicate the matter even more, the headstamp on a case doesn't necessarily indicate who made it. Commercial ammo-loading firms frequently contract with competitors to supply formed brass. Companies like Speer and Hornady do not manufacture cartridge cases, and may buy from one supplier this year and another one next year, although the identifying headstamps will be the same.

Sorting brass by brand and, if possible, by lot is the first step in case preparation. Mixed batches impair accuracy and conceivably can cause dangerous pressures. Note the different headstamps here.

SORT THOSE CASES

All this adds up to one fact of life for the handloader, and this is that he must sort his fired cases by headstamp and, preferably, by lot, and keep his various lots separate. If he assembles ammunition using three or four different brands of brass indiscriminately, he will surely produce widely varying pressures from shot to shot (which wrecks accuracy) and may, in extreme cases, even create dangerous pressures.

Some reloaders have gone to the trouble to sort cases, even within a given headstamp, by weighing or by measuring volumetric differences, but the benefits derived from such painstaking efforts are simply not worth the trouble, even for super-precise benchrest competition. Yet these procedures may be worthwhile once just to convince you that significant differences in case volume do exist. But I have another, much simpler means of achieving the same practical ends. That is merely to purchase cases, whether as virgin brass or as factory-loaded ammo, in fairly large lots of at least 40 to 60 at a time, and to keep those lots separate. I prefer to purchase 100 cases at a time.

It's possible to mark all the cases in one lot so that they can forever be identified, by means of filing tiny nicks in the rim with a small three-cornered file. Some sort of simple system can be devised, such as one notch for one lot and two or three notches for other lots, or by filing the notches opposite certain letters or numbers in the headstamp. Be sure to make permanent notations of your code, however, because it's easy to lose track when you begin working with several different calibers. As long as the notch-filing isn't overdone, it in no way weakens or damages the cases.

Or one can simply keep each lot of brass in its own bin or box; that's the lazy man's way, which is to say, *my* way. However you decide to do it, *do* it; it's important.

It's also important to keep brass sorted according to the number of times it has been fired. Properly loaded, cartridge cases have a long life, but that life is not indefinite, and a few cases will be lost along the way. If you load for the hunting field, you'll probably wish to use only brass that has been fired at least once but not more than about three times, for reasons I will discuss in another chapter. On the other hand, brass that has been fired many times, from

10 to 20 or more depending upon the specific cartridge, is best set aside for use only in low-pressure loadings for plinking or small game.

Cases that fall between these two extremes are suitable for general practice shooting, noncompetitive target shooting, and experimenting. It should be apparent from all this that the times-fired statistic on a lot of cases is important. For this reason, I like to load all cases in a lot, or in an identifiable sub-lot, each time I load any of them, to avoid having to keep track of some that happen to have been through the rifle's chamber five times and others that have been fired only twice. If loading in such quantities isn't practical for one reason or another, I break the lot down to sub-lots and keep them separate as well. All this sounds complicated, but it really isn't much trouble once you establish some kind of system. Perhaps this discussion will at least serve to emphasize the importance of sorting brass. It's the vital first step in any kind of metallic cartridge reloading.

CASE INSPECTION

The second, and equally vital, step is inspection of the cases. Once you have selected a lot of brass for a planned load and have the cases set up in a loading block before you, pick up each case and give it a quick bow-to-stern visual inspection. Check for split necks (or incipient splits), cracks in shoulders, and anything even hinting at a possible weakening in the case body about a quarter-inch ahead of the rim. This may be a shiny ring or partial ring around the case, or any mark that suggests that the brass there has been stretched longitudinally. It appears most frequently in the belted magnum cases and those that have been fired in older, rear-locking rifles of lever- or slide-action types.

It's possible to be confused by the bright ring often left by a full-length resizing die on cases that have been fired at high pressures, especially in maximum-diameter chambers, but with a little practice you'll learn to tell the difference. When in doubt, it's worth making a feeler of fine, strong wire with a tiny hook in one end. Run it along the suspicious part of the inside of the case. If there is an incipient case-head separation, it will be revealed by a thinned ring of brass with a marked depression on the inside. The hook on your feeler will catch on it. If doubt persists—and it probably will, for a while—sacrifice a few of the suspected cases; section them with a fine-toothed hacksaw and inspect the inside visually.

While going over the case, note any obvious deformations, such as folded lips, serious dents, or cases that have been partially crushed or bent. If primers are still in place from the previous firing, note their condition, and especially any blackening around the primer, which would indicate a gas leak. If the case has been deprimed, check for the presence of a flash hole in the bottom of the primer pocket (yes, now and then a case comes through without one), and see that the hole is centered and appears neither oversize nor undersize. If you find not one but two flash holes, with a small teat of brass between them, you're looking at a Berdan-primed case, which cannot be reloaded in exactly the same way as regular, Boxer-primed types. Any of these defects justifies discarding the case if it is a common caliber; in very scarce cases, some of the defects may be worth trying to correct, such as minor dents, out-of-round mouths, undersize flash holes.

If the case is one of the belted magnums or any of the small-bore, high-velocity cartridges and this lot of cases has been fired three to five times or more, check overall case length. The easiest way to do this is to set your micrometer dial caliper (you should have one anyway) to the maximum case-length dimension for the cartridge in question, and use it as a snap-gauge for each piece of brass. Cases tend to lengthen with repeated firing because brass under high temperature and pressure flows slightly. If case length is allowed to grow beyond certain limits, the case mouth can be jammed into the origin of the rifling grooves and lands upon chambering. It then cannot expand to release the bullet as gas pressures build up behind it, and, believe me, those pressures can skyrocket. All major handloading manuals give maximum case length for cartridges they cover, and P. O. Ackley's *Handbook for Shooters and Reloaders* gives lengths for most common and many uncommon wildcats as well.

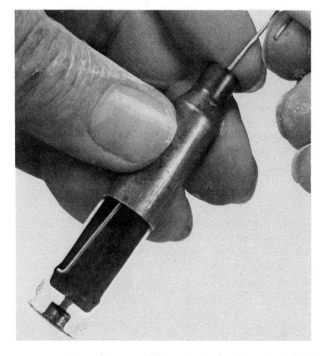

Left: This shiny "stretch-mark" on a .35 Remington case is a sure sign of internal damage to the brass. Trying to get "just one more loading" out of such a case is a short-cut to disaster. Some rifle-chamber/sizing-die combinations, however, can produce a somewhat similar mark. *Right:* A simple hooked wire, shown inside this cutaway case, can be used as a feeler to detect incipient head separations invisible from the outside.

TRIMMING, DEBURRING, AND CHAMFERING

Most manuals also give what is called a "trim-to" length, the dimension below which cases should not be shortened. If your batch of brass proves to be overlength, you'll have to invest in a case trimmer, basically a small endmill with provision for holding the case firmly and precision adjustments for the depth of cut. The cheapest is the Lee tool, and it's a good one. More elaborate trimmers are offered by RCBS, Lyman, Redding, Forster, Bonanza, C-H, Wilson, and other firms. Pacific, RCBS, C-H, and possibly others offer file-trim dies which screw into the press like a loading die. The case is placed in the shell-holder

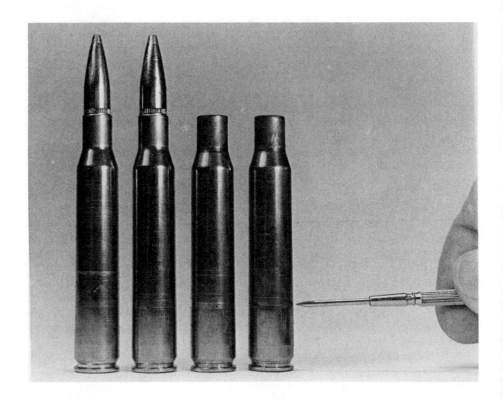

All these cases show incipient cracks at the same place (pointer), but only the right-hand one has actually broken through the case wall. Learn to spot these danger signs during inspection *before* they progress so far.

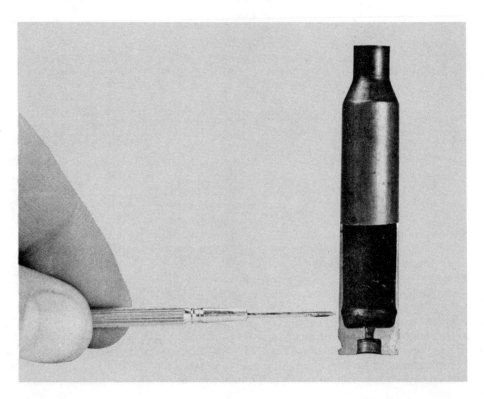

Repeated firing in a sloppy chamber and resizing of a belted case can stretch a case to the breaking point. This case, cut away to show the internal ring of dangerously thinned brass, has nearly reached the breaking point.

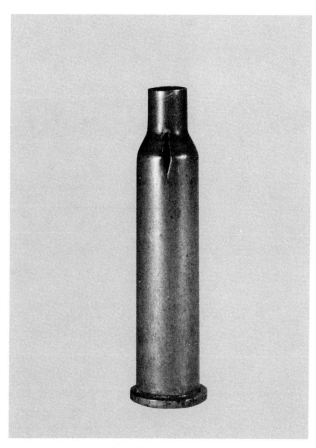

Such gross flaws as this are easy to catch during inspection—if you're not careless. This shoulder split during fire-forming.

and pressed into the die, and any brass that projects above the die top is filed away, the die being hardened to resist the file. (See "Case Length Table," next page.)

Some cartridges are much worse about growing than others, and some need trimming as often as every other firing, although this is rare. Eventually almost all high-pressure cartridge cases will have to be trimmed. It's a nuisance, but it's part of the game.

Cases in a given batch of brass usually lengthen at uneven rates, so that some of the lot will be too long, while the rest will be normal or somewhere in between. If the handload you plan to assemble in those cases requires crimping, as in rifles with tubular magazines or some of the magnum revolver rounds, you'll have to trim them all to a uniform length in order to assure a uniform crimp. On the other hand, cases that headspace on the mouth must never be trimmed below standard length, for to do so would create excess headspace.

Whenever cartridge cases have been trimmed, their mouths must be deburred and chamfered. This is also true of new cases, whether virgin or the products of firing factory loads. The necessary tool is a simple and inexpensive little gimmick offered by most makers of reloading tools, or it can be the blade of an old pocketknife. The purpose is to remove the burr around the outside of the case mouth, and to chamfer lightly the inside to facilitate the starting of a bullet. The purpose is *not* to make a cookie cutter of the case mouth; if deburring and chamfering are overdone, the mouth is weakened and splitting is encouraged, especially in cases that are usually crimped onto the bullet. Deburring and chamfering need not

Cases tend to "grow" in length with repeated firings (some calibers more than others), and may require occasional trimming to keep them within safe maximum lengths.

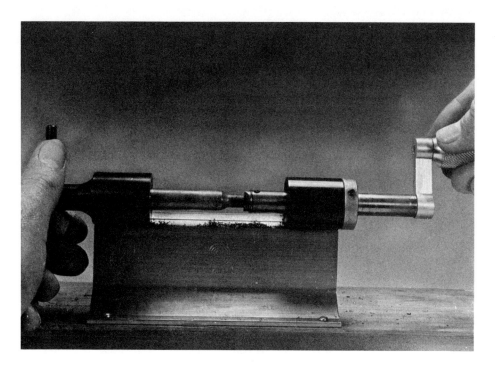

CASE LENGTH TABLE

The Dial Caliper/Case Length Gauge may be used for length, inside and depth measurements with a capacity of 5 inches.

The individual graduations on the outer scale of the dial are equal to .010 inch ($^1/_{1000}$). To measure .005 inch ($^5/_{1000}$), the pointer must center between the graduations on the outer scale.

The individual graduations on the vernier are equal to .1mm.

Popular calibers are shown below. Trim rifle cases (after sizing) .005 to .015 inch less than the maximum length shown. Trim fired pistol and revolver cases .005 to .010 inch less than the maximum length shown. (Courtesy of Speer)

CALIBER	MAXIMUM LENGTH	TRIM LENGTH	CALIBER	MAXIMUM LENGTH	TRIM LENGTH	CALIBER	MAXIMUM LENGTH	TRIM LENGTH
.17 Rem	1.796"	1.79"	6.5mm × 55 S.M.	2.165"	2.16"	.340 Wby Mag	2.820"	2.81"
.218 Bee	1.345"	1.34"	.270 Wby Mag	2.545"	2.53"	.35 Rem	1.920"	1.91"
.22 Hornet	1.403"	1.39"	.270 Win	2.540"	2.53"	.350 Rem Mag	2.170"	2.16"
.22 K-Hornet	1.403"	1.40"	.284 Win	2.170"	2.16"	.357 Herrett	1.765"	1.76"
.22 PPC	1.505"	1.50"	7mm B.R. REM	1.520"	1.51"	.357 Mag	1.290"	1.28"
.22 Rem Jet	1.280"	1.27"	7mm Exp Rem	2.540"	2.53"	.358 Norma Mag	2.508"	2.50"
.22/250	1.912"	1.90"	7mm Rem Mag	2.500"	2.49"	.358 Win	2.015"	2.01"
.220 Swift	2.205"	2.20"	7mm Wby Mag	2.545"	2.53"	.375 H & H Mag	2.850"	2.84"
.221 Rem F.B.	1.400"	1.39"	7mm/08	2.035"	2.03"	.375 Win	2.020"	2.01"
.222 Rem	1.700"	1.69"	7mm × 57 Mauser	2.235"	2.22"	.38 Colt S. A.	.900"	.89"
.222 Rem Mag	1.850"	1.84"	.30 Herrett	1.605"	1.60"	.38 S & W	.775"	.77"
.223 Rem	1.760"	1.75"	.30 M1 Carb	1.290"	1.28"	.38 Spec	1.155"	1.15"
.224 Wby Mag	1.920"	1.91"	.30/30 Win	2.039"	2.03"	.380 Auto	.680"	.67"
.225 Win	1.930"	1.92"	.30/40 Krag	2.314"	2.30"	.38/55 Win	2.130"	2.12"
.240 Wby Mag	2.500"	2.49"	.30/06	2.494"	2.48"	9mm Luger	.754"	.75"
.243 Win	2.045"	2.03"	.300 H & H Mag	2.850"	2.84"	9mm Win Mag	1.160"	1.15"
6mm × 47	1.850"	1.75"	.300 Sav	1.871"	1.86"	.41 Mag	1.290"	1.28"
6mm PPC	1.503"	1.50"	.300 Wby Mag	2.820"	2.81"	.44 Mag	1.285"	1.28"
6mm Rem	2.233"	2.22"	.300 Win Mag	2.620"	2.61"	.44 Spec	1.160"	1.15"
.25/06	2.494"	2.48"	.303 Brit	2.222"	2.21"	.444 Marlin	2.225"	2.22"
.250 Sav	1.912"	1.90"	.308 Win	2.015"	2.00"	.45 Auto (ACP)	.898"	.89"
.256 Win Mag	1.281"	1.27"	.308 Norma Mag	2.560"	2.55"	.45 A.R."	.898"	.89"
.257 Rob'ts	2.233"	2.22"	.32 Win Spec	2.040"	2.03"	.45 Colt	1.285"	1.28"
.257 Wby Mag	2.545"	2.54"	8mm Rem Mag	2.850"	2.84"	.45 Win Mag	1.198"	1.19"
.264 Win Mag	2.500"	2.49"	8mm × 57 Mauser	2.240"	2.23"	.458 Win	2.500"	2.49"
6.5mm Rem Mag	2.170"	2.16"	.338 Win Mag	2.500"	2.40"	.45/70 Gov't.	2.105"	2.10"

be done at every reloading, but only on new cases and after trimming.

CLEANING CASES

I should add something here about cleaning cases. I remember a jovial character who shot at my rifle club range every Saturday morning. He kept a pad of 00000-grade steel wool on his shooting bench, and whenever he wasn't firing—when targets were being changed or he was chewing the fat with another member—he was methodically polishing his rifle cases. We were amused to note that his groups were never much to brag about, but he had the shiniest cases in town!

Which says something about the relationship between clean brass and good performance: There ain't any! However, if shiny cases appeal to you, there are several ways—other than using superfine steel wool—to go about cleaning them. By far the best is a case tumbler or vibrator, using ground nutshells, corncobs, or plastic as a polishing medium (usually with a chemical polishing agent). Such equipment is fairly expensive and takes several hours to do its job, but it will polish a large batch of brass at once and cleans both the inside and outside of the cases, plus primer pockets. It is, in fact, the only safe way I know to clean the insides of cases. Avoid chemical cleaners of the sort that require dipping or soaking the cases. If these are strong enough to really do the job, they may damage the brass, and I know of none that can eradicate the hardened powder residue that blackens the insides of fired cases. Of course, any of the various kitchen-type brass cleaners, such as Brasso, will polish the outsides of the cases, but they require time and elbow grease better reserved for actual loading,

 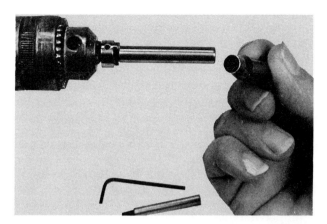

Left: After trimming or when virgin, case mouths need to be chamfered inside and deburred outside. Manual tools like this one from C-H do the job well. *Right:* This tool, for use in an electric drill or drill press, trims, chamfers, and deburs in a single, speedy operation. Different mandrels, shown beneath, in background, are required for different cartridges.

Left: The current generation of vibrator-type equipment does an excellent job of cleaning cases without fuss or muss. Shiny brass may not shoot any better, but it is easier on reloading dies than dirty, gritty cases. *Middle:* Rotary tumblers clean and polish cases somewhat more slowly than vibrators, but have, on average, greater capacity and versatility. Some, like this RCBS Sidewinder, can use either wet or dry media. *Right:* A set of case spinners like these from Sportsman Supply Co. permit cleaning even the grungiest brass almost instantly. With the drill mounted in a vise or stand and the correct spinner chucked up and spinning, slip a dirty case onto the mandrel. A cloth soaked with brass polish (or, in extreme cases, a pad of fine steel wool, with or without polish) is then moved about on the spinning case. When clean, the case can be plucked off the spinning mandrel. The process is fast, safe, and easy.

and, as I said, shiny brass shoots no better than dull brass. However, *corroded* brass, with a green residue over a pitted surface, should be discarded. I've been talking about the dulling and darkening that accompanies normal handling and firing, not actual corrosion, which is chemical destruction of the metal by acids, salt water, or other agents to which cartridges are rarely exposed.

In the long run, a tumbler-type cleaner (such as used by rockhounds for polishing mineral samples)

is the best bet for restoring that virgin shine to brass. (Two of these are shown above.)

PRIMER POCKETS

Cleaning primer pockets is another job that needn't be done after every firing, unless you're a perfectionist. Do it often enough to keep the residue, which forms in the bottom of the pocket, from building up enough to interfere with proper seating of the primers. This means cleaning about every second or third firing, in typical cases. This can be done with the blade of a small screwdriver, although several simple, inexpensive tools are available that do it better, faster, and easier. Primer residue is fairly brittle and easily removed, but take care to avoid enlarging the primer pocket by removal of brass, especially around the walls of the pocket.

While we're on this subject of primer pockets, it's appropriate to point out that military brass (one of the great boons to reloading in such calibers as .223 Remington, .308, .30/06, and .45 ACP) requires special processing because military primers are actually crimped into place. Depriming such once-fired cases is best done with a drift punch just small enough to pass through the flash hole and a hammer, although some die manufacturers offer specially beefed-up decapping pins. In any case, getting spent military primers out of their pockets is a tough job, and seating fresh primers is all but impossible unless the pockets are modified.

This can be accomplished by reaming or swaging. Special tools are available, or the job can be done with a sharp knife. Trim away the lip of brass that held the military primer in place. Great care should be exercised to avoid enlarging the pocket itself, with either the knife or a commercially made reamer. Swaging is the best bet for this work, and, again, several different tools can be purchased for the job. Here swaging is the removal of the crimp by placing the pocket over a solid studlike swaging tool. Some tools are used with a loading press (RCBS) and others with a vise and a hammer (C-H and others), the chief differences being cost and convenience. This is another task that needs to be done only once, before the military case is handloaded for the first time.

You now have a batch of cases in your loading block, sorted, inspected, cleaned, trimmed, deburred, chamfered, and with primer pockets cleaned. Now, and only now, can you begin processing the brass for actual reloading. Of course, since fired primers must be removed for primer pocket inspection and cleaning, and since in most rifle cases depriming is combined with the resizing process, I have necessarily gotten a little ahead of myself in this discussion. Let's go back and discuss that resizing-depriming step, the first part of which is lubrication.

LUBRICATION

I said that clean cases don't shoot any better, but I must add that dirty cases—very dirty ones, with gritty gunk attached—may damage sizing dies, causing scratches that will then be reproduced on every case sized in that die. Cases need not be shiny, but should be wiped clean before sizing. This wiping should not be with a cloth used to apply lubricant, since the grit is then merely distributed throughout the batch of cases.

In fact, using anything except your fingers for lubricating cases is likely to spread grit, including the inking pads so popular for lubrication. Also, nothing offers the reloader so certain a means of controlling lubrication as his fingers, and they are the instrument I prefer for applying sizing lube.

Most manufacturers of dies also sell lubricants, since proper lubrication is absolutely essential in sizing, especially full-length sizing. Making sure their customers have good lubes available saves the die-makers the profitless trouble of removing even more stuck cases than they have to as it is. All lubes sold especially for resizing work well enough, but the two I like best are sold by Hornady and Hodgdon. These have about the consistency and feel of cold cream

Left: Removal of residue from primer pockets ensures proper seating of the primer for the next firing. *Right:* This RCBS equipment swages the crimp from primer pockets in military brass to dimensions correct for normal reloading, without enlarging the pockets.

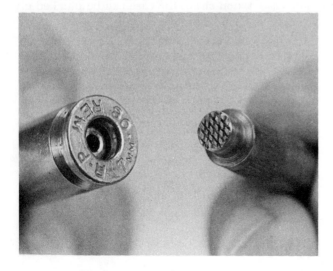
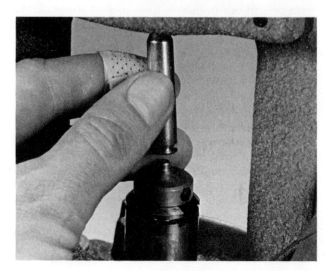

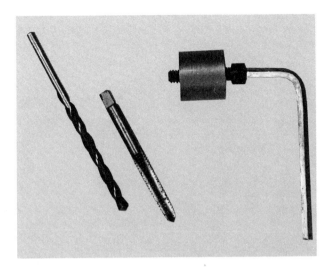

A stuck-case extractor kit is less complicated to use than it may first appear. The die in which the case is stuck is removed from the press and the flash hole of the case drilled out with the drill bit shown. The hole is then tapped, and the sleeve placed over the case head. The bolt is threaded into the tapped hole and turned with the Allen wrench to extract the case without damage to the die.

(but don't try cold cream as a substitute!). They wipe on and off easily, and the red Hodgdon goop actually seems to clean cases to some extent as it lubricates.

The right amount of sizing lube is important; too much produces dents in case shoulders, and too little leads to stuck cases. It's probably beneficial (and inevitable) for a new reloader to stick at least one case in a sizing die early in his career, if only to convince him of the desirability of avoiding that minor catas-

trophe forever afterward. When you do stick one, either buy a good stuck-case extractor and read the directions carefully before proceeding, or return the die to the manufacturer. Any other course of action will fail to remove the case and quite likely will result in a ruined sizing die.

Sizing lube must be applied very sparingly. The lubricated case should feel just slightly greasy, without a visible buildup of lubricant. The simplest method of application is to dip the tip of a forefinger in the lube and spread it over the thumb and fingers, then handle the cases thoroughly. It is not necessary to lubricate the case neck or shoulder nor, of course, the area around the extractor groove or belt since that portion of the case doesn't enter the die. Don't fret about getting your fingers greasy by this method; they'll get greasy anyhow, from handling the cases, no matter how the lube is applied.

The inside surface of bottlenecked rifle cartridge *necks* should be lubricated as well, else the force required to pull the expander button back through the neck as the case is withdrawn from the sizing die can stretch the case significantly. Do not, however, use any oil, grease, or gel-type lube here. A dry lubricant such as graphite or molybdenum disulphide is correct, and can be applied by an appropriately sized, synthetic-bristle brush. Several manufacturers offer such brushes, and at least two—RCBS and Bonanza—make a neat and inexpensive unit for the purpose. The unit has three sizes of brushes mounted vertically within a reservoir for the dry lube.

If you get a nerve-rending screech when you drag a bottlenecked case out of the sizing die, you're stretching cases and hastening the day for trimming. It's best simply to make inside-neck lubing a part of your routine on all bottlenecked cases.

After sizing, the lubricant must be removed from the cases. Most authorities recommend thorough

Left: Fired cases must be lubricated before sizing, and this picture shows two ways to do it. In the background, a stamping pad "inked" with lubricant across which the cases are rolled, while the case in the right foreground is manually lubed. By either method, the trick is not to overdo it. *Right:* One way to dry-lube the insides of case necks is by means of this handy little Bonanza tool with three different-size brushes and a reservoir for graphite or molybdenum disulphide.

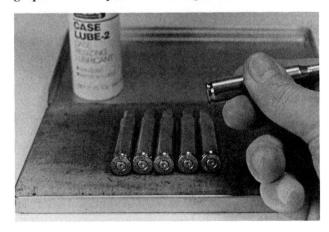

wiping with a soft cloth, but I have never quite satisfied myself with merely wiping dry. Remember that the brass case must expand and cling to the walls of the chamber during the peak pressure period in firing. Too much lubricant, either on the cases or in the chamber, inhibits this action to some degree and produces an abnormal strain upon the gun's locking system. In fact, the thrust applied upon a test gun's bolt by firing a deliberately oiled cartridge was once measured in ballistics laboratories, before the introduction of more sophisticated equipment, as a means of determining total chamber pressure.

Therefore, my own habit is to remove the lubricant from each sized case with a solvent on a paper towel. Anything will do—lighter fluid, cleaning fluid, automotive solvent. Gasoline is much too dangerous for use around a reloading bench, and even the naphtha-based solvents mentioned above should be used with care. Plain old lighter fluid has the advantage of being packaged in small quantities with safe closures and convenient applicator spouts. Cleaned cases should feel bone-dry, "squeaky clean," to the touch.

At this point, the hard work in reloading has been done. What remains—priming, charging, and bullet seating—goes very quickly. For this reason, a handy habit to get into, when you have no other work to do at the bench, is to preprocess cases. When you're in a hurry, or it's the night before you leave on the annual deer-hunting trip, it's a boon to be able to pick up a block full of cases ready to be primed and loaded. I try to keep every empty case I own processed and ready for loading at all times; I don't accomplish it, but I try.

Priming is the next step, and it gets a full chapter unto itself, the next chapter.

ANNEALING BRASS

More space has probably been spent on annealing than the average reloader will find worthwhile, because the process is required only under special conditions. When it is required, however, nothing else will serve. I include annealing here for the sake of completeness and not to scare off a would-be handloader. Many reload for 20 years without ever annealing a cartridge case.

You'll recall the brief discussion in the previous chapter on the microstructure of brass, which can be changed by cold-working. Resizing a case cold-works it, as does bullet seating and crimping. With each reloading, therefore, the crystalline structure of the case neck and, to a lesser degree, the body is changed. The crystals of the alloy grow larger and the brass becomes harder and more brittle. This is probably the major cause of brass failure, via split necks. It is accelerated when the rifle's chamber is too large, relatively, for the specific resizing die so that the brass is cold-worked excessively with each processing. This doesn't mean that either chamber or die is outside specifications, but, manufacturing tolerances being what they are, it happens now and

One method of annealing case necks involves standing them in water, heating the necks with a propane torch, as shown, and tipping them over to quench. Most useful for small lots, this system demands a good deal of alertness and dexterity.

then. Drastic case reforming, such as necking up or down more than one caliber, also contributes to early brass loss through hardening.

The answer is reannealing the neck and shoulder portion of the case. This reduces crystalline size and makes brass sections that are tough and springy again instead of hard and brittle. However, the annealing must not be allowed to extend to the head area of the case; that portion must be left hard. The problem, then, is the application of just the right amount of heat to just the right portion of the case for just the right duration. It sounds pretty formidable, but there are ways to do it.

The one most often recommended is as follows: stand cases on their bases in a shallow tray or pie tin containing from ½ to ¾ inch of water, and heat the necks with a propane torch. As each one reaches the correct temperature, tip it over to quench in the water. This method requires a certain amount of practice in judging just when the correct temperature is reached. Some sources have said to heat the necks red hot. Don't do it. Especially on small cases, this will result in overannealed and ruined cases. The first visible color change will be to a brownish tinge, and then to a bluish one. With the torch flame applied to the mouth of the case, the color change will occur within a few seconds, and will spread to the shoulder. By this time the mouth will show the blue color shift, but as soon as the brownish tint has reached the junction of shoulder and body, the anneal is complete. Ideally, the case should be rotated during application of the flame for an even anneal.

If a large number of cases are annealed in the same pan of water, the water will rather quickly become almost hot enough to boil, and should be exchanged

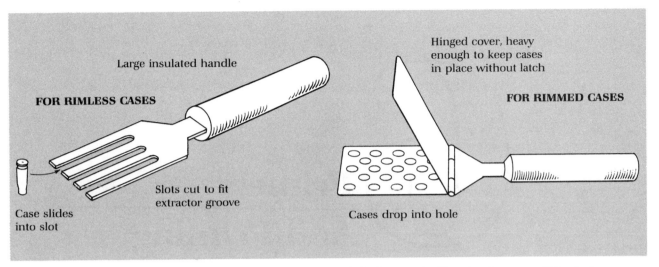

Here are cartridge holders for annealing. The drawing at left shows a holder that lets you slide rimless cases in along the cartridge cannelure. The drawing at right shows a spatula-like holder for rimmed cases.

for cold water. Ordinary tap water is cold enough.

A more satisfactory method of annealing is available if you happen to have access to an electric lead melting pot such as is used in casting bullets. Fill the pot with lead, melt and flux it (see fluxing instructions in chapter 19 on casting), and set the pot's thermostat at 750° to 800° Fahrenheit. Provide yourself with a handy vial of light machine oil, and a bucket of water. Pick up each case by the head, mouth down, and dip it into the oil for about half its length. Shake off the excess oil and dip the neck, shoulder, and about a quarter-inch of the body into the hot lead. Just as you begin to feel an uncomfortable degree of heat in your fingertips, drop the case into the water.

The advantage of this method of annealing is that you know the temperature being applied (assuming the pot thermostat is reasonably accurate), and you cannot stand enough heat to permit overannealing. Even so, it's hot work and something you won't want to do more often than necessary.

If you have to anneal a large batch of cases, a little ingenuity will produce a device similar to those shown above for holding up to a dozen cases in the lead at once, with a quick-release feature so they can be quenched before too much heat spreads to the head sections. With such a device, of course, you lose your built-in heat control and must anneal by time rather than feel. About 8 to 12 seconds (not more than 15 seconds, in any case) will be about right.

The annealed cases will need to be washed thoroughly in a grease-cutting detergent to remove the oil and then dried before loading. Drying proceeds more rapidly if the cases have been deprimed (and then there's no chance of accidentally mixing a live primer in with spent ones). For small batches, a hairdryer speeds up the process. For larger quantities,

The molten-lead technique of annealing cases. Bare fingers ensure against getting the case head too hot, but this is hard, hot work.

the cases can be spread on a cookie sheet and dried in the oven, provided you're quite confident of your oven's temperature controls, and you don't set the controls higher than 200°. One-fifty is safer, but slower. If compressed air is available, the best solution is blowing out the water and air-drying.

Essentially, the annealing process involves applying at least 750° Fahrenheit but not more than 950° to the neck-shoulder portion of the case, without allowing the head portion to reach a temperature higher than about 200°.

6 Primers And Priming

There's an enormous amount of precision, reliability, and power packed into small-arms primers, tiny as they are. The longer you handload, the more respect you'll develop for primer manufacturers, but somewhere along the line you'll probably cuss them a few times too. When a round of reloaded ammunition fails to fire, the first explanation that springs to mind is a defective primer. Such problems exist; in my decades at the loading bench I've seen only one primer without a pellet of detonating compound, and several more that lacked anvils, out of close to a quarter-million examined. However, I've

never had a misfire that I could positively pin on a defective primer. There are so many other factors in the gun, the reloader's technique, and the loading tools that can create firing malfunctions that I'd estimate the odds on a primer misfire at less than one in a thousand. In this chapter, I'll show you how to eliminate as many of those other factors as possible, so that when you do have a misfire, you may be able to gripe to the manufacturer of the primer.

A rifle or pistol primer has three components: the cup, pellet of priming compound, and anvil (for Boxer primers; Berdan types will come later). All three are

The three left-hand drawings show centerfire metallic cartridge primers as they come from the factory and with a firing pin causing detonation. At right is a typical shotshell primer.

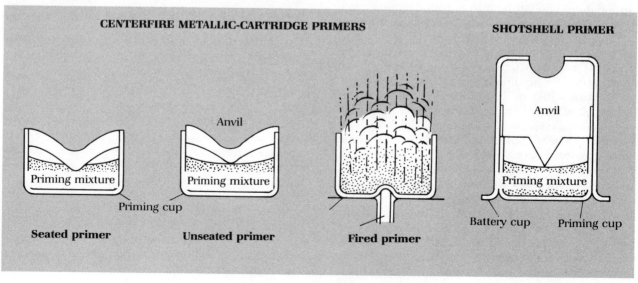

CENTERFIRE METALLIC-CARTRIDGE PRIMERS

SHOTSHELL PRIMER

Priming mixture

Priming cup

Seated primer

Anvil

Priming mixture

Unseated primer

Fired primer

Anvil

Priming mixture

Battery cup   Priming cup

important to proper functioning. The cup must be of correct diameter to fit snugly in the pocket of the case, the correct thickness to contain chamber pressures even when dented by the blow of the firing pin, and the correct hardness to accept a full-depth indentation. The pellet must be of the correct chemical composition for sensitivity and of the correct weight to produce enough flame to ignite the powder. The anvil must be of correct design to seat properly and straight and to support the blow of the firing pin.

THE POWER OF PRIMERS

When the firing pin indents the primer cup, it pinches the pellet between it and the anvil, detonating the compound. A very fine balance is necessary in the compound for just enough sensitivity but not too much, for the sake of safe handling. Never underestimate the potency of priming compounds. Some years ago, I'm told, a workman at a primer manufacturing facility was carrying a bucket of loose primers, an act that would never be tolerated under modern practices. Apparently dust from the pellets sifted down to the bottom of the bucket, and the whole bucket detonated. The report I had was that they never found any part of the workman except his shoes.

An acquaintance of mine had what he estimates at about a hundred rifle primers detonate in a plastic medicine vial in his left hand. He lost his hand and the sight in his left eye, and he underwent a series of operations for cosmetic repairs to his face, arm, and upper body, suffering a great deal of pain, a staggering financial setback, and the loss of a part of his livelihood. He was a gunsmith.

PRIMER PRECAUTIONS

Such tragedies illustrate the inherent explosive power of small-arms primers, but they can be avoided totally by understanding and adhering to a few simple precautions. The first is *never* store primers in *any* kind of container other than the original factory packaging. The second is to go back and reread that last sentence several times. If you find it desirable to decap live primers and intend to save them for future reuse, save a few empty factory primer trays in which to store them. Do not keep live primers, however few, loose in any sort of miscellaneous container, and most especially not one made of glass.

Never have more loose primers on your loading bench than you have cases to prime at that moment. Obviously, it's folly to subject primers to heat, impact, or electrical current.

If these few rules are religiously observed, small-arms primers are no more dangerous than so many BBs; if the rules had been observed, neither of the two tragic accidents I've described, or the many others I've heard of, would have occurred.

With these warnings out of the way, we can proceed to the right ways to employ primers. They are the spark plugs that make our handloads go; without them there would be no such hobby as reloading.

CORROSIVE AND/OR MERCURIC PRIMERS

The principal ingredient in all modern primers, regardless of manufacturer, is lead styphnate. Lead styphnate replaced two earlier compounds, mercury fulminate and potassium chlorate, in all commercial ammunition and in primers furnished for reloading

Left: The wrong way and the right way to store primers. *Never* keep loose primers in any sort of container, as at left. Store them *nowhere* except in the original sleeved trays in which they were originally packed, *as shown.* *Right:* Alertness at the loading bench is important. For example, you must always read carefully enough to catch that word "magnum," which makes a big difference in both safety and satisfaction.

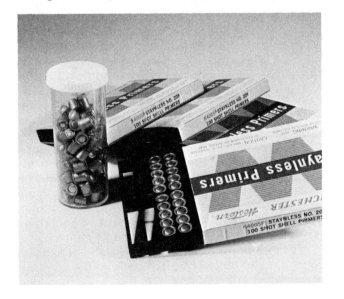

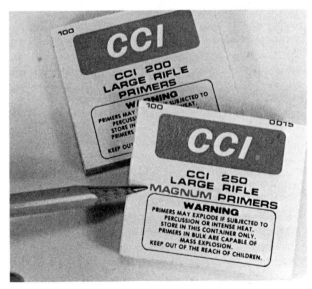

shortly after 1930. This was necessary because the mercury fulminate, upon firing, produced compounds that made the brass case brittle and destroyed it for further use, and the potassium chlorate deposited compounds in the rifle's bore that guaranteed almost instant rust unless immediate and special cleaning procedures were followed after firing. Primers containing these two chemicals are called "mercuric, corrosive."

The significance of all this to the reloader lies in the possibility of old lots of ammunition turning up carrying such primers. The use of mercuric, corrosive primers in certain batches of military ammunition continued until at least 1954, and they may be found in military .30/06, .45 ACP, and 7.62 NATO (.308) cartridges. Caliber .30 M-1 Carbine ammo was never loaded with corrosive primers. Civilian sporting ammunition loaded prior to about 1927 may be assumed to have mercuric, corrosive, or both types of primers. All commercial ammunition having nonmercuric, noncorrosive primers, and all such primers sold for reloading, carry statements to that effect on the factory packaging. Except for a few lots of military ammo that can be identified by headstamp, there is no way to be certain whether old ammo or primers that are loose or that have been repackaged are corrosive or noncorrosive.

Since cases in many of the old-time calibers are quite scarce and expensive, a handloader who discovers a supply of primed cases or loaded ammo for his old buffalo-buster faces a dilemma. If he fires the cartridges and they happen to be loaded with mercuric primers, he has ruined the cases. No known treatment after firing can restore mercury-damaged brass to service. If he is aware of the possibility of chlorate corrosion, he can protect the gun after firing by prompt and thorough cleaning with hot soapy water and a military-style bore cleaner, but he may have destroyed his precious hoard of brass for reloading.

It's best to take no chances. The bullets should be pulled and saved and the powder charges discarded. Then squirt a shot of a lubricant known as WD-40 into the mouth of each case. This stuff is the best primer-killer I know, and after a few hours, more than 99 percent of the primers will be deactivated. Now the cases can be deprimed in the usual fashion, using more than ordinary gentleness in operating the tool out of respect for that remaining less-than-one-percent that may not be quite dead. Actually, even if a primer does fire in this process, no danger to the reloader is involved because the case is safely enclosed in the die. But the case may be ruined (if the primer was mercuric) and the die should be cleaned in the same manner as a gun in which corrosive primers have been fired.

The brass can now be cleaned up and reloaded in the normal manner, with modern components.

The problem is a bit more complicated with mercuric and/or corrosive military stuff with crimped-in primers. After dousing with WD-40, you can try decapping the cases with an extra-stout depriming pin in your sizing die stem. I'd have to recommend against the drift-punch-and-hammer treatment; a single live primer in the batch is one too many when the case is not enclosed in a steel die and your hands are over the mouth. Best deep-six the whole lot and start over with modern brass.

Safe, responsible disposal of unserviceable cartridge cases deserves a sentence or two here. The brass should be crushed between the jaws of pliers or a vise so that it cannot possibly be thought to be serviceable. If primed (with whatever kind of primers), each case should receive an inside squirt of WD-40. After such "decommissioning," a case is nothing more than an inert scrap of brass and can safely be discarded in the household trash. Live rounds, of course, can never be disposed of in this manner; they should be broken down and deactivated as above, or perhaps buried in a place to which the public has no access.

PRIMER SIZES AND TYPES

Primers for modern cases come in two sizes, large (.210-inch diameter) and small (.175-inch diameter). There are also primers made in each size specifically for rifles and pistol cartridges, the latter having a smaller pellet and thinner, softer cups to accommodate the lighter firing-pin blows and smaller powder charges of most handguns. Although they'll fit, resist the temptation to substitute rifle for pistol primers, or vice versa, when you find yourself out of stock. Serious ignition difficulties are sure to result.

There are also a number of special variations in each size and type of primer, the most familiar being the so-called "magnum" versions. These are essentially nothing more than standard primers with about 50 percent more pellet by weight. They are useful when trying to build a fire under massive charges of very slow-burning powders such as are common in the big belted magnum cartridges, among others, or when burning certain hard-to-ignite propellants. These magnum primers may elevate chamber pressures somewhat if substituted in a load established with standard or nonmagnum primers. Follow primer specifications in published loading data. When switching from a standard to a magnum primer in an established load, it's advisable to reduce the powder charge a couple of grains for test firing. Usually, you'll find you can work the load back up to or very near the previously established powder charge without symptoms of excessive pressures, but don't take that for granted.

Another specialty primer offered by several makers is a small rifle type designed for high-pressure loads in .222 Remington-size cases, especially including the various .17 calibers. A fairly recent innovation is the so-called "benchrest" primer, said to be manufactured to exceptionally high standards of uniformity for super-accurate bench rifles and varminters.

Shotshell primers, Berdan primers, and percussion caps are still other types that will be discussed in more detail in the appropriate places. I've included

PRIMER TABLE I (Boxer)

Mfgr.	Small Rifle	Small Rifle Magnum	Large Rifle	Large Rifle Magnum	Small Pistol	Small Pistol Magnum	Large Pistol	Large Pistol Magnum
CCI	400 BR-4	450	200 BR-2	250	500	550	300	350
Remington	6½	7½	9½	9½M	1½	5½	2½	—
Winchester-Western	6½-116	—	8½-120	—	1½-108	1½-108M	7–111	7M-111F
Federal	200 205	—	210	215	100	—	150	—
Alcan (S&W)	SR	—	LR	—	SP	—	LP	—
Hodgdon	SR	—	LR	—	SP	—	LP	—
Norma	SR	—	LR	—	SP	—	LP	—
C-I-L	1½	—	8½	—	1	—	2½	—
RWS-Sinoxid	4003	—	5341	5342	4031	—	5337	—

PRIMER TABLE II (Berdan)

Mfgr.	.175	.177	.179	.199	.201	.210	.217	.238	.241	.242	.250	.251	.254
Eley-Kynoch	—	69	72A 74A	—	78	—	59 60 81	—	34	36	—	41	172
RWS-Sinoxid	—	1548	—	1680	—	—	1674 5601 5603 5608	1698	—	—	6000	—	1775
S&W-Alcan	175PB 175RB	—	—	199B	—	210B	217B	—	—	—	250B	—	1794 645B

a table of primer interchangeability and manufacturer's designations here to help straighten out any confusion that may arise in selecting a primer.

Once the correct primer for the load in question has been selected, all that remains is to poke it into the primer pocket, right? Wrong! Like everything else about reloading, there's more to priming than meets the eye.

PRIMING TOOLS

Most bench-mounted presses for the reloading of metallic cartridges come equipped with some sort of priming device, and these work well enough for all practical purposes. The mechanical advantage of such presses is so great, however, that they impart no "feel" to the operator seating primers. Most of them do not have any sort of positive stop to ensure that all primers are seated to the same depth. These facts explain the availability of a couple of dozen tools, ranging in price from less than $10 to more than $40, whose sole purpose is to seat primers. Most utilize reloading press shellholders, some have gravity-feed

A few of the special priming tools available are, from left, Bonanza, Lee, and two RCBS models.

When gently shaken from side to side as shown, a primer flipper aligns all primers anvil-up. This is an inexpensive and handy accessory, especially for loading primer magazine tubes. If you want your primers anvil-down, just place the lid on and insert the whole flipper.

magazines to speed up production, and a few offer great sensitivity, the importance of which I will discuss shortly.

I must confess I am very nervous around primer magazines of any kind. Once in a great while, a primer may detonate while being seated (as the result of an operational mistake), and the possibility of a whole column of caps producing a chain detonation makes me shudder. Most progressive-type reloading presses necessarily rely on primer magazines, and at least one—the Dillon—incorporates a steel shield around the tube. The Bonanza priming tool carries its stack of primers resting on their sides, their open ends facing an open slot in the aluminum tube. The idea is that if one primer goes, it *might* not set off the whole stack, and the force of the explosion is uncontained and directed away from the operator.

All these are thoughtful and worthwhile approaches to the problem, but I still prefer to handle my live primers one at a time. The design of many of the special priming tools permits the reloader to do this, although at the cost of much speed. That's a trade-off I'm happy to make, having seen what a few primers can do. The reader is, of course, free to decide for himself.

My favorite priming tool of the lot is also the cheapest, the little thumb-pressure-operated Lee priming tool (shown below left), which is so sensitive that I can actually feel the primer bottom in its pocket. More important, I can easily detect the slightest enlargement of the primer pocket.

EXPANDED PRIMER POCKETS

When a handload that produces too much pressure is fired, the entire cartridge case head is swelled, and the primer pocket itself is enlarged slightly. If the same load is fired repeatedly in the same case, the pocket will continue to expand, until it becomes too large to provide a snug press fit for a fresh primer. In extreme cases, you can actually seat a primer in an expanded pocket without tools, using your thumb, and in even more extreme cases, the fired primer may simply fall out of its pocket when the fired case is extracted and handled. How rapidly this pocket-expanding process advances depends upon how much pressure is generated; in severe overloads, a single shot is all it takes to open up the pocket too much to seat a fresh cap. Thus, the condition of the primer pockets in fired cases is a useful indicator of the pressure levels of previous firing. A loose pocket, into which a new primer slips with suspicious ease, even in a tool of low mechanical advantage especially made for priming, is a double warning signal; it mandates discarding that case because of obvious overstressing, and it shouts that the previous loading(s) was too hot. In truth, the feel of inserting new caps into processed cases is a part of cartridge-case inspection.

SEATING DEPTH

Assuming all pockets are suitably tight, the one remaining consideration is the depth to which primers are to be seated. To begin with, they must be seated at least flush with the case head, and ideally a few thousandths of an inch below flush. A "high primer," as one that is not quite flush is called, can cause ac-

Left: This little Lee priming tool offers excellent sensitivity at a bargain price. *Right:* All modern metallic reloading presses have a priming mechanism, most of which are similar to that on this RCBS "Rockchucker"— a swinging arm delivers the primer through a slot in the ram and a hole through the shell holder.

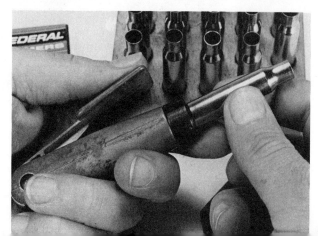

During seating, the anvil of a Boxer primer is intended to be pressed slightly deeper into its cup, stressing the pellet of priming compound for correct sensitivity. This is why the anvil's "feet" protrude slightly from the cup before seating, as seen at left.

cidental discharges, especially in the slam-bang operation of semiautomatic weapons. Such discharges are termed "slam-fires," and they invariably result from high primers, if the gun itself is normal.

If you look carefully at a live primer in profile, preferably with a magnifying glass, you will note that the feet of the anvil legs protrude slightly from the mouth of the cup. When a primer is seated in its pocket, these feet bottom first. Slight additional pressure then forces the anvil to slide into the cup a little, prestressing the pellet of priming compound. This design is intentional, and provides for reliable and uniform functioning of the cap. If the primer is seated so that the anvil feet do not touch the bottom of the pocket, then part of the force of the firing pin must be diverted from its primary purpose of indenting the cup to seating the primer fully. This usually results in hangfires or even misfires, and at best destroys uniformity of powder ignition.

On the other hand, if the primer is seated too deeply, the anvil will be forced into the cup far enough to crack or crush the pellet of detonating compound, also resulting in hangfires and erratic ignition. In short, primers must be seated, not too deeply and not too shallowly, but just right. That's why the sensitivity of special priming tools is valuable, especially to the reloader who is a perfectionist.

Proper seating depth necessarily varies from case to case, since manufacturing tolerances produce slight variations in the depths of pockets, as well as in primers. A depth micrometer is especially made for measuring primer-seating depths, and is the ultimate in precision, but the tip of the human forefinger has more than enough sensitivity to detect, with a little practice, primers that are high or abnormally deep. A suspected high primer can be confirmed by standing the primed case base-down on a smooth surface; if the primer is flush or below flush with the case head, it will stand steadily. If the primer is high, even by a couple thousandths of an inch, it will rock. I know that system sounds too simple to be recommended in a deep, scientific book like this one, but it works.

One other point: If you must err in primer seating, it's best to err on the side of too deep than too high.

You now can see the importance of cleaning primer pockets of the residue of previous firings. If this residue accumulates in the bottom of the pocket, it interferes with proper seating of new primers.

A few years ago, primers were manufactured in two styles, according to the maker's taste. Some had flat-faced cups and others were rounded, and loading-tool makers were forced to furnish priming punches in both styles and, of course, in large and small sizes. Today, almost all primers are flat-faced, and only two punches are supplied. If you purchase a secondhand tool, however, it may have both styles of punches, and you should make certain that you're using both the correct diameter and the proper style.

CAUSES OF MISFIRES

Oil or grease from case lubricants is death to primers. The most probable cause of a misfire in a handload is deactivation of the primer pellet by accidentally transferring lubricants from the case to the primer. This is yet another good reason for using a solvent to remove case lube after resizing. Most primers sold for reloading today are sealed either with a disc of foil paper or a drop of lacquer, but even so, the insidious oil may get through to the pellet.

The second most common cause of misfires is improper seating of the primer which can result from careless use of the tools, as described above, or—more rarely—from incorrect dimensions in the tool, shell-holder, or even the case itself.

Finally, the firearm may contribute to an occasional misfire. The firing pin may be broken or the tip damaged, the firing-pin spring may be broken or weak, or the chamber's headspace may be excessive, so that the case isn't properly supported against the firing pin's blow.

Another obvious cause can be the absence of a powder charge in the cartridge. This may seem unlikely, but don't think it can't happen to you. If you reload long enough, it almost certainly *will* happen to you. When it does, be forewarned that the sound of the primer's explosion cannot be heard if the bullet doesn't leave the case, and the bullet will not be driven out of the case by the primer's force alone in most centerfire rifle cartridges. In some small pistol cartridges, the bullet may be partially displaced or even driven into the forcing cone of the barrel.

In any case, there are so many other causes of misfires that a defective primer is almost never to blame. The precision with which these tiny titans are manufactured approaches perfection, and quality-control procedures are very severe. If you have a misfire, stop cursing the primer maker and begin to examine your equipment and techniques. This advice is not intended to protect the primer manufacturers from being maligned but to speed you on your way to discovering the problem and correcting it.

I will add other comments on primers and priming in the chapters on loading for the hunting field, loading for obsolete cartridges, and reloading safety.

Gunpowder

Readers of this book will be less interested in the history of gunpowder (although it is interesting) or processes for making it than in how to select and use propellant powders.

Nevertheless, an understanding of certain elementary technical aspects of powder is necessary for its intelligent use. Therefore, I'll devote a little space here to the physical and chemical characteristics of this stuff called gunpowder, which has had so momentous an impact upon the history of mankind, and which is the fuel for our handloads.

POWDER TYPES

There are two basic breeds of gunpowder in use today, designated as black powder and smokeless powder. Black powder is a mechanical mixture of potassium nitrate (saltpeter), charcoal, and sulfur. Despite the fact that black powder is man's oldest explosive substance, it is still in use and growing in vogue among shooters of muzzleloading arms in the United States. It was supplanted as a standard propellant in sporting cartridges in the U.S. only in 1894.

The so-called smokeless powder that supplanted black powder is of greatest interest to reloaders today. All smokeless available to the handloader is basically nitrocellulose, formerly called "guncotton." Powders that have no other energy source than nitrocellulose are described as "single-based." The various IMR powders (IMR Powder Company) are examples of single-based propellants.

Some gunpowders have nitroglycerine added to the nitrocellulose for higher energy content, and these are said to be "double-based" powders. Examples on the reloaders' market are those made by Hercules, Inc., and the full line of Winchester-Western Ball powders, among others.

There are advantages and disadvantages to both types of powder. Double-based propellants are non-hygroscopic, almost waterproof, have a higher energy content per unit of volume, and are generally easier to ignite. Single-based powders appear to be somewhat more stable chemically, and distinctly less temperamental at high pressure levels. They will not chemically attack the plastic in powder measures most handloaders use, though double-based powders will. Either powder may appear in the form of sticklike grains or flakes of several possible shapes.

The other major type of powder has a distinctive shape as well as some distinctive properties. Individual granules appear to be tiny spheres, sometimes flattened slightly. This is called Ball powder by Winchester-Western (the word "Ball" is a trademark) and "Spherical" by the other major supplier of such powders, Hodgdon Powder Co., Inc. Ball-type powders are manufactured by totally different methods than the stick-type or extruded powders, but they are made of the same basic materials. All ball-type powders, at the time of this writing, are double-based, and they share with double-based extruded powders the characteristics of waterproofness and high energy content. They are exceptionally stable, however, so much so that the shelf-life is said to be unknown, although ball-type powders have existed for more than a quarter-century. Most ball-type propellants are extremely dense, meaning that with them you can

Canistered propellant gunpowders for handloading come and go on the market too rapidly to keep any photo such as this current. At this writing, more than 60 different numbers are in production, and you may be able to locate small lots of discontinued items. Within this wide selection, one is exactly right for any load you can dream up—if only you can find it!

put more energy into a given case volume, and they meter through handloaders' powder measures with exceptional uniformity. They are thought to give lower rates of bore erosion in gun barrels than other powder forms, possibly because of their lower flame temperature.

Much of the ball type powder currently on the market today is quite difficult to ignite with a small-arms primer, and magnum primers are frequently recommended. The greatest drawback has been that the ball types deposit an unbelievably stubborn and unique form of fouling in gun bores, a fouling that is impossible to remove with conventional bore cleaners. Chemicals that will remove it efficiently may be dangerous to handle, and may damage gunstocks, furniture, or clothing. Ball-type powder of recent manufacture, however, has been much improved in both these areas, so much so that they are really not factors in its use by reloaders. The newer ball-type powders are also said to produce much less muzzle flash than earlier lots, but this is a question of much more concern to the military than to sportsmen.

The shape and size of the individual granules of a gunpowder are critical to its burning characteristics. Consider a perfectly round granule of ball-type powder. It, like all other forms of smokeless, can be thought of as burning in layers, rather than all at once. Therefore, the exposed surface of the granule is what burns to evolve propellant gases. The surface of a round ball is greatest when first ignited and grows smaller as combustion proceeds. This shape is said to be "degressive."

Now imagine a stick of gunpowder of exactly the same mass, but with a lengthwise hole through it to make it into a tiny cylinder. The outside surface is ignited at the same instant as the inside surface. The outer surface grows smaller as it burns, but the inner surface gets larger at the same rate, so that the total burning surface remains about the same until the granule is almost consumed. By adjusting the size of the hole (or number of holes) it's even possible to make the surface *increase* in area as burning proceeds. Such configurations are called "progressive."

Further control is achieved through various chemical coatings, called deterrents, that are applied to the powder granules to delay the spread of combustion across the powder surfaces.

RELATIVE QUICKNESS

All these efforts to control the rate at which the propellant, in solid form, yields up latent energy suggest there is something about it that is very important to the handloader, and there is. The reason that there are some 60 or so canistered powders on the handloaders' market today is that different applications require different degrees of what is called "relative quickness." The relative quickness of a powder is the single most critical property that powder possesses, from the handloader's viewpoint. He will read, in this book among other places, of "slow-burning" or "fast-burning" powders, and he may even see the phrase "burning rate." He will learn that, in general terms, cases require slower-burning powders, that pistols and shotguns use quicker ones, and that heavy bullets call for slower powders if all else is equal. Relative quickness is the concept that will permit him to relate various powders to each other and to their designed purposes in his home-brewed ammunition. It will help him understand that, say, 50 grains of a slow-burning powder may be the perfect charge in a given cartridge, while 50 grains of a much faster powder is certain to blow his gun to bits, even though it's composed of the same stuff. The difference is the *rate* at which the energy is released.

Several tables are included here to show the different manufacturers' powders on relative-quickness scales, but it must be understood that each manufacturer has his own system, and that the RQ numbers *cannot* be used to relate Hercules powders to Winchester-Western powders. Charts have been at-

RELATIVE QUICKNESS OF IMR CANISTERED POWDERS
(From Fastest-Burning to Slowest)

Powder	Relative Quickness	Powder	Relative Quickness
HI–SKOR 700–X	635	IMR 3031	135
PB	390	IMR 4064	120
SR 7625	340	IMR 4895	115
SR 4756	305	IMR 4320	110
SR 4759	210	IMR 4350	100
IMR 4227	180	IMR 4831	95
IMR 4198	160	IMR 7828	90

Note: The relative-quickness index numbers in the right-hand column were determined in closed-bomb tests in the DuPont laboratories, and reveal burning-rate relationships between the IMR Powder Co. propellants on a scale on which IMR 4350 was assigned an arbitrary value of 100.

CANISTERED SMOKELESS POWDERS
(Ranked from Fastest-Burning to Slowest)

Relationships among propellant powders for rifle, pistol, and shotshell reloading in this table have been deduced from the author's experience and exhaustive reference study of handloading literature. But these are only approximate. They can and will change somewhat in different applications. Similar tables from other sources will vary significantly. Furthermore, these relationships are not *quantitative* in any way; a powder may appear here as slower than another powder, but *how much* slower cannot be inferred from this table. The relative quickness of different lots of the same powder may in some cases vary enough to change the order of propellants listed below. Where two powders appear on the same line, they may be considered very similar, but only specific data should be used as a basis for the loading of ammunition. And never neglect standard safety procedures for selecting propellants and working up loads—*John Wootters.*

*Asterisk (*) indicates discontinued or not now distributed in U.S., but supplies may be found for sale, and reliable loading data is still in print.

WARNING: POWDER CHARGES CANNOT SAFELY BE EXTRAPOLATED FROM THIS LISTING.

1. *Norma R1
2. Hercules BULLSEYE
3. *Norma N1010
4. Olin 231
5. Hodgdon HP38
6. IMR HI-SKOR 700X
7. Hercules RED DOT
8. OLIN 452AA
9. Hodgdon TRAP 100
10. Hercules GREEN DOT
11. IMR PB
12. Hercules UNIQUE
13. IMR SR 7625
14. *Alcan AL-5
15. Olin 473AA
16. *Alcan AL-7
17. IMR SR 4756
18. Hodgdon HS6
19. Olin 540
20. Hercules HERCO
21. Accurate Arms NO. 5
22. IMR HI-SKOR 800X
23. Hercules BLUE DOT
24. Olin 571
25. Hodgdon HS7
26. Accurate Arms NO. 7
27. *Alcan AL—8
28. *Olin 630
29. Hercules 2400
30. Accurate Arms NO. 9
31. *Norma R123
32. Olin 296
33. Hodgdon H110
34. IMR SR 4759
35. IMR 4227
36. Hodgdon H4227
37. Olin 680
38. *Norma 200
39. Accurate Arms MP–5744
40. IMR 4198
41. Hodgdon 4198
42. *Herter 103
43. Hodgdon H322
44. Hercules RELODER 7
45. IMR 3031
46. *Hercules RELODER 11
47. Accurate Arms MR–2460
48. *Norma 201
49. *Herter 102
50. Olin 748
51. Accurate Arms MR–223
52. Hodgdon H335
53. Hodgdon BALL C-2
54. Hercules RELODER 12
55. *Norma 202
56. Hercules RELODER 15
57. IMR 4895
58. Hodgdon 4895
59. *Norma 203
60. IMR 4064
61. *Herter 101
62. IMR 4320
63. Accurate Arms MR–2520
64. Hodgdon H380
65. Olin 760
66. *Reloder 21
67. Hodgdon H414
68. Accurate Arms MR–3100
69. IMR 4350
70. Hodgdon H4350
71. *Norma 204
72. Hercules RELODER 19
73. *Herter 100
74. IMR 4831
75. Hodgdon H450
76. *Olin 785
77. Hodgdon H4831
78. *Norma MRP
79. Hercules RELODER 22
80. IMR 7828
81. Hodgdon H870
82. Accurate Arms MR–8700
83. *Hodgdon H5010

This IMR 4350 is typical of slow-burning extruded powders. Granules are tiny, unperforated cylinders with flame-deterrent, flash-suppressing, and graphite coatings. Long granules of this type sometimes cause uneven metering and even bridging (blocking of orifices) in powder measures.

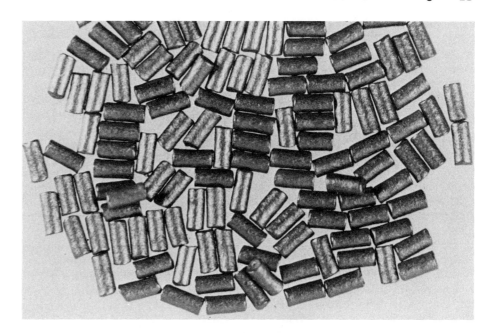

Hercules Unique is an example of a popular flake powder. Most of these are relatively fast-burning and are uncoated, igniting easily. Unique is extremely versatile, with applications in rifle, pistol, and shotshell loading.

IMR Powder Company's SR 4759 consists of short granules that are perforated longitudinally, exposing relatively more surface to ignition. This powder bulks up well and also performs well in reduced loads in rifle cartridges.

tempted that were supposed to rank all powders from all manufacturers in order of relative quickness, and some of them have been reasonably useful, but they were not *quantitative;* in other words, they could show that H380 is faster-burning than IMR 4350, but they could not show *how much* faster. Thus, any attempt to interpolate charges from RQ tables is dangerous, especially among different brands of propellants. Mark this well: No two brands of powder on the market today are exactly alike, and direct substitutions of the same charge of another powder in an established loading are *not* permissible.

There are other reasons for that warning. One is that a given powder is designed to perform within a given pressure range. Within that range, each additional grain-weight of powder added to the charge will produce approximately the same increment of velocity. This linear relationship disappears, however, when pressures rise above those considered normal for the powder; then pressure may rise much more swiftly than charge weight, while velocities may increase little, if any. Any increase in powder charge beyond that point is an overload.

Different types of powder respond quite differently to these factors. Extruded and ball types of approximately similar burning rates may react so differently that the ball may appear to be slower than the stick powder at certain pressure levels and much faster at higher levels. Furthermore, different case shapes may influence the burning rate; a powder may be "slower" in a straight-sided case than it seems to be in a bottlenecked one. You need not know much about the size of such shifts for you will not have to deal with them quantitatively; what matters is that you realize that they can occur. The knowledge can help keep you out of the kind of troubles that generally follow random experiments in propellant substitution.

POWDER DESIGNATIONS AND TERMS

The designations or trade names gunpowder makers apply to their products for the handloader are just that, trade names, even though most of them are numbers. Even within a single brand line, the numbers have no definite relationship to relative quickness, application, or any other performance characteristic.

The term "canistered" is used to describe a powder that is sold at retail for reloading. Actually, it means a powder for which the performance parameters are standardized from lot to lot. That way the handloader can be reasonably sure his pet loads will not have to be redeveloped each time he opens a new canister of that particular powder. Certain popular powders, however, do reveal some changes from lot to lot, usually insignificant. Unless a load is already far too hot, the only precaution indicated when changing lots of a given powder is an extra measure of alertness while firing the first few rounds loaded out of the fresh batch.

Unfortunately, suppliers of powder to the handloading trade have, over the years, adopted some rather confusing trade names for their products, and this practice may lead the unwary reloader into danger. The problem has arisen when one maker labels a powder with a set of numbers identical to those used for a similar, but not identical, propellant by a competitor. For example, there is an H 4831 and an IMR 4831. The "H" stands for Hodgdon, and the "IMR" means "Improved Military Rifle," a copyrighted term of IMR Powder Co. Today, these two powders are different enough in burning characteristics to require a load tested with H 4831 to be reduced by two or three grains, usually, if IMR 4831 is substituted.

Similarly, there are IMR 4350, IMR 4895, IMR 4227,

Winchester-Western 760 is an example of a ball-type propellant in which the manufacturer has controlled relative quickness partially by flattening the balls into thick discs. All globular powders on the market are double-based.

Accurate Arms' MR 2520 is a medium-burning ball-type powder in which the tiny granules are left globular and the burning rate is regulated by coatings. These dense spherical powders meter smoothly in a measure and pack a lot of energy into a case.

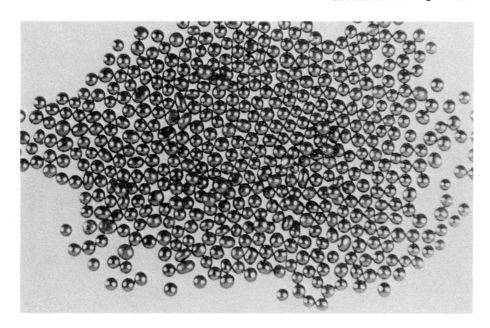

and IMR 4198, while Hodgdon makes a version of every one with the same string of digits! There was a Norma 205 and a Hodgdon 205 too; both have been discontinued, but a reloader might still find a supply of either. I noticed that recent editions of various reloading manuals seldom, if ever, list loads for the same bullet with *both* powders, where there are two with the same numerical designation, probably to avoid any chance for confusion. On the other hand, older data sources may show only the number (with no "H", "IMR", or other prefix). These sources were printed when there was only one and always refer to the older propellant.

If you have an old handbook and don't know which 4831 came first, for example, you should get a newer handbook. In all cases and regardless of the vintage of the manual, it's critical that you *always* look for the prefix before reaching for the powder can. Then look again! Take nothing for granted. Make certain you know which powder a handbook publisher refers to before using that data.

Most manufacturers make many powders that are uncanistered, and thus not available to the public. Winchester-Western, for example, manufacturers about 60 different propellants, but only 11 are canistered. The rest are used in loading commercial and military ammo, for which it's easier to adjust the machines to throw a slightly different charge than it is to painstakingly standardize the entire lot of powder to previous specifications.

INDENTIFICATION

Although a few powders have colored flakes mixed in for identification, do not try to identify any gunpowder by appearance alone. To attempt to do so is to invite serious consequences. The one and only thing to be done with powder from cans with missing or illegible labels, from unlabeled containers, or from cartridges that have been unloaded, is to discard or destroy it. Make no exceptions to this policy, no matter what your buddy tells you about the origins of that coffee can full of powder. Powder costs money, and it's tempting to make a shot-in-the-dark identification to try to salvage the precious stuff; but don't do it. To do so would be little more than Russian roulette, with somewhat less drastic consequences for the loser. By the same token, when you repackage gunpowder be sure the labeling is unmistakable. If you forget to empty the reservoir of your powder measure, discard its contents unless you can be absolutely certain of the powder's identity.

If powders are accidentally mixed, flush the mixture down the toilet. I've heard of reloaders who attempted to interpolate a new burning rate for their new blend and to guess at safe loads. In most cases they plain guessed wrong.

Contrary to widely held opinion, common gunpowder is a relatively weak explosive, containing far less latent energy than ordinary gasoline or any of several other solvents and fluids frequently found around the home. With commonsense precautions, storing and handling propellant powders in the course of handloading operations present very few hazards. Powder is not particularly easy to set off, and when it does ignite while unconfined, the result is rather unspectacular. To satisfy yourself (and/or wife, neighbors, etc.) on this point, pour about a quarter-teaspoonful of a slow-burning powder (4831, IMR 4350, N205, or the like) into a clean ashtray and light it with a kitchen match. Everyone will be thoroughly disappointed with the "fireworks." Do *not*, however, try this little demonstration with any species of black powder because black powder is a different and much wilder animal than smokeless. I'll discuss its traits and tricks in Chapter 21, on loading black-powder cartridges.

8 Powder Selection And Charging

As this is written, there are more than 60 canistered powders on the retail market. So probably the most perplexing question that occurs to the would-be handloader is "How do you know which powder to use in a given load?"

The answer is simple: You work from reliable, tested loading data and use the powder recommended for your bullet weight in your cartridge. If you do not exceed the maximum charge weights recommended, you will not get into trouble.

CHOOSING THE RIGHT POWDER

Some general rules apply, and you will doubtless observe them for yourself in the course of studying reloading manuals. They are *very* general and are not to be relied upon in place of the tested, reliable loading data. Roughly, the larger the bottlenecked case you're loading, the slower-burning the powder. Straight-sided cases including many revolver rounds, the older black-powder cartridges, and some new ones like the .444 Marlin and .458 Winchester perform best with powders that are faster-burning than those used in bottlenecked cases of similar capacity. In a given case, the heavier the bullet being loaded, the slower-burning the powder for maximum velocity. Reduced loads always require faster-burning powders than would be selected for full-power loads in the same case, regardless of bullet weight. These rough rules of thumb apply to handgun cartridges as well as rifle cases, but within a different portion of the relative quickness scale, since even a "slow" pistol powder is faster-burning than the fastest propellants used in most centerfire rifles. Shotshell powders are also very much faster than rifle powders, but are often used in pistol cartridges and occasionally with cast bullets in very reduced loads in rifle cases.

There is not yet any system that will select powders and charges for various bullet weights and case sizes. The closest we have come to such a handy thing is the Powley Computer for Handloaders (see photo, next page).This slide-rule-type calculator selects powders and starting charge weights for any cartridge, even hypothetical ones, but is set up only for the IMR series of propellants. It's useful, but its results should always be checked against reliable reloading data.

Most handloaders gradually accumulate quite a variety of different powders. I try to keep most popular propellants in stock. Otherwise, the one I don't have is invariably the one I'll need when assembling an experimental series of loads late some evening when all the stores are closed. However, at today's prices, a stock of different powders represents quite an investment, and most readers will want to know how to decide which powder to purchase to get started with a new cartridge.

WHEN HANDBOOKS DISAGREE

Remember that different guns exhibit distinctive individual preferences in ammunition components, and guns often perform differently from other, seemingly identical guns. This is true of the test guns used in ballistic laboratories to develop handloading data for publication. If you acquire several different handbooks and make close comparisons between recommended powders and charges for the same cartridge, you'll discover quite a variation in the recommended maximum charges. Speer's test gun may accept several grains (weight) more of a certain

Loads can be planned even for cartridges that do not yet exist if you use this slide-rule calculator or some computer programs described in Chapter 14.

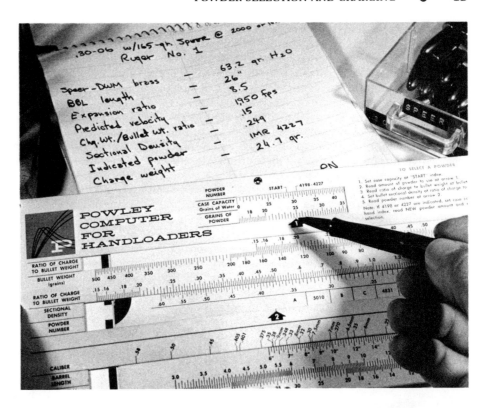

The many excellent reloading handbooks available today are accurate and reliable, except that they may disagree about maximum charges. Furthermore, your own rifle may disagree with all of them, so *all* such loads *must* be worked up individually.

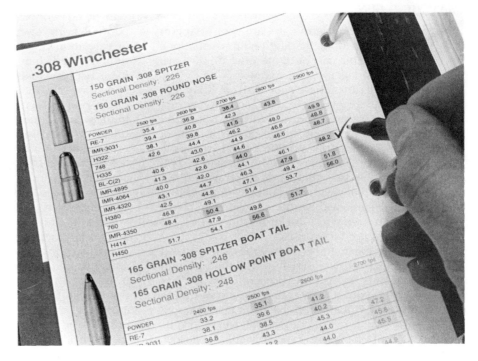

powder behind a certain bullet than Hornady's—and the situation may be exactly reversed with another cartridge a few pages over. You may even find that Lyman's test gun produces highest velocities in a given combination with one powder, while in Sierra's gun an entirely different powder gives top speeds.

These apparent contradictions do not mean that any of the data is wrong. All four of the manuals mentioned, as well as Hodgdon's, the NRA's, IMR's,

Hercules' and others, are meticulously prepared at great expense by experts with the best modern equipment. Contradictions mean merely that no two guns are exactly alike, and the data presented in the manual is right *for the guns used in testing.*

Odds are that your own gun will differ significantly from those used to develop the loading recommendations. This is why you'll find on every page of every reloading handbook a warning that maximum loads should be approached with caution and only after test-firing lighter charges. More about this appears in Chapter 10 on working up loads.

In most instances, however, handbooks will be in general agreement as to the best two or three powders for any bullet weight in a given cartridge, although they may rank those powders in slightly different order. By consulting several different sources of data, you should be able to pin down which powder or two are most promising for starters. Pick the powder (or two) that appears to give near-top velocities for your cartridge and chances are it will be most efficient in that case.

"Efficiency" can be defined in several ways. In this book the word will be used to indicate the powder that offers the highest velocity *per grain of powder.* If two powders seem to be nearly equal in this respect, the one that produces lower pressures will be considered the more efficient. Velocity per grain of powder is easily figured from any reloading manual, and many manuals now include pressure data. If pressure units are not specified, it's a fairly safe assumption that they are CUP (copper units of pressure).

MATCHING GUN AND LOAD

It's very useful to be able to correlate your own gun to the test gun used for loading recommendations in a handbook. This can be done only if you have access to a chronograph, but many shooting clubs and commercial ranges have such instruments these days. If you load a cartridge exactly according to recommendations, paying attention to the case types, primers, barrel lengths, and other factors specified, and discover that your rifle produces nearly the same velocity listed for that charge in the handbook, you can be reasonably sure that loads listed with other powders and bullet weights in that cartridge in that handbook will agree with your own results. Such information can save you a lot of time, money, and components in the future.

Even if the agreement between your own gun and the test gun is poor, you may find that the variation between them is consistent. For example, your gun may accept maximum charges a couple of grains lighter or heavier than the publisher's test weapon; if this is the case, you can crank that factor into your loading plans. Don't take these correlations as gospel, however; there are other factors such as temperature and bullet seating depths, that can distort them somewhat. Furthermore, a change in bullets, even to another brand of the same nominal weight and style, may make significant differences.

You will see the advice, in almost every source of reloading data you read, that exceeding recommended maximum powder charges is unsafe and should never be done. For novice handloaders and those who work from a single data source, this is excellent advice. But "never" is a long time, and if you work a load up to maximums in one handbook, you can almost invariably find another manual in which you have already exceeded the maximums, sometimes by a substantial margin. I will describe reliable methods of determining maximums *in your rifle* in Chapter 10, since they're the only maximums you really want. The point I want to make is that "shopping" a load—that is, thumbing through several data sources in search of the hottest charge listed as safe—is poor practice. Far better to list the "max" load of a certain powder with your bullet weight from each loading manual and average the top charges, and then regard that *average* as your probable maximum until proved different. If you find, with careful testing, that your own gun will safely accept higher charges, you can continue to work upwards. The averaging system will most likely keep you from getting any nasty surprises.

Always remember there is no guarantee that your particular gun will accept even the lighter charges listed in the loading tables, and that custom and wildcat rifles should be regarded with more than average suspicion until you gain some experience with them. I once acquired a very nice custom-barreled 7 × 57mm Mauser rifle and set out to develop a deer load for it. Because I'm conservative, I reduced my starting powder charges a full 10 percent below listed maximums. The first shots blew the primers, a sure sign of horrendous chamber pressures, and I suspended firing operations immediately. Subsequent investigation proved that the rifle had a minimum-dimensioned chamber and that the lot of brass I was using was unusually thick-walled. I still have the rifle and enjoy reloading for it, but neither of those things might be true if my starting loads hadn't been extremely conservative. I recall another custom-barreled rifle, a .243 WCF which I got in a slick trade. At least I thought the trade was a slick one until I found that the rifle would blow primers even with factory-loaded ammo!

Very minute differences in the dimensions of chamber, bore, and rifling can make startling differences in the maximum powder charges accepted by a firearm. The governing rule of handloading is this: Never take for granted that any gun will safely accept maximum handbook-listed charges until that fact is proved beyond doubt by actual firing.

You will have noted by now that powder charges are always measured in terms of weight, and that the unit of weight used, at least in the United States, is the avoirdupois *grain.* A grain is equal to $\frac{1}{7000}$ of a pound. Some confusion is possible between a grain-*weight* of gunpowder and an individual granule, since common usage has "grain" meaning a tiny bit or piece. I shall try to keep the two words separate throughout this text, using "grain" only to indicate a unit of weight and "granule" to refer to the particle.

POWDER SCALES AND THEIR USE

A powder balance, or scale, is essential to any but the most superficial practice of handloading ammunition. All powder scales on the market today are

Typical of the simple powder scales on the market
are these from (clockwise
from left) RCBS, Ohaus,
Bonanza, and Redding. All
are magnetically damped
except the Redding, whose
beam oscillations are
damped by a paddle
swinging in oil.

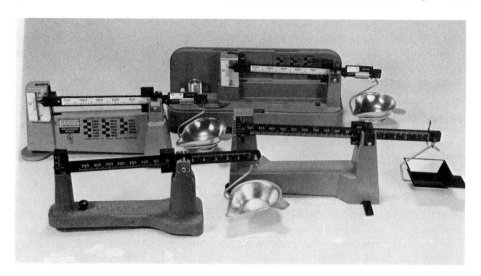

adequate if carefully used, their chief differences being in convenience features. The typical scale is a beam balance with two counterweights, or *poises*, on the beam, and some sort of damping mechanism, most commonly magnetic. The free end of the beam has a pointer relating to a scale and there is a leveling screw in the base. Delicate, usually knife-edge, bearings permit extreme sensitivity in weighing. The scales with extra-large capacities are handy for weighing bullets and complete cartridges as well as powder charges.

The powder scale is the heart of your reloading operations, and it pays to take care of it and learn to use it correctly. First, it should be mounted at about eye level, for convenience in reading and to avoid parallax. (*Parallax* causes a misreading when a scale isn't read from the proper angle.) Second, the powder scale should be kept clean and dust-free, especially the beam bearings. Third, it should *always* be zeroed before use, even though it hasn't been moved since the last use. To do this, set both poises at zero and use the leveling screw to center the beam pointer until it is exactly on the zero mark.

Many scales have a tendency to stick slightly when the beam is in the down position. If powder is gradually added to the pan, they may stick until the weight exceeds the desired charge. Then the beam will go "clank!" to the full-up position and you have to start over. To avoid this, tap lightly with your knuckles on the surface on which the scale is sitting. Do not tap any part of the scale itself. The beam will then usually come smoothly off the bottom position and proceed to balance properly. Take care with your knuckle-rapping, however, that the vibrations are not heavy enough to make the smaller poise jump a notch or two one way or the other.

Magnetically damped scales settle very quickly, usually giving one wide oscillation and one small one before coming to rest. Formerly, powder scales were damped by the motion of a paddle attached to the beam moving in a reservoir of light oil in the scale's base. I never cared for this method of damping, and

prefer to use scales without the oil. Actually, although an undamped scale takes a long time to come to rest, it really isn't any slower than a damped model if you learn to read the pointer swinging rather than waiting for it to settle down. This is probably the most accurate of all methods of reading a simple balance like a powder scale and is the method preferred by laboratory chemists for precise weighing.

An inexpensive but invaluable accessory to a powder scale is something called a powder trickler, which is a simple little gadget for adding powder granules to the scale pan one at a time if need be. With a trickler, you can use a dipper, homemade or otherwise, to drop charges into the scale pan a bit lighter than desired and rapidly bring them up to weight. It's not as fast as a powder measure, of course, but with a

This vibrator-driven, foot-pedal-controlled electric powder trickler from MMC is fast and handy, but not so inexpensive. It's so fast, in fact, that entire small pistol charges of ball-type powders can be thrown with it about as quickly as with a measure. There are also less expensive tricklers that work well.

little practice the difference isn't great enough to justify the cost of a measure for many handloaders.

Sooner or later, of course, you'll get a powder measure, but don't think that you will have dispensed with the need for a scale.

MEASURES AND OTHER CONVENIENCES

The scale must be used to adjust the measure, which throws powder charges volumetrically, to drop the desired charge. Although some measures have micrometer adjustments that are quite accurate, you cannot be certain of returning to a specific charge weight with these adjustments alone. Always set the measure against the scale, using the micrometer adjustments on the measure merely to achieve a rough setting that can be refined with the scale. Then, with the measure set just right, check every fifth or tenth charge thrown to be certain the measure locking screw hasn't loosened up. The scale is the essential final arbiter; the measure is nothing more than a convenience for high production rates. You can reload without a measure, but never without a scale.

Powder measures are peculiar beasts, with a temperament of their own. Basically simple in concept, most of them function by measuring powder that is gravity-fed from a hopper into an adjustable cavity in a rotating drum. A good measure is accurate enough for any reloading purpose. Some are capable of throwing charges consistently within plus or minus

.2 grain, even with the so-called "log" powders, the large-granuled slow-burners like 4831. With smaller-grained powders, and especially with the ball types, the accuracy you get may be even greater from charge to charge.

Consistency depends to a great extent on the operator. Handloaders with their first powder measure are usually appalled at how much the charge-to-charge variation is; then, as their proficiency increases, they discover that the tool is indeed capable of the accuracy claimed by its manufacturer. The secret is in perfect uniformity of operation. The measuring strokes of the handle should be at the same speed and the bumps at each end of the stroke made with the same force for every charge. There is a rhythm and a feel to using a powder measure that can only be gained with practice. The technique that works for me may be all wrong for you, but the key is *consistent* technique, no matter how you do it.

Especially with the long-grained powders, the measure will usually have to cut some granules as the handle is turned. Some measures are better at this than others, having sharper edges for the purpose, but all of them will hang up now and then, breaking your rhythm of operation. When this happens, the charge will almost always be either heavy or light. After a little time on your powder measure, you'll develop the knack of sensing these irregular charges and tossing them back into the hopper with hardly a break in the routine.

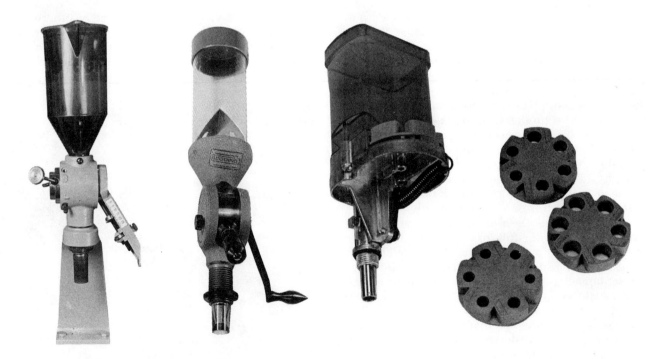

Left: This dual-cavity Ohaus powder measure has served on my bench for many years but is no longer manufactured. The consistency of charges thrown from a measure depends more on the operator's technique than the mechanics of the measure. *Middle:* This Redding BR (for "Bench Rest") powder measure boasts zero-backlash micrometer adjustments of the powder metering cavity. This allows you to return to previous settings with astonishing precision. *Right:* The Lee Auto-Disc powder measure mounts in one station of a turret press and offers 24 different cavities for pistol charges in four interchangeable disks.

The simplest tool for measuring powder is just a dipper. With practice, you can develop pretty good consistency in dipped charge weights, but don't attempt maximum charge levels with dippers unless you check the weight of every charge on a scale.

The very coarse powders will occasionally "bridge" in all measures, meaning that part or all of the charge will hang up where the drop tube narrows below the metering drum. This can be a damn nuisance, with one case receiving half a charge and the next overflowing from a charge-and-a-half. A light tap usually breaks the bridge and allows the full charge to flow through. I know of no way to avoid this nuisance except to be vigilant. Handling gunpowder demands all your attention and concentration, and this bridging business is one of the reasons.

Measures require little or no maintenance, except that you should not leave double-based powders in their hoppers, even overnight. Lubrication is not recommended. Certain powders have a tendency to work their way between the drum and the hole within which it turns and can make the operation somewhat sticky. Cure this by removing the drum and then cleaning the surfaces with an evaporating solvent, but do not oil.

The very simplest part of assembling a handload ought to be dumping the powder into the primed case, but even here there are some special techniques and pitfalls. Many recommended powder charges may turn out to be too bulky for the case. After checking to make certain you're using the correct charge, try pouring the charge into the case very slowly via a funnel with a long spout, perhaps 4 to 6 inches. You'll be amazed at how much more powder you can get into the case by this means, together with a little gentle tapping of the case on the bench top to settle the charge.

DOUBLE CHARGES ARE DISASTROUS

One of the real hazards of handloading is the so-called double charge, which can occur with very fast-burning powders in either pistol or rifle cases. The danger exists whenever there is room in the case for two or more charges of the powder being loaded. If one charge is good, two are distinctly *not* better, not unless you're trying to collect on an insurance policy!

A simple means of guarding against double charges is to arrange two loading blocks, one on each side of the powder measure. In the left block are the primed cases to be charged, standing *mouth down*. Each case is picked up from this position, inverted, charged, and placed (mouth up, of course) in the other loading block. If this is a rigid routine, double-charging a case is impossible. Even so, it's an excellent practice to visually examine all charged cases under a good light before seating bullets. Check any in which the powder level appears to be standing notably higher or lower.

Another good safety rule in reloading is never to have more than one canister of gunpowder on the bench at the same time. This way, you'll never empty the leftover powder in your measure's hopper into the wrong can or inadvertently dump the wrong powder into the hopper.

PROPER POWDER STORAGE

Except when actually pouring powder, keep powder canisters tightly capped. Gunpowder is pretty tractable stuff, but it is an extremely flammable solid, and

 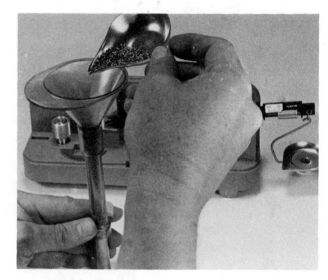

Left: A safe way to avoid double charges is to keep primed cases standing mouth down—and obviously empty—in the loading block, as seen at right, until picked up for charging. ***Right:*** A long drop-tube on a powder funnel permits a heavier powder charge to be poured into a case than a normal funnel will. With some powders, cartridges, and bullets, this is the only way to load recommended charges.

should never be exposed to flame or embers. Reloaders who smoke at the loading bench don't have their heads screwed on right, and are asking to get them *un*screwed! Powder, like primers, should be stored in the canister in which it comes from the factory. If you and a buddy chip in on the cost of a keg or caddy of powder and want to split it up, save a few empty canisters to receive it, and label them conspicuously. Never keep powder in glass, partly because it should be protected from light, and partly because sunlight can be focused by curved glass to ignite the powder. This has happened.

Powder canisters are especially designed to yield before pressures inside them rise to dangerous levels. If you place a closed canister full of powder in a fire, the container will shortly split, issuing a long, bright tongue of hissing flame, but there will be no explosion. My home burned some years ago, but none of the powder canisters in the house went up, not even those whose labels were so blackened that they were illegible. For that matter, not a primer popped (I had more than 10,000 primers and hundreds of loaded rounds of ammunition), and my loading components contributed exactly nothing to the conflagration, although fire damage was very extensive throughout the loading area. That story should comfort you and your insurance man when you begin to accumulate a number of different gunpowders.

Local fire regulations should be followed, of course. Mostly, they pertain to stocks of about 50 pounds of powder or more, and require storage in a powder magazine meeting certain specifications as to construction and heat resistance. An old refrigerator usually meets these requirements. Actually, few handloaders ever have so much powder that they become subject to regulations.

Basically, smokeless powder in the quantities stocked by reloaders should be kept in a cool, dry, dark place in the original canisters. Naturally, a fire extinguisher should be stationed near every location where some quantity of powder is kept, including on the loading bench itself.

The shelf life of gunpowder is unlimited from a practical handloading point of view, but it can deteriorate with age. If you have some canisters of very old powders, watch for rust on the metal portions; when powder begins to break down, some of the compounds released are corrosive to ferrous metals. If you open an old can of powder and notice reddish fumes escaping, consider the powder ruined and get rid of it. In quantities of less than a cupful or so, powder can simply be flushed down the toilet. In larger quantities, lay it out on a cement surface in a trail no more than 3 inches wide and light one end of it. Do not attempt to burn it in a compact pile.

Occasionally, I hear of some shop with large stocks of handloaders' components, including powder, exploding. Since it's almost impossible for smokeless to detonate under this kind of circumstance, such instances are always suspicious. I've investigated a few cases and have never heard of one in which I was convinced that the powder contributed to the explosion. Unless substantial quantities of black powder were involved, explosions have invariably been due to leaking gas, gasoline, or some other explosive. The publicity surrounding incidents of this sort is usually pretty lurid, suggesting that possession of quantities of powder for handloading is hazardous. But anyone with a half-full can of gasoline in the garage is harboring an explosive menace dozens of times more powerful and more volatile than an equal weight of smokeless powder.

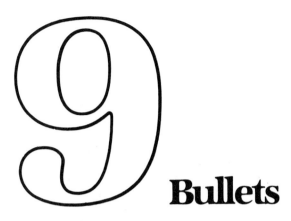

9 Bullets

I once made a rough census on the jacketed bullets available for reloaders and found there were almost 900 different brands, weights, and styles; today, there may well be many more. Somewhere amid that staggering assortment, there should be precisely the correct bullet for any handloading job imaginable. And that's true; the trick is to find it.

BULLET SELECTION IS CRUCIAL

Selecting the one perfect bullet for each load is by far the most crucial aspect of the game. As mentioned in Chapter 3, "Planning the Load," picking the right

These bullet boxes represent only a fraction of the styles, weights, and brands in just .30 caliber. The most important decision made about any loading project is which is the right projectile for the job at hand, amid such confusing abundance.

bullet is the starting point for every handload. The reason is that the bullet is the component that does the work; the purpose of all other components is to direct the bullet to its task with suitable accuracy, velocity, and power. If the bullet fails to perform correctly, however, the load is a failure, regardless of how well case, primer, and powder did their jobs.

And when the bullet does fail to perform, nine times out of ten it's because the handloader sent the wrong bullet for the job. Certain errors in selection are too obvious to require discussion: using a thin-skinned varmint bullet on big game or a full-metal-jacketed slug on any sort of game with certain exceptions. Benchrest shooters will not punch their fingernail-size groups with bullets built for hunting, and long-range rifle competitors are not fond of short, frangible projectiles at super-high velocities. Turkey hunters can't afford such bullets either, no matter what the velocity.

It's desirable that any bullet intended for use on game the size of whitetails and larger have an efficient ballistic shape and that it be pretty accurate, but it's absolutely essential that the bullet offer the right combination of expansion and penetration for the particular size and temperament of the game animal in question. Whitetails, mule deer, and pronghorns are light-bodied beasts that succumb readily to well-placed slugs that open up fairly quickly. Elk, moose, and other species of similar size require bullets that expand more slowly, in order to penetrate to the deep-buried vitals on these muscular, heavy-boned species. Dangerous game such as Cape buffalo, African lion, and the big American bears call for the heaviest slugs with delayed expansion characteristics. Elephants represent the extreme; they're shot with steel-jacketed "solids," which should not expand at all and which provide all the penetration that can be gotten out of a bullet of conventional construction.

Bullets for all these kinds of animals are called "game bullets," but it should be obvious that the right one for any category mentioned here will be wrong for any of the others. A tough bullet that cannot expand properly on an animal as small as a whitetail is neither efficient nor humane, although it may kill, while a fast-opening bullet may not reach the vitals of one of the bigger beasts, inflicting a painful and possibly crippling wound.

Bullets designed for hunting animals smaller than whitetail deer are usually referred to as "varmint bullets," although the varmints may be as large and tough as coyote, bobcat, and javelina. Overexpansion is rarely a problem on such creatures, and never a problem on such pests as jackrabbits, prairie dogs, or woodchucks. Nor is penetration a serious requirement. But these animals are often strafed from extreme rifle ranges, so accuracy, flatness of trajectory, and wind resistance are critical.

INTERNAL CONSTRUCTION IS THE KEY

Hundreds, maybe thousands, of different construction features, gimmicks, and techniques have been tried in the history of smokeless-powder bullet-making to achieve one or more of the above hunting requirements. Many have worked but fell by the wayside in the heat of commercial competition. If you come up with a brilliant idea for promoting expansion along with positive penetration, the chances are it's already been thought of. Everything from soldering cores into their jackets to using two cores of different hardnesses or even two different metals has been tried, along with fancy jackets, metal or plastic wedges to promote expansion, protective nose-caps like the famous "Silvertip" to delay expansion, and dozens more. Cartridge collectors sometimes specialize in the vast variety of ignition systems that have been tried in self-contained cartridges; an even more impressive array could be assembled of trick hunting-bullet designs.

We keep coming back to the basics, a lead-alloy core enveloped in a gilding-metal jacket, with expansion controlled by hollow points, nose shape, amount of exposed lead, jacket profile, scoring of the jacket to create fracture lines, or combinations and minor variations on these themes. The result, for the handloader, is a fantastic selection of custom bullets. Most manufacturers, of course, claim that their bullets will do everything well, and such claims are doubtless sincere. But long, hard experience has proved that certain bullets work reliably on any game to which they are suited, others are remarkably accurate and efficient ballistically, and not too often do the twain meet. I know of no way for a novice handloader to learn the differences except by reading, talking to experts, and testing for himself.

This is no cop-out; it's true that I could categorize bullets available today according to my own experience, but over the life I hope this book will have, so many changes will occur that my information would soon be obsolete. That's how dynamic and competitive the custom-bullet business has become.

Left: Note the subtle difference in color between the dual cores of this Speer "Grand Slam" premium game bullet. The rear core is harder than the front, one of several mechanisms in this projectile intended to control expansion and weight retention upon impact. The specimen at right was recovered from a 750-pound zebra. *Right:* Another famous game bullet style is the Nosler Partition, featuring two separate cores swaged into the jacket from either end. The front core may be lost, but the rear one always remains with the jacket to provide deep penetration. The recovered 7mm sample at right came out of a whitetail deer.

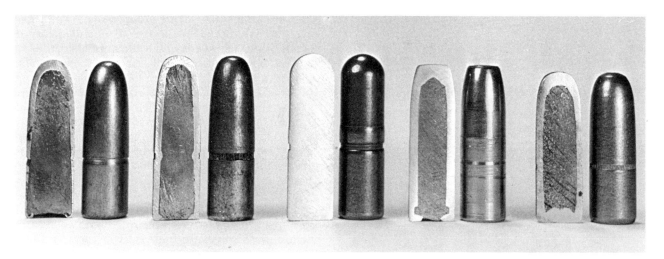

So-called "solid" bullets are used only on the largest and most dangerous game in the world, such as elephant, rhinoceros, and Cape buffalo. Most are not really solid (one metal all the way through), but are merely very strongly full-metal jacketed, as shown. At center in this lineup of 400-grain .416s, however, is a true solid. From left, they are from Ely-Kynoch, Hornady, A-Square, Trophy Bonded Bullets, and Barnes.

"PREMIUM" BULLETS ARE CHEAP AT THE PRICE

One thing will always be true: Elaborately constructed bullets, like those made by Nosler or Bitterroot and others, may seem expensive by comparison with conventional bullets. But the cost of the bullets expended on a long-dreamed-of and expensive hunting trip is trifling at 10 times the usual price. The right bullet for a demanding shot would be literally worth its weight in gold if it meant the climax of the trip and a lifetime memory.

Bullets are *not* the place to economize in hunting handloads!

Nor in target loads, for that matter. A man who competes seriously with a rifle or handgun, whether in benchrest, smallbore, National Match, or whatever kind of tournament, needs a cheap bullet—the one that is likely to cost him that last, vital point for victory—like he needs a chronic case of M-1 thumb!

Plinking and practice loads (which for most of us represent the bulk of our handloading) *are* the spot to save a buck, use up stocks of bullets that didn't pan out for the purpose for which you bought them, or even to try making your own, either cast or swaged.

Assuming a good-quality brand name, I know of no nondestructive testing technique that can predict bullet performance. Concentricity is important, but there probably aren't three dozen men in the United States who can detect significant out-of-roundness with the best micrometer ever made, although there are thousands who *think* they can. It could be done, probably, with an optical comparator, but no handloader has one, and if he did he'd find the comparator slower than actual loading and firing as a method of testing. Uniform weight is important, and a batch of bullets can be sorted into weight groups with an ordinary powder scale, but improvement in grouping ability is sure to be masked by all the other multi-

The Bitterroot Bonded-Core bullets are made by hand, one at a time, of pure copper-tubing jackets and soft lead cores. The two elements are literally soldered together. These bullets expand beautifully (the recovered 7mm samples are from an African gemsbok, or giant oryx) and lose almost no weight. Expensive compared to other bullets—but inexpensive when you consider their effectiveness!

tudinous factors involved in actual firing tests. Only extreme weight variations within a batch, on the order of plus-or-minus half a grain, can be detected on target with less than the finest benchrest rifles. Even then, the bullet may perform beautifully on game, if that's its purpose.

I've already discussed considerations of sectional density, ballistic coefficient, weight, and wind resistance in Chapter 2, "Basic Ballistics." I discuss so-called brush-bucking ability under "Loading for the Hunting Field."

BULLET SEATING DEPTH

All that's left is to plug the bullet into your sorted, inspected, cleaned, chamfered, deburred, primed, charged cartridge case. It's necessary to see that the

The dummy cartridge at left was loaded to fit a 7mm Magnum rifle whose chamber throat had been lengthened. The bullet in the center round is seated to factory dimensions, as shown by the factory cartridge at right. The left-hand round couldn't be chambered and probably wouldn't even enter the magazine of a standard rifle, while the excessive bullet-jump of the shorter round might wreck accuracy. Such must be watched for in secondhand rifles.

expander button in the sizing die has left the case mouth the right diameter to grip the bullet firmly; thereafter the depth to which the bullet is seated is the major consideration.

Many game bullets are cannelured, having milled grooves rolled into their jackets at the point where the mouth of the case should come to make a cartridge of standard overall length. Some bullets come with two different cannelures, for use in two different cartridges; others, especially target and varmint slugs, are uncannelured.

It may happen that "standard overall length"—that is, the overall length to which factory cartridges are loaded—doesn't suit your purposes. You want to seat the bullet deeper or shallower for one reason or another. There is no reason a bullet must be seated to any specific depth except for mechanical considerations. In a repeating rifle, for example, the space in the magazine imposes an overall-length limit on cartridges, and sometimes minor adjustments in seating depth can smooth feeding from magazine to chamber. But the major concern is the relationship of the bullet to the chamber throat when the loaded cartridge is fully chambered.

If the bullet is seated so far out that it is jammed solidly into the origin of the rifling, or "lede," serious

pressure jumps may ensue because the bullet is delayed an additional fraction of a second before it begins to move forward under the impetus of the expanding powder gases. It will also make the breeching system of the gun difficult to lock, perhaps slowing the vital second shot at escaping game or wrecking a target shooter's rapid-fire rhythm. Finally, if the bolt is opened without firing the round, the bullet may be held firmly enough by the rifling to be pulled out of the case, spilling powder into the action of the gun and requiring the use of a cleaning rod to remove the bullet.

On the other hand, too-deep seating can also increase gas pressures somewhat by reducing the volume inside the case. Except in extreme cases, the magnitude of pressure increase will very rarely be disastrous, but it's certainly undesirable and unnecessary. Accuracy frequently suffers from seating bullets too deeply, however, because the bullet must jump so far from the case mouth to the rifling. During this jump, under the impulse of thousands of pounds per square inch, the bullet is completely unsupported, and usually arrives at the lede yawing or slightly cocked. The lede may straighten it out partially, but most likely it will be driven through the bore in a position in which the bullet's center of form no longer corresponds with its center of rotation. It then leaves the muzzle in a condition of dynamic imbalance, and the result is a wild shot.

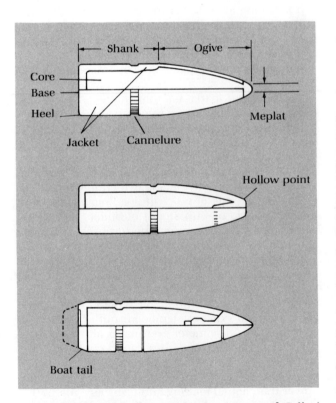

Parts of jacketed bullets: Ogive (pronounced O-jive) derives from French; it originally meant *arch* in a cathredral ceiling. Cannelure (pronounced KAN-ae-loor) means groove or fluting.

Land-marks in a soot coating show that this smok-ed bullet is seated too long for the rifle. (Live rounds, of course, should never be smoked.) A good general rule is to seat so the bullet barely fails to contact the chamber throat, say by .030 inch or so.

Most reloaders, therefore, seat rifle bullets to touch very lightly or barely fail to touch the lands. Benchrest shooters mostly prefer fairly firm contact between the bullet's ogive and the rifling, while hunters like a small but positive clearance. Some experimenting will be required to determine exactly how much clearance gives best results in each different rifle and loading, but a good starting point is somewhere between .030 to .060 inch.

You can determine the amount of clearance in a couple of ways. The easiest is to take a fired case and insert a bullet in the neck with the fingers. The bullet should be an easy sliding fit; if it is too loose, it may be necessary to run the case into the sizing die just enough to size a tenth of an inch of the mouth. The bullet should be seated as long as possible. Then carefully chamber the dummy round and gently close the bolt. Contact with the lands should push the bul-let into the case neck, so that the resulting overall cartridge length can be measured. This round can then be used as a gauge to set the seating die to seat bullets a fraction of an inch shorter.

The other and more precise way of measuring seating depth is to make up a dummy (repeat: *dum-my*) round with the bullet seated to about factory length. Chamber this round in the rifle and insert a cleaning rod down the muzzle until it comes to rest on the tip of the bullet. Mark the rod at the muzzle. Then extract the dummy round and drop a *loose* bullet point-first into the chamber with the muzzle pointed down. With a cleaning rod, tap very lightly a couple of times on the base of the bullet. Now, han-dling the rifle gingerly, turn it butt-down and reinsert the rod, allowing it to come to rest very lightly on the bullet's nose. The rod is again marked at the

muzzle and the distance between the two marks will be the difference between the overall length of your dummy round and the longest feasible seating with that bullet in that weapon. This technique sounds complicated, but it's really rather easy and extremely accurate.

Bear in mind that while all these measurements are *overall* cartridge length, it isn't the tip of the bullet that contacts the rifling (or the seating stem in the seating die, either). Contact is made at some point on the ogive, well back from the tip and just in front of the full-diameter section of the projectile. If you're ever in doubt as to whether all your measurements and calculations have produced a round that is ac-tually touching the rifling lede, there's a very simple method of finding out. Again, make up a *dummy* round, without primer or powder, and smoke the bullet sooty black in the flame of a kitchen match (away from the loading bench, of course). Then gently chamber the round and just as gently extract it. The faintest contact between bullet and lands will show clearly as bright copper spots against the velvety black soot. Confusion may arise in rifles equipped with a plunger-type ejector mounted in the bolt face. Such ejectors will cock the dummy round to the side as it is withdrawn from the chamber and may cause a streak of soot to be scraped off the bullet in some irregular pattern, but the land marks will still be un-mistakable all around the circumference of the bullet.

Once you standardize the seating depth for each

A heavy boat-tailed bullet seated to standard factory overall cartridge length in a case like this .284 WCF can raise pressures by reducing the volume of the combustion chamber.

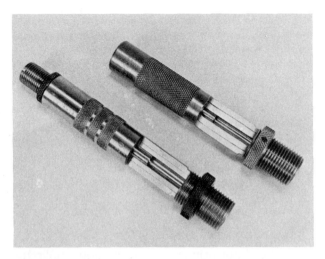

Left: The precision seating dies shown here are designed to ensure that the case is held in perfect alignment with the bullet as the bullet is forced into the case neck. Noticeable improvement in accuracy may result from use of dies. *Right:* A collection of suitably-marked dummy rounds vastly simplifies resetting bullet-seating dies when adjustments have been changed. Just back the seating screw out, adjust crimping shoulder if necessary, insert dummy, and screw seating stem down firmly against the dummy's bullet.

The .44 pistol bullet shown at left has a crimping cannelure for use in revolvers. The 9mm (center) and the .45 (right) do not have a cannelure because the autopistol cartridges for which they are made headspace on their mouths and cannot be roll-crimped.

load, you can save yourself the trouble of going through the entire process again if you'll make up another dummy round and mark it with a felt-tip pen to indicate the brand and weight of bullet. A file of such "length rounds" makes it easy to reset your seating dies to any desired load after having changed the settings.

Each different bullet to be used in a certain rifle, even those of very similar profiles, will require its own specific seating depth. Round-nose bullets, for example, will have to be seated relatively deeper than spitzers of the same weight because their fatter ogives contact the lands sooner when the round is chambered. Unless you use only one particular bullet brand, weight, and style in a rifle, you'll be constantly changing the settings of your bullet-seating die.

SEATING BULLETS FOR HANDGUNS

Handgunners have considerably less leeway in bullet seating than do reloaders of rifle cartridges. Non-standard seating depths tend to jam semiauto pistols, and revolver rounds are limited by cylinder length. There are a few exceptions. But for the most part, handgun bullets are simply seated to give an overall length identical to that of factory loads, and most handgun bullets are cannelured at the correct place for crimping at this length.

If the cannelure happens to be mislocated for your purposes, on either handgun or rifle bullets, simple canneluring tools are offered by C-H and Shooters Accessory Supply. The tool allows you to put a cannelure on any bullet wherever you want it.

CRIMPING

The importance of a cannelure is that the type of crimp used by most reloaders (when they use one) relies upon the presence of a cannelure. This is called a roll crimp, and most standard bullet-seating dies are provided with a shoulder in the die cavity that, when the mouth of the case is forced against it, actually rolls the case lip inward into the cannelure, locking the bullet in place. Without a cannelure, there's no place for the lip to go and the case shoulder is usually bulged, sometimes ruined.

I prefer not to crimp rifle ammunition at all unless I have to. Crimping and resizing as a case is reloaded repeatedly cold-works the brass at the case mouth and eventually promotes split necks. Further, there is evidence that crimping injures potential accuracy. As pointed out earlier, uniform roll-crimping demands absolutely uniform case lengths, and that means regular trimming, chamfering, and deburring.

In most cases, crimping is a waste of time in rifle loads, but there are occasions when it is essential. One of these is when the ammunition is to be used in a rifle with a tubular magazine. Consider what

The bullet at right has been battered by recoil in a box magazine. The bullet at left has not only been battered but also shoved deeper into the case by recoil forces. This dangerous occurrence can usually be avoided by using an expander ball of smaller diameter in the sizing die. (See drawings, page 77.)

happens to a cartridge in such a magazine; when the rifle is fired, recoil drives it rearward but the inertia of the cartridge in the magazine causes it to tend to remain in place. This compresses the magazine follower spring which, when the rifle comes to rest at the rear of its recoil movement, drives the ammo in the magazine rearward, slamming it against the stop. Without a positive crimp, this slam-bang action may easily drive the bullet deeper into its case, which fouls up feeding and may be dangerous.

Cartridges in a box magazine or clip take a beating, too, being hurled against the front of the magazine as the rifle recoils with considerable force, more than enough to batter the soft lead of spitzer points unless the magazine is equipped with a bullet point protector. However, except in rifles of exceptionally heavy recoil, bullets subjected to such treatment will usually not be pushed back into their cases if the resizing die reduces case necks to the proper diameter to hold the bullets by friction.

Certain modern cartridges with extremely short necks simply do not have enough bearing surface to grip long, heavy bullets and so hold them against heavy recoil without a crimp, and a hard one. Except in the case of such cartridges, if you find reserve ammo with bullets pushed deeper than you seated them, crimping may be a temporary answer. But you'll be happier locating the problem in your sizing die and correcting it.

Reloading for any autoloading weapon also re-

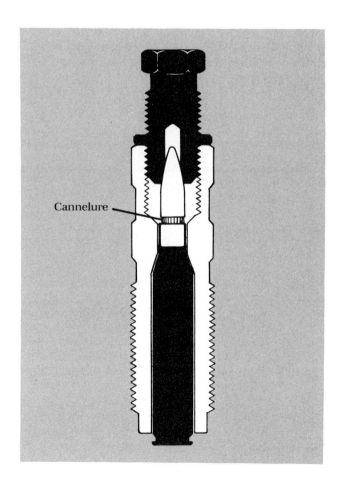

This cutaway view of a loading die shows the case crimped into the bullet's cannelure.

Cannelure

quires crimping. Cartridges are subjected to some pretty violent treatment coming out of the magazine, and uncrimped bullets may be pushed deeper in their cases when slammed against the feed-ramp as the bolt rides forward.

Many handgun cartridges for semiautomatic weapons cannot be roll-crimped because they headspace on their mouths. Several methods may be tried to keep bullets in place. First, the loaded round can be taper-crimped in a special die that squeezes the case neck more tightly around the bullet. No cannelure is necessary for taper-crimping. Second, the expander button in the sizing die may be dressed to a smaller diameter or removed altogether, which will necessitate great care in seating bullets to avoid crumpling case mouths. Third, you can use your canneluring tool to roll a cannelure into the *case* at the point at which the bullet's base should rest. This provides a slight shoulder inside the case to support the bullet. Fourth, you can change lots of brass; a different brand may work better. Fifth, you can change sizing dies.

Sixth, and finally, you can change pistols! Take your pick.

Revolver loads usually require heavy crimping, too, for different reasons. Heavy recoil forces work with the inertia of the bullets in uncrimped rounds to *pull* the bullets rather than to push them deeper. In such cartridges as the mighty .44 Magnum, a couple of shots may cause the bullets in the unfired cartridges to protrude so far that the cylinder cannot rotate. Even more important, with some of the slow-burning pistol powders used in the magnums, a very heavy

crimp is one of the factors in uniform, complete combustion of the powder.

In general, crimping should be avoided whenever it isn't absolutely required. In most rifle cartridges it can be avoided; in many handgun rounds it cannot. When crimping cannot be avoided, there are right and wrong ways to accomplish it. The great majority of dies provide for crimping and bullet seating simultaneously. This would be all right except that the geometry of the dies is such that crimping begins before the bullet is fully seated. With wide cannelures and the most careful adjustment of the dies, it may still work, at least well enough for casual use. But for the greatest precision and best accuracy, seating and crimping should be done in two separate steps, even though the same die is used for both purposes.

In the first step, the die body is backed off a turn or two, the bullet-seating stem is adjusted to proper seating depth, and the bullets are seated. Then the seating stem is screwed *out* a few turns so that it will not contact the seated bullets, the die body is screwed *in* to produce the desired degree of crimp, and the lot of cartridges is run through the die again. Chapter 12, on adjusting loading dies, gives more details on the process, but this brief description conveys the general procedure. The extra step is well worth the trouble, especially with pistol ammo, for increased uniformity and accuracy.

With the seating and crimping of the bullet, the actual process of handloading a round of ammunition is complete. Now we come to the fun part, actually firing to see how well your careful planning and labor have worked out.

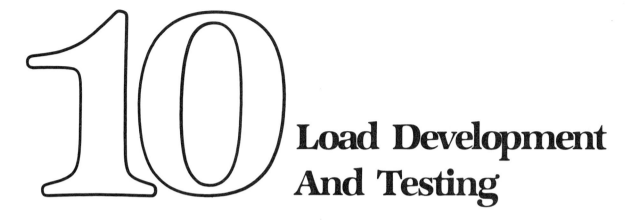

10 Load Development And Testing

oad development is the execution of the planning of a specific handload described in Chapter 3, together with the experimenting and testing necessary to assure that the load is safe, mechanically functional, and capable of its mission. In less formal handloaders' jargon, it's known as "working up a load."

That phraseology is not bad, either, since the process of developing a load literally involves beginning with powder charges well below the expected maximum weights and working, step by step, upward until the specifications for the load are achieved, or until it becomes apparent that they cannot be achieved safely with the selected components.

"MAXIMUM" LOADS

With the correct bullet for the job in mind, and what seems to be the most promising powder for the proposed load, the first step is to estimate the charge weight at which the desired performance will be realized. Please note that I did not say "maximum performance." The word "maximum" is tossed around among reloaders and in their literature with a familiarity that is frightening. Very few reloaders seem to understand what a maximum load is. The truth is that what many reloaders refer to as their "max" is actually an overload. That they get into as little trouble as they do is a compliment to the quality and

Serious load testing, especially for accuracy, can be done only from solid sandbagged rests at known ranges. Pressures and velocities can be checked at the same time.

margins of safety built into modern firearms.

Let's think in terms of 10-shot series, rather than of a single firing. The variables in ammunition being what they are, it's impossible that all 10 shots will register exactly the same chamber pressure and velocity. Instead, we must deal in the *average* pressure and velocity recorded over the 10-shot string. As a sidelight, the smaller the variations in such measurements, the more efficient and accurate most loads will be. In typical hunting-rifle cartridges, a difference between the highest- and lowest-pressure shots of 1,000 PSI (pounds per square inch) is quite good, but differences of as much as 10,000 PSI or more are not at all uncommon. Such a wide variation strongly suggests that something is wrong with the load.

You have to be careful about averages though. If you'll think about it a moment, you'll realize that it's possible for one load having only a 1,000-PSI variation to have the same average pressure for the 10-shot series as another showing a 10,000-PSI extreme range. Here are examples for a couple of hypothetical loads, as tested in a ballistic lab:

TEST A		TEST B	
Shot No. 1–50,400 PSI		Shot No. 1–46,800 PSI	
No. 2–51,500 PSI		No. 2–50,100 PSI	
No. 3–49,200 PSI		No. 3–51,200 PSI	
No. 4–49,700 PSI		No. 4–50,500 PSI[1]	
No. 5–50,500 PSI		No. 5–46,100 PSI	
No. 6–49,600 PSI		No. 6–59,900 PSI[2]	
No. 7–50,100 PSI		No. 7–50,400 PSI	
No. 8–49,100 PSI[1]		No. 8–46,800 PSI	
No. 9–50,000 PSI		No. 9–56,600 PSI	
No. 10–52,300 PSI[2]		No. 10–50,400 PSI	
Average	50,200 PSI	Average	50,800 PSI
Variation	3,200 PSI	Variation	13,800 PSI

[1] = lowest individual pressure
[2] = highest individual pressure
All pressures rounded to the nearest 100 PSI.

Let's assume you are working with a cartridge that has a standard working pressure of 54,000 PSI. Both these loads show an *average* pressure that is well within that limit. But note that in Test B two of the individual shots, 6 and 9, far exceeded it, one of them by a dangerous margin. Note, too, the vastly larger extreme variation for Test B, almost 14,000 PSI as opposed to only 3,200 PSI in Test A.

The hypothetical load in Test B is an overload, even though its *average* pressure is within limits. It will probably prove to be a very unsatisfactory load too, but for the moment the only concern is safety. Each shot fired that exceeds the designed working pressures for a gun stresses some of its components, and those stresses are cumulative. The fact that the gun failed to blow up when the first overload was fired merely means that it's a well-made gun. But it might blow unexpectedly in the future, not as a result of any one shot but as the result of a long series of loads that overstressed its parts.

Therefore, for your purposes, an overload may be defined as any load of which the highest pressure shot in the 10-shot series exceeds the rated limit for that cartridge. If just one shot goes over the limit, it's too hot for continued use. Thus the *average* pressure for a true *maximum* handload will be well *below* the accepted pressure limits for that cartridge.

All references made in this text to maximum loadings should be interpreted in that light.

A PRESSURE SERIES

Let's get back to developing your load. I said that the first step is to arrive at a predicted maximum charge weight, assuming you plan a full-power loading. As described in Chapter 8, this is most easily done by consulting several different reliable data sources and taking the average of their top recommended loads for your cartridge, powder, and bullet as your projected maximum. Let's assume that the figure you arrive at as a reasonable top load is 60 grains.

The procedure is to load a series of cartridges for test firing, with the initial group charged with between 5 and 10 percent less powder than you figure you'll end up with. When using a familiar rifle, 5 percent is a safe figure, and amounts to a 3-grain reduction, or 57 grains for the first firings. Load three to five rounds with 57 grains, another three to five with 58 grains, and still another set with 59 grains of your selected powder. At this point, it's not a bad idea to increase charges by *half*-grain increments, especially with one of the ball-type powders or some of the extruded numbers, which are known to exhibit

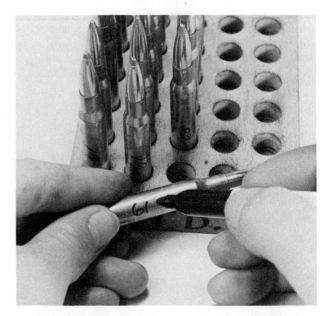

A pressure series is a series of cartridges loaded with progressively heavier powder charges fired to determine maximum safe pressures in a specific firearm. There's no harm in actually writing the powder charge on each case, to ensure against mix-ups.

some lot-to-lot variations in burning rate. In hot weather, or when using a fairly fast-burning powder in full charges, it's a better idea to start the half-grain steps a grain or so sooner in the series. Finally, load another five cases with 60 grains, the projected maximum.

If you're working with a rifle whose characteristics are not known, I'd suggest dropping that top charge back a full 10 percent for starters, and ascending through the last 2 grains via half-grain increases. This makes for more test shooting and the expenditure of more components, but it's worth the trouble.

Now you can head to the rifle range to see if these glittering jewels you've assembled so lovingly really go BANG! when the trigger is pressed. You have loaded what is known as a pressure series. Their sole purpose is to determine the safe maximum charge weight for that set of components *in your own rifle*. Obviously, without elaborate laboratory equipment, the individual handloader is unable to determine absolute pressure levels in his reloads. On the other hand, what he really wants to know is not the exact pressure, to the last PSI, produced by his loads, but whether those loads are safe for regular use in *his* rifle. If they are, it matters not what the numbers say; if they aren't, the numbers still don't matter.

Upcoming text explains how to detect excessive pressures by examining parts of the round after firing and by taking precise physical measurements both before and after firing.

PRESSURE SYMPTOMS

There are quite a few indicators of high pressure, some of which require a bit of experience to interpret. They begin with the sound and feel of the rifle when it is fired. The muzzle blast of a seriously overpressure load will seem earsplitting, and the recoil will be abnormally heavy. If you're firing a familiar rifle in which you've shot enough factory ammo to give you the feel of the normal blast and kick, you should notice immediately the increased sensations of an overload, if similar bullet weights are being used. A shooting buddy of mine once fired three overloads in his .30/06, cartridges that held a full 10 grains too much powder. Not only could he tell the difference, but *I* could tell the difference, sitting at the next bench on the firing line.

A too hot load will often cause a perforated or badly leaking primer. This damaged primer will usually produce a stinging puff of hot gases on the shooter's upper face (one of the several very good reasons to wear protective glasses at all times when shooting).

The effort required to extract the fired case is another index to high pressures. In extreme cases, even a bolt-action rifle with its powerful primary extraction can be locked up solidly, so that the bolt cannot be lifted by hand. Lever, auto, slide, and single-shot actions usually have less extraction power and may be locked up at much lower pressures than a bolt action. In any kind of action, such a condition indicates a

Bottom: Increasing powder charges to destruction of gun is not recommended! This is what's left of a .44 Magnum barrel in a Thompson-Center Contender that was fired with a massive overdose of the wrong powder. That's solid steel you see peeled back like an orange rind. Some of the shrapnel is still in the shooter's leg. *Top:* This is the .44 Magnum case in that wrecked Contender when it blew.

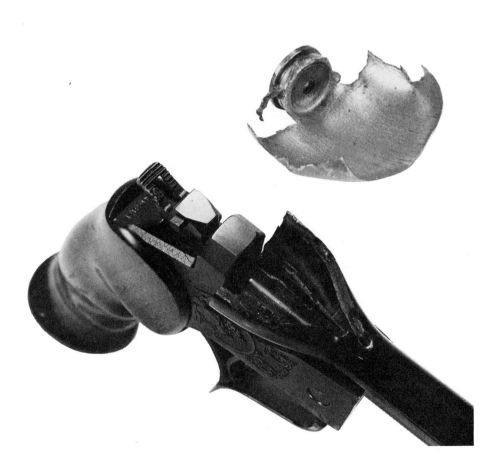

chamber pressure far beyond the boundaries of safety. When this occurs, there is a very good chance that the rifle has been damaged in some way. The locking system may be stretched or sprung, headspace will almost invariably have been increased dangerously, and the chamber and/or receiver ring may be swelled permanently. Certainly, serious permanent stresses have been imposed in the steel of the firearm.

There are all degrees of extraction difficulty, however, ranging from the locked-up bolt I just mentioned to a barely perceptible stickiness on the upstroke of the bolt handle. Even the stickiness, no matter how insignificant, means that the load just fired was an overload in your rifle, no matter what the reloading manual said.

After you extract the case, several parts of its anatomy may offer clues to pressure. If there is blackening around the primer, that primer leaked a little gas even if you didn't feel it on your face, and in normal cases this means the load was too hot. If the letters and numbers of the headstamp appear to be ironed out, so to speak—noticeably less deeply indented than on other cases in the same lot—it means the same thing. On rifles with plunger-type ejectors mounted in the bolt face, excessive pressure usually is revealed by a small, clear circle of brass, which was extruded back into the ejector hole and forced the spring-loaded ejector before it. This circle may be sheared off when the bolt is rotated if the extrusion is deep enough. A fellow in my rifle club once told me that he found these brightly polished ejector marks a convenient way to keep track of how many times his 7mm Magnum cases had been fired! I picked up my shooting gear and moved to a bench at the other end of the firing line.

Some rifles will mark cases in this fashion even with

normal pressures, due to tiny burrs standing above the plane of the bolt face around the ejector hole. If they appear with loads you *know* are mild, suspect this condition, and polish the burrs away with a small, hard Arkansas stone.

General polishing of the case head around the primer usually means high pressure, too. This occurs because high-pressure loads tend to cling to the walls of the chamber, the brass case having expanded permanently. These loads also tend to resist being turned by the rotating bolt head as the bolt is lifted. In varying degrees, this is the explanation of locked-up bolts and of scraped-off ejector-hole marks too.

READING PRIMERS

We come now to the primer itself, a controversial indicator of high pressures. It's true that there are no absolutely reliable means of deducing pressure levels from primer condition, nor of relating two fired primers of different makes to each other. But it's also true that any reloader can, with experience, learn to "read" fired primers, provided they are all of the same brand and lot, and fired in the same rifle. If the firing-pin indentation is surrounded by a pronounced crater, the crater is a warning signal; it *may* mean that the rifle has a weak firing-pin spring or an oversized firing-pin hole in the bolt face. But, again, if you know from experience that your rifle has neither of these defects, that cratered primer in a previously untested load is a sign of high pressures. This is especially true if the primer is also excessively flattened. It should keep some of the radius between the face and the walls of the primer cup; if that's gone, the load was very hot. If it's not only gone but reversed, so that the primer has a flanged appearance when

Left: A circular, brightly polished area on a fired case head, especially from a rifle with a plunger-style ejector, strongly suggests excessive pressures. *Middle:* This is an extreme case of a leaking primer. The dark smudges were made by gas forcing itself out around the primer. Note that the primer itself is cratered but not too flattened, from which we may conclude that the primer pocket was already loosened from earlier high-pressure firings. *Right: This* was an *over*load! A drastic over-charge wrecked the case and flowed the brass into the extractor recess. The rifle was damaged but, fortunately, the shooter escaped injury.

The two primers at left show differing degrees of cratering, while the next two have perforated primers. At far right is an example of a case fired at normal pressure.

The three fired primers at near left reveal varying amounts of flanging at the top. The primer at the extreme right shows normal pressure. Together with other symptoms, a pronounced flanging can be an indicator of excessive pressures.

punched out of the pocket and viewed in profile, the load was even hotter.

The trick to getting useful information out of fired primers lies in using the same brand most of the time. You will gradually learn what different high-pressure levels look like in your primers, and can correlate these signs with the other pressure symptoms mentioned above to construct a quite dependable early-warning system. In fact, you should never rely on just one of these signs alone. If you find the bolt-lift heavier than usual but the case head and primer don't look too bad, don't choose arbitrarily to believe the primer and ignore the sticky bolt. Take everything into consideration and don't fail to heed even a single high-pressure sign, wherever it may turn up.

The most certain information on high pressures that the average handloader can collect from fired cases involves using an accurate micrometer. A very good vernier caliper can also be used, but a "mike" is better. Either instrument requires some practice and skill to apply with reliable accuracy, but every handloader should have a micrometer and know how to use it, if only for his own convenience.

MEASURING CASE EXPANSION

The method of pressure estimation by measurement gauges any permanent increase in the diameter of the cartridge case head after firing. Measurements must be made with considerable precision to be of any value, since even one half of one thousandth of an inch is significant. Several schools of thought exist

as to where the measurement should be taken. On rimless cases, the head immediately forward of the extraction groove is the most popular spot, and on belted cases, the head forward of and adjacent to the belt is most favored. On rimmed cases, the head just in front of the rim is the diameter most often used. These are the locations I prefer, but some experimenters have reported good results miking the diameters of the rims or belts. With careful measurement and experience in the technique, any of these places can be used to get good information, but the

Case-head expansion after firing is the handloader's key to acceptable pressures in his own guns. Shown here is the correct place at which to take diameter readings on a standard, rimless case. Of course, measurements before and after firing must be taken across the same diameter.

values given below apply to the first ones I mentioned and may or may not hold true for any other places on the case head.

All cases expand noticeably in these areas on first firing, whether with factory loads or handloads, so the micrometer technique cannot be used on this firing. That first firing, however, should expand the case to match the particular chamber in which it has been fired, and any measurable further expansion on subsequent shots should be considered an indication of very high chamber pressures. In general, if the case head expands by as much as .001 inch, in *any* dimension, it may be considered ample evidence that pressures were excessive for that shot in that gun. Some authorities suggest that even .0005 inch is too much, but this should certainly be regarded as the outside limit of permissible expansion. I personally prefer to keep working loads under .0001 inch expansion, and recommend such a standard to the conservative handloader.

This case-head expansion, by the way, explains the loosening of primer pockets described in an earlier chapter as a high-pressure symptom.

After the expansion that takes place on the first firing, which is normal and does not necessarily indicate high chamber pressures, it's desirable that case heads retain the same dimensions indefinitely. If a load that is producing, say, .0005 inch expansion is used regularly, it will expand by that amount (or a little less, due to work-hardening of the brass) on each firing. The primer pocket will eventually loosen up and the case will be ruined even though pressures are not necessarily exceeding safety limits on any individual firing.

To reliably detect casehead expansion, it's important to measure the diameter at the same point on the case with the micrometer before and after firing. Probably the very best method is to take two diameter measurements at right angles to each other and average them, but for practical purposes it's enough to take only one, provided that one is made with care. The easiest way to do this is to have notebook and pencil on the shooting bench. Before chambering each cartridge, make a mark with a felt-tip pen on the case and take a diameter reading at that mark. Write down the measurement, preferably to four decimal places. Fire the round, extract it, remeasure across the same mark, and compare the reading to the notation of the prefiring measurement. If there is no difference, no additional writing is needed. If there is some expansion, note it opposite the appropriate notes for comparison. Instead of a mark on the case, you can also use one of the letters or digits on the headstamp as a marker to ensure comparable diameter measurements before and after firing. This is less precise than marking the case, but is adequate for most purposes.

Back to your series of pressure loads, charged with increasing weights of powder. As each group is fired, *all* the indices to possible high pressure discussed above should be checked. If no pressure signs appear, the next heaviest charges are fired, and so on through

This is not the result of excessive pressure, but of insufficient support. When this .270 cartridge was unintentionally chambered in a 7mm Magnum rifle, the extractor managed to hold it firmly enough to allow the firing pin to detonate the primer. Case-body expansion in the drastically oversized chamber exceeded the elastic limit of the brass, and the case split. Such an accident is always possible whenever more than one kind of ammo is on or near a shooting place, and is extremely dangerous.

the series. If no symptoms of excessive pressure occur even with the expected maximum load, you may be able to take the charge up another grain or two, using the same procedures and advancing in half-grain steps. In this way, you may be able to safely exceed the top charge-weight recommendation in any given handbook, which only means that your particular rifle is more tolerant of those maximum charges than the test guns used in compiling the handbook data.

However, if you do exceed recommended maximums, you must realize that you're on your own, with only your own knowledge and alertness to protect you from an overload. Wherever you note high-pressure signs on cases, primers, or in the rifle's operation, even if the charge producing those signs is well *below* recommended maximums, you have arrived at or exceeded practical maximums with those components in your own rifle. When I find a load in a pressure series that produces .0005 inch head expansion, I stop right there, drop back at least one grain of powder, and fire another series of 10 rounds. If none of the 10 reveals as much as .0005 inch expansion, I call that my maximum load. If you're not all that certain of your ability to read a mike to the fourth decimal place, take .001 inch as the warning signal and reduce the load (giving that much expansion) by at least 6 percent. If subsequent firings with that charge weight produce no significant additional expansion, primer pockets remain tight, and case life is good, you have a good, safe maximum load.

COMPONENT SUBSTITUTIONS

Now, if you ever substitute components in that load—change bullet, case, or primer brands or types, for example—the whole load-development procedure should be repeated. The powder charge should be reduced about 2 grains (in typical hunting cartridges, more in magnums) and worked back up by half-grain increments. Chances are, you'll find the old, established maximum is still safe, but maybe not, and in this game it's just as well to avoid nasty surprises. A change to a cartridge case brand averaging heavier (less internal volume) can easily reduce the max load by 2 grains, and tests have shown that 10 different bullets of different makes but of nominally identical weights and styles in the same caliber can alter peak chamber pressures by as much as 7,000 CUP. If the load were already at maximum with the lowest-pressure bullet in this group, switching to the high-pressure one might very well shove chamber pressure through the ceiling.

Factors such as bullet bearing length, core hardness, jacket thickness, and design are responsible for these pressure variations, and they are not predictable. We cannot say that Brand X bullets consistently require lower powder charge weights than Brand Y bullets in all calibers and all rifles. The one and only method of making such determinations with your own equipment is by firing pressure series and measuring case-head expansion. You are certainly right, if it has occurred to you that once a good, safe, accurate load has been established, the standardization of that load and all its components should save an awful lot of time and trouble.

READING A TARGET

Presumably, you will be aiming at a target as you fire the pressure series, and some indications can also be gleaned from the target groups. Each charge level should be fired at a different bull's-eye and the group sizes correlated with the powder charges. It is a very broad, general rule (with many exceptions) that finest accuracy in a given cartridge will appear in loads that are somewhat below absolute maximum. I have seen some magnificent groups shot with overloads too, but it is still not uncommon to see a linear relationship between group sizes and powder charges, when all else remains the same. I will discuss reloading specifically for best accuracy later; for the moment, I'm speaking of group sizes as related to each other rather than in an absolute sense.

Say you expect your maximum load to be around 60 grains of a given powder, for example, and drop back to 55 or so grains for your first pressure firings. You may see a group appear, at 100 yards, of 3 inches center-to-center spread between the widest bullet holes. Fifty-six grains of powder may then drop the group size to 2½ inches, 57 to 2¼ inches, 58 to 1⅞ inches, 58.5 grains of powder to 1¾ inches. Fifty-nine grains might then print a five-shot group just 1½ inches across, while another grain added to the powder charge opens the group up to 2 inches again. These numbers are a hypothetical case, but they're quite representative of results of hundreds of pressure series I've fired. It takes more than a single group to determine anything very definitive about a load's grouping potential, but a correlation between powder charge and group size indicates strongly that the 59-

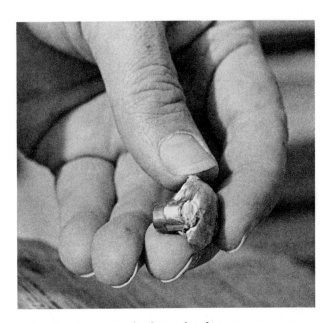

Left: Penetration testing can be done by firing into a stack of saturated telephone books or newspapers. Penetration in wet paper pulp is not necessarily the same as in flesh and bone, but it at least allows easy bullet retrieval and comparisons from shot to shot. *Right:* Bullets recovered from the wet pulp paper can also be compared for expansion characteristics. But you must bear in mind that this test medium makes any bullet look as good as it ever can.

grain charge is worth experimenting with further for top accuracy, and that the load is nearing maximum levels there.

High pressures tend also to be somewhat erratic pressures, as revealed in tests A and B shown in the table earlier in this chapter. Muzzle velocities tend to be related to pressures, and accuracy comes from uniform velocities, among other things. This is an oversimplified explanation, but it shows why maximum safe loads may not deliver maximum accuracy. And it also shows why reading groups shot with pressure series can add one more iota of information on handload pressures generated.

CASE LIFE

The final source of information has to do with the reloading life of the cases. As a rule, the higher pressures mean shorter case life. The causes of failure may be manifold; necks may split, primer pockets may expand, incipient cracks may appear in case bodies. Experience with individual rifles and reloading dies is helpful in evaluating case life. With some combinations, "normal" case life may be almost indefinite, perhaps 50 shots or more. With other equipment, experience may show that about 10 rounds is the normal life of a case, even at moderate pressures. As a very rough index, I expect a minimum of six to 10 shots out of cases used in the high-intensity car-

tridges such as the 6mms and the smallbore magnums, even with top loads, and 10 to 20 shots out of ordinary hunting cartridges such as the .308 and .30/ 06. I often get many more shots out of cases in both categories, but if cases in a certain batch begin to show a high proportion of failures before these figures are reached, I start looking for the reason. High chamber pressures are a prominent cause, although by no means the only one.

Chamber pressures and the elusive "maximum" load level are likewise a prominent source of worry and uncertainty to many handloaders, especially new ones. I hope that the message of this chapter has come across strongly. It is that absolute pressure measurement in your handloads is neither possible nor important. What is important is that you verify that *your* loads are not excessive in *your* guns, and this is easily done by the techniques I've described. If those loads produce good accuracy and long case life with no head expansion of the cartridge cases, they're perfectly safe for indefinite use, no matter how many CUPs, PSI, or "quadriframmuses" of pressure they might develop. Handloads can be classified into only two categories, *safe* and *unsafe*, and the line between those categories can be reliably identified without elaborate equipment or specialized knowledge. Now that I think of it, this chapter might have been better titled "How to Stop Worrying and Learn to Love Your Handloads!"

11 Perfecting The Handload

It is axiomatic that the hottest safe load is not necessarily the best handload for any given purpose. Indeed, for many needs, a maximum load is the last thing you want, especially if you're a turkey hunter or wish to train a woman or children with a hunting firearm. As I pointed out in Chapter 10, maximum loads also do not usually produce the best accuracy.

When we think in terms of absolutes, we may lose sight of practical matters. For example, if you find in your loading manual that one powder can give a certain bullet a maximum muzzle velocity of 2,995 feet per second, and another powder is capable of 3,070 FPS, it's very easy to jump at the latter load because it's over the magic 3,000-FPS mark and appears at first glance to be so much faster than the first one. But I'll give you a written, money-back guarantee that the 75-FPS difference between these two loads (assuming they can be duplicated exactly in your rifle, which is dubious) is absolutely meaningless in actual practice. You will not be able to detect *any* difference in performance due to the difference in initial velocity under any actual field conditions. Nor will any game animal be able to tell any difference either. For practical shooting, the two loads are identical.

IS THERE A PERFECT LOAD?

It may very well come to pass, however, that the slower of two loadings will produce significantly improved accuracy in your rifle, or show some other practical advantage that will more than offset the difference in muzzle velocity (MV). Ferreting out these possible improvements is the real fun in reloading, and I call it "perfecting" the load. At the same time I admit that, out of the thousands and thousands of handloads for rifles, pistols, and shotguns I've developed over the years, I have actually achieved perfection only once. I have only that one loading, a cast-bullet load at reduced velocity for a 7 × 57mm Mauser rifle, that could not conceivably be improved in

A "perfected" handload meets or exceeds all criteria established during the planning stage, including those for such factors as accuracy, trajectory, power, function, recoil, and blast and often gives a favorite rifle a completely new personality.

any way whatever. However, I'm inclined to believe that even one such perfect load in a lifetime is quite an accomplishment.

A nonshooting friend of mine once commented, upon inspecting my loading bench and listening to about two hours of enthusiastic description of the joys and inner satisfactions derived from handloading, that handloading is essentially a search for perfection. Upon long reflection, it seems to me that this noninvolved observer put his finger on an aspect of the game that I'd never heard mentioned before, hence the title of this chapter.

CHANGE ONE THING AT A TIME

There are two fundamental requirements for approaching perfection in a handload. The first is the development of a set of realistic, written specifications as described in the chapter on load planning. The second is varying only one thing at a time during the testing procedure. For example, if accuracy is a major criterion, as in a load for a long-range varmint rifle, the first step is to select a bullet known for its accuracy. If the rifle is in one of the centerfire .22 cartridges, such bullets are available from several makers, including Speer, Sierra, Nosler, Hornady, and others. Say you start with the Speer, and the brand of case and primer is pretty well determined by your current components inventory. Any of two or three powders may prove to deliver optimum accuracy, and with each powder, one particular charge weight is likely to give best results. Testing, however, should involve only one powder at a time, with the only variable the charge weights. With safe maximums already established as described in the foregoing chapter, a series of loads is assembled with charge weights varying across the range that appeared most promising for accuracy purposes. For this type of testing, not less than ten rounds of each load should be put up, to be fired in either two or three groups.

At the end of a day's shooting, you will have a very realistic idea of the charge weight that seems to deliver best accuracy with that powder. Note that during this day's shooting, the one and only variable tested was charge weight. On the next trip to the range, you will compare perhaps the two most promising charge weights, shooting at least four or five five-shot groups with each. At this point, the best possible combination of that particular powder, charge weight, and bullet should be evident. If accuracy of the combination meets your previously written specifications for the load, you have arrived.

Suppose, however, that you suspect an entirely different propellant might give even better groups. The procedure is repeated, and results compared to the earlier tests. This process can go on through the entire range of powders that are appropriate to the particular cartridge and which may number from three to ten. Different rifle barrels will definitely respond to different powders differently, for reasons we cannot explain. A good load in one accurate rifle

is very likely to be at least a better-than-average one in any other accurate rifle, but it may *not* be the very ultimate, perfect combination. It's worth trying several powders in perfecting your load; one of them may reveal a decided advantage in a given gun.

It's even more likely that your barrel will reveal a distinct preference for one particular bullet. Such preferences cannot be predicted; they must be sorted out by experimental firing. But, if bullets are what you're testing, make sure the only variable in the tests is the bullet. Using the same powder and charge weight, fire test groups of two or three different bullets (of the same weight and style, of course). One will usually turn out to hold at least a slight advantage over its competitors. I have a custom-barreled 6mm Remington that delivers decent groups with only one bullet brand, weight, and type. But with that bullet and the powder charge which suits best, the rifle will shoot rings around most other lightweight field sporters. Without the patient testing that eventually revealed the magic combination for this rifle, I might have sold it early in the game, never knowing that it was potentially one of the most accurate rifles in my rack. Not many guns are as stubborn and selective as this 6mm, but almost all of them show similar strong preferences in components.

To repeat, the trick to isolating the one perfect combination is in varying one component at a time, while keeping everything else as nearly the same as possible. If you fire handloads featuring a couple of different bullets, two or three powders, and maybe several charge weights of each powder, you will never know, when you produce a radical improvement in grouping, which factor was responsible.

FACTORS IN LOAD TESTING

Speaking of factors, there are several involved in the shooter himself. The human factor is one of the most difficult to keep consistent from test to test. Interpreting test results may be difficult enough as it is, without having to wonder whether that "flyer" (wide shot outside the group) was the gun's fault, the ammo's, or yours. For this reason, most handloaders get to be pretty good benchrest shooters. Those who don't never really know how well their firearms can perform and are largely guessing as to which is the best load.

The first requirement for serious group shooting is an extremely solid, stable shooting bench. Most rifle clubs have at least a few such benches for the use of their members. It is possible, although difficult, to construct a portable bench for serious load-testing. This is a book about handloading and not about carpentry; information on building a benchrest is available from the National Rifle Association and other sources. Suffice it to say that a rest across the hood of your pickup truck, or an ironing board, will *not* enable you to refine your rifle's accuracy to the utmost.

With an adequate shooting bench available, you'll

Flashlight bulbs taped to the scope and muzzle of the rifle and my shooting glasses trace the movements of recoil during the night firing of a .30/06. Note the involuntary and delayed resistance to the thrust of recoil about halfway up the front two traces and the way my head rocks as my body is driven backward.

need some sort of rest. This can be anything from a $60 fully adjustable shooting stand to a couple of bricks topped with a sandbag, but it must be firm and of the correct height. For years I've shot from an inexpensive, homemade rest constructed of a pipe nipple, floor flange, and section of channel iron.

Whatever sort of rest is selected, sandbags are absolutely necessary for serious testing. Probably the most common and convenient container for sand for this purpose is the canvas bag in which lead shot for reloading shotshells is furnished. Cutoff blue-jeans legs, stitched up at each end, are also about the right dimensions. A friend of mine adds a ritzy touch to his shooting bench by using moneybags from a local bank to hold his sand. Very good leather sandbags are also available commercially.

Two sandbags are needed, one under the forearm of the rifle and the other under the toe of the butt-stock. The rifle should be arranged on these supports so that the sights lie very close to the intended bull's-

eye without being touched by the shooter. The shooter thus uses the very minimum of muscular force to align the sights, which reduces at least one source of shot-to-shot variation in testing.

Every rifle displays slightly different tendencies in how it reacts to being held and fired, and some experimenting is necessary to determine the preferences of an unfamiliar piece. Some rifles do their best when held very tightly against the shoulder of the shooter, with exactly the same forces applied to the stock for every shot. Others deliver best results only when held as lightly as possible, just firmly enough to control them, and others fall between these two extremes. Hard kickers sometimes respond best to some downward force on the forearm, but this is fairly unusual. The key factor is uniformity; however the rifle does best, do it the same for every shot. Ideally, test groups should be fired under roughly the same atmospheric conditions as those with which they are to be compared. Wind, light, and mirage can do mischief with groups, and may deceive you into believing that one ammunition is more accurate than another when the reverse is true.

Shooting from a benchrest is not an art learned overnight, and when you are attempting to determine the absolute accuracy level of a given load or rifle, bear in mind that the human element can never be totally removed from the rifle/ammo/shooter equation. Indeed, it will vary from day to day and even on the same day, due to fatigue, weather, and general mood. If you doubt that, try firing a few groups when you have a headache or on a day when you had an argument that upset you.

However, groups fired on the same day with different ammunitions can reveal significant differences in performance even if you're not shooting your best that day. Negative human factors roughly cancel each other out, or are added in equal measure to all groups, so that a half-inch difference in apparent grouping potential is probably a real difference.

HOW MANY SHOTS, HOW MANY GROUPS?

Shooters often ask how many shots a statistically meaningful group should contain and how many groups must be fired to achieve a fairly high degree of certainty about the findings. Some experimenters insist that three-shot groups are valid, since three is about as many shots as are ever fired at a game animal. Others prefer the more standard five-shot group, while still others contend that nothing very useful can be learned from groups of less than 10 shots. Since the object is to gain the most information from the least expenditure of components and time, the argument is by no means academic.

The answers are known, but they are hidden within the mysteries of the science of statistics, of which I am hardly a master. I have looked into the matter, however, and have found among the complicated mathematical equations a few concepts serviceable to the handloader.

Generally speaking, good, solid data can be derived from five-shot groups, although it is true that ten-shotters do give a better idea of the potential of a given load—better, but not twice as good.

If decisions between two different loads are based on five consecutive five-shot groups, the chances are they will be the correct decisions almost twice as often than if based on only a single group. *Ten* five-shot groups increase the probability of a correct decision by another 60 percent or so. A professional statistician could doubtless quibble with this way of expressing the matter, but it does simplify the idea usefully.

I use five five-shot groups as my standard test. If two different ammunitions reveal a fairly large difference in average group size after five groups of each have been measured, I assume the difference is real. If the difference is still very small after shooting five groups of each load, I load and fire five more of each, and use the average of all 10 groups of each load for a comparison. At this point, I can assume that an *apparent* difference revealed by these average group sizes will be a *real* difference about 90 percent of the time. That's worth knowing and requires no computers, slide rules, or advanced calculus.

Perfecting a load can involve many things besides accuracy, of course, but accuracy in rifles and pistols is a fundamental starting point. Most of the other items on your written list of specifications for a handload, such as point of impact relative to another load in the same rifle, or some specific velocity, will be covered in other chapters. Trajectory and terminal energy can be observed or calculated while working up and accuracy-testing any handload. Possible specifications such as the use of certain powder or bullet (to use up stocks, for example) are merely a matter of decision before actual reloading begins.

In most handloaders' minds, though, "perfecting a load" centers around patient and pleasant testing with the objective of squeezing the last possible bit of performance out of a favorite rifle. There is a great sense of satisfaction to be gained from starting with a rifle that shoots 2-inch groups with factory ammunition and watching those groups shrink, perhaps to less than 1 inch, through the trial-and-error process of reloading experiments.

12 Adjusting Loading Dies

What follows is not intended to replace illustrated instructions furnished with reloading dies. Those instructions are, for the most part, quite thorough and particularly adapted to the design of the dies described. However, some uses of such dies are not usually included in the basic instructions, because discussion of these uses would require a small book. The die manufacturers don't write books, and I don't write elementary loading-die instructions.

Yet I cannot resist the temptation to clarify a point commonly made in those instructions. They usually tell you to install a shellholder in the press ram, raise it to the full-up position, and then to screw the sizing die into the die-station until it makes firm contact with the shellholder. You may finally be instructed to lower the ram slightly and screw the die-body down another quarter-turn or so before setting the locking ring.

The reason for that last action is that all reloading press frames will spring somewhat, even if imperceptibly, under the very heavy loads that can be placed upon them by their own compound linkages. The die-maker has no way of knowing which brand of press you will use with his dies, much less anything about the chamber in your firearm. So the above basic

The standard method of setting a die for full-length sizing involves screwing the die down firmly against the shellholder. If both die and rifle chamber are within tolerances, this is okay, but it may shorten cases too much in a few chambers. I describe an alternative—and better— method in the text.

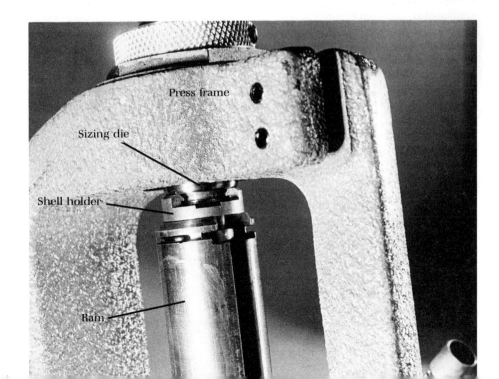

procedure is intended to produce reasonably well resized cases in the greatest number of combinations.

But that procedure does not necessarily produce *ideal* resizing in any particular combination of press, die, and gun. In fact, this process may seriously overshorten the head-to-shoulder dimension of a bottlenecked case in certain guns, shortening case life or worse.

The proper way to do it for your particular gun is as follows. Install the shellholder and raise the ram fully. Screw the die into the station until it's *short* of touching the shellholder by perhaps ⅛ inch. Now lubricate a case fired in your gun, resize it with the die so set, and try to chamber it in your rifle. The bolt should refuse to close behind it. Do not force it. Turn the die down a quarter-turn, size the case again, and try it again.

Repeat this process until the bolt closes easily as the case chambers—but with a slight but definite "feel." Now carefully turn the die in just ⅛ turn, no more, and set the lock ring. Try a few more cases to make certain the adjustment is correct, then leave it alone for as long as you are preparing ammo for that firearm.

Done correctly, this procedure produces a die adjustment that is customized specifically to your die, your press, and your gun. Manufacturing tolerances in all three are effectively eliminated, and cases receive the *minimum adequate* resizing (both adjectives are important), which is the goal.

Loading dies for metallic cases come in either two-die or three-die sets as a rule. Bottleneck cartridges require only two dies, while straight-sided rounds (revolver cartridges and many of the old-time rounds) call for three-piece die sets.

In the former, resizing, depriming, and neck expanding are accomplished by a single pass through the sizing die, and the second unit seats bullets and, if desired, crimps. In three-die sets, the first die usually resizes and deprimes, the second flares case mouths, and the third seats bullets and crimps. In some brands, sizing is the only function of the first die, while the second unit deprimes and performs the flaring/expanding duty. In a few cases, a fourth die is added to the set, which does nothing but crimp case mouths onto bullets.

FULL-LENGTH OR "PARTIAL" RESIZING?

The first question the reloader faces is whether to full-length resize for every loading, or partially resize the case only. (Partial resizing is often miscalled "neck resizing.") I wish I could answer that question once and for all, but I cannot. The theories are that full-length resizing overworks the brass and results in early case failure, and that partially resized cases fit the chamber in which they were fired better and offer better potential accuracy. There are some flaws in both theories. Unless the rifle's chamber is maximum and the sizing die is minimum, unlimited full-length resizing appears not to cause early case failure after all, according to tests. It may be true that partial resizing makes for a better fit between case and chamber the second time around, but it may also make

Straight-sided rifle cartridges like the .375 WCF shown require three-die sets, and so do most handgun cartridges. Die sets for bottlenecked cartridges need only two.

Sizer

Bullet seater

Decapper/expander

These cases have been smoked to make apparent the differences between so-called "neck sizing" in standard full-length (FL) dies (illustrated at right) and full-length sizing, at left. Note base reduction of full-length-sized case, indicated by pencil. True neck-only sizing requires a special die and cannot be done correctly in full-length dies.

for hard chambering after two or three firings. Unless the chamber *and* die are perfectly concentric the bullet is unlikely to be held in perfect alignment with the bore unless great pains are taken to chamber the cartridge oriented exactly as it came out of that chamber after the previous firing.

Furthermore, partial resizing very frequently creates as many problems as it irons out, unless special neck-sizing-only dies are used. These are available on special order. Especially on very tapered cases such as the .257 Roberts or 7 × 57mm Mauser, trying to neck-size only in a full-length-sizing die often results in a case that cannot be chambered in the rifle, and/or one on which the headspace measurement has been altered. Hunters must full-length resize in order to achieve maximum reliability in feeding from the magazine and smooth chambering. As my years at the reloading bench lengthen, I find I tend to full-length resize everything. Accuracy in anything except benchrest rifles is as good as ever, and case life appears normal in the calibers I regularly reload.

In most cases, even if a special neck-sizing die is ordered, cases will require full-length sizing every three or four rounds anyway, if anything approaching maximum-pressure charges is used. I suspect any difference in accuracy potential between full-length and neck-only sizing is completely submerged in the other variables, even in a very accurate field varmint

1. As ram is raised, expander ball enters case mouth, guiding case into die cavity. **2.** Near top of stroke, case walls contact sides of die chamber and are pressed inward. **3.** With about 1/16-inch gap between bottom of die and top of shellholder, case is partially resized. Note: Shoulder has not come in contact with die shoulder and is left in fire-formed position. At same time, depriming pin on expander ball ejects spent primer. **4.** At extreme limit of upstroke, case (including shoulder) fully contacts die and has been returned to factory dimensions. **5.** On downstroke, case is withdrawn and expander ball is drawn through case neck, sizing it to friction-grip a new bullet. Note: If expander ball pulls hard now, lube lightly inside case mouth. If this fails, polish ball with coarse steel wool or emery cloth. (Courtesy Nosler)

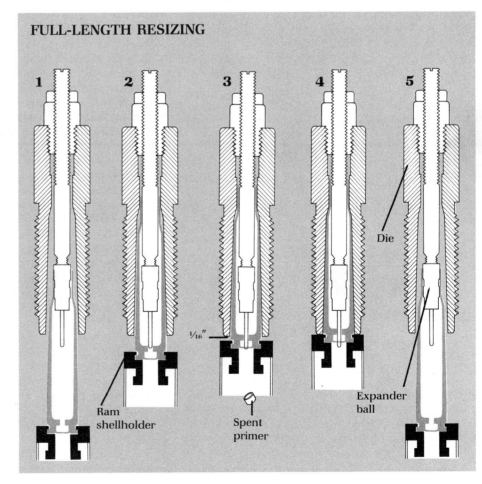

FULL-LENGTH RESIZING

1   2   3   4   5

Ram shellholder

1/16"

Spent primer

Die

Expander ball

rifle. Benchrest guns are in a class by themselves, and loading is usually done with custom-reamed dies and special presses.

The best bet for any confused handloader is to try it both ways in his dies and shoot the results in his rifle. That is, by the way, very good advice for solving most reloading problems: Go and ask your rifle!

HEADSPACING BELTED CASES ON THE SHOULDER

A special problem that arises in loading for many of the modern belted magnums is early case failure via stretched or separated brass even with submaximum loads. This occurs because such cartridges headspace on their belts, and not on the case shoulder area as do rimless cases. Because head-to-shoulder length is not critical, manufacturers of rifles do not hold dimensions in the shoulder region of their chambers to very critical tolerances. When the cartridge is fired, the case shoulder is blown forward to match the chamber shoulder. Then, when the case is full-length resized for reloading, the die may set the shoulder back to factory-standard length. The whole process is repeated with each firing and reloading, but the case is steadily weakened by being stretched upon firing. Ultimately (often in as few as three firings) the case will fail via an annular crack in the brass just ahead of the heavy interior web portion. Most often, everything holds together on firing, and then the extractor jerks the head of the case out of the chamber, leaving the body in place. This can be rather embarrassing when a big bull elk is galloping out of sight over a ridge, since the rifle is out of action until some

A coating of soot from a candle or match flame reveals contact areas in a full-length sizing die (left) and a rifle chamber (right).

sort of rod is improvised to knock the case body out of the chamber. It could conceivably be dangerous too, although I have not heard of a serious accident occurring this way. In any case, case failure is best avoided. The way to avoid it is to reset your sizing die so that the case actually headspaces on the shoulder, in the same manner as for rimless rounds, and the belt becomes superfluous.

This is done by unscrewing the die body in its locking ring until it fails to touch the shoulder of a fired case. Now smoke the case shoulder with a kitchen match (I *did* mean a *fired, empty* case!), after lubricating, of course. Then run the case into the die as far as it will go, withdraw it, and examine the shoulder. The soot should be intact. Screw the die body down a half-turn and try it again. Continue this process, slowly turning the die down a little at a time until just a bare contact between the shoulder of the die cavity and that of the case develops. If this fired case will freely reenter the rifle's chamber, you can set the lock ring at this position and keep the die so set. You can be assured your magnum cases are not being lengthened and shortened like an accordion in the course of firing and resizing.

Experience with a given rifle may reveal that slightly more shoulder-sizing than described above is necessary for smooth chambering, especially after two or three firings. If so, screw in the die body just an eighth or a quarter turn at a time, trying the case in the rifle after each adjustment. The object is the very minimum possible sizing to produce ammunition that feeds from the magazine into the chamber smoothly, and on which the bolt handle closes with its normal feel.

Once this point is reached, lock the die ring solidly and leave it alone. L. E. Wilson, by the way, makes a

The result of normal full-length (FL) resizing of belted cases fired in a sloppy chamber is head separations, often in as few as three firings. This is easily avoided by readjusting dies to headspace the case on the shoulder, as if it were a rimless cartridge, in this instance ignoring the belt.

Because conventional bullet-seating dies do not engage the actual tip of the projectile, different bullet profiles require different seating-stem adjustments to produce a given overall cartridge length.

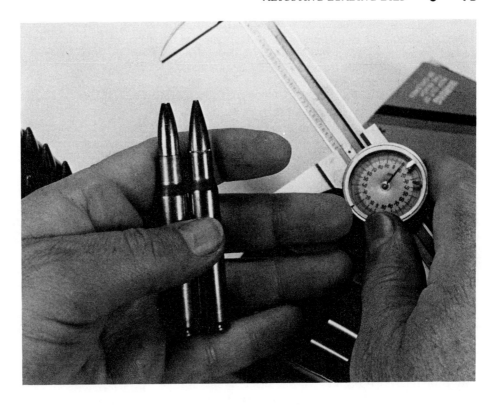

case gauge for belted magnums that has an adjustable shoulder. This is invaluable for returning your sizing die to its previous setting in case you need to change it, as to resize a batch of brass not fired in your own rifle. With the Wilson gauge, the painstaking process

This case gauge for a belted magnum features an adjustable shoulder that greatly simplifies returning a sizing die to a previous setting to headspace the round on its shoulder instead of its belt.

described above is shortened to a few minutes, and accuracy of resetting the die is perfect.

The handloader should be aware of another situation in which early case failure (via cracked or separated heads) may occur, which has nothing to do with die adjustments, or even with out-of-tolerance chambers.

It occurs when loading for a rifle whose breech bolt locks at the rear. Most of these are lever actions of vintage designs, the Winchester M1895 chambered in .30/40 Krag or .30/06 Springfield being a prime offender. Other action styles, even including some bolt actions, may reveal the same tendency to stretch cases. One example is the Danish Schultz and Larsen turnbolt, often found chambered for the 7 × 61 Sharpe & Hart cartridge.

What happens with high-pressure loadings in such guns is that the bolt itself compresses, or springs, under the thrust of chamber pressure, allowing the bolt face (which supports the case head) to move backward slightly. Since the case walls cling to the wall of the chamber during the moment of firing, the case is thus stretched, producing a thinned ring in the case wall just ahead of the case-head web. This is not dangerous when firing factory ammo or handloads in virgin brass, but fired cases are sufficiently weakened to make them a little dicey for even one reloading.

There is no magic die adjustment that can cure this problem. It is entirely in the rifle's design, and the only thing a handloader can do to ameliorate the problem is to keep pressures in his loads very mild. Fortunately, the problem rears its hideous head only in firearms of older designs that happen to be chambered to modern cartridges, and there aren't many of those. The symptoms (stretch-rings and circumferential cracks in cases) are identical to those produced by rifles with sloppy chambers for belted magnums or those with excessive headspace, but the cause is entirely different.

USING REFERENCE ROUNDS FOR BULLET SEATING

In the prior discussion of bullet seating, I suggested that the reloader make up a dummy round for each of his standard loads, mark on it the brand and style of bullet, and file it away. As I said there, each different bullet weight, profile, and brand will require a different seating depth. You can merely measure the overall length of each standard load and keep it in your reloading records. The bullet-seating die can then be adjusted by trial and error to produce a cartridge of correct overall length, but this takes time, is trouble, and wastes a few bullets and cases. The easy way to return to the right setting is as follows.

Screw the bullet-seating stem upward in your seating die at least a half-inch, so that it cannot even touch the bullet in a standard-length round. Then run your reference dummy round up as far as the press permits into the die (if the die is set to crimp, the die body will have to be backed out a turn or so and locked in the noncrimping position). Now simply screw the seating stem back into the die until it makes *firm* contact with the bullet in your dummy cartridge. Finally, with a screwdriver, turn the seating stem *not more* than another half-turn into the die, and lock the stem in that position. Withdraw the dummy round and set it aside. Seat a bullet in a fresh case with the die so adjusted. A quick check with a caliper should reveal that the overall length of this cartridge is within a few ten-thousandths of the overall length of your reference dummy. This whole process takes about 2 minutes, and is reason enough to keep a collection of dummy rounds on hand for all your standard loads.

SEPARATING BULLET SEATING AND CRIMPING

The process of using a seating die in two separate steps to seat bullets first and then to crimp case mouths on them was briefly described earlier. It merely involves using the bullet-seating stem only (with the die body backed off a turn or so) to seat bullets to the proper depth, and then backing out the seating stem and turning down the die body until the crimping shoulder comes into contact with the mouth of an empty case in the shellholder with the press ram fully raised. At this point, extremely delicate adjustments are possible, and you don't need to screw-in the die body much to produce a heavy crimp.

Straight-cased cartridges are flared, as mentioned, to accept the base of the bullet without crumpling. This flaring is easily overdone, and should be nothing more than a faint outward belling of the first 1/16 inch

The mouth of the case shown at left has been flared to facilitate seating cast bullets, and the flare may interfere with chambering. Crimping is undesirable, but the seating die can be adjusted, with care, merely to return the mouth to a straight condition (as shown right) without rolling it inward.

or so of the case neck. When you can barely start a bullet in the case mouth with your fingers, flaring is adequate. With many loads, however, the mouth must be belled to accept the bullet, but no crimp is desired. Cast-bullet loads in bottleneck rifle cases are an example. Set the crimping shoulder inside the die cavity to do no more than iron out the flare, leaving the case mouth perfectly straight rather than crimped inward onto the bullet. This is necessary, since leaving the mouth flared may interfere with chambering the round.

From this point, the crimp can be made as heavy as desired, providing there is a groove or cannelure on the bullet to receive the case mouth. If you attempt to put a roll crimp on a cartridge neck that's holding a jacketed bullet without a correctly placed cannelure, you will get no crimp, and you will ruin the entire round by swelling the shoulder. In general, if there is any justification for a crimp at all, the crimp should be a moderate to heavy one, but it can be badly overdone. Controlling factors are the depth of the cannelure, type of bullet, and design of the die. If these factors are exceeded, the round is likely to be spoiled anyway, even if a cannelure is present. The feel of the loading press on which the work is done will tell you when crimping has gone far enough. Normal crimping offers little or no extra resistance to the operation of the handle, while excessive crimping makes a quite noticeable difference in resistance at the very end of the stroke.

CARE OF DIES

A good loading die is a thing of beauty and a joy for a long time, at least, if not forever, and deserves a little care. By far the most common cause of ruined dies is resizing dirty, gritty, and/or insufficiently lubricated cases. Clumsy efforts to remove stuck cases are probably the next most frequent reason for damage. Depriming stems and pins may be bent or broken by trying to decap Berdan cases or by allowing the stem's lock ring to loosen enough to permit the stem to be badly off-center. Dies are made of very high-quality steel, but none, as far as I know, are of stainless, and they will rust if neglected.

Dies are often marred by use of poorly fitting wrenches or pliers. In the typical arrangement, the locking ring around the body of the die is held in place by a setscrew that presses a small soft lead pellet into the threads on the outside of the die body. These usually jam, but pliers are not needed to loosen them. A few sharp raps on the die ring with a plastic mallet, directed exactly at the set screw after it has been loosened, will allow the ring to be turned freely by finger pressure only.

More and more sizing dies these days are being made with an insert of tungsten carbide that actually does the sizing. These are expensive, but worth it when large volumes of cases are to be processed, since no lubrication is required in such dies. The tungsten carbide insert, although super hard (cases come out looking burnished), may be brittle, and these dies should not be dropped or battered about with any sort of tool.

Manufacturers of reloading dies today make a staggering array of special dies for even the wildest ideas in case forming. Almost any kind of reforming die imaginable can be special-ordered, and I know of no centerfire cartridge for which loading dies cannot be made. In general, the makers are incredibly obliging. They have already learned to solve just about any problem you're likely to run into and a few you're unlikely to even dream of. If you have a problem, a little correspondence with the manufacturer of your dies will usually provide the answer. They also stand behind their products. The lesson in all this is to let the manufacturer use his own judgment in matters of altering or repairing loading dies. Your local machinist friend may be a hell of a machinist, but it's a safe bet he knows less about the requirements for a loading die than the people who made it.

Use your dies as they were meant to be used and with loving care. If something feels funny in the reloading process, stop right there and run it down. Keep your cases clean and lubed, and the dies clean and protected from rust. Use only recommended tools in adjusting the dies. You should consult the manufacturer about any sort of repair, projected alteration, or malfunction, as well as about any special needs in dies. Do all these things, and your dies will last as long as your rifle or pistol will, and usually longer. I have had dies in service for more than 30 years of heavy use, and they're just as good today as when they were new.

The pencil points to the expander button of a sizing die. Its diameter is important. If it is too large, bullets will not be held firmly. If too small, bullets and cases may be deformed by seating pressure.

13 The Handloader's Chronograph

Handloading's most important technical development since about 1950 has been the small, portable, accurate, and relatively inexpensive chronograph. There was a day when shooters had to take the word of ammunition manufacturers on muzzle velocities. I'm not implying that these good folks intentionally misled their customers, of course, but neither did they allow velocities to suffer in the telling. It was remarkable that the published muzzle speeds of certain brands of factory ammo dropped abruptly when personal chronographs came into popular use.

At that time, publicity on new cartridges also became suddenly more conservative. In 1961, a new cartridge was announced as having a velocity about 800 FPS higher than actually could be produced by properly chambered guns available to the public. This fact became general knowledge, and the cartridge fell on its face (for that and other good reasons). That same company's *next* new cartridge, introduced just 2 years later, turned out to deliver slightly *higher* velocities than claimed for commercial rifles, at least in early lots, and has been a resounding success.

VALUE OF A CHRONOGRAPH

A chronograph is nothing more than an electronic bullet speedometer. The only direct information it yields is the velocity of a bullet (or shot charge) at some specific distance from the muzzle. That velocity is called the *instrumental velocity* at that distance, and it can be readily converted to muzzle velocity, if the bullet's ballistic coefficient is known.

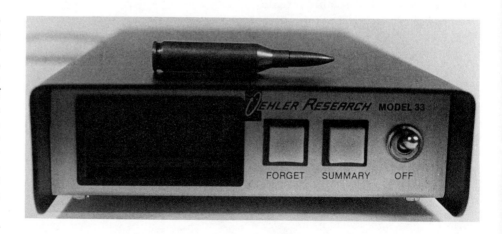

The Oehler Research Model 33 is considered the standard of the handloaders' chronograph industry, even by many of its competitors. About the size of a cigar box, it yields high, low, and average velocities, extreme spread, and standard deviation (unmistakably the most useful measure of ballistic uniformity) for any number of shots up to 99 in a string.

Obviously, a reloader can live without this information (most of us veterans did so for many years). And like powder measures, chronographs are by no means essential to safe and satisfactory handloading. However, once you become accustomed to working with a chronograph, it's hard to imagine doing without one.

The reason is that, besides the instrumental velocity of each round, a chronograph provides quite a lot of indirect information, such as the *average* velocity of a given load and the extreme velocity *spread* within that series. Some models also calculate the *standard deviation* of shots in the string, which is the best statistical measurement of shot-to-shot ballistic uniformity.

Knowledge of the velocity of a handload is virtually useless in the hunting field or on a target range. Moreover, muzzle velocity can be inferred from observed trajectories, if measured according to the simple methods I described in Chapter 2. But that process requires a lot of shooting and the expenditure of time and expensive components. The chronograph provides the necessary information so accurately and quickly that it will probably eventually pay for itself in cash savings, even if you place no value on your time at the loading bench and shooting bench.

A chronograph can actually help predict the performance of a load. With its help, you can evaluate the efficiency and uniformity of a load with just a few shots, and thus save many false starts at reloading. It can help identify maximum safe loads, and it notifies you when you have reached an established velocity goal. Or it tells you that goal is not safely attainable in your particular firearm, which may be even more important. Certainly, when building reduced loads for turkey, for example, in which a very specific velocity range is critical to correct performance, a chronograph is almost indispensable.

The introduction of improved optical screens has had a corollary benefit: because no physical contact between bullets and screens occurs, the measurement of velocities in no way affects the projectiles' flight, and they can be aimed at a downrange target through the screens. Therefore, the velocity of each bullet can be clocked during accuracy testing. Performing two different functions on each shot materially reduces the number of cartridges that must be loaded and fired, saving time and components, and it can also help interpret accuracy results. For example, it's revealing to discover that a "flyer" outside the group also registered an abnormally high or low velocity. I've gotten into the habit of leaving the chronograph on during all test firing, even when I'm not primarily interested in recording velocities. Modern equipment makes it easy.

As this is written, about half a dozen companies manufacture chronographs for handloaders, with prices beginning around $250, complete. Thus you can buy one for less than the price of some telescopic sights, and considerably less than most new bolt-action rifles. Two or three reloading buddies can chip in to reduce the investment even more. A chrono-

graph is no longer beyond of the reach of any serious amateur ballistician.

HOW IT WORKS

The typical chronograph is a solid-state electronic miracle of compactness, low battery drain, and accuracy. In simplest terms, it contains only three elements in its little black box. The first is a crystal "clock" that "ticks" with mind-boggling precision at the rate of 200,000 to 500,000 beats per second. Then there's an electronic means of counting the number of "ticks" during the period a bullet moves a measured distance, and, finally, some method for displaying the count for the operator. Depending on the vintage of the chronograph, this display may be very simple, requiring some manipulation, arithmetic, and reference to tarage tables before you can come up with the actual velocity in feet per second (FPS). Or the chronograph may be quite sophisticated, even incorporating a tiny computer to perform calculations prior to display.

Outside the black box, there must be two sensors to detect the passage of the projectile. All current models I'm familiar with use optical sensors for this purpose. They actually "see" the shadow of the bullet passing over them. These sensors are called screens, because they once were exactly that, woven-wire screens through which the bullet passed. Mechanical screens have taken many forms, including paper with grids printed on them in electrically conductive ink, wire, or even graphite pencil leads. Screens were physically broken by the bullet. This required re-

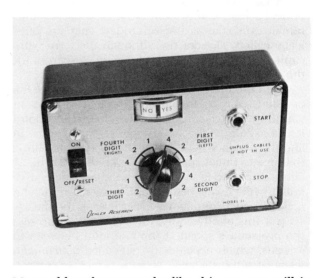

Many older chronographs like this one are still in regular use and giving handloaders perfect satisfaction. Such a secondhand instrument can work if you are economy-minded and if the maker is still in business to service the instrument and provide replacement screens.

The all-in-one-unit Quartz-Lok chronograph offers the simplest imaginable setup with permanently spaced optical screens. The liquid crystal display readout gives velocity only.

placement after every shot (slow and expensive). So if you are considering buying a second hand chronograph, also consider whether you'll be able to obtain suitable screen material in the future.

Sonic screens that detect the shock wave from a passing bullet were tried and, I believe, are still used in some laboratory chronograph installations, but never for handloaders' portables. Development of the optical screen made all other types obsolete, and it remains the standard screen today. They are generically called "skyscreens" although the term with a capital "S" is a trademark of Oehler Research, Inc., the leading maker of reloaders' chronographs.

When the bullet is detected passing over the first, or "start," screen, the chronograph's counter starts counting the ticks of the crystal clock. Detection of its passage over the "stop" screen ends the count, and the distance between screens is used to convert the time to bullet speed in feet per second. The FPS figure displayed is actually the *average* velocity of the bullet while it was between the screens (remember, it slows down continuously after leaving the muzzle). To put this another way, the FPS figure represents the projectile's speed at the midpoint between the screens, which becomes the so-called *instrumental distance*. If this distance is about 12 feet—a common one—the calculated *muzzle velocity* will be about 10 to 25 FPS higher, depending on the bullet's streamlining and real velocity.

The accuracy of the chronograph's output depends upon the precision of screen spacing, and the greater the distance between screens, the better that accu-

racy will be. This is true in theory, but practically speaking, a shorter spacing is accurate enough for a handloader's purpose, which is measurement of velocities of 500 to 4,500 FPS. Improvements in chronograph systems have shrunk the 10-foot spacing once considered minimum to 5 feet, then to 4 feet. And now in at least one commercial model, the distance is only 1 foot. Short spacings are more convenient and much easier to measure precisely and repeatably.

All reloaders' chronographs these days are battery powered, so that they can be used anywhere there's a safe backstop. Again, unlike the older models, they do not require replacement of screens for every shot. Thus you need to move in front of the firing line only to set up the screens at the beginning of a shooting session and to take them down when you're finished, which means a portable chronograph can be used even on a busy public firing range. Chronographs are so simple to operate that anyone willing to read and follow directions can use one and thereby achieve a level of accuracy comparable to that of industrial ballistic laboratories.

SOURCES OF CHRONOGRAPH ERROR

The major bugaboo in using a portable chronograph is in screen spacing, which is up to the operator in most models. An error of $\frac{1}{10}$ inch in a 10-foot spacing will yield an error, in a typical .30/06 loading, of 7 or 8 FPS—double that in a 5-foot spacing. This is usually the largest single source of error in a chronograph. Screens must ideally be perfectly vertical, with the planes of their detection fields perfectly parallel to each other.

Incidentally, the distance of the start screen from the muzzle is not very critical, contrary to first appearances. Even if the midpoint between screens is moved a full foot one way or the other, it will make only a negligible difference in results. However, that start screen should be far enough from the muzzle to allow muzzle blast to dissipate somewhat. Ten feet is about minimum.

There are other sources of error in any chronograph system, no matter how expensive or sophisticated. That crystal clock can have .05 percent error in its ticking and remain within standard tolerance. Crystal aging, ambient temperature, and battery voltage can all contribute to this error margin as well. The counter cannot split a beat, but must register the bullet's passage to the nearest whole count, which adds a potential error of as much as 2 FPS at 3,000 FPS. Screens are not perfect either, and even an optical screen may vary from shot to shot as to how far a spitzer bullet must intrude into the plane of the detection field to be "seen." This can introduce an error that is the equivalent of a $\frac{1}{16}$-inch error in screen spacing, or 5 to 6 FPS. Finally, conversion from the raw count to FPS inevitably involves some "rounding off" of fractions, for another possible 1-FPS error.

If all these internal error sources were maximized

in the same direction, the "worst-case" result would be an error of from about 3 FPS to as much as 14 FPS, even with perfect screen spacing by the operator. This error potential is inherent in all chronograph systems from all manufacturers. Thus, if a manufacturer's advertising claims or implies a worst-case error smaller than about 0.3 percent at 3,000 FPS with screens 10 feet apart, he's pulling your leg!

A couple of other caveats must be observed by a chronograph operator. Intense heat does affect the operation of all chronographs, so it's a good idea to protect the black box from direct summer sun. Also, especially when chronographing handguns and short-barreled rifles, side-blast from the muzzle impacting the box can jar the battery column and cause a momentary loss of circuit. Shield the box from the shock wave.

SOLUTIONS TO PROBLEMS WITH OPTICAL SCREENS

Skyscreens are a great convenience, but they're heir to a number of malfunctions. Oddly, there's much more light in a cloudy-bright sky than a perfectly clear one, and it's the contrast between the bullet's shape and the bright sky that triggers an optical screen.

Thus, your chronograph may begin giving nonsensical—or no—readings around noon on clear days. Obviously, a skyscreen cannot be used anywhere it cannot see the sky—or an artificial "sky" produced by an incandescent light source.

A stubborn and mysterious problem with the early skyscreens involved an occasional failure to detect bullets when the sun was at certain low angles. This was eventually traced to what is called "glint"—a reflection of sunlight from a shiny bullet that exactly cancelled out its passing shadow and prevented the triggering of the screen. This got to be a real nuisance at times, and we reloaders tried everything from darkening shiny bullets with felt-tip markers to erecting cardboard shields to shade bullets when they passed the screens. Today, vast improvements in the sensitivity of skyscreens have greatly reduced the problem, but it can still happen. If sky lighting causes misreadings, the same remedies—felt-tip markers and cardboard shields—still work.

INTERPRETING CHRONOGRAPH RESULTS

The standard number of rounds in a velocity test series is 10, and this number is recommended for a

 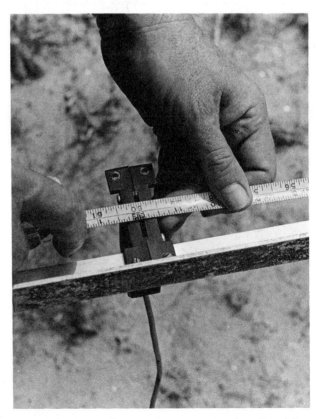

Left: The most important source of error in a portable chronograph system is error in screen spacing. Precision counts here. *Right:* Here I'm measuring the distance from gun muzzle to start screen. This is not a critical distance, but to avoid effects of muzzle blast, the start screen should be at least 10 feet from the muzzle. It's best to keep distances as much the same from day to day as possible for consistent results.

reasonably good average. If you take two consecutive 10-shot averages with ammo from the same lot, you will usually find they vary somewhat, which means that more than 10 shots in the string will give a more accurate average. A 10-shot average, however, yields results that are close enough for most handloaders' purposes. Now and then, with an unusually uniform batch of cartridges, you'll know by the fifth shot that the average is not moving much. In this case, I often settle for five-shot results. However, five (or fewer) shots actually provide pretty shaky ground on which to base handloading decisions.

Even the most painstakingly assembled cartridges with powder charges weighed to zero variation will exhibit some shot-to-shot variation in velocity. In view of this, and remembering the discussion of inherent chronograph error, it becomes obvious that a test series in which the extreme velocity range between the fastest and slowest rounds does not exceed 40 to 50 FPS is very good indeed. The standard deviation of such a string will usually fall between 10 and 20 FPS, sometimes even lower. Extreme spreads (ES) exceeding 100 FPS in typical rifle cartridges begin to cast doubt on that loading, and an ES in the neighborhood of 200 FPS definitely indicates something is out of balance in that combination.

Handgun ammo is, for reasons unknown to me, almost never as uniform as rifle ammunition, even when assembled with the same care. Most handgun velocities are, of course, much lower than rifle speeds, meaning that a given extreme spread represents a much larger *percentage* of a pistol cartridge's velocity. About the same spread standards apply: 50 FPS is good, 100 is dubious, and 200 can only be considered poor. However, if large variations appear, take time to analyze the whole series. If, for example, 9 out of the 10 shots fall into a small extreme variation and the tenth registered either very high or very low, you have grounds for suspecting the validity of that particular reading. More shooting may be required to determine the real ballistic uniformity of the load.

THE IMPORTANCE OF BALLISTIC UNIFORMITY

If you take the trouble to examine the loading data presented in either the Hornady or Sierra handbooks, you will observe that each similar increment in the powder charge produces about the same increase in muzzle velocity, if all else remains equal. This is because there is a roughly linear relationship between chamber pressure and velocity within certain important limits. You may deduce, then, that a handload that produces very uniform shot-to-shot velocity is also delivering uniform pressure. Provided the bullet you are using is known to be accurate in that particular barrel, chances are very good that a low extreme spread in velocity (or a low standard deviation) will translate into small groups on target. Other factors besides chamber pressure do affect rifle accuracy, of course, but uniform ballistics is an excellent starting place in the search for it.

This is why a chronograph can assist in pinpointing load formulae that promise accuracy, and thus save a great deal of loading and shooting time and money spent for test components. When several different powders, for example, are chronographed with the same primer, bullet, case, and gun, and one of them reveals a markedly smaller shot-to-shot velocity spread, it's a strong indication that you should concentrate on that propellant in future experiments. For this purpose, the actual average velocity of the loads is of no more than casual interest; the story is told by individual velocity readings in the series, as related to each other.

In the same way, other components in a handload may be tested. Chronograph data is particularly revealing of primer performance.

SPOTTING UNSAFE LOADS WITH A CHRONOGRAPH

I mentioned earlier in this chapter that a chronograph can help identify maximum loadings. I did not mean that any of the high-pressure symptoms I discussed in Chapter 10 can be ignored when you purchase a chronograph but only that the chronograph makes available one or two more such signs to help you interpret all the rest.

One of these is unacceptable extreme variations in velocities. Actually, quite a number of conditions can produce variations, not the least of which is poor ignition (from the wrong primer, a weak firing-pin spring, etc.). An imbalance between the bullet weight and powder type, overlength cases, and a few other factors may also be responsible. But if the average velocity is near the expected maximum for that combination of components, the culprit is probably an overload. As I mentioned before, *high* pressures usually mean *erratic* pressures, and erratic pressures can be expected to produce abnormal velocity variations. Therefore, extreme velocity spreads are immediately suspect, especially when they show up suddenly with heavier powder charges in a combination that seemed pretty uniform at lower velocities. Like most other high-pressure signs, this one can be deceptive, however, and I've seen some excessive loads not only group well but reveal quite normal extreme variations between the fastest and slowest shots in a string. In other words, erratic velocities may indicate too much breech pressure, but uniform ones cannot be assumed to guarantee its absence.

If your load with a given bullet and standard barrel length registers a much higher velocity than any handbook gives for that bullet weight for any listed powder, the load is almost certainly too hot, even if it seems quite uniform. Handbook publishers are certainly conservative, but all of them take their loads up to the highest pressures (and velocities) they consider absolutely safe in the majority of guns. There is seldom as much as a 100-FPS difference among the different publishers in the fastest loads listed for the same bullet weight in any given cartridge, regardless of powder type. If your load clocks 200 FPS over the fastest load you can find in any book for that bullet, it's a cinch it's too hot. This is not to say that it can't be too hot if it doesn't exceed the published velocities, only that if it does by any material margin, it's probably a serious overload.

Finally, as I suggested above, muzzle velocity is approximately proportional to powder charge weight, but this is true only within the normal pressure range of each powder. Every propellant has a specific range of pressures within which it behaves normally. At pressures below that range, it usually will not burn completely, leaving much residue in the barrel and producing variable, but low, velocities. At pressures above that range, the linear relationship between charge weight and velocity breaks down, and pressure may suddenly go sky-high with a small increase in powder, while velocity climbs little or not at all.

Thus, if your load development with a chronograph has previously shown that each additional grain weight of powder boosted velocity by about, say, 135 FPS when working a few grains below handbook maximum, a sure sign that you're nearing (or have exceeded) absolute maximum is a sudden drop in the velocity increment on adding more powder. If another grain of propellant adds only 75 FPS to that load, and still another produces no more than an extra 20 FPS or less, you have already exceeded a working maximum charge. If these latter loads also reveal progressively greater extreme variations in velocity, the suspicion is confirmed, and will surely be proved conclusively by "miking" the case heads (measuring their diameters with a micrometer).

I have velocity series recorded in my handloading notes that actually reveal a slight *drop* in average velocity when one grain too many was added to the load. At the same time, cases were failing from expanded primer pockets after only one firing. Pressures in these loads were extremely dangerous, but velocities did not increase. I was getting nothing useful for my trouble, money, or the hazard to which I subjecting myself and my rifle, which is the usual case with overloads.

There comes a point beyond which it is not possible to drive a given bullet any faster with more of a given powder, regardless of pressure, and it is at about that point that pressures begin to go out of sight. One of the greatest values in a portable chronograph is the identification of that point.

Again, the careful and systematic use of an accurate micrometer on case heads is the only irreplaceable method of detecting overloads. A chronograph can give early warning signs, but it alone is not capable of surely pinpointing excessive pressures.

Still an inexpensive, portable chronograph *can* do so many things so well that you will quickly come to regard it as indispensable.

14 Home Computer Ballistics

I am writing this chapter on an aging Apple II + computer, which serves as the principal tool of my trade as a writer. Besides performing as a word-processor the computer also serves as an important tool of my handloading hobby because I have software for a large variety of ballistic programs. In fact, with the old Apple (with only 64K of memory) and a few floppy disks, I actually possess more capacity for rapid and accurate ballistic calculations than major professional ballistic laboratories had only until about the 1970s.

We are living amid an ongoing revolution in record-keeping and numbers manipulation launched by computers. Although the revolution really only began in the late 1970s, I rather doubt that modern business or science, or even modern society, could continue to function without these miraculous machines so inadequately termed "computers." In another few years, handloaders probably will not consider being without a computer. It was inevitable, of course, that a few of the new breed of computer programmers would also be avid reloaders and shooters and that they would write programs for their own convenience. It was just as inevitable that their friends and their friends' friends would covet the capabilities in such programs. So small businesses were set up to market the software (the disk programs that allow the calculations). This seems to be exactly how most of the ballistic programs for personal computers wound up on the market today.

Computer programs for handloaders are about the best thing that's come along since the invention of smokeless powder. The reason is that ballistic calculations are extraordinarily tedious and complex, so much so that even simple procedures concerning trajectories, wind drift, and retained energies might take hours or even days with a hand calculator, pencil, and paper. The speed and precision with which a small computer works through the same formidable formulas literally defies belief. A computer does complicated and repetitive mathematical procedures in seconds, and that is exactly the kind of work involved in ballistics. Furthermore, the versatility of a computer in displaying results in useful and comprehensible ways, including charts and graphs, adds to the amazement.

YOU TOO CAN BE A COMPUTER-SHOOTER!

A computer seems to intimidate many people, but it is really just a very smart, yet dumb, machine—a tool that does certain kinds of work easily and fast. Ballistic work on a computer requires no scientific, engineering, or even mathematical background. A child can do it, and many do.

With the right software, it is unnecessary to understand even the general principles of ballistic calculations, much less how to perform them. You don't have to know a drag function from a front sight. All the programs in this field that have come to my attention are so "user-friendly" they're almost cuddly. They're also totally self-prompting, meaning that they ask the operator for the necessary information in step-by-step fashion, present him with the options, and patiently await his commands. You don't have to be a typist or even know simple arithmetic, much less calculus, to extract the most sophisticated ballistic information from your home computer. You do have to be able to read, but that's about all.

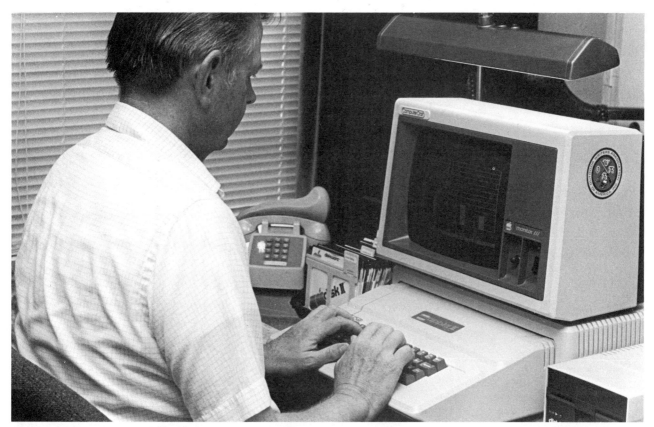

Today's software gives computer users a ballistic calculating power possessed only by major professional laboratories until the late 1970s. This software also gives you many options in handloading records storage, retrieval, and manipulation. I'm here shown with an aging Apple II +.

WHAT BALLISTIC COMPUTERS DO

There are three fundamental classes of shooting-related programs on the market. By far the most common is the general *ballistic* program. Typically, you input the muzzle velocity of your load and the bullet's ballistic coefficient, and the computer calculates trajectories, retained velocities and energies at any range, and the bullet's deflection in various crosswinds. In effect, you have all the data contained in the ballistic tables in the back of most reloading

The program that I modified by trial and error to produce this printout was first published in the June 1983 *American Rifleman* magazine. It's available free to anyone with enough patience to type it into his computer. As a professional firearms writer, I still find this modified program the quickest and most useful ballistic software of all. The topmost block records all parameters for the load. The next block down provides comprehensive data on load performance at the zero range. The next block down is a chart offering velocity, energy, trajectory, and windage dope. And the bottom block gives the six facts of greatest interest to a hunter about any load. The original program is also available from PAB Software (address at end of chapter).

```
- ------------------------------------
           .338 WIN MAG.
    77/MRP/210-GR."BEAR CLAW"
VELOCITY: 3000 FPS,    BALL. COEF.: .32
            STANDARD METRO
- ------------------------------------
MUZZLE VELOCITY (FPS):                 3000
RANGE (YARDS):                          240
REMAINING VELOCITY (FPS):              2325
REMAINING ENERGY (FT-LBS):             2521
TIME OF FLIGHT (SEC.):                 .273
TOTAL DROP (INCHES):                   13.2
MAX HEIGHT ABOVE L.O.S. (INCHES):         3
ELEVATION REQUIRED (MOA):               6.1
DEFLECTION IN 10-MPH WIND (INCHES):     5.7

- ------------------------------------

RANGE   REM.   REM.    BULLET       WIND
YARDS   VEL.  ENERGY    PATH    DEFL.,10 MPH

  0     3000   4196    -1.5         0
 50     2851   3789     1.1         .2
100     2706   3415     2.6         .9
150     2566   3071     2.9        2.2
200     2431   2755     1.9        3.9
250     2299   2465     -.6        6.3
300     2172   2199    -4.8        9.3
350     2048   1956   -10.8        13
400     1929   1734   -18.7       17.4
450     1814   1534   -29.1       22.7
500     1705   1355   -42.3       29.1
- ------------------------------------
- ------------------------------------

FIRST ZERO RANGE IS 27 YARDS

SIGHT RIFLE 2.5 INCHES HIGH AT 100
YARDS TO ACHIEVE THIS ZERO AND
POINT-BLANK RANGE

HIGHEST POINT OF TRAJECTORY IS 3 IN.
BETWEEN APPROX. 118 AND 154 YARDS

ZERO RANGE IS 240 YARDS

MAXIMUM 3-INCH POINT-BLANK RANGE IS
280 YARDS

2000 FT-LBS ENERGY THRESHOLD IS AT
342 YARDS
```

```
000     2983   PROGRAM RUN DATE: 9/21/87

CUSTOM BALLISTICS TABLE FOR: JOHN WOOTTERS
USING THE 210-GR. TROPHY BONDED "BEAR CLAW" BULLET
UNDER THE FOLLOWING ATMOSPHERIC CONDITIONS:

    LOCATION: WYOMING ELK HUNT
    ALTITUDE = 9000 FT ABOVE SEA LEVEL
    LOCAL TEMP = 45 DEG F.
    SEA LEVEL BP = 29.92 IN HG
    RELATIVE HUMIDITY = STANDARD--78%
    ORIGINAL MV @ 59 DEG F. = 3000 FPS
    REVISED MV @ 45 DEG F. = 2983 FPS

BALLISTIC COEFFICIENT UNDER STAND CONDITIONS = .32
BALLISTIC COEFFICIENT UNDER THESE CONDITIONS = .44
THESE NONSTANDARD CONDITIONS HAVE THE EFFECT OF MAKING THIS BULLET
MORE EFFICIENT IN OVERCOMING AIR RESISTANCE DURING FLIGHT--FLATTER TRAJECTORY.
(THESE ARE DIFFERENT THAN ACTUAL SIGHT-IN COND'S--ZERO MAY CHANGE SIGNIFICANTLY)
(NORMAL ZERO IS 240 YARDS)

WITH GUN WT = 8.75 LBS, BUL WT = 210 GR, PWDR WT = 77 GR, & MV = 2983 FPS
APPROX RECOIL OF YOUR WINCHESTER M70
IS 35.4 FOOT-POUNDS.

FOR COMPARISON, 15 OR LESS FT-LBS IS THE ACCEPTED MIL STD FOR SHOULDER WEAPONS

                                                      TRAJECTORY  CROSS
RANGE   VELOCITY   ENERGY   MOMENTUM    TIME    DROP   (W/1.5  IN. WIND
(YDS)   (FT/SEC)   (FT-LB)  (SLUG-FPS)  (SEC)   (IN.)   SIGHTS)    DEF *
****************************************************************************
TRAJECTORY COMPUTED BY USING THEORETICAL 'ZERO' THAT MAY NOT FALL EXACTLY ON ANY
10-YARD INCREMENT--HENCE, NEW ZERO IS APPROXIMATE (BUT WITHIN TEN YARDS).

000     2983       4151     2.78       0.000    0.0    -1.5       0.0
50      2872       3848     2.68       .0513     .5     2.24       .02
100     2762       3560     2.58       .1045    2.054   3.57       .07
150     2655       3288     2.48       .1599    4.747   3.77       .16
200     2550       3034     2.38       .2175    8.671   2.75       .29
250     2449       2798     2.28       .2776   13.933    .4        .46
300     2349       2575     2.19       .3401   20.642  -3.38       .68
350     2254       2370     2.1        .4053   28.927  -8.73       .94
400     2160       2176     2.01       .4733   38.916  -15.76     1.25
450     2070       1999     1.93       .5442   50.777  -24.65     1.61
500     1982       1832     1.85       .6183   64.654  -35.54     2.03
550     1897       1679     1.77       .6956   80.751  -48.64     2.51
600     1814       1535     1.69       .7765   99.243  -64.1      3.05

* DEFLECTION IN INCHES PER 1 MPH CROSS-WIND. MULTIPY BY WIND VEL FOR TOTAL DEF.

MAX ORD FOR THIS TRAJECTORY IS 3.83 INCHES ABOVE L-O-S @ APPROX 130 YDS

YOUR PRIMARY ZERO FOR THIS TRAJ IS NEAR  260 YARDS

YOUR PSEUDO ZERO IS NEAR  10 YARDS

(ZERO HAS SHIFTED FROM ORIGINAL SIGHT-IN RG DUE TO THESE DIFFERENT ATMOS COND'S)
................................................................................
COMMENTS:  100-YD. P.O.I. IN HOUSTON 3.5 IN. HI ... LOAD VERY ACCURATE


::::::::::::::::::::::::::::::::::::::::::::::::::::::::::::::::::::::::::::::::::
         CUSTOM BALLISTICS     COPYRIGHT 1985 BY PATRICK M. FLANAGAN
```

This is a printout from a Flanagan program offers essentially the same data for the same load, shown in the preceding printout, but it is organized differently. Differences in trajectory and energy result from the fact that the preceding printout was for sea level ("standard metro") while this one reflects performance at high elevations and low temperatures. Both programs offer additional features, as well.

manuals, and more—plus it is available more quickly and often presented more usefully. This much is common to all such programs, but most of them also do much more, as I'll show a little farther along.

The second general category comprises programs specifically tailored to *handloading*. For example, the program called "Load from a Disk" acts as a sort of electronic reloading handbook, selecting the powders most suitable for any load, presenting charge weights (starting, intermediate, and maximum loads), and predicting both velocities and pressures. It also does much more, but this is the core of the program and the aspect that makes it unique. This program re-

quires a few different kinds of inputs, including the powder capacity of the case, barrel length, bullet weight and diameter, and additional factors.

The most striking thing about this particular program is that it works as well for hypothetical cartridges as for real ones, which makes it a wildcatter's delight. You can sit down at the computer and predict the performance of some oddball cartridge design for which neither gun nor brass even exists!

Use of this program does not, however, eliminate the need for conventional reloading handbooks, nor for working up and testing handloads. The predicted velocities and pressures for specified load combi-

Given accurate velocity readings from the same firing at two different ranges, most available ballistic programs calculate a bullet's ballistic coefficient, as shown here. This is handy for cast bullets, factory loads, and other projectiles for which such information is not published, because the BC is essential data for all ballistic calculations. The example shown here is a calculation of the BC for Remington's .17 Remington factory load, based on Remington's published velocity data. The program is from Eberlein Engineering (address at end of chapter).

The possibilities of computer ballistics are limited only by the programmer's imagination. This printout results from a run of a Datatech program computing bullet paths of three different loadings in the same rifle, that rifle being zeroed for the load in the left-hand column only.

The Eberlein Engineering program has stored in it all ballistic data on all rifle and pistol bullets (including cast bullets) made by Hornady, Sierra, Speer, Nosler, and Lyman. Data for the bullet for which you wish to compute ballistics is called up merely by tapping in the correct index number in the left-hand column of this menu.

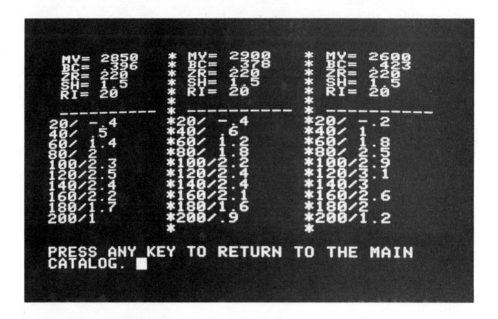

nations are just that—*predicted.* There are too many subtle factors affecting real pressures in real guns for any computer to offer better than a ballpark estimate of actual firing results. Nevertheless, this particular software is interesting to work with and a real timesaver. It's from W. W. Blackwell, noted as a source at the end of this chapter.

Several other programs offer the handloader systems for storing and retrieving not only actual loading records but related data for those loads, including group sizes and actual velocities, as well as the ballistics—trajectories, energies, and so forth—for each one.

My third software category is a catchall. These are *specialty* items that do different things in different ways. One of the most fascinating is one that simulates actual shots at game. It allows you to specify the load, scope magnification, zero range, and the kind of animal—deer, bear, elk, or varmint. It then presents you with a stylized animal on the screen with a set of crosshairs superimposed on it, and informs you of the range, wind direction and force, and uphill or downhill angle. The apparent size of the target is consistent with the scope magnification and the range. You can move the crosshairs around to adjust the hold as you would in real life under those conditions, and you can "fire" the shot. The program then displays the point of impact and informs you of the distance by which your shot missed a theoretical perfect bull's-eye. It also analyzes the miss, so that you can see how much was due to wind effects and how much to wrong holdover or holdunder. After 10 shots with random distances, hill angles, and winds, it calculates your average miss for the series.

DATATECH HUNTING TRAINER/SIMULATOR

1. This is the aiming screen in the Datatech Hunting Trainer/Simulator for a deer-size animal. The target occupies about the same portion of the visual field as it would through a riflescope of the specified magnification. All the parameters of the shot are shown. The crosshairs can be moved around as you wish, compensating for wind, range, hill angle, and the shot "fired." (Datatech mail-order address is at end of chapter.)

2. An analysis screen then appears, showing the POI (point of impact) of the shot and giving the distance from the intended POI in inches and the actual wind drift and bullet path at the specified range. A random circular dispersion, compensating for the rifle's accuracy level and the shooter's, is built in.

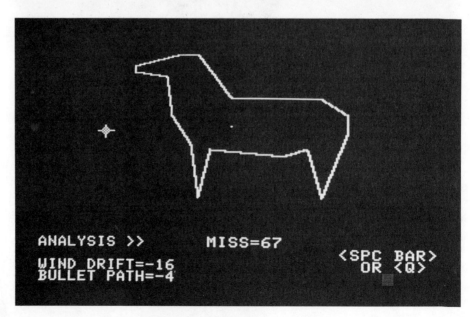

This program is an especially effective educational item, though it has much of the appeal of a computer game. After an hour or two on the Hunter Trainer/Simulator, as it's called, you get a very realistic feel for what wind and gravity do to bullets.

ADDITIONAL FEATURES

The above descriptions of available programs are quite elementary. If programs did only what I have described so far, they would be invaluable to any serious shooter, but in truth the basic functions I've described are only the beginning. Programmers seem to vie with each other to add new and ingenious features to their programs. Following are only a few features available in many ballistic programs:

- Calculation of an unknown ballistic coefficient from velocities at two ranges.
- Calculation of point-blank range for any load.
- Calculation and evaluation of recoil force.
- Calculation of trajectory for one load fired in a rifle zeroed for a different load.
- Calculation of sight changes (telescopic or iron) in minutes of angle (MOA) or clicks.
- Calculation of midrange trajectory height, properly called the *maximum ordinate*.
- Calculation of bullet momentum (different from energy, and of great interest to silhouette shooters).
- Calculation of time of flight to any range.
- Calculation of lead on moving targets at any distance and target speed for any load.

3. The Hunting Trainer/Simulator offers four different-sized target animals, and this is the program's version of a groundhog through a 10× scope at 100 yards. Either factory loads or handloads can be used with this program.

4. This is the analysis screen for the previous "shot" shown. You can gain a lot of valuable knowledge about trajectory and windage using this program.

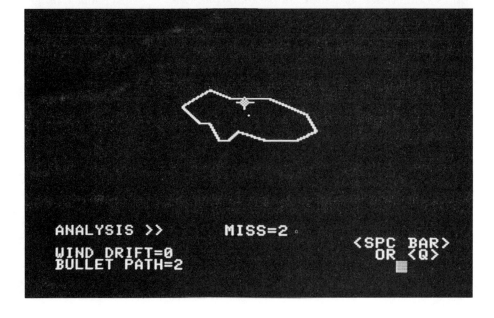

- Correction of ballistic outputs for air density, altitude, humidity, and temperature. With this feature you can properly sight-in your elk rifle for a hunt that will take place at, say, 8,000 feet in cold weather, even though your zeroing is being done at sea level on a hot day.
- Calculation of bullet drop, which is not the same as trajectory or "bullet path."
- Determination of precise value of "clicks" in a rifle or pistol sight.
- Conversion between English and metric systems of measurement.
- Comparison of trajectories of up to three different loads.
- Calculation of the standard deviation, given a series of velocities. (Some portable chronographs also offer this feature.)

And believe it or not, there are still more!

Built right into a single ballistic program, for example, is the data on most rifle and pistol bullets, including cast bullet designs, that are currently marketed by Speer, Sierra, Hornady, Nosler, and Lyman. With this one, you simply inform the computer that you want to use the 130-grain Hornady .270 flatbase spire point, for example. It looks up the ballistic coefficient and other pertinent stored data and proceeds with the requested calculations.

All current programs, as far as I know, will deliver all or most of this information for rifle, pistol, and shotgun ammo, and even for muzzleloading arms. Some can do it for airguns too, and—would you believe?—arrows! Most—but not all—of these programs are geared for printing the output if a printer is available, and some are set up to store output data on diskette for future reference. At least one will create charts, diagrams, and graphs, and will print them out with the right equipment.

Although ballistic software generally will perform most of the functions I've mentioned so far, there's quite a difference in manner of presentation. One program may compute and display full trajectory data for any range and with any interval—every yard, 10 yards, or 100 yards, whatever you specify. Another may show it for no more than five selected distances, at fixed intervals, or only up to a certain maximum distance.

Different programmers also have different ideas about the proper procedures within the program. In other words, in each program you are required to proceed along certain routes of input and output. You may have to command the computer to do a lot of calculations that have already been performed once in order to extract the specific information you desire. This is not bad, since a computer never gets bored or tired, but it does take time, even at computer speed. Even though the same calculation without the computer might require an hour, you can still find a repeated 10-second wait annoying.

What I'm saying is that, if you shop around among the many ballistic software brands, you will find that some of them suit your needs and preferences better than others, even though you can get basically the same information out of all of them. It's a matter of procedures and presentation.

Shopping for software is not easy, unfortunately. I have seen no ballistic programs in software shops where they can actually be run or, at least, the manuals (documentation) read thoroughly. Most of them are sold by mail order from advertisements in shooting magazines (*Handloader* is probably the most consistent source). Sierra Bullets offers a program that presumably could be ordered through any Sierra dealer, as well as by mail. The good news is that this direct marketing materially reduces software prices; ballistic programs commonly cost only one-fourth to one-third what typical spreadsheet, word processing, or database programs do. I know of only one such program that costs more than $100.

WHICH COMPUTER?

Ballistic programs are available for most, if not all, popular home computer models. I know of such software for the Apple, Tandy or TRS (Radio Shack), Atari, IBM PC (and "compatibles"), Commodore, the Texas Instruments Programmable calculator and others, but every program is not available for all computers. If you already have a computer, your selection of ballistic software will thus be somewhat limited. Only a few programs are available in any of several different computer languages. Also, a certain program may not run properly on all models of the same brand of computer.

In my case, I actually selected my Apple partly because I was aware of several interesting ballistic programs available for it alone. That was before the introduction of the IBM line of personal computers, when the Apple owner had by far the best selection of shooting software.

Today, that situation has probably reversed itself. Most ballistic programs being written are for the IBM and its compatibles, and one of these would probably be my choice if I were starting all over again. If the program on the disk is written in the BASIC language used by Apple, TRS, or Commodore and can be operator modified, it will be relatively easy to "translate" into either of the other BASIC versions. Only a few changes will be required, since the three versions are quite similar. I have translated a program originally written in TRS BASIC into "Applesoft" (the Apple dialect of BASIC) without difficulty, and I am certainly not a programming expert.

Any computer software, of course, demands a certain amount of RAM (random-access memory) capacity in the machine on which it will be run. Usually 48K or 64K is enough. Most newer home computers have far more RAM than required by today's programs, and the memory capacity of some older models can be expanded (for a price). Be sure to check on memory capacities before purchasing either software or a computer.

Some computer models are much faster than others, because they have faster microprocessors. I mentioned that many ballistic calculations are extremely complex, and computer speed does make a small but significant difference. My Apple II + has one of the more leisurely microprocessors still current, and certain commercial ballistic programs run on it with annoying slowness. This could also influence your purchasing decision. However, the way in which the program is written may have an even greater effect on speed, regardless of the machine. In any computer project there will always be several different ways to accomplish the same ends, and the particular method chosen by the programmer who wrote the program will affect running speed.

Finally, certain home-computer models have distinctly better graphics capability than others, in case you're interested in a ballistic program with graphics features. The various Apples are particularly noted for their inherent graphics, and I have modified a BASIC ballistic program to draw trajectory curves on a grid on my screen without benefit of any special graphics software.

In shopping for a ballistic computer, be sure to inquire about all these factors and compare different brands. And one more tip: in most larger cities, a lively trade in second hand computers has sprung up. If ballistics are your major, or only, interest in owning one, check your Yellow Pages; you may find you can pick up an older, pre-owned model that will do all you need at a very reasonable price. Recent inquiries around such shops proved that I could exactly duplicate my present setup, except for the printer, for about 15 percent of the cost of my original setup.

SOFTWARE FOR FREE

Not all ballistic software requires a hard-cash outlay. My favorite program, for example, was published in its entirety in the June, 1983, issue of *American Rifleman*, in an article by William P. Davis, Jr. The entire program was in print, so it cost me only several hours of meticulous typing. It was originally written on a Radio Shack TRS-80 computer, but I had to make only a dozen or so changes to translate it into "Applesoft" for use on my machine. Of all the pure ballistic programs I have, this is the one I like best and I usually reach for it when faced with a ballistic question from a reader of one of my magazine articles. It lacks some of the fancy features of the others, but the internal procedures and methods of displaying results suit my purposes perfectly.

Well, *almost* perfectly. As I said, no two programmers see problems in exactly the same way, and I suppose no two shooters do either. In any case, since I wrote—or, more accurately, copied—the program, I modified it here and there as I went along. The output I get now is the information I want, with no data that is extraneous to me. The overwhelming advantage to a program written in BASIC is that it can be listed and modified by the user. Many programs, however, are written in machine language and locked away so that the average user can't even see them, much less change them. This protects the copyright holder by making it difficult for a buyer to make copy disks and give them away or sell them.

At least a few other ballistic programs besides Davis', are in the public domain, having been published in *Handloader* magazine in past years, and there may

I further modified the Davis/NRA program to draw this trajectory graph on the computer screen. Each vertical block equals 12 inches and each horizontal block equals 50 yards. Such personalized modifications require no special training. I have none whatever as a programmer.

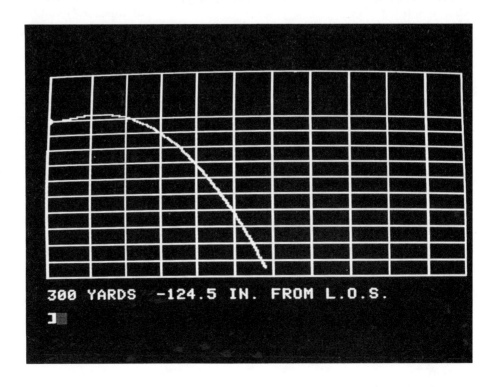

300 YARDS -124.5 IN. FROM L.O.S.

have been some printed elsewhere, that I missed.

When I first got the Apple, I even wrote a few programs of my own, as exercises in elementary programming. I still use one of these from time to time. It calculates recoil energy from any given load in 10 different gun weights simultaneously. Except for my time, it cost me nothing.

A collection of software can become quite an investment, but there are other valuable programs legally available for free. As in the case of a chronograph, several shooting buddies can also chip in on software or even on the computer to run it.

USING A BALLISTIC COMPUTER

There are so many functions available in ballistic software. And there are so many ways of combining them that any effort here to describe them will be inadequate. However, a couple of examples, along with the actual printouts reproduced here, may at least give you a feel for the benefits you could expect from a home computer.

Let's assume a fellow wishes to work up a load for his .300 Winchester Magnum for use on a once-in-a-lifetime, mixed-bag hunt in Alaska, British Columbia, the Yukon, or the Northwest Territories. He hopes to have the opportunity to take mountain sheep, caribou, moose, and grizzly, and he would prefer to do it all with the same handload so he has to memorize only one trajectory. The moose will probably be shot at fairly close range, but it is a huge animal requiring great power and penetration. The sheep and caribou don't take so much killing power but are often long-range propositions where flatness of trajectory becomes critical. The grizzly, of course, demands all the killing power that can be built into the load, this animal being notoriously unforgiving and vindictive when wounded.

Our intrepid hunter thinks immediately of the 200-grain Nosler spitzer bullet, which he knows from experience will do the job on elk-size animals, at least. But he has never fired it at really long range, and has no idea of its long-distance energy delivery or wind deflection. Cranking up the computer, he enters the ballistic coefficient and muzzle velocity (either chronographed or estimated from Nosler's handloading manual data) and asks for the maximum point-blank range and correct zero at sea level. His answer appears on the computer screen (see accompanying printout); the computer suggests he zero the

rifle at 252 yards for a maximum point-blank range of 296 yards.

He now asks the same question, changing the elevation to 6,000 feet above sea level and the temperature to 40° F., these numbers being an approximate average for the area he plans to hunt. This time, the computer gives him the second answer (see printout below), showing only slight changes in recommended zero and point-blank range.

```
POINT BLANK RANGE DETERMINATION
ENTER MAXIMUM ALLOWABLE HEIGHT ABOVE
OR BELOW THE LINE OF SIGHT, INCHES: 3

CALCULATIONS WILL TAKE UP TO 30 SECONDS


MAXIMUM POINT      299 YARDS
BLANK RANGE
SET ZERO           255 YARDS
RANGE AT
2 ITERATIONS REQUIRED
```

So far, so good. He knows now that the zero he establishes on his home range before departing for the north country will remain valid in the mountains. The point-blank range routine in the program asked him to enter the maximum acceptable trajectory height above the line of sight, and his answer was 3 inches. Such a trajectory will therefore allow him to ignore range out to almost 300 yards. He will simply aim for the center of a ram's chest with the certainty that the bullet will neither rise above nor fall below the vital zone to that distance.

He decides on a 250-yard zero, but this leaves him with a problem. He has only a 100-yard range available for final scope adjustments, and he now wonders how high to set his point of impact above center at 100 yards in order to achieve a zero at 250 yards. Without the computer, this problem could be solved only by finding a longer range and expending a great deal of ammunition.

With it, however, he merely enters the necessary data (ballistic coefficient, bullet weight, height of sight-line above the axis of the bore, and muzzle velocity) and requests an analysis of the load at 250 yards. In seconds, he has his answer before him (see printout below), which tells him more than he ever wanted to know about what will happen with that load at 250 yards. Next, he orders the computer to prepare a chart showing remaining velocities and energies, bullet path, and deflections in a 10-mile-

```
POINT BLANK RANGE DETERMINATION

ENTER MAXIMUM ALLOWABLE HEIGHT ABOVE
OR BELOW THE LINE OF SIGHT, INCHES: 3

CALCULATIONS WILL TAKE UP TO 30 SECONDS


MAXIMUM POINT      296 YARDS
BLANK RANGE

SET ZERO           252 YARDS
RANGE AT

1 ITERATIONS REQUIRED
```

```
----------------------------------------
              .300 WIN MAG
         200-GR. NOSLER PARTITION
VELOCITY: 2930 FPS,    BALL. COEF.: .584
            STANDARD METRO
----------------------------------------
MUZZLE VELOCITY (FPS):               2930
RANGE (YARDS):                        250
REMAINING VELOCITY (FPS):            2538
REMAINING ENERGY (FT-LBS):           2861
TIME OF FLIGHT (SEC.):               .275
TOTAL DROP (INCHES):                   14
MAX HEIGHT ABOVE L.O.S. (INCHES):       3
ELEVATION REQUIRED (MOA):             6.2
DEFLECTION IN 10-MPH WIND (INCHES):   3.4
----------------------------------------
```

per-hour crosswind with this load out to 400 yards by 25-yard increments.

Presto! From the display (see printout below), he discovers that he must adjust the point of impact of his load to be 2.6 inches high at 100 yards to achieve a 250-yard zero. He also learns that the highest point of his trajectory will be around 140 yards, and that, depending on the size of the target animal, he'll need to begin to hold a little high on any shot past about 325 yards.

The chart offers a good deal more information, as well. Our man is pleased to note that his projected load carries a full 3,500 foot-pounds of energy to 50

```
--------------------------------------
              .300 WIN MAG
          200-GR. NOSLER PARTITION
VELOCITY: 2930 FPS,    BALL. COEF.: .584
             STANDARD METRO
--------------------------------------
RANGE   REM.   REM.    BULLET      WIND
YARDS   VEL.   ENERGY  PATH    DEFL.,10 MPH
0       2930   3812    -1.5        0
25      2889   3707    -.1         0
50      2849   3604    1.1         .1
75      2809   3503    2           .3
100     2769   3405    2.6         .5
125     2730   3309    2.9         .8
150     2691   3215    2.9        1.2
175     2652   3124    2.7        1.7
200     2614   3034    2.1        2.2
225     2576   2947    1.2        2.8
250     2538   2861    0          3.4
275     2501   2778    -1.5       4.1
300     2464   2696    -3.4       4.9
325     2427   2616    -5.7       5.8
350     2391   2538    -8.3       6.7
375     2355   2462    -11.3      7.8
400     2319   2388    -14.7      8.9
--------------------------------------
```

yards, which is comforting should he get grizzly charged, and 3,000 foot-pounds all the way out to 225—more than enough for any of his intended game, even the moose. A glance down the listed wind deflections informs him that, if the wind is really blowing (as it usually does in the mountains), he'd better remember to give 'er a little Kentucky windage on any shot past about 250 yards.

All of which is quite a bit of information, considering that he hasn't even *bought* those bullets yet, much less loaded or fired any! And, considering the price of cartridges these days, our friend would be dollars ahead if his computer study happened to reveal that his first choices of cartridge and bullet were not the correct ones, after all. In fact, it would be just as simple for him to sit at the computer and "test" half a dozen different cartridges and/or loads until he found the best fit. Outfitters and guides would sleep better if all their clients did just that before booking a hunt. Some wise shooters might also print out or copy down the dope and tape it to the buttstock of their rifles, just in case.

And how accurate are these numbers, considering that they came out of a bunch of electrons moving around? The answer to that may surprise you: naturally, the numbers should be double-checked by actual firing as far as possible. But they will be considerably more precise than the handloader could gather with any amount of shooting, because they ignore the wobbly, flinching, trigger-jerking human behind the rifle.

SOURCES

There is no more dynamic or fluid business today than the computer/software business, and I know that I will contribute to the early obsolescence of this volume by even attempting a listing of ballistic software sources. Nevertheless, I know of no other such listing anywhere, and the following is offered for your convenience.

I can only suggest that, if you're interested, you contact the sources shown here. If they're out of business or have moved, merged, or vanished, I'm sorry, but that's the way the world is.

● W. W. BLACKWELL, 9826 Sagedale, Houston, TX 77089. Offers several programs including "Load from a Disk I," which is the electronics handbook I mentioned earlier. It calculates internal and external ballistics for any rifle, commercial or wildcat. "Load from a Disk II" calculates optimum rifling twist, bullet velocity from trajectory, ballistic coefficients from shape, and more. "Ballistic Coefficients on a Disk" provides just that from major U.S. ammo manufacturers. Pro-

grams run on Apples, Laser 128, IBM PC's and clones, and Commodores 64 and 128.

● DATATECH SOFTWARE SYSTEMS INC., 19312 East Eldorado Dr., Aurora, CO 80013. The Hunting Trainer/Simulator mentioned in the text and on the same disk a general ballistic program. Both for Apple computers.

● DYNACOMP INC., Dynacomp Office Building, 178 Phillips Rd., Webster, NY 14580. "Reloading Database" is a user-friendly handloading analysis program originated by Redfan Inc. for IBM PC's and compatibles, as well as for CP/M systems. Allows quite sophisticated manipulation of load component and test data, and provides a variety of charts, graphs, and tables showing results. This standard program can be customized by Redfan, if you have special additional needs.

● CULLEN Q. LEE, PO Box 215, Scooba, MS 39358. An extremely sophisticated general ballistic program for the Apple Macintosh, IBM, Leading Edge, and others.

● PAB SOFTWARE INC., PO Box 15387, Ft. Wayne, IN 46885. A variety of excellent shooters' and handloaders' programs, including the NRA-published

Davis program mentioned in this chapter, for TRS-80 Models I, III, and IV, Apple II, and IBM PC (and possibly others by now). New programs added to the line from time to time.

● EBERLEIN ENGINEERING CO., PO Box 607, Saulk City, WI 53583. The program is "Exterior Ballistics for Small Arms," for the Apple II and IBM PC families of computers. A very versatile ballistic program designed for reloading applications and containing ballistic coefficient data for most bullets by all major bullet-makers.

● PATRICK M. FLANAGAN, 7056 Yucca Circle, Twenty-nine Palms, CA 92278. The program is "Custom Ballistics," illustrated on page 90.

15

Loading
For Accuracy

he word "uniformity" contains the real secret to accurate and satisfactory handloads. The greatest advantage a reloader has over the ammunition factories is that he doesn't have to make a profit on his time and so can go to any lengths he wishes to preserve cartridge-to-cartridge uniformity. True, he can hand-tailor loads to the demonstrated preferences of his individual firearms, but even that is to no avail unless he can assemble the ammo to considerably closer tolerances than a manufacturer.

To be candid, the gap between handloads and factory stuff has narrowed dramatically since about 1980. It's no longer as easy as it once was to build reloads that routinely outshoot the commercial product. I'm not certain exactly how the manufacturers have caught up—better bullets in certain loads, no doubt, and an overall improvement in equipment and processes—but they have. Now and then these days I receive a batch of factory-made ammo for testing that is so good I'm glad I don't have to beat it with a handload in order to preserve my reputation! This is most often true in the varmint calibers, especially .223 and .22/250 Rem., and in certain brands. I've recently gotten super-accurate stuff from Norma, Frontier (Hornady), and especially Federal.

It may be worth noting too that there is a trend within Remington, Winchester-Western, Federal, and Weatherby ammo to use the same bullets handloaders do, and I can think of factory ammunition today that is actually loaded with Hornady, Speer, Sierra, or Nosler bullets (although the box usually won't say so). The reloader can no longer be confident of cutting factory-ammo groups in half in his own firearms merely by clapping a few components together; he has to work at it.

Still, when we speak of accuracy we're talking about

uniformity; it is the great key to accurate ammunition. Only when techniques for uniformity have become a handloading habit can you begin to search more esoteric realms for new breakthroughs in accuracy.

WHAT IS "ACCURACY?"

First, you must answer the question, "How accurate is 'accurate'?" Obviously, the answer varies widely. A woodchuck shooter who does most of his shooting on the far side of 300 yards would laugh out loud at the African professional hunter's concept of accuracy. The former demands at least minute-of-angle accuracy, while the latter is only interested in minute-of-rhinoceros accuracy in his big .470 double rifle. A far-gone benchrest competitor might sneer at both of them. Joe Deerhunter worries more about the carryability and handleability of his rifle than its grouping ability, and may cheerfully settle for 3-inch groups at 100 yards, knowing that such a weapon will reliably put every deer he'll ever shoot at on the ground if he does his part. Obviously, there is no absolute standard of accuracy against which any and all rifles and pistols can be judged. It's up to each individual handloader to decide, in planning his load, what degree of accuracy is necessary to the load's purpose. If he finds he can exceed his minimum requirements, so much the better; if not, he at least knows whether the load has succeeded or failed.

Accuracy in rifled arms is usually described in terms of minutes of angle (MOA). If you imagine yourself standing at the center of a perfect circle, that circle can be divided into 360°, each degree with 60 minutes. A minute of angle, being a measurement of arc, is a minute of angle at any range. At 100 yards, it figures out to 1.047168 inches. For practical purposes, this is so close to an even 1 inch that hand-loaders consider a rifle that groups inside 1 inch at 100 yards to be a *minute-of-angle rifle*. However, to be a *true* minute-of-angle rifle, it should also group in 2 inches at 200 yards, 3 inches at 300 yards, and so on, out to its maximum practical range. One minute of angle at 1,000 yards, for example, is 10 inches, and there are rifles and riflemen capable of minute-of-angle performance even at that range.

You will *hear* of a great many more standard, off-the-shelf sporting rifles that are capable of minute-of-angle accuracy than you will ever *see*. If you worry a lot about the apparent fact that everybody else's deer rifle is good for a "minute" (according to the owner) while yours seems to average no better than, say, 1.75 minutes of angle (MOA), your distress will be considerably relieved by actually shooting those other red-hot sporters. A couple of 1-MOA groups do not an minute-of-angle rifle make; the long-run average is what counts.

BARREL TIME AND GOOD VIBES

The accuracy potential of a rifle is inherent in many different parts of the gun and ammunition. The quality of the barrel itself is probably the most important single item, along with the bedding of wood to steel throughout the arm, the trigger, the lock time, and several other factors. An entire book could easily be written on the subject of "tuning" a rifle for optimum accuracy, and I have no room here for such a discussion. However, proper load development is an essential part of such tuning, and that *is* relevant to our topic.

One thing must be understood about the barrel. This is that even the stiffest, most massive rifle barrel vibrates like a tuning fork when fired. A lighter barrel's vibrations have a greater amplitude than those of a bull barrel (an extra-thick barrel), but they all vibrate. The vibration causes the muzzle to move, but the direction of the movement is unpredictable. In the case of a perfectly bedded barreled action, the movement should be perfectly vertical, assuming a perfect barrel. Most barrels have some lateral component to their vibrations, with the muzzle swinging in a circle or an oval at some angle.

Now heed this carefully, for it will explain some seemingly mysterious things you will experience in your load testing. The barrel begins to vibrate as soon as the powder charge begins to burn, and the vibration continues throughout the time the bullet takes to move down the barrel and depart the muzzle. This period is called the "barrel time" of the bullet, and it varies from load to load, depending upon the burning characteristics of the powder and the quantity being burned. Let's assume you have one of those perfect barrels, perfectly bedded, which vibrates only in the vertical plane. Furthermore, let's assume that the first shot fired delivers the bullet at the muzzle when the muzzle happens to be at its maximum upward displacement on its vibration cycle. If the next

shot fired happens to have a very slightly different barrel time, the bullet may arrive at the muzzle when it's at its maximum downward displacement. Although the physical displacement of the axis of the bore at the muzzle may be very small, it is nonetheless a real factor in grouping; those two bullets were actually launched in slightly different directions and the first will arrive at a measurably higher impact point on target than will the second one.

From this you can appreciate the importance of consistent barrel time from shot to shot. And near-perfect uniformity in all factors in the load is the key to consistent barrel time. If the barrel in question happens to vibrate in, say, an oval pattern (which most of them do), the displacement of successive shots due to varying barrel times will be lateral as well as vertical.

This vibration phenomenon, by the way, explains why a lower-velocity load with a heavier bullet will occasionally register a higher point of impact at 100 yards than a speedy, light-bullet load, contrary to apparent logic and the laws of physics. It also explains why a given powder and charge will sometimes shoot to a different point of impact than another load that drives the same bullet at an identical velocity. This is a matter of some importance to handloaders striving to adjust the point of impact of a low-velocity small-game load relative to that of a full-power loading in the same rifle.

ELEMENTS OF ACCURACY

Accuracy in rifles, of course, involves a host of factors other than consistent barrel time. Probably the most important single element in accuracy after a high-quality, well-bedded barrel is the bullet. Some of the characteristics of "good" bullets have already been discussed, as has proper bullet seating relative to the rifling. The keys to accuracy could be said to be good bullets in a good barrel. It's true that one rifle may shoot smaller groups with one bullet while another, identical arm does its best work with a different bullet, but these differences are usually quite small. A good bullet is a good bullet in *any* rifle, and a rifle that shoots small groups with one good bullet almost always does nearly as well with any other equally good bullet. Bullet selection is critical to accuracy, but reading and talking with handloaders experienced with your cartridge shortens the search for the right projectile for your purposes.

As I have said, the right powder and charge weight is also important to finest accuracy, and here individual rifles may show rather wide differences. It's well worth experimenting with as many powders as may be appropriate in the cartridge in question, because now and then one of them will turn out to be exactly what a particular rifle prefers, delivering dramatically better groups than any other propellant. This will not regularly be the case, but it happens often enough to be worth trying when the very finest possible accuracy is the goal in a given rifle.

A CASE FOR CASES

Most of the rest of the factors recognized as vital to best accuracy lie in the cartridge case and the techniques for preparing and loading it. The neck is the portion of the case's anatomy most critical to accuracy. It holds the bullet. Ideally, all case necks in a lot should be exactly the same length, exactly the same thickness all around their circumference, and should grip their bullets with exactly the same tension, not too much and not too little. Uniformity in case-neck length is easily achieved by careful trimming, deburring, and chamfering.

Case-neck thickness is another matter. The right thickness must be related to the rifle chamber in which the cases are to be fired and to the internal dimensions of the die in which they will be resized. If necks are thinned too much, the die may not reduce the internal diameter enough to provide proper grip on the bullets. Necks can be thinned and evened up by inside reaming or outside turning with the neck supported on a close-fitting mandrel. Inside reaming can be performed with special attachments offered for use with several of the case-trimming tools on the market, with special reamers furnished by die manufacturers, or with a boring-bar tool made by Lee. Any of these tools will do a good job, but the benchrest shooters who tend to go to the ultimate extremes in search of accuracy almost universally prefer the outside turning technique. This can be done on a lathe, of course, but several small, ultraprecise, hand tools are available (from Marquart Precision, Dewey, Hart, and others). These tools are capable of holding neck thickness all the way around a case to plus or

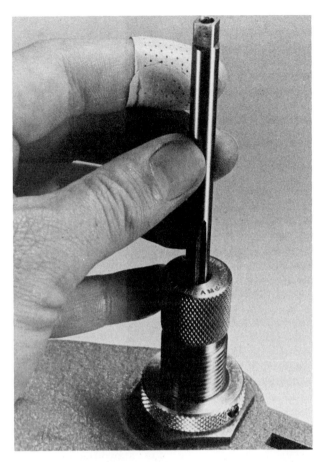

Case necks can be inside-reamed instead of outside-turned, using a special RCBS die and a precision reamer rotated with a tap wrench.

This Marquart outside neck turning tool shaves case necks to uniform thickness within .0001 inch, which is a must for ultimate accuracy.

minus .0001 inch. Neck turning is tedious work at best, and is not worth the trouble, according to my experiments, on hunting rifles. Very accurate field varmint rifles, say those averaging under ¾-inch groups at 100 yards with unaltered case necks, will show a small but definite improvement in accuracy with processed necks, and serious bench rifles absolutely demand the turning of necks. Some winning benchresters do nothing special to their brass except to use cases from the same lot and to trim and turn case necks, but they regard these things as essential.

The other end of the case comes in for attention from other serious accuracy buffs. The flash hole, through which the primer flash reaches the powder charge, should be uniform from case to case in terms of both diameter and length. The idea is that this contributes to uniformity of ignition. Flash holes can be gauged so that cases can be sorted into lots with holes of uniform diameter, or a twist drill of the correct diameter can be used to enlarge all flash holes in a lot of cases to the same diameter. However, flash holes that have been materially enlarged will cause high pressures, and should be avoided. On small rifle cases (the only kind, usually, which deserve such meticulous treatment) flash holes are best kept not smaller than .081 inch or larger than .089 inch. A #45 twist drill will produce a uniform .082-inch hole, which seems about right. The latest rage among benchresters is tools that chamfer the inside end of the flash hole for uniform length as well as diameter.

The seating of the bullet is of considerable impor-

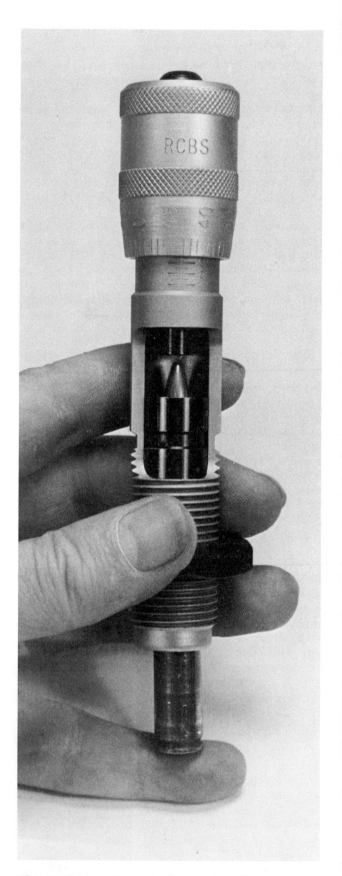

This RCBS Benchrest bullet-seating die maintains case/bullet alignment during seating, as illustrated in Chapter 9, but adds micrometer adjustments that permit a quick, precise return to a previous setting.

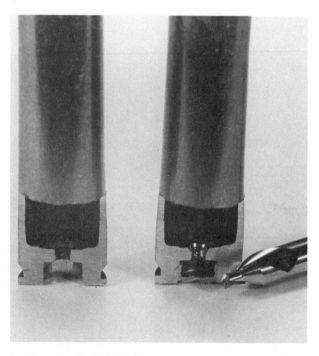

"Uniforming" flash holes removes internal burrs and produces flash holes of uniform length as well as diameter. The tool shown is from Brown Precision. Several makers offer a similar tool.

The Brown "Little Wiggler" measures straightness and concentricity of a loaded round, and uniformity of neck thickness.

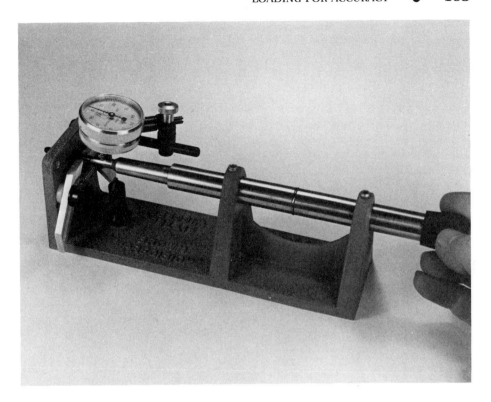

tance to accuracy, not only as to the matter of seating depth, but also of seating straightness. There are special seating dies for use in bench-mounted tools that have provisions for holding the case and the bullet in perfect alignment throughout the process of seating. This is supposed to result in better concentricity and a loaded round in which the axis of the bullet is parallel to and identical with that of the case. There's no doubt at all that this does indeed reduce group sizes, but again, it's mostly the super-accurate rifles that can benefit. Varmint shooters may find special seating dies a good investment, but no big-game hunter ever will find them worthwhile.

ACCURACY TOOLS AND TECHNIQUES

There are tools for everything in handloading, including those that measure the crookedness of loaded ammunition. The Brown Precision "Little Wiggler" is especially useful for this purpose, because it not only indicates the amount of "runout" or crookedness of a seated bullet, but also incorporates a little jack for straightening the round by the few thousandths of an inch usually required. This tool will also measure the thickness of case necks to within .0005 inch; even benchresters concede that .002 inch is adequate case-neck uniformity. If loaded rounds are crooked enough, no gauge is needed to spot the problem; simply roll the round across a smooth surface and watch the point of the bullet. If it rotates in a small circle as the cartridge rolls, it is tilted enough to affect

accuracy. The rule of thumb is that each .001 inch of crookedness in the bullet as seated will result in a displacement on target at 100 yards of about ⅛ inch. Most factory ammunition reveals a misalignment of from .002 inch to .006 inch, and military ammo is about the same. Each shooter can decide for himself how important this element of accuracy is, but a fair rule might be as follows: for benchrest shooting, maximum acceptable bullet tilt of .0005 inch; for serious long-range varminting, not more than .001 inch runout; for general hunting, including big game, not more than .004 inch, preferably less.

Of course, all these cunning efforts to build the utmost accuracy into handloaded ammunition will be for naught if the cases used have not been carefully sorted, and preferably all of the same lot. It might be worth repeating here too that uniformity of powder charge weight is crucial to accuracy. Charges should be within .2 grain of the same weight for any sort of shooting where accuracy is a factor, and within plus or minus .1 grain where it is paramount. Handweighing each charge is the way to be certain, but a skilled operator with a familiar powder measure of high quality can learn to throw charges this uniform, at least with certain powders. No benchrest shooters I know of handweigh charges, even for match shooting.

One more thing: handloads for the ultimate in accuracy are never crimped, except in a few handgun cartridges.

And what has all this to do with reloading for ordinary hunting and plinking? Well, every rifleman is interested in accuracy as a general concept, and most

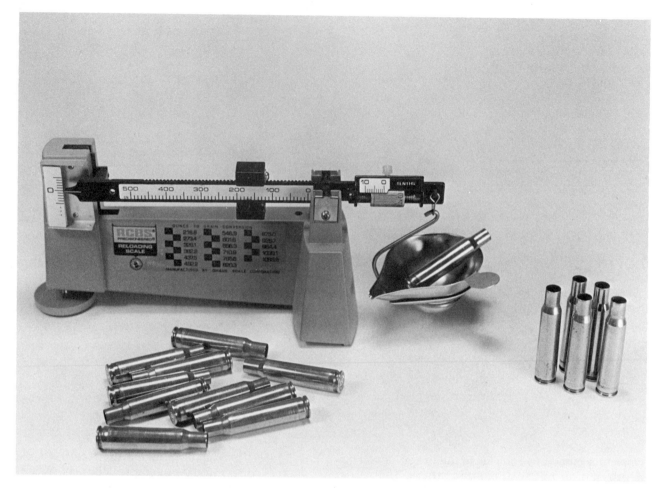

Many benchrest competitors select a batch of cases by weight, process them, and then use the same 10 cases for all firing for record. Cases of uniform weight and identical exterior dimensions will also have identical internal volume and so help promote uniform firing.

of us get the bug, sooner or later, to see just how well our sporters can be made to shoot. The real accuracy buffs have improved the breed, so to speak, in the same way that improvements pioneered in the superspecialized Indianapolis racing cars have filtered down to the family station wagon. If this chapter has done nothing else, perhaps it has given the hunter and the plinker the information he needs to judge whether his guns are doing their best, however good that may be. It may also help show him where to look for improvement when the accuracy virus bites. *No* handloader ever becomes immune to that virus.

16 Loading for the Hunting Field

Since about 1960, I've not fired more than a handful of factory cartridges at live game— and I've been blessed with an exceptionally full and far-ranging hunting career on four continents. That career has included several African safaris and the taking of most of the world's most glamorous game animals. It's both surprising and amusing to have people express concern for my physical safety when they learn that I intend to hunt dangerous animals with my "homemade" cartridges.

These well-meaning folks seem to think that handloads may be okay for plinking and target practice, or for common game and varmints, but that there must be something inferior about them for "serious" hunting. I take *all* hunting seriously. And I think we owe it to any hunted animal, whether a lowly coyote

Dangerous game, such as this African Cape buffalo, calls for the utmost in power, bullet quality, and mechanical reliability. And that means handloads.

or a lordly greater kudu, to use the most efficient ammunition available. That invariably means a handload.

Indeed, if rimfire ammo is included, I've had far more trouble with factory ammo than with handloads over the years. And while hunting, I have yet to experience a misfire or mechanical malfunction with a reloaded round. I once went up against a wounded and very angry African lion at 30 yards with a magazineful of handloaded cartridges in a wildcat rifle. The lion lost. The Cape buffalo is surely the toughest and probably the most dangerous animal in the world, and every one of the many I've collected has fallen to handloads. Ditto one record-size male leopard. In all of these and many other encounters with potentially dangerous animals, the fact that I was shooting handloaded ammo was the very least of my worries.

I once surveyed some 30 of America's most famous, worldwide hunters, a group of men and women whose combined experience totals several centuries and thousands of head of game of every imaginable species, and all except one told me they use cartridges that they load themselves or that are custom-loaded for them.

MECHANICAL RELIABILITY IS CRUCIAL

One of the reasons for this confidence in handloads is that I am aware of one paramount fact as I assemble cartridges for the hunting field, and this is that nothing less than absolute mechanical reliability is acceptable in such rounds. *Perfect* functioning, feeding from the magazine, chambering, firing, extraction, and ejection are the *first* considerations in hunting handloads. These things must not be compromised for any other performance factor. If they are, the trophy of a lifetime on the hunt of a lifetime may be lost, not to mention the fact that such compromises can get a hunter killed.

Mechanical reliability is not at all difficult to ensure. For hunting loads, I prefer to use brass that has been fired once in the hunting rifle, but that has not been fired more than two or three times at most. Ideally, brass that has been fired, resized, and reloaded for the hunt delivers the smallest odds of a malfunction. That first firing is likely to reveal any inherent flaw in the case (extremely rare, but possible) and to expand the case to fit that particular chamber.

For hunting, I always full-length resize my cases; this avoids the occasional swelled case, which may not only fail to chamber but may jam the rifle hopelessly under a hunter's frantic efforts to force it home. Naturally, I make certain that cases for hunting are duly sorted and carefully trimmed, chamfered, and deburred. If my dies are adjusted correctly, these few precautions take care of about 99 percent of all potential mechanical malfunctions. I can positively eliminate the other 1 percent by making certain that the loads I'm using are not too hot, and by careful attention to correct seating depths of the bullets (really a part of die adjustment).

TEMPERATURE AND PRESSURE

A powder charge that develops excessive pressure, remember, can cause difficult extraction or even stick a case solidly in the chamber, making the opening of the rifle's action impossible. Extraction problems can be avoided, of course, by keeping hunting loads distinctly below maximum levels. But there's another factor that I have not discussed before, and this is ambient temperature, or more precisely, powder temperature at the moment of firing. This temperature can make quite a bit of difference in chamber pressures, so much so that artillerymen must compensate for temperature in calculating the range of howitzer shells with a given muzzle elevation. The hunting rifleman has no such intricate problems, but extreme temperature variations must be kept in mind when developing handloads. If, for example, he's working up a load at his home in Michigan on a chilly spring day, and intends to use that load on a javelina hunt in the Arizona desert where temperatures may be 50° to 60° higher, he'll do well to keep that differential in mind as he approaches maximum charge levels. It's very unlikely that intelligently developed loads will be pushed into dangerous pressure regions, even by a temperature variation of 100°, but the point of impact may vary significantly. Conversely, a hunter who develops loads during a Texas summer should keep in mind that his zero may shift quite a bit when those cartridges are fired at a mule deer in the Colorado Rockies on a frosty November morning.

This is an extremely complex subject, and any general rule is likely to have all sorts of exceptions. Some types of powder are much more sensitive to temperature variations than others, and the type of cartridge and density of loading can affect results. Temperature vs. velocity tables have been published in the *Speer Reloading Manual*, in Ackley's *Handbook for Shooters and Reloaders*, in *Handloader* magazine, and by IMR (formerly du Pont). They do not necessarily agree in detail, and as I mentioned, warn of many exceptions.

Here are some *very* rough rules that may help a little. Only extreme variations are significant, say powder temperature changes of more than 30° from a "normal" 70°F. From 70° down to about zero, a typical load may lose about 100 FPS, or gain about the same amount of velocity from 70° up to 100°. Certain powders must be watched more closely than others, and these include all the ball types, most double-based propellants, and the old, surplus H-4831 and IMR 4350. Heavy charges and high loading densities tend to increase pressure changes with changing temperature.

In general, temperature variations are unlikely to change 100-yard points of impact more than a couple of inches, at most, between 0° and 100°, but at very long ranges could conceivably cause a miss on deer-size targets. They are also unlikely to bring about dangerous pressure rises, but this shouldn't be taken for granted where loads are already maximum. Best bet is to cut back a grain or two of powder for hunting in very hot climates. Handloaders used to believe that a change in primers, from standard types to magnums, was necessary even with nonmagnum-type propellants in extremely cold weather. Recent tests have cast doubt on this theory, but they haven't given any indication that such a primer switch is undesirable either.

The point to remember is that the actual temperature of the powder at the moment of firing is what's important, not the air temperature. Ammunition carried inside a hunter's outer clothing in subzero weather will be much warmer than the air, and ammo left in the direct rays of the sun, even in mild weather, can reach temperatures of 150°F, which can be dangerous. Even cartridges stored in the closed trunk of a car in direct sunlight may get much too hot for safety. All these things are as true of factory ammunition as of handloads, of course.

HUNTING BULLETS— SELECTION, SHAPE, AND SEATING

Bullet seating has an effect on mechanical reliability that must be determined in each individual rifle, just as temperature variations in zero should be checked out in *your* rifle. A fairly common lament among reloaders is that they did all load-development firing on the rifle range by single-loading the cartridges and failed to test the load's feeding qualities until it was too late. Sometimes a roundnose bullet will be balky in a magazine in which spitzers of the same weight and seating depth behave beautifully, or vice versa. Occasionally, seating a bullet just a tenth of an inch deeper or shallower will smooth out the all-important quick trip from magazine to chamber.

The only way to make certain is to load five or so dummy rounds that are identical to the planned

These bullets, I recovered from big game animals, can all be considered failures, having shed their cores, tumbled, broken up, or flattened laterally. They tended either to reduce penetration or cause deflection from the line of aim. A similar failure on the next shot might be disastrous.

These are all 300-grain .375-caliber softpoints (from left: Sierra, Nosler, Hornady, Bitterroot, and Winchester), shown intact and in typical condition after recovery from saturated telephone books. Note differences in original shape and final frontal area. Weight retention varies just as widely but is less obvious here.

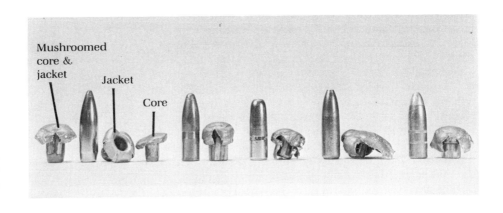

Nothing is more important to the hunter than his bullet's impact performance, which depends upon internal construction. These sectioned bullets show typical differences, and are (from left) from Sierra, Bitterroot, Speer, Winchester, and Nosler.

Each and every round of handloaded rifle ammo you want to take on a hunt should be run through your rifle's magazine, action, and chamber (with appropriate safety precautions, of course) to ensure mechanical dependability. A remote mountaintop or the African veldt is a poor spot to discover that bullets are seated too long or that the cases weren't sized quite enough!

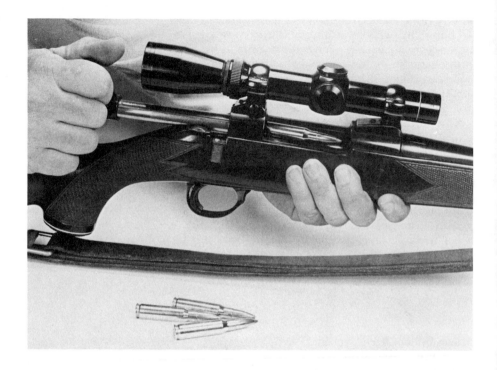

loading except that they have no primers or powder, and run them through the rifle. Try working the action at different speeds; now and then a load will feed perfectly when the action is slammed open and closed but hang up when it is worked deliberately. Or it may be the other way around. In any event, try everything you can think of to cause trouble in feeding—holding the rifle muzzle up and muzzle down, even on its side. If your round feeds flawlessly in such tests, it's a safe bet for the hunting field.

Finally, work every single cartridge through the magazine and into and out of the chamber when you have finished loading the lot for your hunting trip. Make no exceptions; take not even one round that hasn't successfully made the trip through the rifle at least once. Do this with due consideration of the fact that you are handling live ammo and that the rifle will be fully loaded for a few seconds with each round. This should be done in a safe place with the muzzle pointed in a safe direction at all times, and with your fingers nowhere near the trigger. If the gun has a three-position safety, so much the better. In the middle position, usually, the bolt can be operated but the arm will not fire. Even so, the whole operation is best carried out on a rifle range with the muzzle pointed at the backstop. When you have successfully completed the test, you can be certain that there will be no malfunctions in the field, no bullets seated too long, no cases sized not quite enough, and no other oddball foul-ups to cost you a shot at game.

I was following my own advice with a lot of .350 Remington Magnum cartridges I'd loaded for a jaguar hunt in Mexico when I discovered that the bolt would not close behind two of the rounds. Examination revealed that a self-operating "universal" shellholder I'd been using in my loading press had deformed the rims of these two cases so that, although they cham-

bered properly, the bolt could not close. Needless to say, those cartridges never saw the interior of Mexico. A jaguar can be a formidable beast, especially when wounded in his jungle strongholds at night, and the thought of one of those freakish rounds on top of the magazine stack still gives me the shudders. I have not seen that particular cartridge deformity before or since in my reloading and certainly would never have been looking for it in a visual inspection of the loaded

These are Trophy Bonded Bullets' .416-caliber "Sledgehammer" solids, the left one unfired and the other recovered from the carcass of a Cape buffalo. Except for the rifling marks, the fired sample shows no dimensional change at all, which is ideal for a solid bullet. The large nose flat not only offers more shock but also penetrates straighter. By contrast, an ideal expanding game bullet (not shown) would at least double its frontal diameter and retain 100 percent of original weight for maximum penetration.

rounds. But my inviolable rule of checking *every* round of hunting ammo through the rifle alerted me to a totally unforeseen problem.

The importance of selecting the right bullet for the hunting job at hand has been mentioned before, but I should reemphasize it here. Although accuracy, flatness of trajectory, retained energy, and similar good things are certainly important, a hunting bullet is no good if its expansion and penetration capabilities are not matched to the game and the hunting conditions. Fortunately, it's not necessary to make a choice between all these qualities; most good hunting bullets *are* accurate and have good ballistic coefficients. Where some lingering doubt may exist, however, you will never err by choosing the bullet of known impact performance, even if you must give up an unimportant half-inch or inch in grouping or 100 foot-pounds of muzzle energy.

BRUSH BUCKING? FORGET IT!

Deer hunters in particular concern themselves with what is called "brush-bucking" ability in their bullets, as though they expected a certain slug to cut a cord of firewood and stack it enroute to a whitetail in the thickets. The truth is that there is really no such thing as a real brush-buster of a rifle bullet. In shooting at a Botswana Cape buffalo in 1974, I had a .41 caliber, 400-grain bullet at 2,400 FPS deflect from a small mopane tree. This slug had all of the usual qualifications listed for a brush-bucker—fat, heavy, roundnose, and traveling at a modest velocity—yet it deflected about 6 feet in traveling only 12 yards from where it struck the tree before hitting the buff. Fortunately, this was my second shot and the buff was already heart-shot and dying from the first, but neither he nor I knew it at that moment. That it hit him at all was pure luck,

Even the most ferocious of big-bore bullets can be deflected by obstacles. When I hit this mopane sapling in Africa, it caused my 400-grain .416 round-nosed bullet at moderate velocity to deflect almost 6 feet in the next 12 yards of travel.

and would have been very bad luck if he'd not been mortally wounded.

The selection of very heavy bullets in hopes of improving penetration in brush may be self-defeating, since such slugs in a rifling twist to which they are barely suited may be inadequately stabilized. A marginally stable bullet tends to be deflected by a greater amount and from a smaller encounter with a twig than a normal-weight bullet humming along, sound asleep. In the last analysis, it's far better to pick a hole in the brush than to count on any bullet's bulling its way through a heavy screen of brush to a half-seen target. If you doubt me, try a few rounds of your favorite brush-buster through heavy brush on a cardboard box or some similarly large target. You'll be disappointed, but at least you'll be relieved of the need to worry about the obstacle penetration of projectiles for your hunting handloads and can concentrate on more important decisions.

LOADS FOR NON-TURNBOLT ACTIONS

Loading for semiautomatic rifles for hunting is one of these, since such arms have several special problems. Most semiautomatics on the market today are gas-operated, but some older models use the long-recoil system. In either case, the pressures developed by handloads must be regulated rather delicately for satisfactory functioning. If pressures rise too high, some parts of the rifle may be battered in the slam-bang of autoloading operation. If they fail to reach proper levels, the rifle may not cycle at all, in effect becoming a rather elaborate single-shot, or it may fire and jam with each shot. Also, the semiautos do not have the powerful initial extraction effort of a bolt-action, and high pressures may stick cases in an auto more quickly than in manually operated types. Maximum powder charge weights in self-loaders usually turn out to be about 2 to 4 grains below those that work well in a bolt gun, but your particular rifle can provide the answers with careful experimenting. Full-length resizing is usually mandatory in a semiauto, and a special small-base sizing die may be required. To some extent, these same remarks may apply with equal strength to slide-action weapons and, in lesser degree, to certain lever-actions.

In many ways, loading for the hunting field produces ammunition more like that made in commercial ammo factories than does any other phase of handloading. If Remington, Federal, and Winchester could tailor ammo specifically to your rifle, however, you would still have one major reason for reloading your hunting cartridges, and that would be the opportunity to select precisely the right bullet for your game species, under the conditions and in the terrain in which you hunt it, and according to your personal technique and style of hunting.

And that reason alone is well worth the trouble, entirely aside from the satisfaction all hunter-reloaders derive from using ammunition they figured out and built with their own hands.

17 Special-Purpose Loads: Rifle and Pistol

A "special-purpose" handload is one of such limited applications that little or no loading data can be found for it in standard reference material. There are many such loadings, and they provide some of the real fun in handloading.

RIFLE LOADS FOR TURKEY AND SMALL GAME

A fairly common example is the turkey load for a big-game rifle. In many areas, turkey season coincides with deer season and the rifle is a legal weapon for gobblers. But an expanding bullet at full velocity through the middle of a turkey makes such a mess of a magnificent gamebird, not to mention a Christmas dinner, that no turkey hunter tries it a second time. A bullet in the head or neck, or carefully placed to break the back, will do a clean job on the bird, but such shots are difficult, to put it mildly, beyond about 50 yards, even for experts. The answer is a separate handload especially formulated for the purpose. The load should have a point of impact relative to the big-game load in the same rifle so that it can be used without changing the sights and, hopefully, without all sorts of mental gymnastics. Finally, it must not be destructive even with a center shot, so that the hunter can simply aim where the bird is biggest at any reasonable range.

For most cartridges, these loads are no great trick to work out. The overriding consideration is muzzle velocity, which should not materially exceed about 2,000 FPS regardless of caliber or bullet type. Even full-jacketed military bullets can do unacceptable damage at high velocity, as anyone knows who has tried standard military ammunition on turkeys from

The payoff for the time and trouble spent developing a special turkey load for a centerfire big-game rifle: Thanksgiving dinner collected beyond shotgun range without meat destruction. The load? A .308 110-grain full-jacketed carbine bullet at 2,140 FPS.

Here are four different possibilities for a non-expanding turkey-load bullet for centerfire rifle cartridges. From left, a full-metal-jacketed military bullet in the .222 Rem., a Speer FMJ sporting bullet in the 6mm Rem., a Hornady .30 M1 Carbine FMJ for a .308 WCF, and finally a hard-cast pistol bullet in the .35 Rem.

his .308 or .30/06. Velocity alone is destructive. Indeed, if forced to the choice, I'd prefer a softnose slug at 2,000 FPS to a high-speed "solid."

As usual, the first decision is the bullet. Nonexpanding bullets are available in almost any caliber from at least one of several sources. They are—or were—manufactured for target-shooting purposes by Norma in many popular calibers, and by a few custom bullet makers in a more limited selection of diameters. Cast bullets made of some such hard lead alloy as Linotype metal serve very nicely, and molds are available in most sizes. Military bullets can occasionally be purchased either loose or in obsolete ammo that can be broken down for components, and the range of calibers is greater than you may suppose, including 6.5 and 7mm, .303, 8mm, .30 caliber in several weights, and others. Several manufacturers sell full-jacketed bullets in .224 and 6mm diameters. If there's a choice, the lighter bullets in any given caliber work better in standard rifling twists at the modest velocities I have in mind for turkey loads.

Powders for reduced loadings must *always* be selected from among the medium- to faster-burning propellants suitable for that cartridge. The reason is that under certain circumstances, reduced loadings of slow-burning powders have been known to produce something very much like a detonation. This phenomenon, sometimes called "secondary explosion effect" (SEE), is mysterious but is positively known to occur. Many attempts have been made to explain it, but all remain theoretical, and SEE has been difficult to reproduce at will under laboratory conditions.

Three conditions apparently must be present simultaneously to produce the dreaded SEE: (1) the powder must be slow-burning, not faster than about

IMR 4320; (2) the charge must be reduced at least 10 percent below maximum; and (3) the cartridge must have a large case capacity relative to caliber. Such cartridges include, but are not limited to, the .243 WCF, .25/06, .270, and all the belted magnums of calibers .257, .264, .277, and .284, as well as any similar wildcats.

Such pressure excursions (another name for the phenomenon) are easily avoided, simply by switching to a powder having a relative quickness faster than 4320 when building reduced loads in a candidate cartridge.

Again, never reduce the charge weight more than 10 percent for any of these slow-burning powders or any others in this same relative-quickness range: IMR 4350, IMR 4831, Norma 204, 205, or MRP, Hodgdon 4350, 4831, or H 450, or any other propellant from Accurate Arms, Bofors, Nobel. SEE is rare, but the risk remains too great, especially since the quicker powders often give better accuracy at less cost for reduced loads.

With one or more powders selected, the charge weight that will deliver about 2,000 FPS must be determined, usually by extrapolation since loading data for most high-velocity cartridges do not extend downward to this range. At this point, one of the reloading manuals that has data arranged for each combination of cartridge, bullet, and powder in a horizontal line of ascending velocity levels comes in handy. Hornady's and Sierra's manuals are examples. A little close study of the data for your turkey cartridge with the bullet weight closest to the one you plan to use will reveal that there is a more or less linear relationship between powder charge weight and velocity. For example, you may find that approximately 1.5 grains of powder are required to produce each additional 100 FPS. Although the lowest listed charge may give a velocity considerably higher than 2,000 FPS, this relationship should hold pretty well down to that speed. Thus, if the lightest listed charge gives 3,000 FPS at 47 grains, you can try reducing the charge by a multiple of, say, 10 times 1.5 grains—in other words, 15 grains less than 47, or 32 grains of that powder for an expected 2,000 FPS. Such downward extrapolation is quite safe, although *upward* extrapolation of charges is never recommended.

Another possible source of data on low-velocity loads is the fairly voluminous literature now published for cast-bullet shooting, especially including the *Lyman Cast Bullet Handbook*. However, much of this literature deals with the fastest-burning powders, and some caution must be exercised in substituting jacketed slugs for cast bullets at maximum levels. The jacketed bullets will produce more pressure, and usually, lower velocities. Also, a seemingly small charge of a fast-burning powder can produce high pressure, even in a big case if warnings about maximum charges are ignored.

There is, of course, no way to adjust velocities to a precise level without access to a chronograph, but these turkey-load velocities need not be on the money. If the point of impact in your rifle is usable, it really doesn't matter whether the velocity is 1,850 or 2,100 FPS. Properly placed, either will make short work of a turkey and leave an edible bird.

Sometimes the first load tried will work out well in terms of relative point of impact. If I can get a turkey load to strike within an inch or so below or above my regular big-game loading for the same rifle at 100 yards, I'm satisfied. With such a load, any gobbler I get a fair crack at up to about 150 yards is meat for the freezer. More often, the turkey load will display a maddening tendency to strike several inches low and perhaps to one side or the other. This signals the need for some patient experimenting, with different charges of the same powder or with other propellants. Remember the discussion of barrel vibrations and barrel time in Chapter 15? The experiments are simply an effort to find a load that enjoys a serendipitous relationship with that particular barrel. The solution may come anywhere, unpredictably, but you can almost invariably find it if you keep looking. Of all the rifles I've loaded for over the years, only one absolutely defies my every attempt to work out a turkey load that can be used without making a sight adjustment. And, although I've tried more than a hundred different combinations in this rifle, I still haven't given up.

What we've termed a "turkey load" here has many other uses. It will work equally well on small and medium-size game like fox (without destroying the pelt) up to about javelina. It's usually a good pest load for porcupines, armadillos, and the occasional quail-eating feral domestic cat. And, being cheap, it's a first-class informal target and year-round plinking load, without much recoil and blast. Many of my rifles remain zeroed for the "turkey" load at 100 yards at all times except during big-game seasons.

"SQUIBS" ARE HANDY

Another useful special-purpose load is the "squib," which is nothing more than a centerfire rifle load designed to approach absolute noiselessness. It's entirely possible to develop a squib in most big-game cartridges that are so quiet that the sound of the bullet striking the target is actually louder than the muzzle "blast." These loads are necessarily for very short range, usually no more than about 25 yards, but they can be surprisingly accurate at such ranges. They usually require a sight change, but now and again I've had one take the same sight-setting at 25 yards that my full-power loads required for a 200-yard zero.

The obvious use for a squib is gallery shooting (with an appropriate bullet trap) in the basement or garage, where target practice can be carried out without attracting the ire of the neighbors or the attention of the police. Squibs are also suitable for shooting the smallest pests, such as sparrows or rats.

Velocity is hardly important in a squib, since the noise level is the controlling factor, but most squibs will chronograph somewhere between 500 and 900 FPS, and energy delivery will probably approximate that of a .22 rimfire cartridge—which means that these silent little loads mustn't be treated with contempt. Every safety precaution required for any kind of firearm is indicated.

The bullet is the chief problem in a squib-loading

Ultra-low velocity squib loads call for abnormally lightweight projectiles to stabilize in normal rifling pitches. Several approaches are feasible, including (clockwise from top) cast lead-alloy wadcutters, military pistol bullets for rifle cases (where diameter is correct, of course), commercial "plinkers," and even sized buckshot. The lightweight jacketed bullets can stick in the barrel at squib velocities, but can be used for plinking and small-game loads.

Squib loads often develop too little pressure to expand the brass case for good obturation (adequate filling of the breech), resulting in an accumulation of soot on the case (shown left) and in the chamber. Thus, chambers should be cleaned thoroughly before firing high-pressure loads again.

project. Jacketed slugs are out because, at these velocities, they may stick in the barrel! The lightest possible cast bullet for the caliber should be chosen for any kind of stability at such reduced velocities in normal rifling twists. The powder charge is easy; in just about any cartridge of .30/06 volume or less, a good squib load will be found somewhere between 1.5 and about 4 grains of Hercules Bullseye powder. Start at the lower charge weight and vary the load by .2-grain increments until you locate a satisfactory compromise between noise and short-range accuracy. Bullseye being one of the fastest-burning of all powders, care must be taken to avoid double-charging.

Brass that is used for squib loads should be segregated or marked, or both, so that it cannot be used again for full-power loadings. The reason is that the force of the firing-pin blow in some rifles can drive the case into the chamber so that the shoulder is set back slightly. The pressure of the squib is insufficient to fire-form the case again, and a rimless case may wind up with excess headspace. This is no problem with squib loads, but could be dangerous at high pressures. Squib cases need not be resized at all, usually, but they tend to get very sooty since they don't obturate the breech very solidly; that is, they don't expand enough to fill the breech. The chamber will get just as sooty, and needs special cleaning after a session of squib firing.

Turkey loads and squib loads are just two examples of types of ammunition that you cannot purchase from Remington or Winchester, and that extend the versatility of your rifle to previously undreamt-of limits. Only your needs and your imagination restrict the variety of low-velocity loads. Would you like to use your deer rifle on squirrels during the off-season, just to keep your eye in? No reason not to; just use your squib bullet (which might even be a buckshot run through the correct bullet-sizing die) and adjust the velocity wherever in the range of 1,200 to 1,400 FPS you find minute-of-squirrel's-head accuracy at about 50 feet.

"FULL SPECTRUM" LOADING

These two loads form the low end of what might be termed a full spectrum of loads for a single rifle. The other parts of the spectrum would include a varmint load using lightly jacketed, lightweight bullets at maximum velocity. This one is for jackrabbits and woodchucks at ranges of at least 200 yards, depending on your rifle's inherent accuracy and sighting equipment. There would also be the standard deer load, of course, which is probably the first one you developed. It is the only one ever worked up by all too many handloaders who haven't realized that you don't have to make a big bang to have shooting fun. Another load in the spectrum might be a heavy-game load, if the cartridge is suitable, utilizing a heavy, strongly constructed bullet at medium velocities.

Obviously, some cartridges lend themselves to full-spectrum loading better than others. Those that do are the medium-capacity cases between the calibers of .264 and 8mm, roughly. You will never make a brown-bear cartridge out of a .243 or .250 Savage, nor will your .338 or .350 Remington Magnum prove to be an adequate varminter, but the vast majority of rifles in use today as big-game weapons can be far more flexible, more fun, and more use throughout the year than factory ammo alone can make them.

Some of the belted magnums, especially the 7mm, work reasonably well as full-spectrum rifles, although their cavernous cases make development of squibs and turkey loads somewhat trying at times. But all of them lend themselves to what may be called "stairstep" loading. This simply means loading them down to duplicate the performance of smaller cartridges of identical caliber. The 7mm Remington Magnum can be made into a perfectly good 7 × 57mm Mauser, .284 WCF, or .280 Remington. The .300 Winchester or Weatherby Magnums convert nicely to .30/06s, .308s, .300 Savages, or even .30/30s. The .350 Norma Magnum can handily duplicate the .350 Remington Magnum, the .35 Whelen, the .358 WCF, or the .35 Remington. There's even a .38/55 WCF lurking in your .375 Holland & Holland Magnum, and a .45/70 inside your mighty .458 Winchester Magnum!

The first question, of course, is "Why bother?" If you had wanted a .300 Savage, you say, you'd have bought one in the first place, instead of springing for

A "full spectrum" of handloads for the .308 WCF cartridge: From left, a 500-FPS squib with size 0 buckshot, a plinking load with the Hornady "Plinker" bullet, a turkey load with .30 Carbine FMJ bullet, a practice and small-game load with a cast bullet, a varmint load with 130-grain Speer HP, a long-range load for deer-size game with 130-grain spitzer, a medium-game load with 150-grain bullet, a general-purpose big-game load with a 165-grain slug, and a big-game 200-grain Nosler Partition.

a .300 Winchester Mag, right? Well and good. But think back over the last year or so, and see just how many shots you've fired with your thundering magnum. Five? Ten? Maybe a couple of boxes? If you're like most shooters, your magnum hangs on the rack, reserved for big-game season only, while you shoot something a little pleasanter and more suitable for nonmagnum purposes—or *wish* you had something for such shooting. Stairstepping the magnum down to lesser performance levels through handloading is at least one good answer for shooting more and shooting more cheaply.

Stairstep loading is very easy. Again, stay away from the slow-burning powders. Find charge weights that duplicate velocity levels of the cartridge you're aiming to imitate by downward extrapolation. Of course, any jacketed bullets may be used, but those used in the smaller cartridge you're duplicating are most suitable unless a serious difference in rifling twist rates appears. That's really all there is to stairstepping, besides the fact that you'll find you're enjoying your magnum rifle about 10 times as much as ever before and that your skill with it is growing by leaps and bounds.

RECOIL—ACCOMMODATION LOADS

Handloading is the best and perhaps the only sure way to acclimate a shooter to a magnum rifle's recoil, without risking development of a serious flinch. Flinching is a completely involuntary effort on the part of the subconscious mind to protect the shooter's body from pain or possible injury, and no amount of willpower can overcome a tendency to flinch. The one and only way to avoid it is to convince the subconscious that the rifle's recoil isn't going to hurt or harm you. And the best way to accomplish that psychological selling job is to do a lot of shooting with

the magnum thunderstick, but only with very reduced loadings.

First trials should be with about half charges (one more time, do *not* reduce slow-burning powder charges by more than 10 percent), and enough loads should be fired to become completely accustomed to the recoil. When you find you don't even notice the kick, increase the powder charge in your light loads by, say, 5 grains, and remain at that level for a while. Then go up another 5 grains, and so forth. Somewhere in this process, you will need to change back to the normal, slow-burning powder to achieve maximum velocities, but by that time you will probably have learned to deal with the recoil unconsciously. It is possible to recoil-proof a youngster or a novice lady shooter in exactly the same way, regardless of the cartridge. Let them shoot light loads year-round to develop confidence and familiarity with the rifle, then put up some full-power hunting ammo, rezero the rifle yourself, and take them hunting. They will never notice the increased recoil, from then on.

REDUCED LOADS FOR HANDGUNS

Although most of the magnum revolvers can be fired with factory-built reduced loadings, the same thing can be accomplished with handloads. The mild .44 Special factory load works well in the .44 Magnum, and .38 Special commercial ammo in several different power levels can be used in a .357 Magnum. The .41 Magnum comes in two different loadings from the factory, one of which is a somewhat reduced load with a lead bullet. Factory rounds cost money, however, and there's no reason a reloader can't increase the flexibility of his big revolver in exactly the same way he extends his rifles' performance. Full-blown, "planet-wrecker" loads will eventually knock even the finest revolver out of time and produce unnecessary wear on its parts. For plinking, practice, small-game

Here stand six good reasons for loading reduced-velocity ammunition; these are among the hardest kickers of today's big-game rounds. *Any* shooter will find practice with them more pleasant when using reduced loadings. Magnums all, they are (from left) .460 Weatherby, .458 Winchester, .378 Weatherby, .340 Weatherby, and .358 Norma.

shooting, and recoil-proofing, mild handloads are not only easier on the shooter but easier on the gun, as well. Most loading manuals give a good selection of mild loadings for the big six-guns.

Unfortunately, semiautomatic handguns don't respond to reduced loads very readily, at least not if you wish them to function as semiautos. On the other hand, having to operate the slide of a pistol by hand for every shot isn't all bad; at least you don't have two-thirds of your precious fired brass flung into deep grass from which you can never recover it.

SNAKE LOADS AND OTHER ODDBALLS

Another project for owners of revolvers is the loading of shot loads for them. The easy way is with the empty shot capsules sold by Speer for use in .38s and .44s, and with the prefilled Remco shot capsules in these and other calibers. Plastic capsules protect the shot from the rifling and deliver better patterns as a rule, but they are not essential to homebrewed shot loads. Hodgdon sells plastic cup wads for use in .38s for just this purpose. In the .357 Magnum, for example,

Two different approaches to snake loads for a .357 Magnum revolver: At left is a commercial pre-filled shot capsule that is seated like a bullet. At right are two plastic bullet jackets (used as shot cups) and a charge of pellets. Such components may be difficult to find, but make good ammunition when loaded as I describe in the text.

This .38 Special snubbie threw this pattern of No. 9 shot at three yards, using handloads featuring the Speer .38–.357 plastic shot capsules, which are sold unfilled. Not many rattlesnakes can survive a load like this at this range.

one of these is seated, skirt up, over a charge of 4 grains of Hercules Green Dot powder (see Hodgdon's reloading manual for other loads) and about 86 grains of #9 pellets are poured in. Then another Hodgdon wad is seated, this one skirt down, flush with the mouth of the case, which is heavily crimped. Even homemade cardboard wads can be made to serve. The resulting loads are murderous against venomous snakes, for example, at ranges of up to about 5 yards. If I had a dime for every rusty-backed old rattler I've stretched out with just such revolver shot loads over the years, I'd be rich.

The only rifle cartridge in which I've ever developed satisfactory shot cartridges is the .45/70, using unprotected shot charges and cutting filler wads from sheet cork or fiber. Results were so-so, even more deadly than the pistol shotshells at short ranges, but without much additional range despite the greater number of pellets in the charge. If velocities are boosted much above 1,000 FPS, patterns become very patchy even at 10 yards, and I doubt that I will ever make my .45/70 a suitable quail gun. However, it is death on sparrows and rats at short distances.

BLANKS

I get a few inquiries about making up blank cartridges, mostly in shotshells for small cannons used in starting yacht races and in handgun cartridges. These latter were once employed extensively for starting and ending athletic events, but regular starter's pistols and .22 blank cartridges especially made for the purpose have largely taken over that service.

I worry about another possible use of the centerfire handgun—they may be carelessly employed in reenactments of western-style gunfights. Non-bulleted blanks still require a wad of some sort to hold the powder in place, and at close range these wads can be dangerous. So can the muzzle-flash and unburned powder granules. Movie producers use special blank cartridges (and, often, specially-modified guns) loaded with powders and wadding not available to the handloader.

All canistered smokeless powders require some confinement to reach the pressure levels to produce the report required in blank cartridges. Special fast-burning powders for blanks are manufactured for the military, but they are not sold to handloaders. Powder

Left: The Speer shot capsules are sold empty in .38 and .44 for reloaders who fill and cap them and seat them like bullets over powder charges recommended in the Speer handbook. *Right:* If no shot capsule is available, shot loads for revolvers can be improvised, using plastic bullet jackets, as shown here, or even gas checks.

Left: Straight-cased rifle cartridges like the .45/70 Government can be turned into fair short-range shotshells by a cunning handloader, as I describe in the text. *Right:* I made this "hockshop" load for the .45/70. This propels three soft lead .457 balls (sold for muzzleloaders) at moderate velocity. Results are surprisingly good as far out as 75 yards, with all three balls grouping inside 3 inches.

salvaged from military blanks must *never* be used in any quantity to drive a bullet of any weight! To attempt this is almost certain to result in serious gun damage and probable shooter injury.

Black powder is probably most satisfactory for most blank shooting and is my usual recommendation. It goes bang very nicely without confinement and produces smoke for a visual, as well as an audible, effect. A caseful of FFFg black powder will be safe enough and creates maximum commotion and smoke. If the rounds must withstand much handling, a wad can be fashioned from shirt cardboard, cork, or felt, and glued in place with what we used to call airplane cement. For most purposes, a rolled-up wad of toilet tissue will serve as well. The trouble with black-powder blanks is that the firearms in which they're fired must immediately be disassembled and thoroughly cleaned, inside and out, with hot, soapy water and solvent to avoid disastrous corrosion.

I admit to having experimented briefly with blanks loaded with a few grains of Hercules Bullseye powder. Results have been pretty satisfactory in the cartridges in which I've tried them (mostly for handguns), provided the top wads were quite firmly tamped down and cemented in place. In calibers from about 9mm up, 5 to 6 grains of Bullseye produces a nice crack. However, Bullseye is a very much more potent propellant than black powder, so you're entirely on your own if you choose to make up blanks with it.

In the realm of special-purpose handloads, the sky's the limit. Most such loadings are working at low-to-medium pressure levels, which gives you more freedom to experiment than with maximum loads, and a little deep thought can devise a way to accomplish almost anything. This is the best area in which to get "creative" in your handloading, rather than with hot stuff that is crowding the limits of safety to begin with. Reduced loads inherently offer more room to exercise your imagination, and the products are uniquely useful.

Handloaders who never put together anything but gut-busting maximum-recoil ammunition are missing some of the most enjoyable and most interesting aspects of their hobby.

18 Wildcat Cartridges

Sooner or later, every handloader of metallic ammunition will hear the siren song of the wildcat cartridge. Most of us suspect that we can design a cartridge that will be better than anything the commercial ammo manufacturers have produced, and, even if it won't be *better*, it will at least be *ours*, a one-of-a-kind upon which our hope for reloading immortality may rest.

Such hopes are usually disappointed. Wildcat cartridges are rarely better than commercial rounds ex-cept for very specialized purposes and almost never unique. About 95 percent of the thousands so far devised have proved all too mortal, as have their fond designers.

On the other hand, a few wildcat rifle and pistol cartridges, past and present, have turned out to be extremely useful. In many cases, they have had a profound influence on commercial ammunition development, and some have passed into commercial manufacture with little change. Today's wildcatter

For many years, the 7mm/ .300 Weatherby Magnum wildcat held the world record for smallest benchrest group at 1,000 yards.

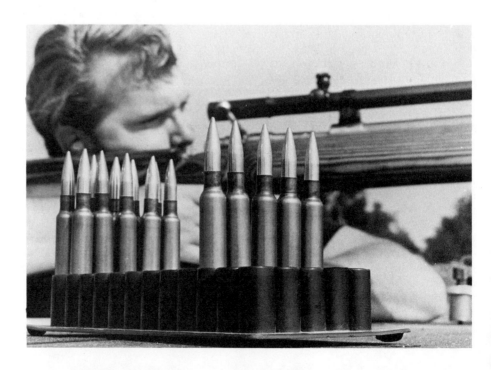

follows an honorable trail blazed by such early experimenters as Ned Roberts, Wotkyns, Ackley, Whelen, Sharps, and many other illustrious names. And who knows but what some real breakthrough in ballistic efficiency still remains to be discovered by a private experimenter?

WHAT IS A WILDCAT?

A wildcat cartridge can be defined as one for which commercially manufactured cases are not available. One trouble with this definition is that, as it stands, it must include a host of obsolete cartridges that once were manufactured but for which brass is either nonexistent or so scarce that it is a collectors' item. The only difference between these rounds and true wildcats is that the wildcats have never had factory-produced guns chambered for them (there are a few scattered exceptions to this rule), while many old rifles are still floating around with chambers cut for the obsolete calibers. From the handloader's viewpoint, there is no difference; cases for either must be formed from some other kind or caliber brass that is still available.

SUCCESSFUL WILDCATS

Among the commercial cartridges that enjoyed long-lived popularity as a wildcat prior to legitimization by Remington or Winchester are the .22/250 Remington, 6mm Remington, .243 WCF, .257 Roberts, .25/06 Remington, .280 Remington, 7mm Remington Magnum, and .308 and .350 Norma Magnums. These became standard factory cartridges with little or no change from their wildcat forms. Others, such as the .17 Remington, .225 WCF, .264 Winchester Magnum, and several of the Weatherby Magnum series, were clearly inspired by wildcats but had their case dimensions altered somewhat, usually to simplify mass production. Although quite a few wildcat cartridges for handguns have been devised from time to time, only one that I can think of has become a standard factory item, and that is the .44 Auto Mag. Several others, such as the .30 and .35 Herrett wildcats, have factory guns chambered for them, the Thompson-Center Contender single-shot interchangeable-barrel pistol in both these cases. Other handgun wildcats that have achieved a measure of popularity are the .357/.45 ACP and the .357 Bain & Davis, on a necked-down .44 Magnum case.

"IMPROVED" CARTRIDGES

The simplest form of wildcat is the so-called "improved" cartridge. Cartridges that have considerable body taper and long, sloping shoulders are candidates for such treatment. The wildcatter has a new chamber cut that has minimum taper and a sharp shoulder, but that will accept and properly headspace commercial ammunition. Factory cartridges are simply fired in the improved chamber. The brass is "blown out" to fit the new chamber by firing pressures and comes out of the chamber with a more modern appearance and increased powder capacity. It can then be reloaded to higher performance than the original form. An advantage to an "improved" rifle is that, in a pinch, factory ammo can be used in it with safety and relatively small losses in velocity. The .257 Roberts cartridge is the classic example of one that benefits greatly from such "improvement." So do

Standard factory cartridges identical, or nearly so, to long-popular wildcats are, from left: .280 Rem., .25/06 Rem., .257 Roberts, 6mm Rem., .243 WCF, .220 Swift, .22/250 Rem., .225 WCF, and .17 Rem.

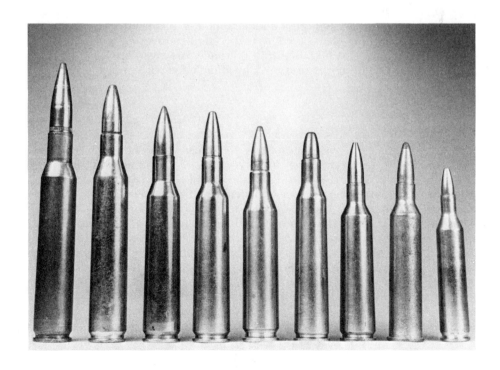

Dies are available for most of the more popular wildcats, and can be custom-ordered for almost any conceivable design, often including elaborate case-forming die sets. From left, these FL (full length) sizers are for the .30 Herrett, .35 Whelen Improved, .416 Taylor, 6.5mm/284, .17/223.

Left: One way to establish safe headspacing for fire-forming when moving a shoulder forward is illustrated in the center case here, where a double shoulder has been formed at a point where a crush-fit will occur when the cartridge is chambered. A ¾-throttle fire-forming load will then blow the shoulder forward to a perfect fit for future loading. *Right:* RCBS made this ingenious die for necking a case upward from .30 to .40 caliber without splitting the brass. It's invaluable for wildcatters.

the .250 Savage, .25/35 WCF, .30/30, 7 × 57 Mauser, and even the .30/06, to greater or lesser degrees.

The next step upward is cutting a new chamber that not only reduces body taper and sharpens the shoulder of a bottle-necked case, but relocates the shoulder forward, shortening the neck and increasing powder capacity considerably. The Gibbs line of wildcats exemplifies this idea. Fire-forming cases for such cartridges is a bit tricky, since some means of headspacing the unimproved cartridge in the chamber is necessary. The safest method is to neck the case up to a caliber larger than the final version will be, and then run it part way into a sizing die of the correct caliber to produce a funny-looking double

shoulder. The forward shoulder makes the cartridge a crush-fit in the chamber. The case is then loaded with a three-quarters-throttle load and fired. If all goes well, it will come out of the chamber perfectly fire-formed to the new configuration. Case loss through split shoulders is quite high during fire-forming with some lots of brass.

WILDCAT CASE FORMING

By far the most common procedure in forming wildcat brass is necking-up or necking-down—expanding or reducing neck diameter to hold a bullet of a di-

Left: Most case-forming for wildcats involves neck and shoulder alterations of standard cases. This sequence, producing .35 Whelen Improved brass from the parent .30/06, is fairly typical. From left, an untouched .30/06 case, the same with neck expanded to .40 caliber, the same necked down to .35 caliber, the same after fire-forming to sharpen the shoulder, and, finally, a loaded .35 Whelen Improved round. *Right:* There are wildcat handgun cartridges, too. This is the .30 Herrett, made especially for the Contender single-shot pistol. Starting with an unmodified .30/30 case at left, the shoulder is set back, the neck trimmed, and the case fire-formed and sized for normal reloading. For more details, see Chapter 22.

ameter different from that the original case held. The .22/250 and .25/06 Remington cartridges were created as wildcats during the 1920s and '30s, by necking the .250 Savage down to .22 caliber, and the .30/06 case down to .25 caliber, with no other changes. Another of the great wildcats of all time, the .35 Whelen, came about when a handloader simply enlarged the neck of the .30/06 to accept a .35 caliber bullet. The one and only wildcat cartridge that I can claim to have invented (chiefly, I suppose, because nobody else was willing to bother with such an oddball) is the .25/222 Copperhead, made by necking .222 Remington brass up to take .25 bullets. Two more of my favorites, the 6.5/284 and the .416 Taylor, are made by reducing the .284 WCF case neck to take .264-diameter slugs and the .458 Winchester Magnum case to hold .416-inch bullets. Far more wildcats have arisen from necking-*down* operations than from necking-*up*. Most wildcatters are looking for higher velocities, and necking-down adds velocity potential up to a point, while enlarging the bore diameter relative to case capacity increases efficiency but adds very little to velocities.

WILDCAT JUSTIFICATIONS

There are other reasons than mere speed for wildcats, however, and it may be that today they are the most valid reasons for the trouble and expense of developing a nonstandard cartridge that requires custom-made chamber reamers, barrels, and reloading dies,

among other things.

Most of these reasons are mechanical. I built a .25/222 Copperhead not because it would do anything some factory round couldn't do, but because it could do it in a type of rifle to which no similar factory cartridge was adapted. I wanted to drive the lighter .25 caliber bullets at velocities of 2,600 to about 3,000 FPS (while retaining good cast-bullet capabilities) in a modern, short-action, box-magazine turnbolt rifle. The game I had in mind for this little rifle was the entire range of pests and edible game up to about the size of the bobcat, coyote, and javelina, and especially wild turkey. I also wanted to be able to load cast bullets at squirrel-killing speeds and do it all without undue destruction of meat and pelts. The .256 Winchester Magnum could have done everything I wished—but that's a rimmed case and rimmed cases are a nuisance in box magazines because they don't feed reliably or at all. Since I planned to reload all ammo for the new rifle anyway, it was no more trouble to assemble .25/222 stuff than .256 Winchester Magnum cartridges.

The little Copperhead has been a practical success, performing exactly as I'd hoped—even better, in many respects—and now has more than 20 years of hunting behind it. Though it's been manufactured, I have no illusions that it will ever elevate my name to the ranks of such great ballistic pioneers as Roberts or Niedner, but it's been a lot of fun. Which is not a bad reason for a wildcat, in itself.

The .416 Taylor is another great wildcat that exists

This is my wildcat .25/222 Copperhead, shown with the variety of bullets it's adapted for. The round is flanked at left by four cast bullets from 60 to 90 grains for squirrel, plinking, and practice loads, and on the right by jacketed slugs of 100, 87, 75, 60, and 60 grains. The Copperhead is an extraordinarily versatile small-game cartridge.

Big-game wildcats include (from left) .505 Barnes Supreme (.460 Weatherby neck up), .416 Taylor (.458 Win. Magnum necked down), .35 Whelen Improved, .30/338 Magnum (almost identical to .308 Norma Magnum), 6.5/284.

for purely mechanical reasons. It is the .458 Winchester Magnum necked down slightly to drive 400-grain, .41-caliber bullets at velocities around 2,400 FPS. The .416 Taylor rifle is strictly for the heaviest and most dangerous game on earth, and I've used it with perfect satisfaction on Cape buffalo and African elephant and lion, among other game.

I constructed my .416 Taylor rifle in 1973 when there were rumors that this wildcat might be adopted by a major manufacturer. Those rumors did not come

true then, but oddly, the .416 caliber is suddenly a hot big wildcat on the scene again. New rumors of standardization have begun. I won't hold my breath, but the cartridge has proved itself and surely deserves such recognition.

However good it may be, the .416 Taylor (named for its developer, gun writer Bob Chatfield-Taylor) exactly duplicates the performance of a 1911-vintage British cartridge called the .416 Rigby, so why bother? Well, the Rigby is an enormous cartridge that requires very expensive oversize rifle actions, and cartridges range upwards of $7 *per round.* Even reloadable brass is rare and costly. The Taylor wildcat works in any .30/06-length bolt-action, which means a lighter rifle with a shorter bolt-throw (important when a lion is charging), and a cheaper rifle even when the cost of special gunsmithing is included. The ammunition uses cheap, available components and has proved very tractable and efficient, so why not? In this case, the wildcat is simply more practical.

Many, perhaps most, benchrest competition rifles are chambered to wildcat cartridges. These are ultra-high-grade rifles anyway, and it's no more expensive to barrel one in a nonstandard cartridge than to a factory number. Benchresters are finicky about things and are rarely satisfied with anything factory built; their fondness for such wildcat cartridges as the .222½ Shilen arises from an effort to *exactly* match case capacity, brass design, and bullet diameter to the precise, optimum requirements of their demanding sport. What they seek is absolute perfection, and no factory cartridge (or wildcat, for that matter) is perfect. It's as simple as that.

One of the most interesting stories of wildcatting began around 1975 when a pair of active benchrest competitors, Dr. Lou Palmisano and Ferris Pindell, began to work with modified Russian 7.62 × 39mm cases for the stated purpose of developing the world's most inherently accurate cartridge. It seems demonstrable now that they succeeded.

Their theories—considered a little radical at the time—called for a short, fat combustion chamber with a 10-degree body taper and 30-degree shoulder, small rifle primers, and long flash holes smaller in diameter than formerly considered "normal." Originally the "PPC" cartridges, as they were called, were necked to .22 and 6mm. They have set more accuracy records than you could carry in a wheelbarrow.

The Finnish firm of Sako now makes PPC cases and chambers rifles for the cartridges, so that the PPCs have moved out of the realm of wildcats. Palmisano unceasingly researches the most rarefied realms of accuracy though and has expanded the line to three different case lengths and added 7mm to the calibers. Some of the American international shooting teams are looking hard at the PPCs, and it seems quite reasonable to predict that PPCs are here to stay, at least as proprietary cartridges (like the Weatherby magnums) if not exactly standards.

In the heyday of the wildcatters, no American-made rifles were chambered to such calibers as 6mm, 6.5mm, 7mm, or high-performance .22s, .25s, .30s, or .35s. Wildcatters could then almost pick a caliber at random and work out a wildcat that would shade its commercial counterparts with ease. Since World War II, however, the picture has changed, and it's difficult to find any spot in the lineup of calibers in which the factory-designed incumbent isn't already close to maximum performance levels. Today's wildcats, if they are to be of any value, must be designed for some fairly specialized purpose, one for which the general market is not likely to be inviting to a major manu-facturer. There's still room for wildcats, but it's getting harder to find.

PROBLEMS WITH WILDCATS

Wildcat cartridges present the handloader with several problems other than the mechanical one of reforming brass. One is the fact that, except for a few very popular wildcats, there is little or no published reloading data available, at least from the same reliable sources from which you can pick loads for standard rounds. The articles written in shooting magazines about this or that wildcat, usually by its nonprofessional inventor, have tended to some pretty giddy claims. Velocities may have been produced as claimed, but little is said about pressures. Furthermore, since wildcat cartridges are by definition non-standard, no standardized dimensional data on chambers and cases exist. Every wildcat rifle chamber is a law unto itself, and even sound data developed in other rifles or pistols may be dangerous in yours. In general, you're on your own in working up loads, and you're working without the benefit of the sophisticated laboratory equipment available to Remington and Winchester researchers. Wildcatting, then, can be seen as a venture in the wild blue yonder and is best reserved for the mature, the cautious, and the experienced handloader.

This is not to discourage the ancient and almost uniquely American art of wildcatting. Far from it;

A promising family of wildcats that never got off the ground: The brainchildren of RCBS's founder, Fred Huntington, and based on the German 9.3 × 64 Brenneke case, they would have been efficient *nonbelted* magnums of (from left) .375, .308, and 7mm calibers.

A few small-game wildcats enjoying varying degrees of popularity are (from left) 6×47mm, .30 Herrett, .25/222 Copperhead, .17/223, .17 Mach IV (.221 Fireball necked down), .22 Stark (.44 Magnum necked down), and .25 Hornet.

wildcatting has contributed a great deal to the present-day richness of our shooting sports, and I hope it will continue to do so. There's a great deal to be found out about the efficiency of the small-capacity cases. There's work to be done in making varmint rifles quieter, as the population grows and expands into areas with woodchucks and jackrabbits. There's room for at least one more revolver cartridge, a long-cased, straight .25-caliber "magnum," and maybe for more than one more auto pistol round. Who knows what else some ingenious wildcatter will turn up?

Besides, wildcats are interesting, fun, and extremely informative, and if you can learn something more about your hobby from it, a wildcat project may be justified on that point alone. I once spent more than a year and hundreds of dollars on developing a 6.5mm wildcat on the then-new .284 case. I remember the feeling that came over me when I realized that I had succeeded in producing a cartridge that was not quite as good, all-round, as the .270 WCF, which had been around for almost 50 years!

Wildcats are expensive, and wildcat-chambered custom arms are not eminently salable, to put it mildly. You'll not likely recover any substantial portion of your investment when you decide to sell your super-duper, cab-over-engine .293 Jones Planet-Wrecker.

On the other hand, the very existence of the wildcat idea is a symbol of a treasured American freedom; most foreign governments would grow faint at the very thought of permitting their people to possess cartridge components, much less to invent their own calibers and build firearms around them. Even in free nations, a discussion of your latest wildcat will get you some uncomprehending stares from shooters. The idea just never occurred to them, as I well know from dealing with customs officials and safari staffs when I took my .416 Taylor to Africa.

On the whole, modern wildcatting may be less rewarding than it was during the 1920s, but it's still a lively game and a sort of postgraduate study in ballistics and handloading. Long may it live!

19 Cast Bullets

They say more game, large and small, and more men, good and bad, have been killed with plain lead bullets throughout history than with all the fancy jacketed slugs ever concocted. That's quite likely to remain a fact too, as long as .22 rimfire ammunition continues to be loaded with lead bullets. Lead projectiles, usually cast, were the standard bullets for all firearms, including artillery, for the first 500 years of the Age of Gunpowder. Every major war from about 1700 to the beginning of the 20th century was fought entirely or largely with plain lead bullets. Every species of game on earth has been taken with cast bullets. Cast bullets wiped out the "numberless" American bison and wrote an end to the glory days of the Plains Indians. Whole continents were conquered and colonized with cast bullets. In short, such bullets made firearms as we know them possible and then made the improvements practical. Many sporting cartridges besides the rimfires are still loaded with plain lead bullets, in the most modern ammunition plants.

A CAST-BULLET REVOLUTION

Considering their history and archaic image, it's a little surprising that cast bullets are enjoying a definite renaissance among sophisticated reloaders, but

Molds are available for cast bullets that are suitable for use in virtually every metallic centerfire cartridge ever developed in the world. In many revolver and obsolete rifle cartridges, cast bullets are the best bullets available and can serve some purpose in even the most recently developed rounds.

The variety of calibers, weights, and styles of cast-bullet molds is almost endless—and increasing annually!

it's true. A vast amount of individual research since about 1975 has produced breakthroughs in cast-bullet technology and has elevated cast-bullet performance to levels undreamed of by our forefathers. There is a national Cast Bullet Association whose members consider five-shot groups as large as one minute of angle disappointing, and who routinely fire benchrest groups in competition that are not easily equaled with jacketed slugs in good hunting rifles. Special cast-bullet wildcat cartridges have become fashionable and so have special chambers in rifles designed to fire nothing but cast bullets. There have been major innovations in bullet design, lubricants, bullet styles, gas checks, techniques, and equipment.

Many people today hunt big game with cast bullets in both rifles and handguns. Cast slugs are becoming

more and more the standard projectile among knowledgeable hunters using powerful, large-caliber revolver cartridges.

None of this has anything much to do with nostalgia, either. It may have something to do with economy, as prices on factory-made jacketed bullets escalate alarmingly, but I suspect that cost savings is often only the initial impetus toward casting bullets. Lead-alloy bullets can be fully justified on grounds of performance alone, but it's a real challenge to make them perform.

The fascination of the challenge is, I think, what keeps most casters sweating over hot lead pots. Although serviceable bullets *can* be produced with a minimum of inexpensive equipment, most bullet-casters actually wind up with quite an investment

Arrayed here is an absolute minimum-cost collection of equipment necessary to cast, size, gas-check, and lubricate cast bullets. From left, mold with handles, lead dipper, lead pot, Lyman 310 tool with sizing chamber, sprue-knocking stick, homemade "kake kutters," and a spoon for skimming the melt. The only remaining equipment required is a heat source and a pan in which to lubricate the bullets.

in molds, dies, and other specialized gear, so that (especially if they place a value on their time) jacketed bullets may really represent cheaper shooting. But the bullet is the only component of a cartridge that you can manufacture from scratch; so making your own bullets is the ultimate do-it-yourself step in reloading.

ALLOYS

The critical factors in cast-bullet performance are alloy strength, hardness, diameter (relative to bore dimensions in the gun), and bullet shape. I will have more to say about shape later in this chapter in the section on selecting a mold. All the other factors are related to the nature of the metal used for casting the bullets. The basic ingredient of course is lead, but pure lead is used only in muzzleloading firearms. For all cartridge arms, the lead is alloyed with other metals, mostly tin and/or antimony with occasional traces of arsenic and other elements.

A bullet metal is usually a rather complex three-part alloy. For a thorough technical discussion of such alloys, I recommend *Cast Bullets*, by Col. E. H. Harrison, published in 1979 by the National Rifle Association of America, the *Lyman Cast Bullet Handbook*, and various issues of the newsletter published by the Cast Bullet Association. Suffice it to say that the specific alloy of a bullet affects its accuracy; expansion characteristics upon impact; its tendency to deposit leading in bores; and its weight, diameter, and ease of casting.

Both antimony and tin, to different degrees, increase the hardness of the alloy. Both also increase the fluidity of the molten metal and contribute to sharper, better filled-out bullets. Antimony contributes more to strength and hardness. Tin's main effect is to reduce surface tension in the melt for a higher percentage of good bullets in a production lot. Antimony also causes less shrinkage during cooling in the mold, and antimony-alloyed bullets are both lighter and larger in diameter than pure lead ones from the same mold.

For very low velocities in rifles and pistols (usually below about 1,000 FPS), almost any alloy will work at least fairly well. As velocities increase, stresses on the bullet are magnified and the strength of the alloy becomes important. Even the hardest lead-alloy bullet is relatively soft and weak compared to a jacketed bullet, and a major key to success is delivering cast bullets to the muzzle of the gun in as pristine and undeformed condition as possible.

Printers' Linotype metal (12 percent antimony by weight, 4 percent tin, and the rest lead) is an almost ideal alloy for cast rifle bullets, provided expansion upon impact is not required. I prefer it for hot handgun loads as well, but nothing softer than a mixture of 1 part each by weight of tin and antimony to 10 parts lead is likely to be satisfactory. Moderate loads and midrange practice ammo can use a somewhat softer metal, say 40 parts lead to 1 part each of tin

and antimony. For the battering bullets get in semi-automatic pistols, a 20–1–1 alloy is about as soft as can be expected to function properly.

Tin and antimony are quite expensive; so, where economy is the goal, casters try to use the smallest percentages of these metals in the melt that will yield bullets of acceptable performance.

Another time-honored source of bullet metal is used wheelweights, formerly available at no cost from service stations and tire companies. No longer free from most sources, wheelweights are at least still cheap and available in considerable quantity. The trouble is that the composition of wheelweight alloys varies considerably today. Once pretty standard at 90 percent lead, 9 percent antimony, and 1 percent tin, they are now mostly lead with an unpredictable admixture of other metals. They are still useful, however, because they contain a tiny percentage of arsenic, and arsenic seems to be necessary to successful hardening of cast bullets by heat-treating. I will say more on this later.

Incidentally, cast bullets actually harden with age, usually achieving maximum hardness about 20 days after casting and, depending upon the alloy, picking up as many as 5 or 6 Brinell Hardness Numbers (BHN) in the process. At that age, pure lead measures about 5 on the Brinell scale, a 1–10 tin-lead alloy reads 11.5, a 1–20 alloy about 10, a 1–30 mix about 9, and a 1–40 tin-lead mix about 8.5. Virgin Linotype runs around 22 BHN, and reclaimed wheelweights from 12 to 16 in most cases. All references in this text are to the "aged" hardness of bullets, rather than the "fresh" readings.

SOURCES OF BULLET METAL

As photo-offset printing has almost completely replaced the old letterpress printing mode, Linotype has become harder and harder to find. Not even many small-town newspapers or print shops still use it. Virgin Linotype can still be purchased occasionally from commercial metals supply houses, and is sold specifically for bulletmaking by such firms as Taracorp and Division Lead. In either case it's expensive, especially when it must be shipped. Home alloying with antimony is difficult because of the very high temperature required to melt it. It is also extremely poisonous (as are most of the elements of bullet alloys), and care must be taken in handling it, molten or solid.

If you do luck into a source of type metal, make certain it's *Linotype* because Stereotype, Monotype and some other printers' metals are largely useless for bullets. Linotype that has been remelted many times may have changed its composition, become softer; so try to find out from your source whether the metal is fairly new or oft-used.

There are many other sources of bullet metal for ingenious scroungers, mostly for lead. A few are lead pipe, cable sheathing, flashing, plumbers' lead and old wiped joints, Babbitt metals, and salvaged bullets

Here we see the materials for cast bullets, again at the minimum-cost level. Clockwise from lower left, scrounged Linotype bars, alloyed ingots, gas checks (not always necessary), homemade beeswax-and-Vaseline lubricant, and an old candle for fluxing. Believe it or not, I've produced thousands and thousands of satisfactory bullets over many years from such scrap.

Alloyed ingots

Gas checks

Beeswax/Vaseline

Linotype bars

Candle for fluxing

from range backstops. One source that must be avoided is salvaged storage-battery plates. The high percentage of calcium found in them in recent years may in some situations create a lethally poisonous gas where the dross skimmed from the lead pot is exposed to moisture and allowed to accumulate, as in a covered garbage can. Old books may recommend battery-plate lead for bullets, but be assured that the hazard is now too great to risk.

I mentioned wheelweights of car tires already, but should mention them again, since they probably represent by far the biggest source of scrounged bullet metal in use today.

HEAT-TREATING BULLET METALS

As Linotype became scarcer, a few handloaders who were also metallurgists discovered that certain relatively cheap and plentiful alloys could be hardened by heat-treating. Plain old wheelweight metal, for example, properly cleaned and with enough tin added to make up as little as 1.5 to 2 percent of the mix, can be made to exceed the hardness of Linotype, perhaps by as much as 5 to 6 Brinell Hardness Numbers (BHN). As I've mentioned, a trace of metallic arsenic must be present, and most wheelweights do contain about 0.05 percent arsenic.

There are two ways to heat-treat lead. Where the bullets will be shot without sizing, they can simply be knocked out of the mold directly into a large container of cold water. *But ensure that no possibility exists for a splatter of water to reach the lead pot, because a tiny droplet of water (or most other liquids, including perspiration) in molten lead will cause a vi-*

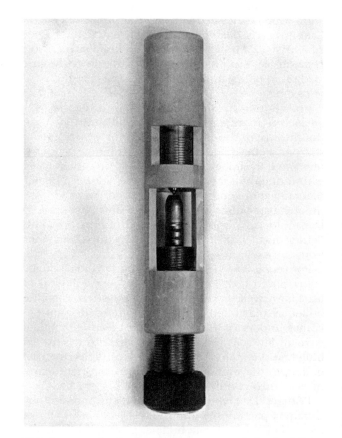

This is a cast-bullet harness tester made by Redding-SAECO. The vernier scale gives an arbitrary hardness reading not directly related to Brinell or other hardness-measuring systems. On the SAECO scale, pure lead tests 0 and virgin Linotype tests 10, with wheelweights and other alloys falling in between.

olent explosion as the water is converted instantaneously to steam. This first method of heat-treating does not produce bullets quite as hard as the method I describe below, but they should equal or slightly exceed Linotype.

Where the bullets cannot be fired as cast, but must be sized, another method is required. Lead is one of the few metals that softens when worked, rather than becoming work-hardened like brass or iron. Therefore, sizing an already heat-treated bullet defeats the purpose by resoftening the surface layer of alloy. The procedure, then, is as follows: Cast, inspect, sort, and size bullets in the appropriate die. You can affix gas checks, but do not apply lubricant. Then heat-soak the bullets for 45 minutes to 1 hour in an oven preheated to about 450°F. Finally, dump them as hot as possible into a bucket of tap water. This rapid quench leaves them very hard, and they can then be lubricated (either in the die used to size them or by the cake-cutter method, I'll describe later in this chapter) and are ready for loading.

The thermostats of household cooking ovens are not to be trusted, however. Determine correct temperature setting experimentally by setting a few reject bullets on their bases on a cookie sheet and "cooking" them at various settings on the dial. When they soften and begin to slump, lower the setting slightly and start with fresh bullets. The idea is to get the temperature only a few degrees below the melting point of the alloy. Also, ovens rarely produce uniform heat, but will exhibit hot and cool spots. Always position your bullets for heat treatment in the same area in which you performed the tests.

Bullets can be cooked in large batches, if desired. I use a homemade tray of hardware cloth lined with metal window-screen mesh. It permits heat to circulate through the layers of bullets and also allows instant quench when the whole container is dropped into the water.

Heat-treated bullets also "age," gaining hardness for the first 10 days or so after treatment, but the gain is not as significant as with non-heat-treated ones.

SELECTING A CAST-BULLET DESIGN

Bullet molds are available in literally hundreds of different designs, calibers, and weights from Lyman, RCBS, Hensley & Gibbs, Lee, Shiloh, Saeco, Hoch, Old West, Northeast Industrial (NEI), and others. Selection poses a problem to the beginner in bulletmaking, but it can be reduced somewhat by observation of a few general rules. The first is to always choose, for general purposes, a bullet in the upper half of the normal bullet-weight range for that caliber. Thus, for caliber .30 where the normal range is from 110 to 220 grains, best results can be expected with cast bullets of 180 grains and up. Lighter bullets have their uses, as in small-game and squib loads, but serve poorly for general shooting. For handguns I prefer the very heaviest designs made.

The second rule is this: Always select a blunt-nosed

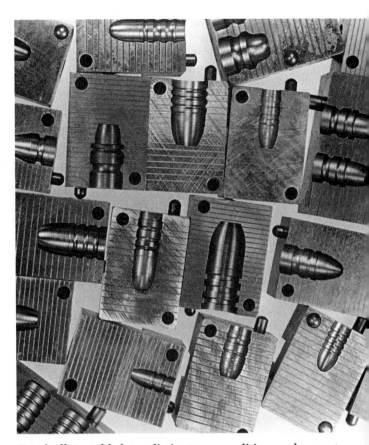

Cast-bullet molds have distinct personalities, and no two are exactly alike. Once they are well broken-in and delivering good bullets, treat them tenderly and never, never loan them out.

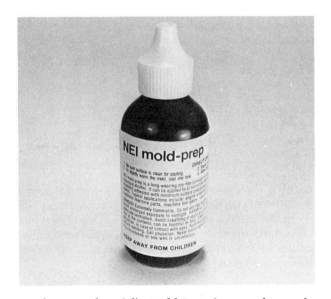

Northeast Industrial's Mold-Prep is a modern substitute for the age-old practice of smoking mold cavities with a candle or wooden match. The exact mechanism isn't definitively understood, but either process improves bullet quality. Smoke can rust on iron mold. But Mold-Prep won't.

The monstrous 4-bore bullet, cast in a Northeast Industrial (NEI) mold, and its .224 cast companion share certain anatomy despite the contrast in size. The top groove in each case, with slanted rear wall, is for crimping, and the other, square-shaped ones are for lubricant and are called "grease" grooves although grease is rarely used these days.

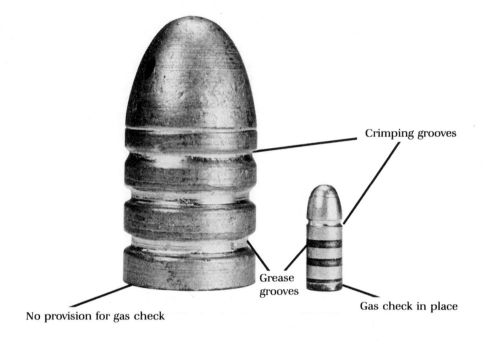

Crimping grooves

Grease grooves

No provision for gas check

Gas check in place

Left: Of the same weight and caliber, these two cast bullets show different design features. The flat-nose design will consistently outshoot the pointed spitzer, but the spitzer will retain velocity and energy farther from the muzzle. Cast bullets are seldom used at long range; but at longer ranges, the flat-nose is the better choice. *Right:* The multigrooved Loverin-style bullet at far right has not been as satisfactory in my experience as the so-called Keith-type slug next to it, especially in loads that require seating that leaves one or more of the grease grooves uncovered.

design. Long, sharp spitzers rarely work nearly as well in cast bullets as round-nose or, better yet, flat-nose designs. The flat-noses not only shoot more accurately but are also more effective on game.

Molds are available for several styles of bullets. The so-called "Loverin" style, featuring many narrow grease grooves, is much less popular than formerly but is still made. The "Keith" style revolver bullet is a semiwadcutter with a single, wide grease groove and is almost standard in revolvers. The most successful rifle bullet might be called the "two-diameter" shape; the bullet shank or body is sized to exact

This special casting-pot from Lead Bullets Technology (LBT) is a recent effort to expand the usefulness of cast bullets. Here a hot, base-pour mold is placed under the spout and the weighted handle at right is lifted and dropped. It's bounce meters a uniform dollop of pure, soft lead into the mold. The mold is then quickly filled from a second, conventional lead pot with a melt of harder alloy, producing a sort of soft-nosed cast bullet that performs surprisingly well.

groove diameter of the barrel while the nose portion comes from the mold at the "bore diameter," as measured across the tops of the rifling lands. For a typical .30 caliber barrel, the nose portion of such a bullet would mike (measured with a micrometer) .300 inch, while the shank would measure .308 inch in diameter after sizing. This design seems to offer the bullet best guidance during its trip through the barrel.

If you plan to carry cartridges loaded with cast bullets in your pocket, design the bullet so all grease grooves are inside the case neck when seated. That way the grease cannot pick up grit that could damage a bore. Also, current conventional wisdom holds that the base of a cast bullet is best not seated below the juncture of case neck and shoulder. According to these two warnings, therefore, case-neck length must be considered in selecting a mold, which means that the perfect bullet for the .30/06 may not be so good for the .308, with its shorter neck.

A few specialty molds are made for bullets without grease grooves, the bullets to be patched with either paper or Teflon plumbers' tape, but those techniques are a bit esoteric for this book. Lyman has also made mold sets for casting the body of a handgun bullet

This innovative NEI mold actually produces jacketed cast bullets! The jackets are cut from ⅜-inch copper tubing, placed in the mold, and warmed with a propane torch. Then the mold is closed and the alloy poured. These bullets can be driven at full jacketed-bullet velocities. Expansion is controlled by the hardness of the alloy.

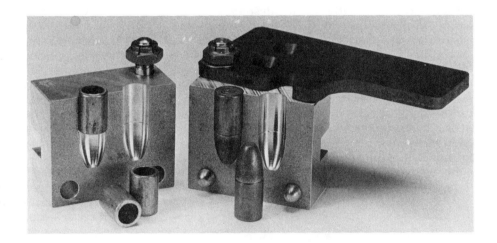

Left: The two-piece Lyman bullet I mentioned in the text consists of a hard (Linotype) base and pure-lead nose, next to it, epoxied together to form an expanding pistol bullet that doesn't deposit lead in the bore of the firearm. *Right:* The bullet at far right, with its rolled paper "patch," is a holdover from the late 19th century. Like most aspects of cast-bullet shooting, however, the technique has been receiving new attention in recent years, with paper and such materials as Teflon tape. Overall, though, the plain, old, lubricated design at left still does most of the work.

in Linotype and the nose portion in pure lead. The two sections are then epoxied together to produce a projectile that can be driven fast without leading and yet will still expand on impact. NEI makes molds for .375 bullets using lengths of ⅜-inch copper tubing. Hot metal is poured into the tubing to produce a kind of jacketed cast bullet, if that isn't too great a contradiction in terms.

I mention these specialty molds here because you may encounter them on the secondhand market. They represent interesting and sometimes successful innovations in cast-bullet technology but definitely fall into the "advanced" category.

CASTING PROCEDURE

Let's begin with a few words about safety. Always wear eye protection and heavy gloves when casting. I've already mentioned the hazard of moisture in a lead pot, and I was not joking. One drop of perspiration in that melt and you'll think somebody threw a small bomb at you! Finally, never cast in an enclosed space without forced-air ventilation. Lead is a systemic poison, as everyone knows now, and breathing the vapors from a potful of it in the molten state doesn't figure to lengthen your lifespan. I do my casting in the garage with doors open and a small electric fan blowing across the top of the pot. You should do likewise.

With a stock of suitable metal on hand and a good bullet mold chosen, the next matter is melting the lead alloy and preparing it for actual casting. This can be done in many ways, ranging from an inexpensive cast-iron pot on a stove to a thermostatically controlled electric melting pot especially designed for bullet molding. Good results can be had with either type of equipment and with any number of options in between. An ideal compromise is the cast-

A conventional mold is warmed by casting and discarding bullets until they come out shiny and fully filled-out. Always wear gloves and safety glasses or goggles, and cast only in a well-ventilated area.

iron pot on a portable gasoline or propane camp stove. Casting bullets on the kitchen range produces good enough bullets, but the inevitable deterioration in family relationships probably isn't worth it. Again, the fumes are toxic.

I think I can produce a higher *percentage* of usable bullets with a pot and dipper, but I can cast them so much faster with a bottom-draw electric pot that I get *more* good bullets in a similar period of time. Consequently, that's the method I use.

Whichever you choose, the basic procedure is the same. Turn the heat up and add alloy to the pot. A few small pieces, such as imperfect bullets saved from the last casting session, speed up the melt. When the metal is completely molten, it will have a gray scum on the surface. If you skim this away without fluxing, you will lose some of that precious antimony and tin and will soften the alloy.

Fluxing merely means adding a lubricant to the molten metal. This can be paraffin, a chunk of candle wax, a nugget of beeswax or bullet lube, or one of the modern powdered fluxes used in printing foundries and by bullet-casters (one is trade named Marvelux). They all work about equally well, differing principally in the quantity and obnoxiousness of the fumes given off when added to molten lead. As soon as the flux has liquefied, the alloy should be stirred vigorously, preferably from bottom to top with a dipper or wooden-handled tablespoon. The smoke created by the flux can be ignited to reduce vapors; it will burn merrily. The fluxing and stirring help to remix the various elements of the alloy, which tend to separate upon melting. Now, and only now, the slag can be skimmed off the melt. The wooden-handled tablespoon, with a few holes drilled in the bowl, is perfect for the job. Finally, the metal is ready for actual casting.

If the mold, fitted to its handles, is of ferrous metal (some are aluminum), it will probably have a coating of some sort of rust-resisting oil. Clean this out before casting begins; it can be burned out by actual casting, but the burning takes a while and the residue may be undesirable. Denatured alcohol does a fair job of degreasing molds, but one of the aerosol degreasers sold in gunshops is quicker. In any case, the first bullets cast in a new mold will not be usable, because traces of the rust-inhibitor will remain despite your best efforts and because the mold blocks will still be cold.

Management of temperature is one of the arts of bullet casting. Ideally, mold and alloy should be kept at a constant temperature; if either is too cool, the bullets will be wrinkled and poorly filled out. If they're too hot, the bullets will have a frosted appearance. A thermostatically controlled electric pot is good at keeping the melt within a fairly narrow range of temperature, and the mold's temperature can be controlled by adjusting the speed of casting and by developing a regular rhythm in the operations.

If you use the dipper-and-pot method, fill the dipper from the bottom of the pot, place the spout against the filler hole in the sprue plate of the mold,

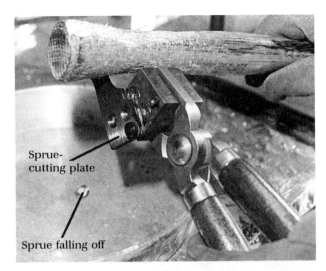

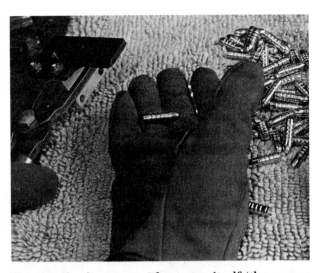

Left: The sprue-cutting plate should be knocked over with a single sharp rap. The sprue itself (the excess casting) will drop into a receptacle for recycling into the melt. *Right:* In a quick preliminary inspection you can cull out obviously defective bullets. Hot bullets fresh from the mold are soft and should be dropped onto a padded surface, as shown.

which has been rolled 90 degrees to the horizontal position. Rotate both dipper and mold as a unit to the upright position so that lead can pour into the mold. Allow the mold cavity to fill and overflow slightly, and replace the dipper in the pot. Now watch the puddle of lead remaining atop the sprue cutter closely. As the freshly cast bullet "freezes" in the mold, you will see a distinct color change on the sprue, and a crystalline texture will appear at its exact center.

Now tap the sprue cutter lightly with a hardwood mallet (I use a hickory hammer handle without the hammerhead) and knock the sprue into a receptacle. Open the mold handles and allow the bullet to drop gently onto a soft surface (a folded towel is ideal). The hot bullet is still very soft and can be damaged by striking a hard surface, including another bullet. Close the mold gently, push the sprue cutter back into position with your mallet, and repeat the process. Casting with a bottom draw pot is essentially the same except that no dipper is used.

I mentioned rhythm. Casting should be a rhythmic process, the rate of production varying according to the size of the bullets being cast. A 500-grain .458 mold gets hotter and cools off faster (because there's less metal in the blocks themselves) than a 50-grain .22 mold. The key is the time required for the sprue to harden properly. It should require a few seconds after the last molten lead is added, but if the sprue is knocked off too soon, a ragged hole will be torn in the base of the bullet and it will be ruined. Different molds perform quite differently. Some drop perfect bullets as soon as they're brought up to temperature and produce very few rejects, while other—apparently identical—molds will never deliver more than half their bullets in usable shape, no matter what you do to or with them. You have to get to know the char-

acteristics of each individual mold and adjust your techniques and timing to suit them.

One more thing: a good mold is a rare and precious possession. Treat it tenderly, care for it as though it's a jewel of great worth, and never, never lend it out!

Fluxing cannot be overdone. It should always be done when fresh metal is added to the melt to keep the level in the pot uniform, and, of course, always before skimming. Regular and thorough fluxing is one of the secrets of consistent cast-bullet quality, which in turn is one of the secrets of satisfactory cast-bullet shooting.

Another of those secrets is careful inspection of the finished product. Basic inspection is by eye, in a good light, looking for wrinkles, improperly formed bullets, flaws in bases, or base cavities or raised sprues. The former are due to striking off sprues before the metal has frozen, the latter from too-loose sprue-cutter plates. Bases are crucial to good shooting, and nothing less than perfect bases should be retained. In fact, casting *perfect* bullets is easy enough that a serious reloader need not settle for even minor imperfections. If real target-grade accuracy is the object, bullet inspection may extend to actual weighing of every bullet to detect lightweight specimens, which probably have concealed internal air pockets.

SIZING AND LUBRICATING

The next step is sizing and lubricating. Usually both operations, plus seating gas checks, are accomplished by a single stroke of a lubrisizing tool such as those offered by Lyman, RCBS, or Saeco. Sizing is necessary because bullet molds tend to drop bullets at least a couple of thousandths oversize. Bullets must be reduced to correct diameter, which varies according

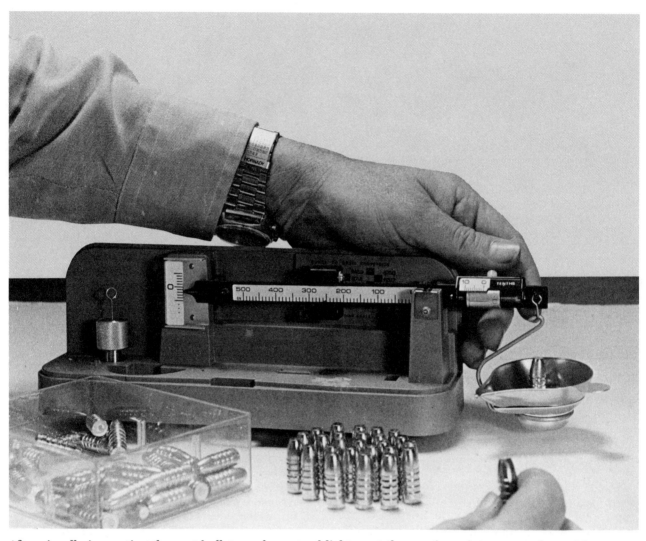

After visually inspecting the cast bullets under a good light, sort the survivors into groups by weight.

Left: Gas checks are shallow copper cups fitted to the bases of cast bullets to protect the lead from the powder gases. Only bullets designed to accept gas checks can, like those at left. Those at the right of the box of gas checks, described as "plain-based," are designed to be fired without gas checks. *Right:* Lubricating, sizing, and, if desired, affixing of gas checks is most easily performed in a lubrisizer. This is Lyman's Model 450.

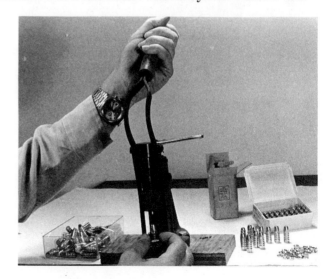

to the individual barrel in which they are to be fired. Expert opinions vary, but, as in the case of so many other aspects of handloading, the rifle or pistol itself is the final authority. Personally, I favor bullets that exactly match the bore (that is, groove diameter) and prefer not to shoot cast slugs more than .001 inch over that diameter. Others standardize at .001 inch and accept .002 inch, but very few shooters get good results with bullets larger than .002 inch over groove diameter.

Sizing, however, damages bullets, and excessive sizing ruins them. Modern sizing dies do a good job, but reducing bullet diameter more than about .002 inch below original as-cast girth almost always produces inferior accuracy. These numbers rightly indicate that if your bullet mold drops bullets that mike more than about .004 inch over the groove diameter of your rifle and top accuracy is your goal, you'd better get yourself another mold!

Plain lead-alloy bullets, without jackets, must be lubricated to avoid rubbing off hard-to-remove lead deposits in the barrel. In the old days, bear grease and buffalo tallow had large followings and would probably still work today. The search for the perfect cast-bullet lube has extended itself into every sort of slick substance known to man, and some of the secret formulas for bullet lubes read like something out of

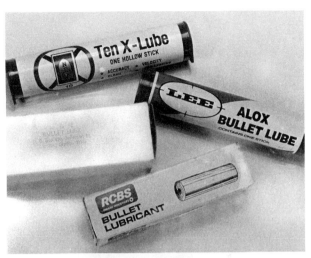

All of the many brands and types of bullet lubes come in perforated sticks for use in lubrisizing tools. Almost all are based on a beeswax-and-Alox 2138F mixture. A few have secret ingredients.

an alchemist's notebook. The best thing found so far, however, is not only fairly simple but readily available. It is a 50–50 mixture of pure beeswax and a synthetic substance known as Alox 2138F. The mixture is available in dozens of different brand names; just ask for "Alox lube" and you'll have one that's so good that further experimenting seems to be a waste of time. It is not too much to say that the discovery of Alox 2138F, together with tapered sizing dies (the common kind, these days), has revolutionized cast-bullet shooting.

Perhaps I should say that Alox lubes are the best readily available and in widespread use. Several smaller specialty firms produce lubricants, mostly with a secret ingredient or two, for which some strong velocity and accuracy claims are made. Among these are Red Rooster, LBT, and NEI. I have not tried all of them and cannot verify the claims for those I have tried. Nevertheless, lubrication remains one of the most promising areas for cast-bullet advancements, and at the rate such technology is progressing, I do not discount present or future claims by manufacturers.

GAS CHECKS

Gas checks are shallow gilding-metal cups fitted to the bases of cast bullets designed for them. They protect the soft metal from the tremendous heat of the powder gases. In general, any alloy bullet driven faster than about 1,600 FPS should have a gas check to help prevent leading in the bore and to improve accuracy. If a bullet has the stepped heel for a gas check, use one; despite references in the literature to successful low-velocity use of gas-check-type bullets without their gas checks, I have never achieved anything better than peach-basket grouping with na-

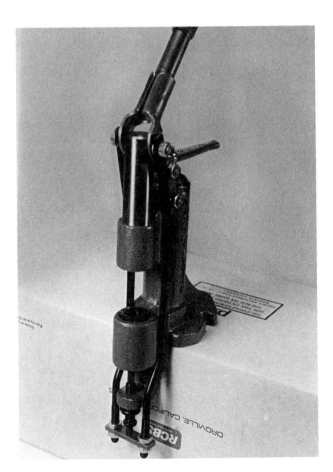

RCBS's lubrisizer is one of the best.

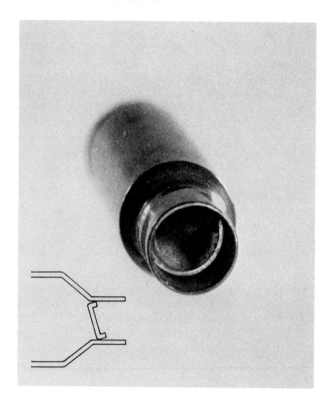

The 7 × 57 case in the photo holds at a gas check, cocked and jammed in the base of the neck, better shown in the drawing. The check was simply ripped off the bullet. This is a visual reminder that, if a cast bullet's base must be seated below the juncture of neck, a crimp-on gas check is desirable. I was not aware of any abnormality during the firing of this cartridge, and do not know why this occurred.

ked metal, at *any* velocity, if the design called for a gas check.

Two types of gas checks are marketed today, the standard type offered by Lyman and the so-called "crimp-on" type sold by Hornady. The latter are literally crimped into the soft alloy of the bullet when the combination is forced through a sizing die, the theory being that gas checks that are shed in flight destroy accuracy. There may be merit in this idea, but it's also true that very hard bullet metal such as Linotype resists the crimping action so determinedly that bullet and check may be deformed in the effort. I have actually broken the handle of a lubrisizer trying to crimp Hornady gas checks onto slightly oversize, hard bullets. Therefore, I use the crimp-ons when I can, and the noncrimping Lyman gas checks when I can't, depending upon the metal and design of the bullet itself.

A company named Hanned Precision has introduced a novel idea in gas checks; they sell tooling for making gas checks out of aluminum beverage cans and applying them to the bases of *plain*-based bullets. They're called "frechecks," and represent an intriguing approach to the protection of cast-bullet bases.

With a goodly batch of gleaming new bullets cast, inspected, sized, lubricated, and, if necessary, gas-checked, you are ready to move on to an examination of the special techniques involved in assembling accurate ammunition around them. Obviously, if you place any sort of value on your time, cast bullets are not exactly free, even if you can scrounge all the materials that go into them. To be worth the effort, they'd better have something to offer besides economy, and they do, as you will see.

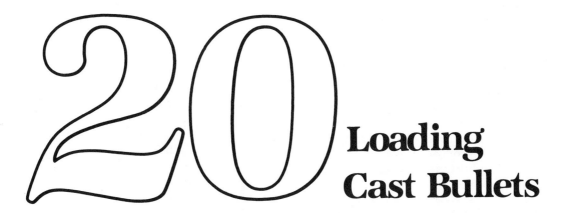

20 Loading Cast Bullets

Some veteran handloaders regard the loading of cast bullets as a sort of postgraduate exercise in the art of reloading. After all, anyone can pick a jacketed-bullet load out of a handbook, follow the recipe, and wind up with ammunition that will deliver at least acceptable results in his rifle or handgun. Not so with cast bullets. They seem to require a certain cunning and technical expertise that are not possessed by every handloader.

CAST-BULLET VELOCITIES

Perhaps the key word should be patience, instead of cunning. In any case, I have known reloaders who could make cast bullets do everything except deal poker hands while others, equally knowledgeable, never seem to have any "luck" with these fascinating chunks of lead.

Cast bullets have traditionally been for moderate-

Careful selection of a weight and style permits use of cast bullets from the same mold in several different cartridges of the same bore diameter. Lyman's 85-grain #257312 (at right) works well in such .25-caliber rounds as (from left) the .25/06 Rem., .257 Roberts, .250 Savage, .25/20 WCF, and .256 Win. Magnum.

to low-velocity loadings, at least in rifles. Until recently, about 2,000 feet per second was taken as the general upper limit of cast-bullet velocities. This means, of course, that some of the older cartridges such as the .30/30 WCF or .35 Remington can be loaded to full *normal* velocities with cast bullets, but more modern rounds relegated cast-bullet loads to reduced-velocity status.

This is not entirely true any longer. Alox-based lubricants, modern cast-bullet designs, and new loading techniques have unquestionably raised the practical velocity limits. Some experimenters have reported good results at velocities of 2,600, 2,800, and even 3,000 FPS, but other reloaders have been frustrated in trying to duplicate those results. A newcomer to the world of cast bullets is still well advised to keep his velocities under about 2,200 FPS, at least until he learns some of the tricks of the cast-bullet trade.

The reason for this is that the very strongest lead-alloy bullet is still relatively soft and weak compared to jacketed slugs and is easily deformed by the heat and pressure of firing. The higher the velocity, the greater the heat and pressure. And the more deformation of the bullet, the wilder the shooting. It's *possible* to get good results with lead bullets at high velocities, but that's not *easy*.

Most uses for home-cast slugs don't require high speeds anyhow. The majority of these loads are probably for plinking and practice shooting with a big-game rifle during the off-season, with shooting generally done at 100 yards or less. Cast bullets are ideal: they're cheap, they are easy on the barrel, and they can have more than enough accuracy for these purposes. The second most common use is small game, for the pot or for pelts, and modest velocities are a must for this kind of hunting.

CASE PREPARATION

Cases for normal cast-bullet loads are prepared in exactly the same manner as for loading jacketed bullets, except that case mouths must be flared or belled slightly. If they are not, a soft lead bullet even slightly cocked during the seating process will catch the lip of the case and crumple it. I discussed flaring already in Chapter 12 on die adjustments, but there is another way to flare case mouths if you don't wish to invest in a special sizing die (dies for straight cases normally come with provisions for belling mouths, but those for bottleneck cases ordinarily do not). It is done simply by tapping a bullet (not a whole cartridge) of considerably greater diameter nose-first into the case mouth. I use a .35 caliber bullet for everything up to caliber .30, and keep a full-jacketed .50 caliber machine-gun bullet on hand for everything larger. This must be done *before* the cases are primed, for obvious reasons. A little practice will teach you just how much tapping is required to flare the mouths the correct amount; overdo it and you cold-work the case mouths excessively and may have difficulty inserting them into the bullet-seating die.

So-called "M-type" sizing dies for bottlenecked rifle cases, sold by Lyman and others, are specially engineered for loaded cast bullets, providing a bit of flare on the case mouth and expanding the neck slightly larger than is usual for jacketed bullets.

POWDERS AND PRIMERS

Notes on powder selection for various cast-bullet and other low-velocity loadings are included in the chapter on special-purpose loads. Quite a bit of loading data is published for cast bullets, in a special handbook by Lyman, by Hodgdon, and in many popular shooting magazines, especially *Handloader*. A few notes on primers may be helpful here. Since most of the powders used in reduced loadings are fairly easy to ignite, it might seem that primer selection would be no more critical in cast-bullet loads than in full-power loads with jacketed bullets, but this occasionally proves to be untrue. For reasons I cannot explain, now and then a reduced load turns out to be very finicky about primers. The phenomenon and its cure are both unpredictable, but it may be worth the trouble to substitute primer makes or types in a load that shows promise, as a part of the final fine-tuning of the formula. This is especially true if that load reveals a tendency toward vertical stringing of groups.

FILLERS

One of the major breakthroughs in cast-bullet performance in the last 20 years has been research and

Powders selected for cast-bullet loads tend to be of the fast- to medium-burning types, resulting in low-density loadings. In such situations, changing primer brands or types may tighten groups.

development on the use of filler materials between the reduced powder charge and the base of the seated bullet. In certain loads, improvement in grouping with fillers can be astonishing.

However, I can proceed no farther without running up the warning flag. There appears to be a possibility that fillers can be hazardous. The mechanisms are poorly understood, but some rifle chambers may have been "ringed" by loads featuring fillers, and I have heard rumors (and only rumors) of rifles blown up under circumstances that seem to indict the filler as the villain.

Unfortunately, I can offer no serviceable rule of thumb for staying out of this kind of trouble with fillers (such as the rules in Chapter 17 for avoiding pressure excursions with reduced loads of slow-burning powders), except to place myself on record as advising against the use of fillers. However, I must confess that I consider the hazard sufficiently remote that I use fillers quite regularly in appropriate cast-bullet loads for my own guns, and have done so for a couple of decades without a trace of a problem. I do observe certain precautions, however: I never use any kind of hard wad, such as a card, and I avoid the use of fillers in straight-walled rifle or revolver cases, confining them to bottleneck rounds only.

To repeat, because I am prepared to accept what I consider a minute risk in my own reloading, it does *not* mean that I commend a practice to you. Also, the fact that I will now proceed to describe the proper way to prepare loads with filler should not be taken as advising you to use them. There have been many discussions of fillers in print (including in an earlier edition of this book) that are now understood to be incorrect. More is known about the subject today, and what follows is to be regarded merely as an update, and probably not the last word at that.

There is not really anything new about the idea of filling empty space in a case with inert material. The technique was developed decades ago when pioneer handloaders started filling up excess space in cases with cornmeal or Cream o' Wheat cereal. What's new about today's practices are the filler materials employed and the systematic testing that has quantitatively proved the value of fillers.

The original idea behind the use of fillers is still valid. This is that a small charge of powder in a large case will assume varying positions in the case, and varying shapes, from shot to shot. The primer flash may thus impinge upon a different surface area of powder and at a different angle from shot to shot, and variations in ignition can undermine ballistic uniformity. The filler, in the old days, was thought of as nothing more than a device to hold the powder charge in a uniform shape and uniform relationship to the primer. This is still a useful goal, but we now know that the filler serves another, perhaps more important, purpose, and that is to insulate the cast-bullet base from the heat of combustion.

We could still use cornmeal, but its weight must be added to that of the projectile in compounding loads since it is not consumed in firing. Experimenters a few years ago began working with kapok, a natural fiber, to lighten the total ejecta of the load, and got good results. Next, the synthetic fiber Dacron was tried, and this has now become standard among serious cast-bullet loaders. A dollar or two will buy almost a lifetime supply of Dacron from most upholstery shops, since no more than 1½ grains is used in most loads even in the largest cartridges. One-half to 1 grain is more common in typical cast-bullet loads in rifle cases. Dacron is not used in handguns much, because normal powder charges usually fill most of the available case space.

The procedure is simple enough. What follows, however, differs in important ways from earlier writings by competent handloading authorities. They, and I, formerly suggested that the filler tuft of Dacron be balled up, stuffed into the mouth of the charged case, and *tamped down firmly on the powder*, using something like the eraser end of a lead pencil. We now suspect that practice to be wrong, and possibly dangerous.

Instead, current instructions are as follows: pluck a tuft of Dacron from your supply and weigh it. You will quickly develop the knack of plucking very close to the correct weight by eye, but verification on a powder scale is still a good idea. Spindle the tuft so

Current thinking concerning inert fillers such as Dacron is that, if used at all (see warnings in text), they should *not* be tamped down on the powder charge but should fill the entire space between charge and bullet base.

that it can be started into the case mouth, but *do not* roll it into a tight ball. Start it into the case and gently push the tuft down far enough that a bullet can be started in the case mouth. The bullet's base will now complete the seating of the filler. The idea is to have the entire space between powder and bullet base filled up with the Dacron fiber.

In cases up to the .308 in capacity, start with ½ grain of Dacron. In .222-size cases and smaller ½ grain will be about maximum. In .30/06 and larger cartridges, the right amount will usually be found between 1 and 1½ grains in most loads. Not surprisingly, shooting in hot weather may require more Dacron than the same load needs on cool days. Only personal experimenting with your own rifle can reveal the just-right loading. Careful group-shooting should show distinctly smaller spreads as well as rounder groups (without marked stringing tendencies, either horizontal or vertical) with Dacron if the load is accurate enough to make such distinctions to begin with.

Cast bullets are seated in the same manner as their jacketed counterparts, but care should be taken to see that the seating punch in your die does not deform the bullet's nose. If you don't happen to have

the correct punch on hand, improvise. The right shape can be built into the existing punch with sealing wax or epoxy putty, using a cast bullet as a mold to form the material before it hardens. The results should give good service. The material can be removed any time you wish by applying heat.

SPECIAL CONSIDERATIONS

Excess lubricant on cast bullets may be squeezed or cut away from the sides of the bullets in seating, and tends to build up on the face of the seating punch. If lubricant buildup is allowed to continue, it causes successive bullets to be seated deeper and deeper. Watch closely for lubricant buildup in loading a large lot of cast-bullet ammunition, and clean the face of the punch occasionally if you detect buildup.

Watch also for thin rings of lead being shaved from the bullets as they're forced into the case necks. Chamfering and flaring the mouths should prevent this, but since cast bullets are often sized a thousandth of an inch or two larger than jacketed bullets in the same caliber, the meticulous handloader may wish to get a special expander button for his case-sizing die for use in cast-bullet loads, to avoid squeezing his slugs down in the process of seating them in too tight case necks. Many manufacturers of reloading dies furnish oversize expanders on special order, and Lyman even offers a special series of sizing dies, designated by the letter "M," for loading cast bullets.

Cast bullets will give best results in uncrimped cases, and crimping is to be avoided except in heavy magnum revolver loads, when the ammunition will

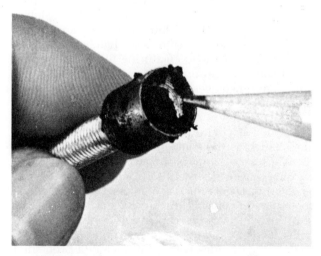

A buildup of bullet lube on the stem of the seating die can cause the seating of bullets progressively deeper, resulting in varying ballistics and accuracy as well as possible pressure increases.

Left: Bullets of lead alloy must be lubricated to prevent rubbing off of soft lead in the gun's bore during firing. In the po'-boy style of lubricating cast bullets shown here, bullets are stood on their bases in a pan. Then molten lube is poured to cover all grease grooves. *Right:* When the lubricant hardens, the projectiles are cut out of the resulting cake with a neck-expanded case of proper caliber, though with the head sawed off. Lubricant, usually a beeswax mixture, can be remelted indefinitely.

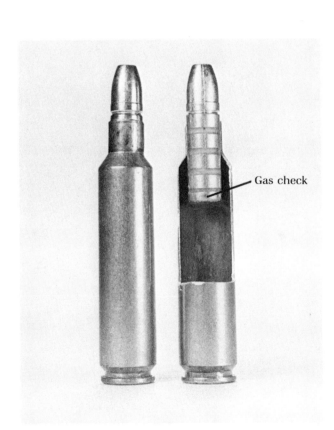 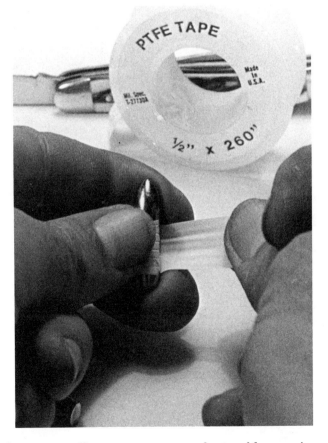

Gas check

Left: Gas-checked cast bullets that must be seated deeply to cover all grease grooves can be troublesome in short-necked cases. In such situations, only gas checks (see previous chapter for photos) that crimp firmly onto the bullet's base should be used, to avoid stripping in the neck. *Right:* Teflon patching with plumbers' PTFE tape is new and experimental. It's the modern twist on the old paper-patching technique. NEI offers special molds in several calibers designed for tape patching.

be subject to rough handling and similar circumstances. The flare can be removed from the case mouths as described in Chapter 12, on die adjustments.

Remember, too, the warning about using cases for full-power loadings that have been fired with squib loads. Don't do it.

The "secret" to cast-bullet success, it should be obvious now, is in the delivery of perfect bullets at the muzzle. Careful casting of metal of the proper hardness, meticulous inspecting and rejection of all except perfect bullets, minimum sizing, protection of the metal from deformation by heat and pressure in firing, and adequate lubrication add up to good shooting, and it can be very good indeed. In fact, there's no particular reason that a rifle shouldn't shoot cast bullets as well as or better than jacketed slugs. Many cast-bullet shooters are disappointed with groups that exceed a minute of angle at 100 yards or even farther.

These comments must be qualified by caliber, for the reason that the smaller the bullet in mass and diameter, the more crucial very minor, almost imperceptible, flaws become. I have never achieved really top performance from .22 caliber cast bullets, and only rarely with 6mms. Conversely, 7mm and .30 caliber slugs have given beautiful results, and .35 and larger ones even finer accuracy.

BORE CONDITION

Another factor that is often ignored is the sensitivity of cast bullets to barrel fouling from firing jacketed slugs. If you've been blazing away with the latter, take time to thoroughly clean your bore before switching to cast bullets. The difference in grouping may amaze you. Incidentally, the reverse is also true: jacketed bullets will not group well from a barrel in which a great many cast bullets have been fired, at least not for the first few rounds. Eventually, the high-velocity jacketed bullets will clean the cast-bullet fouling from the bore. This is also the easiest way to clean a bore that has been leaded by cast bullets that were too soft, too fast, or insufficiently lubricated. If the bore is heavily leaded, firing a high-velocity jacketed slug through it may produce dangerous pressures, but if there is only a minor deposit of lead, a couple of full-power jacketed bullets will eliminate it.

Cast bullets are a challenge; no doubt about it. They require more know-how, more patience, and more effort for good results than jacketed bullets. But he who asks "Why bother?" has never known the feeling of driving home the fifth shot in a 1-inch group with bullets he molded himself and of observing the expression on the face of the shooter at the next bench who can't seem to do better than 2 inches with the finest modern jacketed slugs.

21 Loading for Black-Powder Guns

Sooner or later, almost every handloader either acquires an old black-powder breechloading rifle or some friend asks him to help in providing ammunition for one. In most cases, handloading is the only hope for restoring these old-time smokepoles to service because factory ammunition is not available except in collectors' quantities and of course at collectors' prices.

THE BRASS PROBLEM

The first problem is always cases. A couple of years ago a friend brought me a magnificent old Winchester Model 1886 rifle chambered for the .40/65 WCF cartridge, vintage of 1887. He had the original bullet mold and hand-type reloading tools, both marked "Winchester Repeating Arms Co.," and a couple of boxes of original factory ammunition. He wanted to shoot the old buffalo killer, but he was aware of its considerable value on the collectors' market and consulted me to make certain that nothing he did might damage the gun.

A quick check in Frank Barnes's *Cartridges of the World*, an invaluable reference in such matters, revealed that .40/65 WCF ammo had been discontinued by the manufacturers in 1935; so the cartridges my friend had couldn't have been younger than that. This posed the possibility that primers in that ammunition were mercuric and corrosive; therefore, we decided not to run the risk of firing the factory loads. If there had been no other choice, we could have broken down those cartridges, salvaging bullets and cases and discarding powder and primers, and reloading the cases. As it happened, however, we did have a choice, since modern .45/70 brass can be easily re-formed to fit the .40/65 WCF chamber. Accordingly, we disassembled a couple of rounds to double-check correct bullet diameter (there were several common in the many early caliber .40 cartridges) and to satisfy our curiosity about other aspects of the loads. These proved to be black powder.

Greatly enlarged, black gunpowder appears to consist of irregular chunks, in contrast to the uniform granule shapes of smokeless powders.

Old factory-loaded ammo for black-powder cartridges may have corrosive and/or mercuric primers that can damage the barrel of a fine antique rifle when fired. If modern brass can't be bought or reformed, it's safest to deprime and reload the old cases with modern components.

At left is an original factory .40/65 WCF cartridge, loaded with black powder. The other two rounds are handloads with cases reformed from modern, Boxer-primed .45/70 brass and loaded, respectively, with jacketed and cast bullets.

While waiting for a set of RCBS loading dies in this caliber, I molded a number of bullets in the original mold that came with the rifle, and a few more in Lyman's #403196 mold. The latter weighed 260 grains in Linotype, while the same metal came out of the old mold weighing 235 grains. All were sized .406 inch.

When the dies arrived, I sized a few brand-new .45/70 cases in them and tried them in the rifle, finding that they would not quite chamber. The bases were not being squeezed down quite small enough due to interference between the shellholder and the face of the die. Consultation with RCBS produced a sizing die for the similar, but longer, .40/82 WCF cartridge. The .45/70 cases were then driven into this die with a bench vise (properly lubed, of course) and knocked out with a steel punch. This technique sized the cases all the way to the rim and produced .40/65 cases that worked perfectly in the old rifle. From that point on, we were home free, having only to select a powder and charge. I even discovered that jacketed bullets in the correct diameter were available from Colorado Custom Bullets (now Barnes Bullets). The original ballistics of this cartridge called for a 260-grain bullet moving 1,325 FPS at the muzzle, and this was easily duplicated with 26 grains of IMR 4198 powder. Since this old Winchester has an extremely strong action and was in almost new condition, we cautiously experimented with heavier loads, successfully—and safely—achieving just under 2,000 FPS with the 250-grain jacketed Colorado Custom bullet.

Left: High-quality loading (and, if necessary, case-forming) dies are available for almost any obsolete cartridge. **Right:** It was common practice in the late 1800s to furnish the customer of a high-grade rifle with a set of reloading tools and a bullet mold. Note that this mold, which came with the .40/65 WCF rifle that I mention in the text, carries the "Winchester" mark.

At near left is a cast bullet from the original mold obtained with the rifle in question, compared to a lead bullet pulled from a round of old .40/65 WCF factory ammo. At right appears a pair of modern jacketed bullets of correct diameter and weight from Sailer and from Barnes, respectively.

This rifle would make an effective and interesting arm for whitetail deer at normal ranges, or even for the bigger game it was originally designed for, if the owner cared to risk damage to the finish. The whole project was great fun, and a fine old rifle could roar again, after more than half a century of silence.

In that story are inherent several important points in load development for black-powder arms. First, make certain of the mechanical condition of the weapon, preferably by having it inspected by a competent gunsmith. Second, watch out for obsolete factory ammunition. If mercuric, corrosive primers are fired, the brass cases are hopelessly ruined, and the rifle will be damaged unless meticulously cleaned immediately after firing. If the ammunition is loaded with black powder, cleaning is all the more necessary. Furthermore, the primers may be deteriorated, and the cases themselves are probably not as strong as new ones. Wherever possible, it's worth the trouble

to make new ones from current brass. More about this later in this chapter.

BERDAN PRIMERS

If the cartridge in question is British or European, the primers are probably of the Berdan type. If you attempt to deprime such cases in the conventional manner, you'll break your decapping pin and possibly damage your sizing die as well. It will sometimes be possible to form cases for your obsolete cartridge from modern, Boxer-primed brass for some other caliber, which will save an enormous amount of time and trouble in the future. An amazing number of original black-powder case designs can be made from new brass for .45/70, .30/40 Krag, or 9.3 × 74mmR. Best of all, an outfit called Brass Extrusion Laboratories, Limited (B.E.L.L.—operated, surprisingly enough, by

Brass Extrusion Laboratories, Ltd. (B.E.L.L.) specializes in providing rare foreign and obsolete brass such as this for reloading.

a fellow named Jim Bell), makes a great many exotic cases with Boxer primer pockets, from which almost any obsolete caliber can be formed. Bell's list is too long to include here and new numbers are added regularly, but if you've a rifle for which you cannot buy loaded ammo or cases elsewhere, Bell would be worth checking. Because of the relatively low demand for these oddball cases, Bell's prices must necessarily be fairly stiff. But the cases are often the only way to shoot a certain old rifle, and I consider them bargains at the price.

There are a few other sources for sound, Boxer-primed cases in obsolete calibers. For example, Dixie Gun Works sells newly manufactured .50/70 brass, and now and then a lot of the big, rimmed ".45 RCBS Basic" brass turns up. Almost two dozen common and not-so-common black-powder rounds can be made from this straight-walled case.

If none of these sources can provide boxer-primed cases for your black-powder veteran, there remains one last hope, and that is to remake some other case into the one you need. There is hardly a cartridge for which acceptable cases cannot be mangled up out of some other caliber, and you will probably be astonished to learn how much can be done with a few simple tools and a little ingenuity.

To learn this, you must find a copy of an out-of-print book by the late Maj. George Nonte, entitled *Home Guide to Cartridge Conversions*, published in 1961 by Stackpole. There is said to be a revised edition, published by Gun Room Press of Highland Park, NJ. If any book can be called "definitive" on any subject, this is the one, and I regard it as an essential component of any handloader's library.

If even the Nonte book lets you down, you can

probably still shoot the old rifle. RCBS offers a tool for decapping Berdan-primed cases that works well enough, but the job remains a nuisance. Furthermore, the tool cannot be used to remove live primers. This can best be accomplished by removing the depriming stem from your resizing die and running the unloaded case all the way into the die. Then turn a steel rod to a sliding fit in the case neck. Fill each case with water, insert the rod, and administer a whack on the rod with a large hammer. Theoretically, hydraulic force will force out the primer. It will also spew water all over everything in sight, but it's the only safe way to decap live Berdan primers.

If no Boxer-type case can be converted to fit your Berdan-primed cartridge, you're stuck with using the latter primers, which are scarce on today's market. You'll need the RCBS tool for removing fired primers.

The sure way to pick a powder charge for a black-powder cartridge is to use black powder, which is also scarce but available in most areas. Use FFg granulation in a quantity that fills the case to the base of the bullet or a little above, so that seating the bullet will compress the powder charge about ⅛ inch. Having arrived at this charge volumetrically, you can then set your powder measure to drop this quantity without worry about charge *weight*. Personally, I don't care much for using a rotary powder measure with black powder; the stuff can be set off by static electricity and, conceivably, by the mechanical action of the measure. I know reloaders who get away with measuring powder this way, however, and have never heard of such an accident. I still prefer to use a dipper. Lee offers a graduated set of powder dippers which are quite handy, or you can make your own by soldering a wire handle to an old case that has been trimmed to hold the desired volume of black powder.

PYRODEX

There is now a product labeled as "the *replica* black powder," trade named "Pyrodex" and distributed by Hodgdon. Pyrodex is not exactly a substitute black powder, although it can be substituted volume for volume for very similar ballistic performance, and although it smokes, smells, and fouls guns (and gunners) about as much as "black." It is, however, a much safer product to ship, store, and handle, so much so that it has earned an entirely different classification from the Department of Transportation.

Moreover, Pyrodex can be handled by shops in many municipalities whose fire codes effectively prohibit possession of practical quantities of black powder, making it available to some shooters who might otherwise have to drive for hours to purchase propellant for older rifles legally.

Pyrodex comes in a number of grades, labelled "P," "RS" (for muzzleloading pistols, rifles, and shotguns) and "CTG" for handloading cartridges. The rule, mentioned above, is that *Pyrodex is always substituted*

Pyrodex, as of this writing, is the only substance I know of that can safely and satisfactorily be substituted for black powder. "Cartridge" grade is the correct granulation for reloading black-powder cartridges.

for black powder on a volumetric basis, never weight for weight. Used thus, it usually provides approximately the same ballistic performance as black powder. The so-called replica black powder also replicates black powder's corrosive bore and case fouling and requires the same kind of prompt cleaning, although Pyrodex's fouling seems to be less accumulative. It has a higher ignition temperature, which sometimes causes a problem with muzzleloading guns, especially flintlocks, but this is of no consequence in centerfire cartridges.

Pyrodex has performed extremely well for me in original black-powder cartridges, so well that it's my first choice for that application even though I have plenty of real black powder on the shelf.

The success of Pyrodex may have flushed one or two competitors out of the bushes, one of which is called Golden Powder. The long-promised and much-heralded appearance of Golden on the market has been repeatedly postponed, and I have not been able to gain any practical experience with it. Who knows, though? By the time you read this, Golden may be the smash hit of the century.

If the gun is in sound mechanical condition, the method described of arriving at a propellant charge should give very similar pressures and velocities to original ammo, with points of impact that coincide with the factory sights on the guns, some of which are not adjustable. However, continued use of black powder in any gun will almost inevitably result in some deterioration of the bore and finish unless you're willing to spend an ungodly amount of time in cleaning after every firing. This involves washing the bore out with hot soapy water and the use of any of the newly developed black-powder solvents (thanks be to the muzzleloaders!) on all parts of the action, inside and outside, followed by thorough oiling with corrosion-inhibiting lubricants, plus occasional in-

spection for a few days after each firing, just to be sure that you are on the safe side.

SMOKELESS LOADS FOR BLACK-POWDER CARTRIDGES

If all that maintenance sounds a bit laborious, the solution is the use of smokeless powder, and that brings about a whole new set of problems. The principal one is pressure, specifically pressures beyond the capacity of obsolete actions. This is complicated by the fact that different models from the black-powder era that were chambered for the same cartridge are of radically different strengths. A .45/70 load, for example, is perfectly safe in an 1886 Winchester lever-action but is quite likely to convert an 1873 trap-door Springfield's receiver to shrapnel on first firing!

Therefore, I'd recommend that reloaders wishing to develop smokeless loads confine their activities to the aforementioned Winchester 1886 (and later lever-actions) and 1885 single-shot "High Wall," the Sharps 1878 (Borchardt), the Marlin Models 1893, 1894, and 1895, the big Martini actions, the Stevens 44½, and the Remington-Hepburn and similar rifles, assuming breeching, headspace, and firing pins are perfect. All other original black-powder arms are best fired with black powder only, including the old Colts, Bullards, Wessons, Maynards, rolling blocks, Whitneys, Ballards, Sharpses, and the Stevens, Winchester, and Marlin arms not on the above list. I concede that some of these *can* be fired with light charges of smokeless, but I consider the risk of doing so less desirable than the work of cleaning up after a black-powder-burning session.

There are several excellent sources of information on loads for the old cartridges, including the aforementioned Barnes book, *Cartridges of the World,* a

Use of a priming charge of smokeless powder to ignite the main charge of black powder reduces fouling and usually improves velocities somewhat. For this, many shooters use the IMR Powder Company's SR 4759, not exceeding 10 percent of the total weight of the charge.

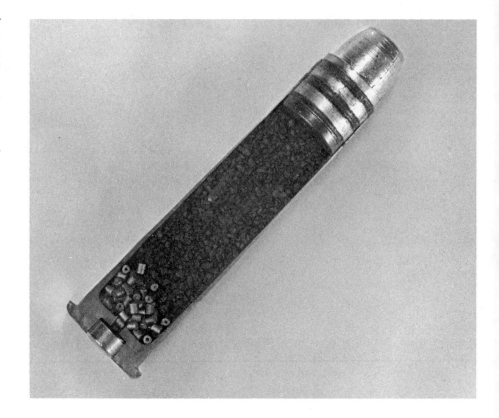

large-format, softcover volume essential to any reloading program with any obsolete or foreign cartridges. Another is Major George Nonte's hardback *Home Guide to Cartridge Conversions* (Stackpole, 1961). Also, *Handloader* magazine (bimonthly) and *Handloaders Digest* (annual) publish some loading data for black-powder cartridges.

CORRECT BULLET DIAMETER

Bear in mind that steels in use during the black-powder days were by no means as sophisticated as those in modern guns. Some of the old barrels are relatively soft and may be worn out quite rapidly by driving jacketed bullets through them at high velocities (for those cartridges). For this reason, cast bullets should be used for most shooting in the old guns, and powder charges kept below maximum to reduce throat erosion from hot gases as much as possible. For most purposes, the cast bullets will do anything within the range of the cartridge anyway. Furthermore, bore diameters varied quite a bit more before the turn of the century than today, and the handloader's ability to size cast bullets to almost any desired diameter may produce better results with lead-alloy bullets than with jacketed ones.

The bore size can be determined by slugging the bore of the rifle. To do this, carefully drive a soft, *pure* lead ball a bit larger than the bore through it and measure the largest diameter of the slug with a micrometer. Very worn bores often do their best work

with slightly oversize bullets, sometimes as much as .002 inch over groove diameter.

The description of efforts to restore my friend's .40/65 WCF Winchester to service included some of the problems arising from trying to find shootable, reloadable brass for an obsolete caliber. For most handloaders, simple reforming and trimming to a new length, plus a bit of inside neck reaming and fire-forming, constitute the limit to which they'll go in manufacturing cases for black-powder rifles.

STORAGE & HANDLING

Perhaps a few words on storage and handling of black powder here will save someone an unfortunate experience. I advise against storage of black powder in the home, and especially near any other combustibles. "Black" can be ignited, as mentioned, by an electric spark (including static electricity), heat, percussion, and fire. Unlike smokeless, it is officially classed as an explosive, and it need *not* be confined to burn violently. Keep stored quantities small, keep it separated from primers and smokeless powder and preferably in a magazine of approved design, and handle it cautiously. Black powder is far less forgiving than smokeless, and can never be taken for granted. When handling it, one must be *thinking* at all times. For example, it's best not to use a plastic funnel to transfer black powder between two containers, because common polyethylene funnels can build up static charges. Instead, use a metal one, preferably brass. Ferrous metal, which can cause a spark if struck sharply, should be avoided around black powder; remember, that's how a flintlock rifle ignites the stuff. With the exception of the containers in which black powder is sold, it has for good reason been stored traditionally in horn, brass, or copper.

Of course, being wetted destroys black powder, unlike most smokeless. It's hygroscopic and picks up moisture easily from humid air. "Keep your powder dry" is still good advice where black powder is concerned, and that means storing it in a relatively cool, dry place.

Many old-time rifles have fixed sights, having been regulated at the factory for what was probably the only loading available in commercial ammunition. Today's black powders are not exactly the same as the ones in use in the 1880s, despite carrying the same granulation designations. This means that, unless a shooter wishes to alter his original black-powder rifle by adding adjustable sights (which may considerably reduce the value of the piece), he'll have to experiment with powder charges to try to find a load that strikes where the sights look at some useful distance. This can be a particular problem with the old British double-barreled rifles, in which there is not only a question of zeroing but one of trying to make both barrels shoot to the *same* zero. This can be a maddening procedure with smokeless powder, but can usually be achieved with a little experimenting with black powder. Unfortunately, there is no easy way around it. You just have to try everything you can think of until something works. Varying bullet weights may help.

In any case, many reloaders consider loading for the old-timers to be one of the most rewarding aspects of their hobby. There is an aura about the guns that fought the Civil War, wiped out the buffalo, and subdued the Apache, Sioux, and Arapahoe that's well nigh irresistible to any dyed-in-the-wool gun buff. These rifles spanned the brief period between the end of the muzzleloading era and the coming of smokeless powder. They're a part of our history and a part of our shooting heritage.

22 Loading for Handguns

From the handloader's point of view, most handgun ammo falls into one of three major categories: hunting loads (mostly for revolvers), competition loads (mostly for semi automatics), and defense loads, which may be for either pistols or revolvers. The single-shot handguns—bolt-action, falling block, or break-actions—appear extensively in both hunting and metallic-silhouette competition. Each of these handgun categories has its own specialized requirements, and no other aspect of metallic-cartridge reloading is changing as rapidly as this one. Let's take a look at each category separately.

SINGLE-SHOT SPECIALTY PISTOLS

These guns are really stockless rifles and are commonly chambered for rifle cartridges. Reloading for them is done exactly as if they were rifles, with a couple of exceptions. For example, loads for a single-shot pistol chambered to 7mm–08 Rem., .30/30 WCF, .35 Rem., or similar rounds (including the many wildcats in use) will use rifle primers, even though they'll be fired in something that is at least technically a pistol. Also, contrary to the expectations of many, powders that yield highest velocities in a given cartridge when fired in a rifle will usually do so in a pistol barrel as well, bullet weight being equal. Some of those same powders, however, may produce truly fearsome muzzle flash and blast when touched off in a 10- to 14-inch single-shot pistol barrel. The ball-type propellants as a group tend to deliver the most impressive fireballs from pistol muzzles, and the slower-burning powders (for the caliber) can be expected to produce higher muzzle pressures and thus louder

bangs. It's an individual judgment, but many find it worthwhile giving up a few FPS to avoid these effects.

For hunting big game with the single-shots, the rules for bullet selection are quite different from those in effect when loading the same cartridge for a rifle. This is because of the difference in attainable velocities. For example, the 150-grain spitzer is beyond question the best all-around big-game bullet for a .308 rifle, but out of a 10- or 12-inch pistol barrel, it will not necessarily expand reliably. The deer hunter carrying a .308 Pachmayr Dominator, for instance, or a Contender with a .30 Herrett or .30/30 barrel is better off with one of the 110- to 130-grain bullets.

But those are varmint bullets, you say. Exactly. They're more lightly jacketed and are designed to expand at long range where velocity has dropped far below muzzle speeds. Velocity from the pistol barrel is relatively low to begin with; so the lightweight slugs do not over-expand at shorter ranges, as might be expected, and penetrate well on large game.

This approach pays off across the board. Lower-velocity rifle cartridges such as the .30/30 WCF and .35 Rem. are very successful in single-shot pistols largely because the bullets have always been designed to work well at low speeds. The wildcat called the .375 JDJ is tremendously useful on nondangerous deer-size game because of the availability of bullets intended for the low-velocity .375 Winchester cartridge in rifles.

Sierra Bullets recognized this need and introduced no fewer than six new bullets for the handloader. They are specifically (and so marked on the boxes) for single-shot pistols in 6mm, 7mm (two), .308-inch, .312-inch, and .375-inch diameters. Perhaps other weights, styles, and calibers will be added to this

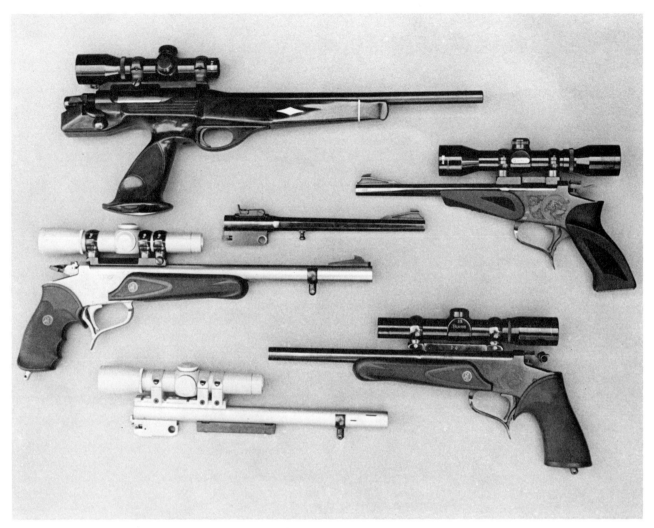

Today's specialty single-shot pistols are actually stockless rifles, often chambered for rifle-type cartridges. Bolt actions, like the .35 Remington XP-100 at top, require rifle loading techniques, as well. Other styles, like the Thompson-Center "Contenders," make slightly different demands. The lower complete gun on the left is a Contender with 14-inch .30/30 WCF barrel. Scoped barrel at bottom is a custom, Mag-Na-Ported .375 JDJ from SSK. The scoped Contenders at right are, from top, a .221 Fire Ball and a .256 Win Magnum.

list from time to time, with other manufacturers following suit.

Selecting bullets for International Handgun Metallic Silhouette Association (IHMSA) or NRA Hunter Pistol or Long Range Pistol courses of fire is a different ball-game. Expansion is not important, but accuracy, flatness of trajectory, and sufficient momentum to topple heavy steel rams at 200 meters are. In most cases, match-grade bullets in the heavier weights (for the caliber) are the proper choice, and careful, comparative testing will determine the best one.

Mechanical Considerations. Reloading for a bolt-action pistol (such as Remington XP-100, Wichita, Kimber) is mechanically identical to doing it for a bolt-action rifle. If it's a break-action Thompson/Center Contender, however, there is one handloading operation that requires a bit of extra attention, and that is the case-forming step. If the cartridge is one of the several popular wildcats (.30 Herrett, .357 Herrett, .375 JDJ, etc.) for which Contender barrels are available, the process will involve necking-down, at least, and often such tasks as resetting shoulders and shortening as well. Even when the case is a rimmed one, the brass should be sized so that it headspaces on the shoulder.

This requires initial setting of the full-length sizing die ¼ inch or so above the shellholder with the press ram in the full "up" position. The Contender's action shouldn't close on a case sized at this setting. Turning the die in (down) ⅛ turn at a time, resize the case and try it in the pistol. Repeat the process until the action will *just* close freely. A "snap fit," in which an extra effort is required to close the action, is incorrect. So is a fit with any headspace "play." What you're seeking is actually zero headspace, a perfect fit, with

Contrary to some expectations, the chronograph usually shows that the same powders that produce highest velocities in a rifle barrel also do so in the same cartridge chambered in a 10- to 14-inch handgun barrel.

a case body that is neither too long nor too short. Both accuracy and optimum case life depend upon setting case shoulders so that they exactly fill the chamber, no more, no less.

Actually, having set the shoulders thus during initial case-forming, I prefer to back the sizing die off a "hair"—⅛ turn or less—and lock it there for resizing fired brass. With rimmed cases, which routinely headspace on the shoulder anyway, be sure to set your sizing die so that it doesn't set those shoulders back during resizing.

HUNTING REVOLVERS AND CARTRIDGES

Repeating handguns used for hunting big game are usually revolvers, either single- or double-action. They are generally chambered for one of the magnum rounds—.357 ("Magnum" or "Maximum"), .41, or .44—or the .44 Special or .45 Long Colt. Recently, the .454 Casull has, in the superb five-shot revolvers from Freedom Arms, redefined the term "magnum." It uses

The superb Freedom Arms single-action is the ultimate in revolvers for big-game hunting, as is the .454 Casull cartridge to which they are chambered. As usual, the key to effectiveness is in bullet selection and carefully developed handloads.

This 11-year-old girl, Christy Smith, of Alice, Texas, in 1983 shot the first perfect 40 × 40 score by a Junior Lady in an IHMSA sanctioned silhouette match, setting state and regional, as well as international records. Christy shot handloads, naturally, in a 7mm TCU specialty pistol.

the most powerful cartridge for production revolvers that can be purchased over the counter. There have been a couple of powerhouse semiautomatic handguns, such as the Wildey (9mm and .45 Magnum) and the Automag (.357 and .44 AMP) that were big-game worthy. But not much is seen of them in the hunting field these days, partly because of their value as collectors' items.

As always, bullet selection is the first consideration in loading revolver ammo for hunting large animals, regardless of caliber. With slugs of light-to-normal weights for the caliber, expansion has always been a problem at handgun velocities. Lately, bulletmakers have made great strides in assuring good expansion, at least from about 1,200 FPS up, even to the point of reducing penetration to a dubious level.

HEAVY CAST BULLETS FOR HUNTING

While handgun hunters were waiting for problems of expansion and penetration to be solved, a few of us began monkeying around with very hard cast bullets, and from there began to experiment with heavier and heavier bullet weights. J. D. Jones, of SSK Industries, deserves credit as a pioneer in this field, just as he merits loud huzzas and kudos for his "hand-cannon" cartridges. To make a long story short, we went around plunking our heavyweight revolver slugs into assorted large and sometimes hostile beasts and discovered that they're very reliable killers from any angle, even though they are much too hard to expand noticeably—that is, assuming one could shoot well enough to put them where they belonged.

In calibers .44 and .45, particularly, it was found that the wound channel is wide enough to get quick results after passage of a semiwadcutter at nominal unfired diameter. If that bullet also happens to be a

In revolver cartridges for really big game, many knowledgeable reloaders are going to very heavy, very hard cast bullets. In each caliber grouping here, the left-hand slug represents the "conventional" heavyweight. From left: *(1)* .357 158-grain, 200-grain SSK, and 215-grain Lyman; *(2)* .41 210-grain and 275-grain SSK; *(3)* .44 240-grain, 310-grain and 320-grain SSK; *(4)* .45 255-grain, 295-grain Lyman, and 330-grain SSK.

heavyweight, it can be counted on to drive on to the vitals even from an awkward angle and, usually, to make an exit hole. A large flat nose on this bullet, furthermore, seems to multiply the shocking effect and produce quicker kills, and finally, it damages little or no edible meat. The result is that many of us have abandoned jacketed bullets almost entirely for hunting large, tough game with a .44 or bigger caliber. That word "almost" leaves a little room for the well-shaped but non-expanding jacketed silhouette bullets offered by Speer, Hornady, and Sierra.

How heavy is "heavy?" In caliber .357, 200 to 215 grains; in .41 Magnum, 275 grains; in .44, 310 to 320 grains. In .45 caliber, about 300 to about 350 grains, my personal favorite being 330 grains. Talk about flying sledgehammers! If those weights sound a little scary, especially when I tell you that we drive them pretty close to the handbook velocities for *standard-weight* slugs, I can only suggest you try them. Sure, recoil goes up a little (sometimes a lot!), but you'll be surprised how quickly you get used to it.

A couple of *caveats*: these are cast bullets only (Linotype or heat-treated alloys testing a minimum of about 21 BHN). Jacketed bullets raise pressures and reduce velocities. Also we are *not*, repeat: *not*, using these loads in any but the very strongest, modern, single-action revolvers—Rugers, North American Arms, Sevilles, and Freedom Arms. They are not for the classic SAA Colt (even newly manufactured) nor any of its clones, at least not at top velocities.

Not long ago, I walloped a huge wild boar with a handgun. This animal was shot because he was vermin, although I was pleased to have his trophy-size tusks. Since his flesh was not edible, I decided to utilize his carcass as a test medium for revolver bullets and loads. As you may know, an old boar has a gristle shield, a thickened section of horny hide over his neck and shoulders, as armor against the tusks of other males in dominance battles. This gristle shield can be as much as one full inch thick, like this one, and it is not uncommon to blow up a 240-grain jacketed hollow-point bullet at full velocity from a .44 Magnum on the shield without further penetration.

On this specimen, which weighed about 350 pounds, I tried quite a variety of revolver ammo in hunting calibers, factory and handloads, from 25 yards. All shots were broadside, placed in the shoulder. Exactly one load consistently achieved full penetration and exit, and that was a .44 mag from a 10½-inch-barrel revolver featuring a 310-grain SSK cast bullet at 1,400+ FPS. No jacketed .44 load of any weight got through, nor did any standard-weight .41 Magnum bullets. Nor would a 215-grain Linotype .357 slug from a 10½-inch-barrel Ruger SRM revolver at 1,500+ FPS; I didn't waste time or ammunition trying anything lighter or softer. The runner-up to the heavyweight .44 was a 330-grain .45 at 1,300+ FPS from a Freedom Arms pistol; this one was usually found under the hide on the far side.

For game of the temperament of deer, which are deer size or smaller, these big cast slugs may offer too much penetration, and it is for such game that the excellent jacketed slugs of normal weight offered by all bulletmakers excel. I must say, however, that the older I get and the more game I see shot with handguns, the less use I have for light bullets, for any purpose.

SPECIAL CONSIDERATIONS IN RELOADING HUNTING REVOLVERS

Almost all hunting loads for revolvers are near maximum permissible pressure levels, which calls for care in charging, seating bullets, and crimping. Top quality brass is a requisite, and that means recently manufactured cases in .44 Special and .45 Long Colt. Very old cases in either caliber may be found to have folded or "balloon" heads. Avoid them for anything save mild plinking loads. Better yet, throw 'em away. A tip: I use Federal brass as my standard for quality and strength for the big-caliber revolver cartridges; this is also true in .45 Long Colt.

In selecting a load for heavy hunting bullets, either jacketed or cast, the slowest-burning powders are the first place to look—Winchester-Western 296, Hercules 2400, and Hodgdon's H110 are all universal favorites. With 296 or H110, however, optimum combustion requires three things in the load: a high loading density (100 percent is ideal), a heavy bullet, and a very heavy crimp. All three things contribute to the confinement of the evolving powder gases, which is necessary to attainment of appropriate and consistent pressures.

A heavy bullet forcement, or "pull," is also desirable. This is the force required to push the bullet out of the case neck. Different lots of brass may have different neck thicknesses, and the whole operation involves a little juggling of bullet diameter, case lots, and expander-ball diameters.

The crimp has additional importance in the heavy-bullet loadings. In these, recoil converts the entire

Insufficient flare on the mouths of straight-sided revolver cases often results in crumpled and ruined cases during the bullet-seating step.

"Practical" pistol shooting, placing great emphasis on speed and power, is one of the fastest-growing of all target-shooting games in America. Handloads are the almost-universal choice of top competitors.

With careful development, cast bullets can be made to work well enough in auto pistols to provide a lot of very inexpensive practice. In some well-tuned guns, cast bullets can be as reliable as jacketed slugs.

pistol into a powerful inertia-type bullet puller, and the last round in the cylinder must withstand as many as five firings before its turn comes. If a bullet jumps the crimp and slides forward, it will prevent rotation of the cylinder and put the gun out of action, which can be embarrassing—at the least! Needless to say, the bullet must have a crimping groove to work at all, and with the heavyweight bullets I mentioned earlier, you have to get *serious* about your crimping. The correct crimp actually looks over-crimped. Even when the crimp is correct, it's not a bad idea to rotate the firing order of cartridges in the cylinder and, if possible, to inspect the remaining rounds after a shot or two. The precaution might save you the trophy of a lifetime and a lot of frustration.

TARGET LOADS

Handgun target shooters have little choice but to reload, unless they were fortunate enough to be born rich. Mastery of the pistol requires so much practice that the price of factory loads virtually precludes acquisition of championship skills.

Until fairly recently, almost all serious target competitions were shot with one (or both) of two calibers: .38 Special and .45 ACP. Today, there are so many classes and categories of handgun competition that I must make a distinction between formal, NRA-type "bull's-eye" shooting and the many popular styles of so-called "practical" shooting.

"Practical" simulates combat and includes a variety

of bowling-pin, steel-plate, and other targets under several different sets of rules. All shots are fired against the clock and "from the leather," meaning that the competitor starts with his hardware holstered, and his draw is included in the time. Most practical pistol courses are shot at relatively short ranges, require at least one reloading operation, also against the total time, and have some power restrictions on ammunition that force shooters to deal with realistic recoil levels.

Obviously, the world of pistol competition has undergone quite a few changes since the NRA card-carriers first stood up for leisurely one-handed plinking at scoring rings on paper targets! Nevertheless, bull's-eye shooting still has its followers, and a national championship won at Camp Perry is still a prestigious accomplishment.

The competitor is, of course, concerned with accuracy first and foremost, although mechanical reliability is certainly not unimportant in a match where a malfunction means losing. Handloading ammo that equals the accuracy of industry-loaded match cartridges is not easy. In fact, the goal in such handloading is merely to *equal* factory stuff, and it's likely that most handloads fail to do so. Serious accuracy testing

By eliminating the human variable, a machine rest like this Ransom can compare the accuracy of different ammunitions in a handgun. The rest permits the gun to recoil normally and to be returned precisely to battery, and accepts almost any pistol by means of interchangeable grip adapters (foreground).

requires the use of a return-to-battery mechanical rest for the gun, such as the Ransom or Lee models, to sift the human factor out of the testing, and relatively few reloaders invest in such equipment. Without it, you'll never really be sure of the quality of your loads.

In pistol ammo even more than in rifles, quality results from application of the most painstaking efforts toward absolute uniformity from round to round in the ammunition. As usual, everything begins with good bullets, and since these are usually cast by the reloader, extra care is mandatory in fluxing, temperature control, casting technique, bullet inspection, lubrication, and sizing. Bullet styles are important; most target bullets are either full- or semi-wadcutters, and the hollow-based designs are more difficult when trying to cast target-quality projectiles. Since feeding in autos is involved, the metal must be hard—at least as hard as Linotype to avoid deformation when driven against the feed ramp. Uniform bullet weight is much more important than exact weight. If you weigh all cast bullets and segregate them into groups that vary by ½ grain in average weight, you'll probably discover that both groups shoot about equally well, but that they shoot to measurably different points of impact. Many match-winning handloaders hold the weight range within any one lot of cast bullets to plus or minus .1 or .15 grain.

For match purposes, cases must be the best you have, carefully sorted, all of the same lot and age (if possible), trimmed to identical length. Primers should be all of the same manufacturing lot.

Many powders are used in match .38 and .45 loads, including several so-called shotgun powders, Norma's 1010, Hercules Unique, and others, but Hercules Bullseye still seems to win most of the matches. Charges are very light to reduce recoil and bullet deformation. Depending upon the particular gun, from 2.7 to 3.0 grains of Bullseye are common for the .38 Special with the wadcutter bullets of about 150 grains, and 3.0 to 3.5 grains are used behind typical target bullets in .45 ACP. The determining factor is the pistol itself; use as little powder as needed to work the action, provided accuracy remains good.

The .38s are best crimped lightly to keep the bullet from being driven back into the case when it rams against the feed ramp. Since the .45 headspaces on the case mouth, it cannot be crimped in the usual manner, which rolls the case lip into a groove on the bullet. A long taper crimp is preferable if bullets show a tendency to be seated deeper during feeding. A better idea, if it will work, is reducing the diameter of the expander button in the die so that case mouths have a tighter grip on the bullet. If overdone, however, such cases can squeeze bullets down too much even when the mouth is properly flared before seating bullets. Obviously, a fairly delicate adjustment between various factors is required here, with some experimenting necessary with each gun. A sort of last-resort possibility is rolling a cannelure deeply into the case at the point at which the bullet's base should rest. In the end, it's perhaps a combination of techniques that will best solve the problem.

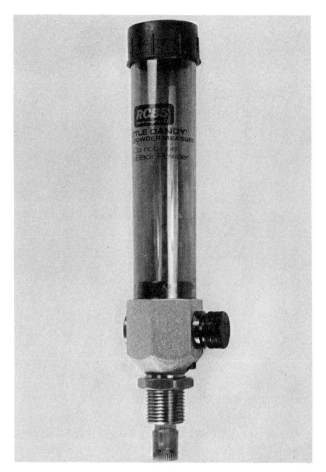

The RCBS Little Dandy is typical of powder measures made especially for the loading of handgun cartridges, using interchangeable, fixed-cavity rotors for fast and precise metering of small charges.

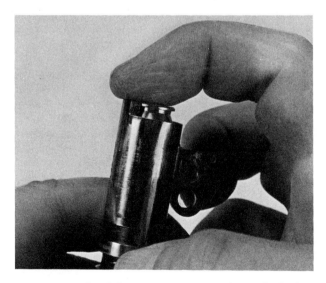

In auto pistols of the common Browning-Colt design, the barrel itself can be used as a headspace gauge for handloads. When a round is dropped into the chamber, the case head should be perfectly flush with the barrel extension.

Even though the .45 target loads will not be roll-crimped, cases must be of uniform length, again because of the headspacing system in these pistols. Short cases can cause weak ignition, and long ones can tie up the pistol. Yet .45 cases may not be trimmed much below normal length in an effort to make them uniform because excess headspace can result. Best bet is careful sorting of cases within a large lot of empties, to find enough that are the same length for loading match ammo.

On the whole, loading competition-grade handloads for target pistols is a tall order, but so many of today's finest target shooters succeed at it that it must not be impossible.

COMBAT AND DEFENSE LOADS

Loading for the practical pistol games and for personal defense are almost the same—almost, but not quite. The major differences are the need for *absolute* mechanical reliability for the latter purpose (a malfunction in a match merely means you lose the match!) and a concern about excessive penetration for home defense. Accuracy is not paramount in either situation because most such shooting is done at targets only a few yards distant. But accuracy is never out of place in a handload if the price is not too high.

The handgun kept for purely defensive purposes may literally be almost any make, model, or caliber ever manufactured, of widely varying quality and characteristics, whereas the gun for most popular combat games will probably be a 1911-style .45 Auto, highly tuned and customized. Still, loads for the game and the grim reality are similar enough in general characteristics to be treated together. Certainly, most loads that are suitable for serious defensive work will be excellent for "practical" shooting, provided the firearm qualifies under the rules.

One more time, everything—literally *everything*—else is subordinated to the need for unfailing mechanical functioning. The gun must not fail to fire, each and every time the trigger is pulled, as long as ammunition remains in the magazine or cylinder.

In sixguns (a few are *five*guns these days), this means careful case preparation and super-careful priming, making certain no lubricant reaches the primer pellets and that all primers are correctly bottomed in their pockets but not crushed. Bullets are carefully crimped in place, for the same reasons that hunting loads are—to hold them firmly against recoil.

Bullet selection is according to different criteria, however. Most encounters in which this ammunition will be fired are at point-blank range, and too much penetration (on either hits or misses) may endanger innocent people elsewhere in the house or vicinity. This, then, is the place for the lighter bullets in each caliber, and, I think, the place for hollow-points at maximum velocities. Some authorities differ; this is my own opinion and my practice. Remember, these cartridges will never be fired except in the direst

This line-up of handloads for the old .45 Colt cartridge suggests the versatility available to a pistol shooter through reloading. At left is a shot load built from a cut-down .410 shotshell. Next, a general-purpose, economical load featuring a cast bullet, followed by a commercial swaged hollow-point load for high performance in the older revolvers. Finally, a low-velocity round-ball load for short-ranged practice, plinking, and pest shooting.

emergency, and the intent is not to inflict a quick and humane death upon a game animal, but to disable a human being bent upon murder, rape, or assault, whether the shooter is an officer of the law or an honest citizen defending his home and family.

In the autoloaders, you have the same problems mentioned in the remarks on autoloading target pistols. You must be certain each round reaches the chamber smoothly, except that here you can accept a bit of bullet-nose deformation at ranges that average about 5 to 7 yards. In general, the same solutions apply as well. The important thing is that the load be tested in the gun in which it will be fired until no doubt whatever lingers about its reliability in feeding, extraction, and ejection. This will involve firing not less than 50 rounds of the load from the clip. Even a single jam or failure to feed is one too many, and the cause must be identified and a cure found. In some cases, the cure will be found in alterations of the pistol itself—a new magazine, polishing the feed ramp, or a new extractor spring. Perhaps the most common alteration is a set of adjustable sights for a handgun that has fixed sights that do not put the most effective defense load on the point of aim.

The reason for my earlier comment that handgunning is the most rapidly changing of all areas of shooting is now apparent. There are pistols now that were hardly dreamed of a few years ago, chambered for cartridges an old-time pistolero wouldn't recognize. Radically new, different, and demanding handgun competitions have become popular. Handgun hunting is no longer a stunt, but a serious discipline on at least the same level as bowhunting. Handgun scopes have yet to catch up with the guns, but the sight of one in a gunshop showcase raises no eyebrows these days. During the firearm-sales doldrums of the early 1980s, *handgun* sales held up better than any other kind.

Patterns of sport shooting are still swirling like smoke from a genie's bottle. It's too early to say what shape they'll take. But one thing is now clear: Americans' love affair with the one-handed gun, once thought to have died with the Old West, is just getting started! And this is despite the best efforts of the Coalition to Ban Handguns; Handgun Control, Inc.; and all the other gun-haters. Of all the chapters in this book, this one would be easiest to expand into a whole volume of its own.

23 Tools for Reloading Metallics

Rifle and handgun cartridges can be reloaded, in a pinch, with a few simple tools scrounged or homemade from bits of scrap metal. I suspect that I could find all the necessary items to assemble reasonably functional cartridges in the rear end of my station wagon at this moment. Decapping can be performed with an ice pick or long, slender nail. Case necks can be squeezed down by forcing them into any sort of orifice of a diameter not too much smaller than the bullets which are to be seated in them, even a hole drilled through a piece of hardwood. Primers can be started in their pockets with the fingers and seated by cautiously tapping the case against a piece of hardwood. Powder can be measured—in loads well below maximum—in any sort of makeshift dipper, and bullets can be started and seated by hand. The result may not be as sophisticated or as pretty as ammo loaded with good tools, but it will function and fire safely and might, in a raw *emergency* survival situation, save your life.

That's doing it the hard way, however, especially with the variety and quality of relatively inexpensive tools on today's market for the home-processing of metallic ammunition.

PORTABLE PRESSES

The basic tool is a press, which can be visualized as nothing more than a simple machine to multiply the strength of a man's fingers and to direct that force conveniently. The simplest are the various portable, or tabletop, models that do not require permanent mounting. The Lee Loaders, the ancient Lyman 310 "tong tool," and the English "Pak-Tool" are examples. These can be used anywhere and stored in a container no bulkier than a cigar box. Some years ago,

after my home had been severely damaged by fire, I lived in a rented apartment for several months while the house was rebuilt. In the apartment, I had no place to set up a regular reloading bench, and much of my equipment was in storage. I did have most of my components available, and I had an English Pak-Tool, plus a powder scale and a set of Lee's graduated powder dippers. With that equipment, I merrily reloaded handgun, varmint rifle, plinking, and even big-game rifle ammo for more than three months. True, I kept loads well below maximum, but they were by no means pip-squeak loadings, and they delivered accuracy equal to the accuracy my guns had demonstrated before. With them, I punched a lot of paper and a few jackrabbits, coyotes, bobcats, crows, and javelinas during those months and felt in no way handicapped, at least for that off-season shooting.

The only drawback to such tools is that production of loaded rounds is somewhat slower than with a good bench-mounted press, and that they cannot full-length resize large rifle cases. The precision possible with these tools may be illustrated by the fact that those far-gone accuracy nuts, the bench-rest shooters, routinely load their ammunition with somewhat more carefully made versions of them. Portable presses are also somewhat less expensive, on the average, than bench-mounted presses and dies, and represent a way for a beginner to get into reloading without an elaborate bench or a large initial investment.

BENCH-MOUNTED PRESSES

Despite the virtues of the portable tools, however, virtually all serious reloading hobbyists sooner or later acquire a bench-type unit, and these are available in quite a variety of styles and price ranges. The simplest

A hand-held reloading tool like this was often furnished with a specific rifle on a custom order about 100 years ago. The separate, L-shaped piece has a decapping pin on one end and a screw-type primer seater on the other.

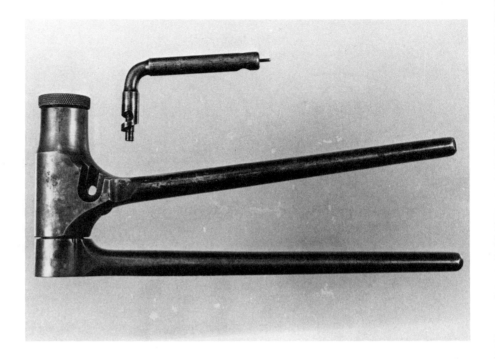

Here is everything necessary to assemble good, safe, accurate handloads without a permanent bench setup. The tooling is a Lee Benchrest set. For submaximum loads, the powder scale could be eliminated and the dipper used alone. The funnel, chamfering tool, and mallet complete the needs for "kitchen-table" handloads.

If you practice with them, a set of Lee graduated powder dippers can provide surprisingly accurate powder charges.

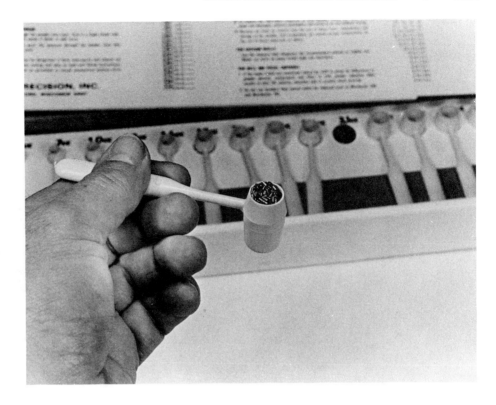

is the so-called "C" tool, which forms the basic element of almost every reloading-equipment manufacturer's line. This is essentially an open-faced frame with the die held in place at the top in alignment with a vertically moving ram, which carries the shellholder. It is driven via a more or less elaborate mechanical linkage by a hand-operated lever. There is a swinging primer-seating arm that enters a slot in the face of the ram and delivers a primer through a hole in the center of the shellholder. About the only possible elaborations of the C-press are a spent-primer catcher and some sort of automatic primer feed. Some presses can be made to operate with either an upstroke or a downstroke, depending upon the operator's preference and type of mounting.

A well-made C-press will serve about 98 percent of anyone's handloading purposes and will do it for a lifetime. Different models may vary somewhat in their mechanical advantage. but all have enough power for normal reloading jobs. The *potential* liability in this type of press is that it could spring slightly under very heavy pressure (only applied in bullet-swaging or extreme case-reforming jobs) and thus lose perfect alignment between die and ram. Most C-tools are heavily built and well designed, and springing is definitely not a problem in normal operations. This is the type of press most reloaders start with, and probably the majority never see any reason to change.

If they do change, it will most likely be to one of the so-called "O" frame presses. They are much like C-presses except that the frame is cast with a structural element to resist that potential springing mentioned above. The open face of the O is usually to the sides or slightly angled, but is to the front in a few models. Leverage and other features, within a given manufacturer's line, are usually the same as on the C-press. The disadvantage of the O-frame (some makers call it a D-frame) is that it interferes to some extent with manual access to the shellholder, especially for left-handed people.

A distinctive and special O-frame press is the RCBS "Big Max," an extremely heavy-duty tool with exceptional mechanical advantage in its linkages, a self-acting "universal" shellholder, overhead priming, and an extension handle for even greater leverage. Of the popular handloaders' presses, this is the one to choose if you contemplate heaviest-duty case forming, bullet swaging, and similar operations.

The next step in this alphabetical galaxy of tools is the "H"-style press, which really differs little from a sideways "O" except that the frame is not in one piece. Instead, the die-holder portion is supported at the top of a pair of sturdy posts which serve as guides of the shellholder portion, which slides up and down. Some H-presses have as many as three die positions, with three corresponding shellholder stations, which speeds up production, especially of handgun ammo.

Then you have the turret presses ("T"-frames?), which carry from four to six die positions in a rotating turret. These are particularly useful if you reload for only one or two calibers. You can leave all dies in place and correctly adjusted at all times. You may also mount your powder measure in one of the turret's die positions, for accelerated production. The Lyman T-Mag turret press offers the added feature of quickly interchangeable turrets.

Left: The RCBS "Rockchucker" is a classic example of the "O"- (or "D"-) frame metallic press. *Right:* This is Lee Precision's lightweight "O" press.

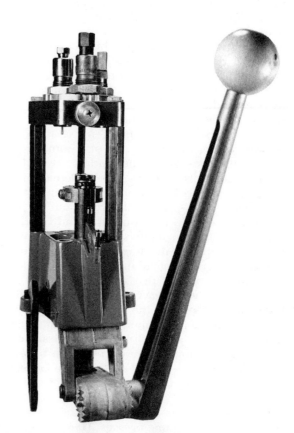

Left: The RCBS "Big Max" is one of the heaviest and most powerful presses, especially suitable for the heaviest-duty reloading jobs, such as bullet-swaging and radical case-forming. *Right:* Lee's three-legged "H" entry is actually a self-indexing turret tool.

Left: The Texan "H"-style press features three die positions with matching shellholder slots. *Right:* Redding makes this turret-style tool.

This complete reloading kit from Lyman features their powerful, six-position turret press.

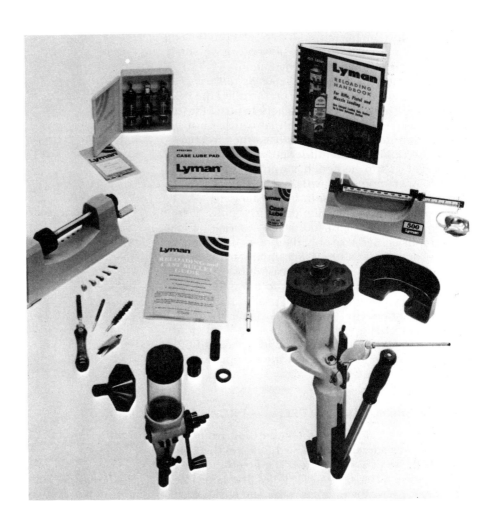

Left: The Huntington "Compac" W-style press can be used as a hand-held tool, or it can be C-clamped to a bench or table. *Right:* Also from Lee, this portable tool utilizes standard dies and shellholders, and has enough power for many full-length sizing jobs.

Turret presses suffer from the same springing problem as other C-type presses, which is essentially what any turret press is, plus the turret must have an axle with some tolerance for free rotation. Deflection under normal workloads, however, is so small that it's not a factor to be worried about.

Continuing the alphabetical analogy, there is also what can be described as a "W" press, called the HDS "Compac." This one is in a category by itself for the following reasons: it's portable and need not be bench-mounted, but unlike most other freehand tools, the Compac can full-length resize large rifle cases. Yet, it can be bench mounted, either with screws or temporarily with a C-clamp. Furthermore, it's engineered to use industry-standard $7/8 \times 14''$ dies and standard shellholders. In contrast the Lyman, Lee, and English portables described a few paragraphs earlier, take only their own, unique dies.

The Compac has a surprising amount of power for a hand-held tool; with a good case lubricant, it requires no extraordinary exertion to move the shoulder of a .30/06 case down to the proper position for a .308 shoulder! The "HDS" in its name stands for "Huntington Die Specialties," the same Fred Huntington (and family) that founded and managed RCBS. So it comes as no surprise that the Compac works.

UNALPHABETIZED—BUT USEFUL—PRESSES

However, the Compac has competition from Lee, which makes a freehand tool with most of the Compac's features at a lower price. The Lee Hand Press, as it's called, also uses standard dies (the same ones you already have for your cartridge) and shellholders.

The Bonanza "Co-Ax" features quick die changes and a universal, self-acting shellholder.

It is lighter than the Compac yet has plenty of power. It has no provision for even temporary mounting on a table or bench. Try as I may, I can't assign an alphabetical designation to this latest offering from Dick Lee, the resident genius at Lee Precision.

Another item that defies alphabet categorization is the Bonanza Co-Ax, a press that's unlike anything else on the market, although it's reminiscent, at a glance, of a modified H-press. It's a light-duty press that handles all but the toughest reloading jobs with ease and speed; I've used a Co-Ax for many, many years with perfect satisfaction. Its most attractive features are its unique snap-in, snap-out die installation, the self-acting, universal (almost) shellholder, and sensitive overhead priming.

PROGRESSIVE PRESSES

The area in which competition between tool manufacturers rages most fiercely these days is that occupied by what have come to be called "progressive"

presses. "Progressive" is a word that has been chosen to distinguish this class of tools from the simpler ones I've been considering until now. Those are called "single-action" presses, because the handle must be operated once for each operation in processing a round of ammunition—each handle cycle, in other words, produces a single action.

In a progressive tool, a cycle of the operating handle does different things to several different cases at one stroke, producing a completed round with each yank. Logically, then, it should be termed a "multiple-action" press, but "progressive" is the word that has stuck. However, brands of presses display several different degrees of progressiveness. In the ultimate degree, everything is automatic. Fired cases, primers, powder charges, and bullets are all fed as needed and assembled into completed rounds that are then automatically dumped into a receptacle. All such a machine requires, other than keeping its magazines and powder hopper filled, is someone to pull the handle. Even that operation can be automated with a hydraulic actuator.

 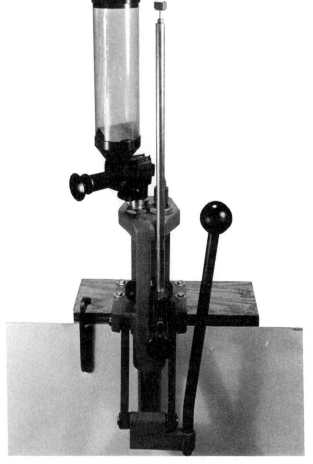

Left: Close to being the ultimate in "progressive" cartridge manufacturing equipment, this from R.D.P. Tool Co. is simply called "the Tool." *Right:* The "progressive" concept in metallic reloading was pioneered by Dillon with this Model 450. Newer Dillon models have been introduced, but this one gives me good service.

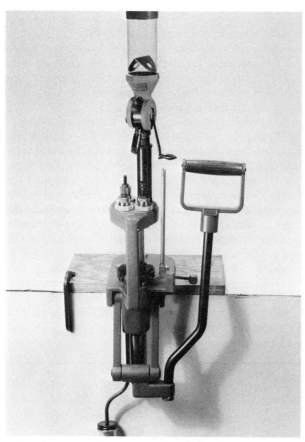 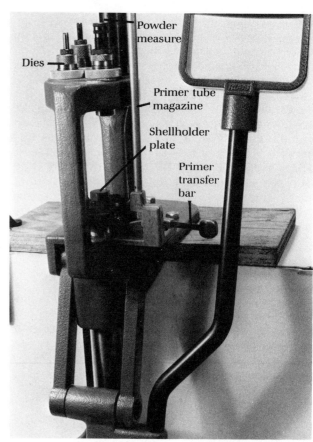

Left: The RCBS "4×4" progressive is one of the best in the business. *Right:* This close-up of the RCBS 4×4 shows primer-handling mechanisms and rotary shellholder plate.

Equipment of this degree of automation is most suitable for shooting clubs, police departments, and small commercial ammo-manufacturing businesses. Few private individuals use ammunition as fast as these machines can produce it, and Joe Handloader will discover that the more automated the equipment, the slower and more tedious is changing over from one caliber to another. Finally, tooling with this capacity is expensive, ranging upwards of $1,500 as of this writing, depending on which bells and whistles are installed. If you're interested, however, by all means look first at "The Tool," made by R.D.P. Tool Company, Inc., of East Liverpool, Ohio. Chances are, you'll need to look no further.

From that level of automation, the progressive loaders range downward through many stages and degrees, and through decreasing price levels as well. The most typical progressive tool requires the operator to feed cases, rotate the shellholder plate or table through the various stations, feed primers manually, and position bullets for seating. He may or may not also have to operate a powder measure and remove completed rounds from the machinery. Such tools—which include the RCBS 4×4, Dillon 550, Hornady Pro–Jector, and Lee 1000—offer a useful increase in production rates (over single-stage equipment) at somewhat elevated prices. All the tools listed

are dressed up O- or D-frames, and all can load any metallic case, from the smallest pistol to the largest rifle calibers. In fact, pistol shooters and survivalists may be about the only shooters with a real need for so much capacity.

In calculating production rates, however, do not forget the time needed to fill primer magazines, powder measures, and other tubes and hoppers, and for installing and adjusting dies when changing calibers. Unless you have an assistant to keep those things full, you'll actually spend more time doing that than loading cases, and all operations must be taken into account in calculating a *sustained* production rate. Even so, 200 or more rounds per hour is not difficult to achieve, with no sacrifice at all in ammo quality. (Single-stage equipment might allow production of 50 to 75 rounds per hour.)

I must point out that tools listed above differ in features offered and price. Some are sold only factory-direct by mail, some include a powder measure; others may include a set of dies. Some feature interchangeable die-plates that materially speed up caliber changeover. Shop carefully to match the tool to your needs.

To me, these progressives are a mixed blessing. I'm distinctly uncomfortable working with any kind of primer magazine, and all the progressive tools employ one. I've seen the destruction a few primers detonating simultaneously can cause, and I'm wary of them outside their factory packaging. If shopping for a progressive reloading tool, I'd pay close attention to the nature of the devices that transport the primers from the magazine to the priming punch.

Another thing that bothers me a bit about progressives—all progressives—is my inability to efficiently inspect cases at any stage of the reloading process, to clean primer pockets, or to visually examine the level of powder in each case after charging. These may not be major criticisms, but they must be considered. They must also be balanced against the real need, if any, for the one feature all progressives offer, which is speed.

I did not intend to leave the impression that progressive tools are a new idea. They are not, in fact; I understand the Star press has been around for years and still sells briskly.

Generally, quality in the press (ram-die alignment, no skimping on material in the frame, finish, and linkage power) is more important to serious reloading than fancy features, and I prefer to pay my money for the former. If extra-heavy-duty service is required, such as swaging jacketed bullets or unusually severe case reforming, by all means select an O-press or H-press; it will be cheaper in the long run.

MISCELLANEOUS TOOLS

I have discussed powder scales and measures, case trimmers, priming tools, and various gauges elsewhere in this book. There are, however, a few other small or specialized tools and necessaries that will facilitate any reloader's work, regardless of his choice of presses.

One of these is the powder funnel, customarily a short-spouted plastic funnel with an inside diameter in the spout which tapers so that the funnel can load almost any case from .22 caliber through at least .45 caliber. Special .17 caliber funnels are on the market, but cases larger than .45, such as the black-powder buffalo cartridges and some British big-game numbers, will require a bit of improvisation. A firm named MTM Moulded Products offers a powder funnel with a detachable 4-inch drop tube. It is invaluable for packing heavy charges into cases in which the best loads are often compressed by seating the bullet. Occasionally a recommended powder charge will actually overflow the case; when this happens, recheck your loading data and, if you find it correct, reach for the long-spouted funnel. It's amazing how much more powder a long drop tube can deposit in the same case volume.

Bullet pullers. Sooner or later, every reloader will find himself faced with the problem of *un*loading ammunition, either to salvage the components or because a loading has proved too hot in his gun. There are two kinds of bullet pullers common today. One is mounted in the loading press and grips the bullet firmly while the shellholder pulls the case away from it. The other resembles a hollow-headed hammer with a device to hold the case head. When the puller

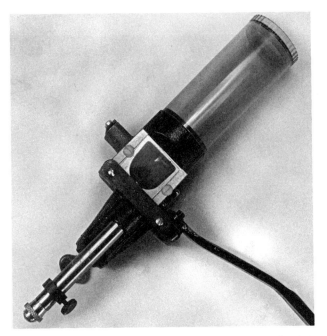 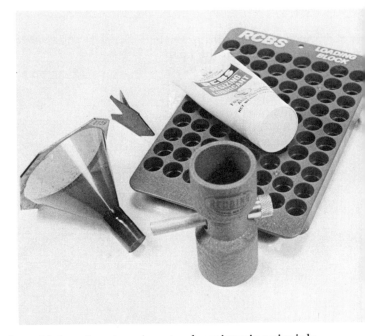

Left: This Belding and Mull powder measure, long popular with benchresters, is not only unique in principle but is also one of the oldest reloading tools still in manufacture. *Right:* Essential small tools and accessories include (clockwise from left) powder funnel, chamfer-deburring tool, loading block, primer-pocket cleaner, and powder trickler. A tube of resizing lube rests upon the loading block.

For correcting mistakes, an inertia bullet puller is as handy around a loading bench as a pencil eraser on a writing desk.

collet for each caliber. *On rimfires, don't use inertia pullers because they grip on the rim and rimfires have soft rims containing priming compound.*

If your inertia puller seems stubborn on old handloads, factory loads, or surplus military stuff, set up your bullet-seating die in that caliber and adjust the seating stem to seat the bullets just ¹⁄₁₆ inch or so deeper. This will break whatever seal may have developed and make pulling the bullets much easier.

Micrometer and caliper. I've mentioned measuring equipment from time to time, but it really cannot be overemphasized. The two basic tools are a machinist's micrometer for ultra-precise measurements on bullets or case-head diameters to the fourth decimal place, and a precision caliper, either vernier or dial-reading, of at least 4-inch capacity. These normally cannot be read closer than about half a thousandth of an inch, but that's sufficient for many handloading jobs. The greater capacity of the caliper also makes it handy for use as a snap gauge in sorting cases by length and similar tasks. Any serious reloader of metallic cartridges should have these two tools, at least, on his bench.

is banged against a hard surface (just as though the operator were driving a nail with it), inertia pulls the bullet. Of the two types of bullet pullers, the press-mounted is probably faster and requires less effort, but the inertia type delivers all components undamaged and ready for reuse. The inertia type is also adaptable to almost any cartridge *except rimfires*, while the press-mounted pullers require a different

Loading block. An obvious essential is the loading block, a wooden or plastic tray with holes in which cases will stand steadily. Blocks with different-size holes are necessary for standard, small-rifle, and magnum cases. The .45/70 and similar cases require a size larger than the belted magnums, and usually have to be homemade by the reloader. It's best to have two of each size, one in which primed cases stand neck down until they are picked up for charg-

Accurate measuring tools are essential to the handloader. Top: A 4- to 6-inch dial caliper reading to .001-inch is probably the all-around most useful, but an 0–1-inch micrometer (left) has advantages for certain jobs. An inexpensive vernier caliper (bottom) is the minimum in precision measuring.

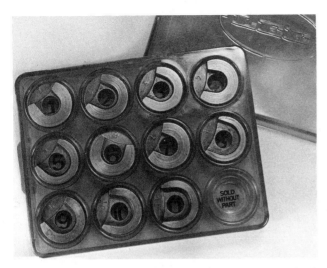

Left: The list of useful minor accessories around a loading bench seems endless. This is a set of shellholders, sold by Lee, which offers the correct size shellholders for more than 99 percent of popular reloaders' calibers. *Right:* This "Nexspander" is a simple way to flare case mouths for seating cast bullets. The case is slipped over the appropriate end and tapped against the bench top.

ing, and another to hold them after powder has been added. If you put one block on each side of the powder measure or scale, you have a built-in procedure for guarding against double charges or no-charge rounds.

Case polisher. I made reference in Chapter 5, on case processing, to tumblers and vibrators for cleaning and polishing fired cases. There is another way to accomplish the same end, and it's probably faster for lots of less than about 200 cases. Sportsman Supply Co. of Marshall, Missouri, sells a set of turned, tapered steel mandrels that can be used in the collet of an electric drill (or other electric motor) as case spinners. Called the Show Me Case Spinners, the set includes seven different spinners to clean any case from .17 caliber through 20mm antiaircraft, shotshells included.

Spinners are easy to use. A case is slipped onto the spinning mandrel, and a cloth loaded with a brass polish is passed up and down the case a time or two, followed by a dry cloth. The case is then slipped off the mandrel, bright and dry. The entire operation takes from about 10 to 30 seconds per case, probably an average of about 15 seconds. When you consider that with a tumbler one still has to sort the cases out of the polishing medium and dump the medium out of each case, the hands-on time for 100 or 150 cases is probably about the same with the case spinners.

Nexpander. Paco Kelly, of Tucson, Arizona, offers a thing called a "Nexpander," which is simply a pair of tapered studs of different sizes mounted base-to-base in a handle. This thing is the fastest way I know to flare the mouths of a batch of brass for seating cast (or jacketed, in straight cases) bullets if the expander stem of your sizing die lacks a flaring step. Effectively,

the case is slipped over whichever of the studs it fits best and its base is tapped on the bench top. With a little practice, it's easy to get just the desired degree of flare with a single tap. My old friend, and managing editor of *Gun World* magazine, Dean Grennell, claims paternity for this gadget, and it has the look of something he'd dream up!

Primer flipper. Another handy and inexpensive item is the primer flipper, a shallow plastic tray with concentric ridges molded into the bottom. Primers (rifle or pistol only; shotshell primers will not work) are dumped into the tray, which is shaken gently from side to side. All the primers will be turned anvil down, which facilitates loading them into a primer-feed tube. If the system requires that they be anvil-up, the lid is put on the tray and the flipper inverted. Even if an automatic primer feed is not featured on your loading equipment, a flipper is useful in reducing the necessary handling of the caps, which, in turn, reduces the chance of primer contamination by oil or grease on the fingers. Offered by RCBS, Hornady, Bonanza, and others, primer turners are all essentially identical.

Case graphiter. Bonanza sells another gadget I've been using for a long time, called a case graphiter. It's a small plastic tray with three different-size bristle brushes mounted in it pointing upward. Powdered graphite is placed in the tray and a case neck pushed down over the brush of appropriate caliber and withdrawn just before sizing. The graphiter deposits a bit of graphite both inside and outside the neck, for quieter, easier sizing and less stretching of the case upon withdrawal of the expander button from the neck. This gimmick costs just a few dollars and is well worth the investment. Only dry lubes should

Such case trimmers are required. These trimmers are typical, from RCBS (left) and Forster.

be used inside a case neck, since liquid or gel-type lubricants catch powder grains when the case is charged and may even inhibit ignition and burning of the powder.

As time goes by, every reloader accumulates a collection of other gimmicks and gadgets, according to his own experience and needs. There are far too many available to be discussed here, but you can bet that if there's any conceivable use for a certain gilhickey on the loading bench, somebody makes and sells it. Now and then one comes to my attention that doesn't even seem to have any conceivable use. Some of these do exactly what their manufacturers claim they will, but I can't imagine why anyone would want to do it. But it may be just what you have been needing. If you have a problem, ask around; chances are there's something on the market that will solve it, no matter how abstruse or exotic your need.

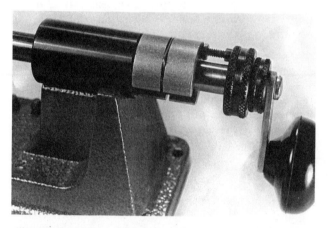

The gray sleeve around the case-trimmer shaft is an RCBS gauge. It eliminates the tedious job of resetting a trimmer to the exact thousandth of an inch after every change.

24 Organizing the Loading Bench

Every reloading book has a chapter on this subject. But the text usually winds up reflecting the author's particular preferences and habits, being less applicable to another reloader's needs or to the space he has available. I promise to try to avoid inflicting my own idiosyncrasies upon you and to confine myself to the Great Universal Truths of organizing a bench.

THE IMPORTANCE OF ROUTINES

The first truth is that systems and routines are vital to satisfaction and safety in reloading. I mentioned one example in the previous chapter, in the discussion of loading blocks. Imagine yourself with a tray full of primed brass, ready for powder charges. If the brass is sitting neck up in the block, and each case is picked up, charged, and returned to the same block, there's an obvious danger that one or more cases will receive a double charge of powder or that some will receive no charge at all. A friend of mine once hurriedly loaded 20 rounds on the night before deer season opened, and somehow managed to skip a row of five cases in the charging step. He also neglected the visual inspection of charged cases, and wound up with one-quarter of his hunting loads duds. Fortunately, this oversight did not cost him a big buck that season, and he didn't discover the powderless cartridges until he began to shoot up that ammunition on the range after the season, but marks on the cases made it clear that those five rounds had been in and out of the rifle's magazine and chamber several times.

This sort of thing couldn't have happened if he'd used the two-block charging system. In this proce-

I built my loading bench into a closet. Its organization results from a couple of decades of experience.

The "two-loading-block" system for positively preventing double charges (and no charges) is shown here, on a very efficient small bench top. Empty cases are turned neck down on the left of the powder measure. Charged cases are turned neck up on the right.

dure, the primed cases would have been standing neck down in one block on the left of the powder measure. Being upside down, none of them could have a powder charge before being picked up and positioned under the measure's drop tube. A second block on the right of the powder measure would have received the charged rounds. This sort of routine becomes a fixed habit, and the reloader comes to consider any case neck up in a loading block as charged, which is not a bad thought pattern to form. The formation of habits at the loading bench is inevitable; so you might as well strive to form those that contribute to efficiency and safety.

Another example is the habit of having no more than one can of powder on the bench top at any time, that one being the can from which the powder in the measure came. Then there can be no chance of emptying the measure into the wrong can. Serious consequences can arise if the handloader happens not to notice the difference in appearance, if any, when next he loads his measure from that can. If he dumps full charges of what he assumes is slower-burning IMR 3031 but is really faster IMR 4198 into his large rifle cases and fires them, he's staring disaster in the eye at close range!

Many routines are established not so much to avoid accidents as to speed up loading. In setting up a shotshell press, for example, the fellow who devotes a little deep thought and study to the placement of his various components—primers, empty hulls, and wads—so as to reduce the number of hand motions required in processing a round of ammunition will very easily be able to increase his output by about one 25-round box per hour with most common loaders.

And he, like the metallic reloader, makes certain that only the correct components for the load being assembled are within reach, to preclude absent-mindedly stuffing the wrong goodies into the case.

TEMPORARY MOUNTING FOR SOME TOOLS

You will have to devise your own procedures and routines to fit your needs and the available space. The important thing is that you be conscious of the value of routines, habits, and systems, and work out those that suit you. Some experimenting with the placement of major pieces of equipment on your bench is well worthwhile before permanently bolting down the tools. This can usually be done by using C-clamps to hold things in place while ammo is actually being loaded, making minor adjustments as you go to suit your right- or left-handedness, your reach, and your manner of doing things. In fact, I never bolt or screw anything down at all, except for my press and powder measure. Everything else is mounted on ¾-inch plywood bases and affixed temporarily with C-clamps. This includes case trimmers, bench-mounted separate priming tools, case gauges, and even shotshell-loading tools. If you are blessed with unlimited bench space (especially "frontage"), you can save a little time by permanently mounting all these items so that they don't interfere with each other, but not many of us are that fortunate.

The placement of powder scales is important; ideally, they should be mounted at eye level, so that you don't have to bend over like a heron stalking a frog to read the swinging pointer without misreading due

A small-parts cabinet, built into the storage space of a loading bench helps organize many small items, such as primers, bullets, tools, and parts.

to angle of view. I built a special shelf for two scales above my bench, and never move them.

DIE STORAGE

Another special shelf is a die rack, drilled with ⅞-inch holes to accept reloading dies. A 6-inch-wide board, ¾-inch thick, will take three such holes (for three-die pistol sets and such) on 2-inch centers. It's probably better to keep dies in their original boxes, but when your collection of calibers exceeds about four, the process of rummaging up the right box from a drawer becomes laborious, and at 20 is intolerable. A cloth can be draped over the die shelf when the bench is not in use to keep dust off the precious dies, and they should get an occasional light spray of corrosion-inhibiting lubricant.

LIGHTING

A really good light is absolutely essential at the loading bench. In addition to whatever area lighting is available, by all means invest in a gooseneck or draftsman-type fixture that permits some flexibility. With it, you can position the bulb properly for in-

RCBS's sheet metal die rack holds enough dies and shellholders for most reloading needs and can be moved about or wall mounted.

specting the level of powder in charged cases, for example, and read delicate verniers, without going blind. Inspecting brass before loading demands good light, as does inspecting cast bullets. All in all, I probably could have begun this chapter with mention of lighting; it's that important.

MAGNET

One of the world's handiest gadgets on a loading bench is a small permanent magnet screwed to the front of a shelf or to the wall. I use one of these to keep track of the assortment of small tools, especially

One of the handiest and simplest gadgets is a small magnet or two for holding small tools such Allen wrenches and screwdrivers.

Lyman sells the wooden organizer rack shown here, a portable item on which a loading press, powder measure, and other tools can be mounted. This makes for a compact and efficient loading setup when no permanent installation is possible.

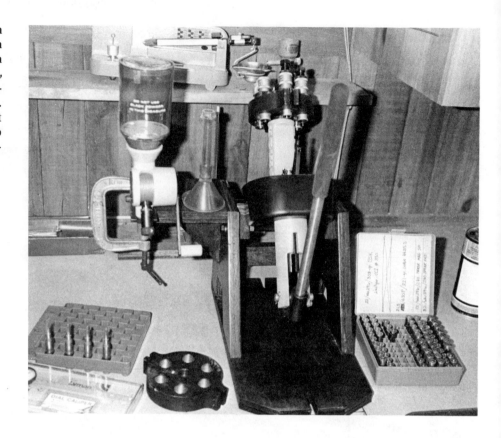

the various Allen wrenches every reloader uses constantly, plus small screwdrivers, flash-hole gauges, and primer-pocket tools. A row of such magnets would be a very neat way of keeping the various shell-holders sorted and easily available, but I use a simple row of small finishing nails driven into the front of the shelf. The same system serves for powder and shot bushings for my shotshell loaders; these bushings are seldom made of ferrous metal, so the magnet idea won't work for them.

BENCH SPACE IS A LUXURY

A perfectly efficient loading bench can be set up in a surprisingly small area. While living in a townhouse with limited space, I once divided a closet in the spare bedroom and built a loading bench into one half, leaving the other half for clothes. The bench top measured only about 27 × 28½ inches, but I happily performed all my reloading there for more than 10 years and never really felt cramped. The secret is to provide sufficient storage for tools, components, and other items above and/or below the bench surface. That way nothing need occupy the bench top save the necessaries for the job immediately at hand.

At the moment I have a secondary handloading center in very tight, makeshift quarters in my "cabin in the woods." Unwilling to devote countertop space to permanently-mounted tooling, I use a Lyman T-Mag turret press bolted to a sturdy, movable workstation (also sold by Lyman). This particular press

must be mounted at the angle shown in the photograph, but many current models can be mounted vertically, and the workstation is adjustable. I mount the powder measure to a shelf on the mounting, so nothing need be tied down to the bench top, and the entire rig can be stored away when not in service. This might not be an ideal setup for permanent, or heavy-duty, loading operations, but it serves my purposes ideally. It would serve many handloaders as a full-time arrangement in an apartment, for example.

COMPONENTS STORAGE

Components storage on, under, or around the loading bench should be given a bit of thought from the point of view of safety. Primers of various sorts and sizes are probably best organized in one of the multidrawered small-parts cabinets whose plastic drawers will hold about six boxes of rifle or pistol primers. If you buy primers by the thousand, store the rest elsewhere. Keep only those types of powder that you use regularly within reach of the bench, and store other types and quantities in your powder magazine. Never keep more powder in an open container, including your powder measure, than you have immediate use for, and never store primers and powder in close proximity to each other. Warnings about storage of primers *only* in the factory packaging bear repeating.

Finally, keep a fire extinguisher within easy reach at the loading bench and close to every other area where powder or primers are kept.

Reloading Record Keeping

I am not a guy who enjoys keeping records. I have trouble keeping my checkbook balanced and am the despair of the IRS when it's audit time. But I can show you, in 5 minutes or less, the full dope on *every* handload I've ever put together, without any exceptions. Record keeping is a pain in the posterior, but it's vital to handloading progress and safety. If you neglect it, the day will come when you will regret it, and you can write that down and say I said it!

THE POSSIBILITIES ARE ENDLESS

For any single cartridge, there are literally thousands of different possible combinations of powder, charge weight, and bullet, not to mention primers, brass, and other variables. Even if you stick with only one bullet weight, brand, and style, there are hundreds of possibilities. No human being can keep in mind forever every formula ever tested in a given cartridge, much less group sizes, velocities, trajectory data, recoil sensation, pressure symptoms, and all the other observations made while firing each combination. If a reloader loads for four or five cartridges, or 20, he'll have to have the mental storage banks of a computer to get by without record keeping.

Good records are more than a convenience or merely a means to avoid duplication of past efforts; they can facilitate the development of a new load by presenting data on past experiments in an orderly fashion to suggest logical avenues for further improvement. They can save a great deal of work by reminding the reloader that a certain rifle seems to prefer one powder over another, that a given bullet in that rifle needs a certain minimum velocity to sta-

bilize properly, or that a specific lot of brass has been fire-formed in one particular rifle.

Most custom bullet manufacturers pack gummed labels with their bullets; labels can be attached to an ammo box and filled out with the pertinent data. Labels are handy for identifying the load in the box, but they are not intended to serve as adequate reloading records. Some sort of permanent records system is still required, and it should be complete, easily stored, and capable of preserving your data in readily retrievable form. This is fairly easy to do.

MINIMUM DATA REQUIRED

At the very minimum, this system should include *all* of the following for *each* loading:

Date loaded	Notes on pressure
Number of rounds	signs, purpose
Charge weight	load, etc.
Powder designation	Case brand
Bullet brand	Times fired (cases)
Bullet weight	Range
Bullet style	Group sizes
Primer brand	Velocity
Primer size and type	

Additional data on the load that is desirable if not absolutely necessary include powder lot number, primer lot number, an identifying number or code for each different loading, and sundry other notes and observations from firing tests, such as recoil, blast, consistency, case-head expansion measurements, temperature and weather conditions during firing, and anything else that will help in future load development.

EVOLUTION OF MY DITTO DATA SYSTEM

Quite a few manufacturers have attempted to publish handloaders' record books, most of them set up with one or perhaps two loads per page. This demands an enormous amount of writing, especially in a pressure series in which nothing changes from load to load except the powder charge weight. Being lazy, years ago I developed a reloading record system of my own that spared me vast amounts of repetitive scribbling. This system arranged all the data for each load in vertical columns, so that I could use ditto marks for those elements that did not change. I have used this system for about 30 years, and it has proved to have quite a few advantages. And some of them were unforseen.

It keeps data in a very compact form, so that many years' experience with dozens of different cartridges is easily stored in a single loose-leaf binder. Furthermore, the data is presented so that it's easy to retrieve, merely by running a finger down a column. For example, if I'm curious as to whether I ever tried

IMR 3031 powder in the .308 WCF case, I can run down the "powder" column on my home-designed, mimeographed form over three or four pages and extract data on every 3031 load I ever fired in that cartridge.

I may very well not be the originator of the ditto-data idea (there's very little new under the sun in any aspect of handloading), but I was certainly the first writer to present the idea in various magazines and annuals catering to shooters. Recently, not one but two firms have introduced handloading record books patterned directly on my system, accidentally or otherwise. Although I am in no way connected with these companies and receive no royalties or other compensation (my form was never copyrighted and was offered freely in my articles), I shall refrain from mentioning the names of these products here. Your reloading dealer doubtless can show them to you. They may or may not be an improvement on my original system, depending on your personal needs. In any event, my own form is reproduced here and you are free to adopt or modify it as you choose. My form has stood the test of my own experience with thousands of different loads for scores of cartridges, and I can think of no way to improve it for my own needs.

My "Ditto Data" system is so fast, compact, and easy to retrieve data from that, to date, no computer program that has come to my attention has been able to match it.

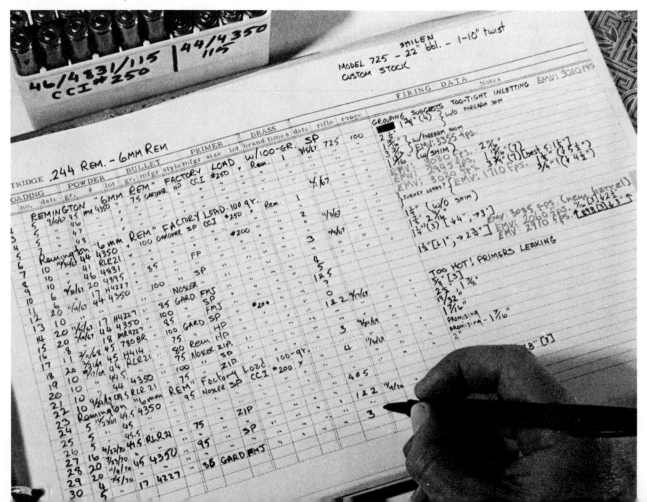

SETTING UP THE DATA SYSTEM

From left to right, under the heading *LOADING*, you will find columns headed *#*, *No.*, and *Date*. The first is my numerical code for the particular loading, the *No.* refers to the number of rounds of that combination assembled, and *Date* is the date I put them together. Totaling the numbers under the *No.* heading gives the total number of rounds fired in that rifle (or caliber, at least), and may eventually give an indication of barrel life, among other things.

Under *POWDER*, we have columns headed *Gr.* (charge weight in grains); *#*, which refers to powder designation (usually a number); and *Lot*. Lot numbers are stamped on powder canisters, and, since certain powders are known to change characteristics from lot to lot, this may be a valuable bit of data for safety purposes or to unravel the causes of mysterious pressure signs.

The *BULLET* heading is self-explanatory, including columns for *Gr.* (weight), *Mfgr.* (maker), and *Style*. The last column may be filled with such notes as *RN* (round-nose), *HP* (hollow-point), *FMJ* (full metal jacket), and *SPZ* (spitzer).

Under *PRIMER* will be found three columns, which seem to me to be self-explanatory, *Mfgr.* (brand), *Size*, and *Lot*. Most manufacturers give their large rifle magnum primers a different size designation from that of their large rifle standard caps, and this number goes into the *Size* column. Primer lots are stamped on the boxes.

Surely the *Brand* heading under *BRASS* requires no explanation. *Times* refers to the number of times these cases have been fired.

The final major heading, *FIRING DATA*, includes columns for the date fired, the particular rifle in which the tests were conducted, the distance at which the firing occurred, and a space for notes. The *Notes* column always includes group sizes (and number of shots per group in brackets) and velocity (if chronographed). In browsing back through my data book, I find many other notes to myself in this column, concerning observations of seating depths, warnings that certain loads are "TOO HOT!" or that the load was worked up for African game and slew this or that animal. Sometimes I refer myself to "Load #103" of the same cartridge for a comparison of velocity or some other aspect that interests me.

THE JOURNAL

My "Ditto Data" book always goes to the rifle range with me, and I enter appropriate data while it's fresh

This reduced reproduction of my Ditto-Data system of records on my handloads may also work well for you. I've not run across another that would serve me better.

CARTRIDGE

LOADING			POWDER			BULLET			PRIMER			BRASS		FIRING DATA			
#	no.	date	gr.	#	lot	gr.	mfgr	style	mfgr	size	lot	brand	times	date	rifle	range	Notes

One feature of a handloading journal is its record of powder-scale settings, for quick return to previously established charge weights.

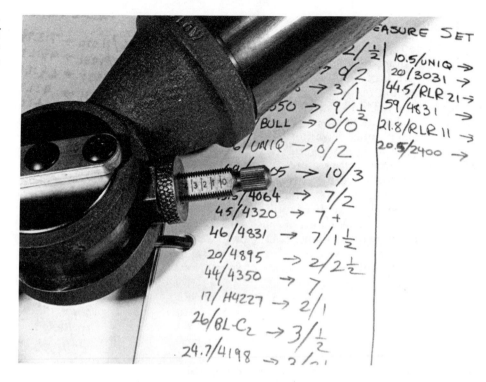

in my mind. I also maintain a 5 × 8-inch loose-leaf notebook as a journal of shooting activities and catch-all notebook for any dope that does not appear on the data forms. In this book I keep all manner of odd-ball observations, outline future loading programs, maintain complete chronograph data (only corrected muzzle velocities go into the data book forms), record powder-measure settings for pet loads, and jot down theories and speculations on how to improve performances in various guns.

In this book, by the way, I keep all shotshell reloading data (all the above applies to metallic cartridges only), including all components of each shotshell load plus patterning analyses, pressure and velocity where known, and general performance notes.

These two books represent the distilled experience gained from about 30 years of handloading ammunition, and there is a rather peculiar effect that develops through such note-taking. Each bit of information recorded comes to amplify and illuminate all the other bits, so that the body of data accumulated really does exceed the sum of its parts. Over the years, the contents of these binders have proved to be by far the most valuable source of reloading information I have, far more useful in my guns and for my purposes than any amount of commerically published handloading dope. With faithful and meticulous record keeping, so will yours.

The real worth of my collection of data was painfully brought home to me when my home burned. I was away from my home at the time, and had several hours' drive to get back after news of the fire reached me. All the way home, through the small hours of the morning, I found myself wondering fearfully if my reloading records had been destroyed. I was con-

The MTM Handloader's Log, a commercially published reloader's record-keeping system, is one of several that use a modified version of my form.

cerned, of course, about all the contents of the house, but those irreplaceable records worried me most.

When I discovered that they were safe, I speedily had every page of both my data book and my journal photocopied and tucked the copies away in a safe place. It may be argued that I make my living writing about such matters, and that my accumulation of data was more valuable to me than a hobbyist's. That may be true from a dollars-and-cents viewpoint. Still, every reloader's records are priceless for his own purposes, and the idea of photocopying them for safe storage, perhaps annually, is a very sound one.

26 Loading for The Shotgun

According to somewhat dated sales figures on all kinds of small-arms primers, at least half of all cartridges handloaded in the United States are shotshells, and the total amounts to more than half a *billion* rounds annually. The great majority of these are target loads to be fired at clay pigeons over skeet, trap, and sporting clays ranges. A serious competitor at any of these games has little choice but to reload his practice ammo, unless he happens to be blessed with a six-figure income, simply because it is necessary for him to shoot so much. At a minimum, he'll probably average 50 to 100 rounds per day, perhaps three or more days each week, all year. For the rifleman-reloader, by contrast, four or five five-shot groups is a fair day's shooting.

DON'T OVERLOOK PERFORMANCE

Except for those who go after mourning doves and pests such as crows, most hunters hardly fire enough shells in the field to justify a loading setup, unless they have need for some special kind of load, which isn't available on the commercial market, or unless they just happen to enjoy experimenting, refining, and perfecting shotshell loadings in the same way that riflemen do. Therefore, many gunners reload all practice target ammo, and purchase factory cartridges for hunting.

If economy is the major motivation for handloading shotshells, performance should not be slighted, and it need not be, these days. When I began reloading shotgun ammunition, it was looked upon in most quarters as a sort of occult art. In those days, plastic cases were unheard of, folded crimps were brand

The two extremes of pattern-changing handloads: At left is a spreader load with the shot charge divided by "B" cards, while at right is a special, long-range load with perforated cushion wad, plastic wrapper, and copper-plated shot.

new, and one-piece wad columns may have been a gleam in somebody's eye but were certainly not available over the counter. We were lucky to get three or four loadings out of a single waxed-paper hull, and we laboriously built up wad columns of nitro cards and filler wads made of fiber, felt, or cork. Plastic shot wrappers were beginning to look like a good idea, and the most revolutionary development in sight was the cupped plastic overpowder wad.

All that has changed. Indeed, shotshell loading has been the fastest-moving of all reloading areas. Tooling, components, and techniques have all seen radical improvements. In the old days, we were reasonably well satisfied if our handloads went BANG and broke an occasional claybird or peppered a hapless tin can. Today, it's possible to load shotshells that are the full equal of the best factory loads in every respect.

I did say "possible," not "easy." Whereas a rifleman or pistolero routinely expects to improve on factory performance with handloads, at least in his own guns, the shotgunner does well to *match* commercial ammunition and very rarely betters it. A good deal is written in the sporting press about super-shotshell handloads. Such results can be achieved through careful experimenting with an individual gun, but the truth is that the same amount of experimenting with factory loads of various brands and types will usually deliver about equally good results.

Why, then, bother with loading shotshells, except for the cost savings? Well, lowered shooting costs constitute a pretty good reason when we're talking about savings of at least $30 to $40 per case of ammo. Then, too, there are many special-purpose loadings, which the factories cannot market economically but an individual gunner may find useful. "Brush" or

"spreader" loads that can throw improved-cylinder patterns from a Full-Choke barrel are still cataloged but rarely seen on dealers' shelves. Furthermore, they are available only in 12-gauge with 1⅛ ounces of No. 8 shot, at only one velocity. If you'd like choke-opening loadings for decoyed ducks with No. 6 shot, or with a heavier shot charge, you'll have to put them together yourself. Conversely, if your barrel is Modified and some of your duck shooting is at long range, handloads can probably come closer to delivering really good long-range patterns than factory ammuniton. Very light loads for maximum savings and minimum recoil are not commercially made but can be handloaded very simply. In short, there are quite a few excellent reasons for reloading shotshells besides economy.

The handloader must shift mental gears when going from metallics to shotshells. Velocity, in and of itself, is not very important in shotshells. I suppose that all of us go through a phase of playing with ultra-high velocities in shot charges, but we get over it when we discover that we're killing no more birds, if as many, and soaking up prodigious quantities of recoil in the process. I long ago standardized velocities of all my shotshell loads, in all gauges, between about 1,165 and perhaps 1,215 FPS. The reason is simply that shot pellets, being spheres, have the poorest possible ballistic coefficient. The difference in striking power at game ranges between a pellet that started out at 1,200 FPS and one launched at 1,350 FPS is so small as to be negligible. In the meantime, the high-velocity loading kicks like a mule and rarely delivers patterns as dense and uniform as those from normal-speed ammo.

Another difference between metallic and shotshell

Height of the components column inside a shotshell before crimping determines the success of the crimp, if hulls are equal. The left-hand pair show correct height and good crimp, the middle ones show too-short a column and resulting dished crimp. Those at right: too high a column and poorly closed crimp.

cartridges is that the latter must come out at a fixed length, whereas overall length in a rifle cartridge can vary somewhat according to the seating depth selected for the bullet. The contents of a shotshell (powder, wadding, and shot) must stand at exactly the right height in the uncrimped hull, in order to get a good, firm crimp and complete closure. If the volume of one of the components is reduced, that of one of the others must be increased by the same amount. Otherwise, the crimp will be bulged and may open up enough to leak shot, or it will be dished and loose. Either condition is likely to cause abnormally high variations in velocity from shot to shot, since a firm, uniform crimp is perhaps the most important factor in uniform ignition and combustion of shotshell powders. Adjustment of the total volume of components in a shell using one of the one-piece plastic wad columns is simpler, since most of these incorporate a collapsible cushioning section that can be compressed enough in crimping to achieve the desired results. However it's accomplished, though, the reloader must fix firmly in mind the concept of a good crimp—not too deep, not too high, but just right. Good crimps are among the keys to good results in shotshell loading.

PATTERN IS CRUCIAL

The critical concept in scattergun feeding is *pattern*. In a rifle, accuracy, velocity, and trajectory are everything. In a shotgun, they're nothing. Pattern is the whole ball game. A good pattern is what breaks targets or kills birds. A load that patterns poorly in a given gun barrel is useless, regardless of velocity or energy figures. Each of the components in the load has its effect upon patterns. Cases themselves are least important, but a worn-out case cannot hold a firm crimp and thus contributes to variable shot-to-shot performance. The type of powder used does not, in general, make much difference in patterns, but the pressure it generates and the rate at which it generates it can make quite a difference. Fast-burning powders with short, high time-pressure curves accelerate the shot charge more violently, deforming more pellets and causing flyers. Slower-burning propellants get the whole column moving a little less abruptly and tend to preserve the perfect roundness of more of the pellets. Deformed pellets are fatal to both density and uniformity in the pattern.

The wad column, whether one piece or built up, serves several functions. First, it must contain the powder gases behind it. Gas that leaks into the shot charge raises hob with patterns. Second, the wad column must cushion the onslaught of the gases, permitting the shot charge to begin its acceleration down the barrel as gently as possible. Otherwise, the pellets at the rear of the charge will be mashed together, deformed, and perhaps even fused into clumps. Third, most modern wad columns incorporate either a plastic cup which carries the shot safely clear of the muzzle or a plastic wrapper intended to protect the pellets from contact with the barrel walls. Either element reduces the scrubbing effect of such contact and, again, delivers more undeformed shot.

Finally, the shot itself has an effect on patterns. Most shot pellets are alloyed to at least a minor degree, rather than being pure lead, but certain brands and kinds are deliberately made much harder than usual. The harder pellets, of course, resist deformation better than soft ones. Some kinds of pellets are copper- or nickel-plated for the same purpose and, although expensive, do pattern better if all else remains the same.

Soft iron, usually called "steel," shot is in a class by itself, by far the hardest of all commercially accepted kinds of pellets. It does not deform at all during firing, and all pellets arrive at the muzzle in perfect shape. This results in short shot strings and uniform, relatively dense patterns. However, this is not to say that steel is the ideal pellet material, as I will point out later in this chapter.

If this brief discussion suggests that the number-one goal in a shotshell load is to get as many of the individual pellets in a shot charge as possible out of the muzzle in a state of pristine sphericity, it has served its purpose. Round pellets fly true; flat-sided or mashed ones spin away at divergent angles and are lost to the pattern.

SHOT-MASS FLUIDITY

The second major concept in shotshell patterns that must be firmly grasped is that of the shot charge as a *fluid* mass, rather than a solid. As the charge begins to move under the impulse of powder gases, it is shortened as the rear pellets move before the front ones in the mass. The charge is then driven out of the case and through the forcing cone in the chamber, being lengthened again as the diameter is reduced. Finally, the shot column must pass through the choke restriction, if any, and again its diameter and length are changed. As it leaves the muzzle, the charge immediately begins to expand in diameter, but it also begins to lengthen as deformed pellets slow down more rapidly than perfect ones. By the time a charge of lead shot has reached 40 yards it may be as much as 10 feet long and 40 inches or more wide. Steel-shot strings are much shorter.

Throughout this rather violent journey, the pellets move in relation to each other, and the charge itself, as a whole, does react somewhat as a fluid. Anything that tends to preserve this fluidity (such as cushioning wads or extra-hard pellets) also tends to improve the density and uniformity of resulting patterns. And any element that tends to disrupt the fluidity of the shot charge tends to reduce pattern density, at least, and usually injures pattern uniformity as well. Salt that idea in the back of your mind and never forget it; it will explain many mysteries and open many doors on the way to shotshell-loading satisfaction.

PATTERN TESTING AND EVALUATION

Patterning your handloads in your shotgun is, obviously, the fundamental process in load-testing. Patterning is a bit of a nuisance and certainly time consuming if done correctly, but it's the one and only way to know whether you have reached your goal. You can fire one shot at an old cardboard box at some unknown distance, step up and eyeball the little holes, and learn exactly nothing whatsoever. Shotshell patterning must be done as systematically as group-shooting with a rifle. There's a great deal more information than one might suspect contained in a stack of fired pattern sheets. It's right there before your eyes, but a little knowhow is required to extract it.

First, pattern evaluation should be based on not fewer than five shots with each load, perferably 10. Basic patterning is done at a measured 40 yards, although some special-purpose loads may also be tested at greater or shorter distances. The best and cheapest testing medium is brown wrapping paper, which can be purchased in 4-foot-wide rolls. Sheets of this 4 feet square are suitable for pattern testing and can be stapled to a simple wooden frame before a safe backstop. Mark an aiming point at the center of the sheet, step back 40 yards, shoulder the gun, and fire quickly.

The usual instructions at this point urge you to draw a circle, 30 inches in diameter, that encloses

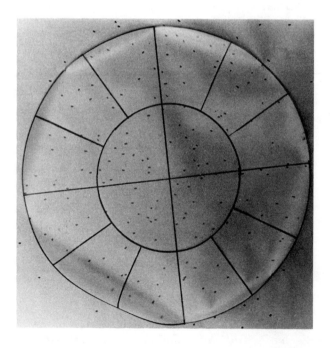

The quickest means of applying the 16-field pattern-evaluation target is to draw it on translucent acetate. When you lay the acetate over a shotgun pattern on brown wrapping paper, you can see pellet holes and count them without needing to draw the 16 fields on each pattern.

the greatest possible number of pellet holes. The relationship of the center of this circle to the aiming point provides information as to whether your guns shoot where they look, something that's worth knowing. The number of pellet holes inside the circle, as a proportion of the number originally launched, gives a good idea as to whether your barrel actually delivers the degree of choke that's marked on the barrel, with that load and particularly with that shot size. The accompanying tables of pellets per load and choke percentages will facilitate that determination. About the only other bit of information available from your marked-off circles is an eyeball evaluation of any gross patchiness or gaping holes in the pattern.

There is much more to be learned from those riddled sheets of paper, however, knowledge that the serious reloader needs, and here's how to derive it.

THE 16-FIELD TARGET

Acquire a large sheet of clear plastic such as engineers and draftsmen use for overlays on engineering drawings. This can be had slick both sides, matte both sides, or matte one side, and it really doesn't matter which you can get. On this sheet, with a felt-tipped marking pen, draw a 30-inch circle. Using the same center, draw another circle inside the first one, with a 7½-inch radius, or half the diameter of the outside circle. Now quarter the whole figure with a horizontal and a vertical line, as shown, like crosshairs in a rifle scope. Finally, divide the outer ring of the pattern into 12 panels with lines at 30-degree intervals. This sheet of plastic can now be laid over a pattern and moved around to catch the greatest number of pellet holes, and no longer do you need to actually scribe circles on the paper itself. Pellet holes are visible through the plastic.

You now have something called a Berlin-Wannsee 16-field target, a remarkably useful instrument for wringing information from a bunch of sheets of paper with shot holes in them. Each of the 16 areas marked off in the target is equal in area to each of the others, and the ratio of the area of the inner circle to that of the outer, doughnut-shaped ring is 1:3. Specifically, the whole pattern encloses about 707 square inches, the inner circle encloses about 176 square inches, the area of the outer doughnut is about 530 square inches, and each of the 16 fields amounts to about 44 square inches.

The first measurement to be made after determining the total number of hits inside the 30-inch circle is the distribution of those hits between the inner circle and the outer doughnut. If the doughnut has about three times the number of pellets as the inner circle, that pattern can be considered at its most efficient range. If the inner circle has, say, the same number of hits as the outer ring (in only one-third the area, remember), the pattern is markedly denser in the middle, and will probably spread to maximum uniform coverage at a greater distance. This is one of the marks of a good long-range load, but is highly undesirable in a skeet load where the average range will be about 21 yards.

The evenness of the patterns is revealed by how nearly similar the pellet counts are in the 16 fields. If the patterns show as few as 2 or 3 pellets in some fields and perhaps 20 or more in others, consistently, you can only conclude that this particular loading seems not to deliver uniform patterns in this particular gun. Such patterns will usually reveal several large holes through which a dove or clay pigeon might escape. There is no such thing as a perfect shotgun pattern, however, so that a ratio of about 2:1 between the densest and sparsest fields can be considered about normal. Anything better than that is probably coincidental.

Finally, the 16-field target can show whether the load being tested has sufficient saturation for the game in question. Many years ago an Englishman named Sir Gerald Burrard devised a formula by which you can approximate the target area in square inches of various gamebirds. According to Burrard, 88 percent of the bird's weight in ounces roughly equals the target of head, neck, and body from typical angles, in square inches. This proportion permits us to relate the areas of our 16-field target to the game we intend to hunt with a given handload. A mourning dove weighs about 4.5 ounces. By Burrard's formula, this translates to a target area of only 3.96 square inches, which means that there's room inside our 30-inch circle for no fewer than 178 mourning doves! That gives some insight into just how dense and uniform a pattern must be to reliably kill doves.

On the other hand, an average wild turkey gobbler presents about 261 square inches of target, and would fit into the 30-inch circle 2.7 times. However, more than one body hit is obviously required to down a turkey, and pellets for this must be large for the necessary energy to penetrate heavy feathers. Not less than 8 pellets, not smaller than No. 2, are needed which means that a perfectly distributed pattern of only about 22 pellets could do the job on a gobbler. This is the saturation concept. Naturally, since perfect distribution cannot be expected, you'd like to see 30 or 40 pellets in the load. Since even a 1¼-ounce load of No. 2s contains 112 pellets, this suggests that for the turkey load, you could go up to one of the smaller buckshot sizes, assuming the gun patterned the large shot equally well. (Most of us, of course, prefer a head shot with smaller pellets on wild turkey, but Burrad's formula does not apply to *heads*.)

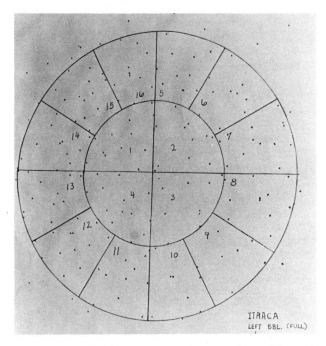
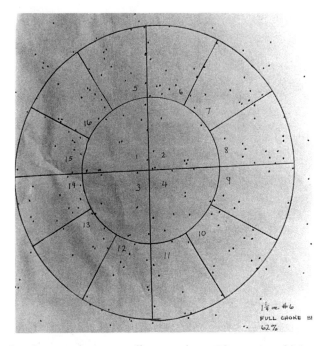

Left: The 16-field target superimposed on this pattern clearly reveals an excellent pattern. The ratio of hits in the inner circle to the outer ring is 1:2.8, showing very little central thickening in pellet distribution. Pellet counts in the individial fields are, in numerical order, 12, 11, 10, 13, 11, 10, 12, 11, 7, 7, 11, 13, 14, and 11. Uniformity is thus exceptional, with plenty of coverage for any sort of game on which such a load is suitable. This pattern is even, dense, well-balanced, and saturated. *Right:* At a glance, this pattern might not appear too bad, but superimposition of the 16-field target shows it to be pretty poor. First, it's a weak modified pattern although fired from a full-choke barrel, with only 173 of the original 280 pellets (62 percent) in the 30-inch circle. The 1:3.6 ratio between hits in the center and those in the outer ring indicates the pattern is already beyond its optimum range, even at 40 yards. Pellet counts in the various fields show poor distribution, with many gaping holes through which a bird could fly unscathed. A hunter firing this load could blame his gun-pointing, when the trouble is actually in his ammo; the 16-field target tells the story.

One more example: A drake mallard weighs about 45 ounces, which equals just under 40 square inches of profile, or approximately the area of one of the 16 fields in the Berlin-Wannsee target. Tests have proved that such birds require four to five hits from No. 4 shot for dependable kills. Therefore, a saturated duck load must produce that many holes in each of the fields, at a minimum, plus a safety margin to take care of unequal distribution of shot over the whole 30-inch circle, say a total charge of 120 pellets. Even

a ⅞-ounce shot charge of No. 4s has about that many individual pellets, and a 1⅞-ounce 12-gauge 3-inch magnum load has more than twice the maximum necessary lead for ducks.

All these things the 16-field target can make apparent when it's laid over an innocent-looking sheet of peppered paper. This is the heart of pattern evaluation of handloaded shotshells, and patterning is the backbone of shotgun performance. Based on information from such testing, intelligent decisions can

The key to satisfactory shotshell loading is in proper matching of all the components in the load: the right wad in the right hull with the correct powder, charge, and primer. These rounds all do the same thing, employing three different case types, three different wads, and three kinds of powder. Follow load formulas to the letter for best results.

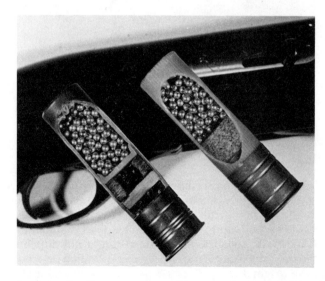

Left: A reloader can often add as much as 10 full yards to the effective range of his shotgun. These loads may be tedious to assemble, but relatively few will be required in a hunting season. *Right:* Factories once loaded special "brush" or "spreader" loads to adapt tightly choked guns to short-range shooting. If you need such ammunition today, however, it must be handloaded.

The range of shot charges for the 20 gauges—standard and magnum—is shown here.

be made about shot size, gauges, and chokes. The testing must, of course, be done at the range at which the game in question is most often fired upon.

Every barrel will handle different sizes of shot a little differently. In fact, the choke designation stamped on a shotgun barrel is really only a mechanical measurement of the actual constriction in the choke, and is not a reliable indication of the patterns that barrel will throw. Every barrel has at least two or three different performance levels, depending upon shot size, type, velocity, and other factors in the load. Reloading can, therefore, actually change the choke of a shotgun barrel. In the hands of a handloader, a modified barrel, for example, can usually be made to pattern anywhere from improved cylinder to full choke by varying components.

Considering the cost of additional shotguns, or even extra barrels, that alone isn't a bad reason for reloading shotshells.

27 Shotshell Components

Shotshell loading doesn't lend itself well to "creative handloading." The name of the metallic-reloading game may be trying different combinations until the right one is found, but the reloader of shotgun ammunition is much more limited. The reason is that shotguns are not constructed with the inherent margins of strength of rifles, or even of pistols, and shotshell powders are very fast-burning. For example, centerfire rifles chambered to modern cartridges may be expected routinely to contain more than 50,000 PSI, and some of the single-shot handguns work at the same levels. Even garden-variety .44 Magnum revolvers are built for 40,000 PSI (and up, in a few cases), but a 12-gauge shotgun is being overpressured at 12,000.

STICK TO PUBLISHED DATA

Random substitutions of shotshell components, even seemingly innocuous ones, in established recipes can produce completely unexpected results, most of which will not be happy. This is not to say that such substitutions are *necessarily* disastrous, or that it's impossible to produce a useful load in this way. It is merely that size and direction of pressure changes cannot be predicted on the basis of any indicators now available to the reloader. One of the best-performing loads I ever worked up, for example, combined a Remington hull, CCI primer, Alcan powder, and Winchester wad. Pressure was normal and the PSI spread a very low 700 PSI. Velocity was right on the money at 1,205 FPS, and velocity spread (from the fastest to the slowest shots in a 10-shot string) was an unbelievable 8 FPS. I should add, however, that I had access to a modern ballistic laboratory with

pressure- and velocity-measuring equipment when I developed that loading. Very few handloaders are lucky enough to have such an advantage, and their best—indeed, their *only*—insurance against nasty surprises lies in faithfully executing reliable published loading recommendations *exactly* as printed.

In another test in that ballistic lab, I once assembled some 20-gauge target ammo precisely according to the Winchester-Western book, using all matched Winchester components. The average velocity of 10 consecutive shots fell within 3 FPS of published Winchester factory ammo. Better than that no handloader can hope to get!

One reason that sticking to authoritative published data is profitable, these days, is that there's so much more of it now. A few years ago, a certain, well, daring was fashionable among scattergun loaders, simply because the available dope was pretty sketchy. Various powder manufacturers offered a little data, but mostly only with their own components. Now, most data publishers include combinations of all kinds and brands of components. Some very comprehensive data is published by independent sources, such as SKR Industries of San Angelo, Texas, which offers the excellent *Handbook of Shotshell Reloading* even though they manufacture neither hulls nor wads, powders nor pellets. The always reliable Lyman shooting library brings out the *Shotshell Handbook*, now in its third edition, as well. Most makers of powder and wads have also seen the light and provide tested data for using their products with a variety of (sometimes) competing items.

Today, Winchester-Western, Remington-Peters, Federal, Hercules, Hodgdon, Fiocchi, and others offer reams of excellent data for almost any practical combination of components you could imagine. There

These special shotshell hulls of transparent plastic are used here to suggest the tremendous variety of combinations of components available to the reloader today. All six loads use the same powder and shot charge and deliver approximately similar muzzle velocities, but they throw very different types of patterns even in the same gun, due to the different wads.

simply is no longer anything to be gained from wild-card substitutions or wild-eyed combinations of components. The smart money says: find the load you want from among the thousands of published recipes and load it, precisely as listed. It may not be as exciting as the old days, but it's safer, cheaper, and more satisfactory all around.

SHOTSHELL HULLS

Shotshell cases have changed radically over my shooting career, and the technological revolution appears to be continuing. When I started, rolled paper cases were the only kind available. Now, only Federal still makes paper cases at all, in 12- and 20-gauge only, and only for target loads. Once-fired specimens can sometimes be purchased in quantity at skeet and trap ranges at attractive prices. Paper loads and crimps very nicely, but it wears out faster than plastic. Watch for pinhole burn-throughs where the paper body meets the brass head, and for burned or torn mouths. Expect no more than two or three good reloads from even the best paper case. Special tools are sold for "ironing" the waxed paper hulls back to good condition, but they're still likely to swell and refuse to chamber if they get wet. I like them very much, but confine their use to informal claybird shooting.

Manufacturers are now into about the third or

fourth generation of plastic shotshell cases and reloaders can find hulls on the market made by at least three different processes. All of them share certain characteristics. They're more expensive than paper hulls but last much longer—about five to eight reloads. Repeated loading and firing does weaken their mouths somewhat, the main result being a minor reduction of muzzle velocities. Plastics are practically waterproof and much stronger than any paper hulls.

Shooters now have plastic cases with smooth or corrugated surfaces, with or without integral basewads, with or without metal heads, skived or unskived (sharply thinned at mouth), and tapered or untapered inside. Furthermore, various combinations of these features are available in different colors and markings from various manufacturers.

To complicate things more, quite a number of "new and revolutionary" ideas in shotshells may still be found occasionally, strange-looking affairs bearing such trade names as "Eclipse," "Wanda," "Whitney," or others. In most cases, their revolutions were short-lived. Some of this stuff is actually unsafe to fire in factory-loaded form, much less suitable for reloading. Most of it is also beginning to have some collectors' value, so the best bet is to hoard it for future capital appreciation. Do not shoot it, and do not attempt to reload the fired cases if you must ignore the no-shoot vital safety advice.

Finally, occasional lots of European ammo may find their way into this country (or may be imported in the future). It's probably of excellent quality if you can figure out what sort of shooting it's good for, but no tested reloading data is available, at least as I write this. Shoot it if you will, but resist the temptation to reload those nice-looking once-fired hulls with "creative" combinations of components. The rule is that if you can't find loading recommendations specifically for any type of case (describing it by brand name, basewad type, markings, head, and other details), don't reload it.

There is one type of exotic shotshell, however, to which these admonitions do not apply, and which you may be seeing in ever-greater quantities. It is the "ACTIV," made by a Puerto Rican company named Rainel. The first thing you'll note about it is that no metal appears anywhere on it. The second is that there may be colorful pictures of gamebirds on the tube. Or maybe not. In any case, this is the only kind of shotshell case currently being sold as a handloading component in unfired condition. Manufactured by an interesting new combination of technologies, this shell may prove to be a wave of the future. Load data is scarce but should quickly become more available. The importer, the J. C. L. Zigor Corporation, has published some data, which is reproduced in the *Handbook of Shotshell Reloading*, an SKR Industries handbook.

Correct identification of the empty hulls in hand is the first step toward safe and satisfactory reloads, and this is not as simple as it might appear. For this, you'll undoubtedly need to do some careful research in the identification section of your shotshell handbook. With the identification accomplished, you may find that only one or two wads are suitable for use in that hull. It all boils down to the fact that *standardization* is the way to go in shotshell loading. Find a steady source of supply of any satisfactory type of hull, and build all your loads around it. This will allow you to stock the appropriate wad (or wads), powder, and primers in sufficient quantity and, perhaps, to get a price break. In any event, you will avoid the fate of the handloader who has to stock a carton of everything. His shotshell components quickly accumulate and crowd his cars, lawnmowers, and everything else out of his garage. Believe me, I speak from experience!

SHOTSHELL WADS

Wadding made the difference in shotshell loads in the 1930s and in the 1950s, and it still does today. But the word "wadding" covers an awful lot of ground. In loading muzzleloading shotguns, yesterday's newspaper crumpled up and rammed home atop the powder charge produces good ballistics and lots of confetti. In my novice days at the loading bench, I used "built-up" or multi-element wad columns, which might have included card wads of various thicknesses and hardnesses, cushion wads of fiber or cork, overpowder cup wads of plastic, and,

The plastic, one-piece wad, shown here at left, may be the most significant development in shotshell loading since the late 1930s. An "old-fashioned" built-up wad column is shown at right.

sometimes, separate shotcups. In the absence of shotcups, polyethylene shot wrappers were in vogue.

This sort of wad column was, in fact, extremely versatile and quite satisfactory, but it took a lot of time to assemble manually and demanded a staggering inventory of components. Then, almost overnight, it seemed, the plastic one-piece wad column was upon us, incorporating overpowder sealing cup, collapsible cushioning element, and petaled shot cup, all in a single unit. These dinguses literally revolutionized shotshell loading. Everybody and his kid brother rushed into production and marketing of a plastic shotshell wad, and scores of different brands, sizes, colors, and designs appeared on dealers' shelves to confuse us.

And that they did! Today, I'm happy to report, the market is down to fewer than 40 different wad designs from perhaps eight makers. That may not sound like much of a simplification, but it is, especially when you recall that six different shotgun gauges are involved. In any case, some wads are highly specialized, doing only one particular job, while others attempt to be more universal within gauge and shot charge weight. Some tend to fit only one kind of case, just as some hulls demand a single kind of wad. What I'm saying is that wad selection can still get a little confusing and deserves some study.

These one-piece plastic wads are certainly convenient and fast to load, but they're hardly the ultimate answer to all reloading problems. For one thing, they tend to tighten patterns, so much so that some older shotguns no longer deliver their marked degrees of choke with factory ammo or conventional

A few of the scores of brands, sizes, gauges, and types of available one-piece plastic wads.

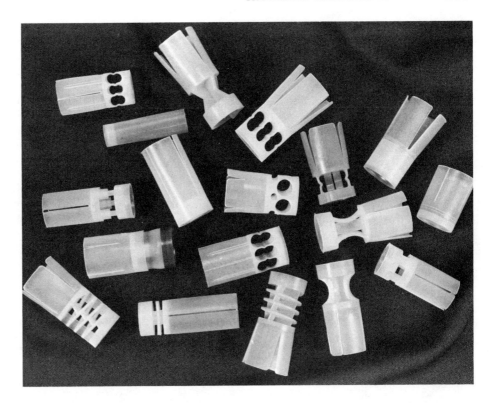

handloads with one-piece wads. For another, they're relatively expensive. Unfortunately, I am aware of no commercial source of all the necessary components for multi-element wad columns.

There are, however, rumors of new, built-up wad columns in some factory-loaded target loads. Let some "name" shooter win the national skeet championship with such ammo, and all those crates and cartons of old wad components in my garage will be worth a fortune!

SHOTSHELL PRIMERS

For years there have been two common sizes of shotshell primers in use in this country. One is the Remington 57*, a small primer that is being phased out of production and may be gone from the market by the time you read this. It is suitable only for Remington and Peters SP hulls and early paper-tube cases with the small primer pocket. Those hulls have been discontinued and will soon disappear. The only primer manufacturer besides Remington making the small primer has been CCI, which will shortly discontinue its CCI 157.

From that time onward, all American shotshells will use the so-called 209, or Winchester, size primer. CCI, Federal, and Winchester all make a primer designated "209." Remington's 209-size is called "97*," however, and if that isn't confusing enough, let me point out that CCI also makes 209-size primers called "109" and "209M," and Federal offers one in this size designated the "410."

All will become clear, however, if you remember

All shotshell primers in these boxes are of the same size, but they're far from interchangeable!

that no substitutions are permissible in shotshell loading recommendations. If the data calls for a Winchester 209 primer, you may not safely use a CCI 209 or a Federal 209. The sizes may be the same, but performance isn't. In fact, the only true interchangeability between primers, as this is written, is between the CCI 109 and CCI 209 Trap and Skeet. These are actually the same product except for the plating on some metal parts of the primer, and they perform identically (except that the cheaper one—209 T&S—will corrode quicker if gotten wet).

SHOTSHELL PROPELLANTS

Shotshell powders are not unlike those used in rifle and pistol cartridges. In many instances, in fact, they are the same powders. Almost all shotshell powders have applications in handgun cartridges, and some (IMR 4227, SR 4756, etc.) are actually designated as "Improved Military Rifle" or "Sporting Rifle" powder. You see among the shotshell propellants all the same variations in granule form—flake, "ball," and extruded—and in chemical content—single- and double-based—that appear in "pure" rifle or handgun powders.

Likewise, the same considerations in storage, handling, and identification that apply to powders for metallic cases apply with equal force to those designated as shotgun powder. There will be more in the following chapter on actual use of these shotshell powders, but nothing more need be added here.

COMPONENT SHOT

There is a great deal more to know about shot itself. In the previous chapter, I showed why it's desirable to get as many of the pellets in a charge as possible out of the muzzle in reasonably spherical shape. Well, the reloader actually has some options in the selection of his shot that will make a difference in this effort. Shot, in fact, might be considered the one component in a shotshell that can be substituted, as follows:

There are three hardnesses of pellets available in bags for handloading. "Soft" shot contains no more than 0.5 percent antimony (a common hardening agent for lead alloys) and is readily deformed in the firing process. It thus spreads faster in flight, and its pattern deteriorates closer to the muzzle, limiting soft shot's usefulness to ranges of about 25 yards or less. Since antimony is much more expensive than lead, soft shot is the cheapest kind of pellet one can use in a handload. Its low cost, however, is not its sole virtue; the fast-spreading tendencies of its mashed and battered pellets may actually be an advantage for such close-range game shooting as quail or woodcock.

"Hard" shot contains from 0.5 to as much as 2 or 3 percent antimony. Most bagged shot sold to reloaders is in this range, and most good factory ammunition is loaded with pellets about this hard. Being harder, it resists deformation better and patterns better to longer ranges than the soft shot. Having more antimony in its makeup, it's more expensive too.

"Extra-hard" shot has up to 6.5 percent antimony, and naturally is the most expensive of the unplated shot types. This is the kind of shot found in some premium grades of factory ammo, and performs best where tight patterns are needed out to the longest ranges at which unplated shot is suitable. Remington's "RXP Grade," All-American's "High Antimony

Samples of some of the shot sizes and types available for handloading include (top row, from left) #9, #7½, and #6 lead, #6 copper-plated lead, (bottom row) #8 lead, #4 steel, #2 and 0 Buckshot lead.

Magnum Grade," Hornady, and Lawrences's "Magnum Brand" are the only types of bulk shot available to reloaders in this hardness class.

Unfortunately, shot packaging today does not include the exact percentage of antimony anywhere on the label. It should, though, because current practice includes some rather creative use of vocabulary concerning performance characteristics. Simple words such as "soft" and "hard" seem to acquire new meanings in such use. It's all relative, I guess. Even soft lead shot *is* harder than something—a marshmallow, for example.

The highest-quality shot you can purchase is plated with either copper or nickel. With reputable manufacturers, pellets selected for electroplating are graded for roundness and uniformity, and the final result is very costly—so much so that some types are sold in quantities as small as 5 pounds (as opposed to the 25-pound bag standard for lesser pellets). However, plating over dead-soft lead does not produce a pellet sufficiently hard to deliver best performance. The lead alloy under the plating must have a fairly high antimony percentage and some foreign brands of copper-plated shot sold at bargain prices did not. They turned out to be no bargain, after all.

Good shot is not as mysterious and difficult to judge as it may seem. If the quality is high, the hardness can be sensed—not quantitatively, admittedly. But you can check hardness by squeezing a pellet between the jaws of a pair of long-nosed pliers. Do the same to another of the same size and *known* antimony content. The quality pellets will mike out

(measure in a micrometer) very close to the correct diameter for the size and will visually be very uniform in size and quite spherical in shape. If you wish to see what the other kind looks and feels like, just pry the crimp open on any major ammo maker's promotional "Dove & Quail" cartridge and examine the contents.

I said at the beginning of this section that shot is the only shotshell component that a reloader can safely substitute, and that's true. His selection from among the different grades of pellets discussed here will make no difference in the safety or ballistics of his load. Even shot sizes, within broad limits, can be substituted, with the following proviso. Shot charges in the data tables are given in ounces, but the actual pellets are measured volumetrically. A bushing or charge-bar setting that delivers, say, 1¼ ounce of No. 7½ shot will drop a lighter charge of larger pellets, simply because they do not "pack" as closely and leave more air space in the filled bushing. Conversely, switching to smaller shot increases the weight of the payload. This lighter payload may make a little difference in velocity. If you're one who's comforted by precision, you may wish to switch bushings or readjust the charge bar to drop the nominal *weight* of the larger (or smaller) pellet.

I find it very convenient, and perfectly satisfactory performance-wise, to leave a shotshell loading tool set up and adjusted for a specific load at all times. The load is a well-tested one, using a standardized hull and wad, that delivers the velocity I prefer (usually my standard 1,200 FPS). The load will probably

With just this equipment, the home-shop handloader can actually make his own shot of various sizes and hardnesses.

This close-up of home-made shot pellets reveals irregularities, but patterning deficiencies resulting from lack of roundness can be partially offset by making pellets very hard.

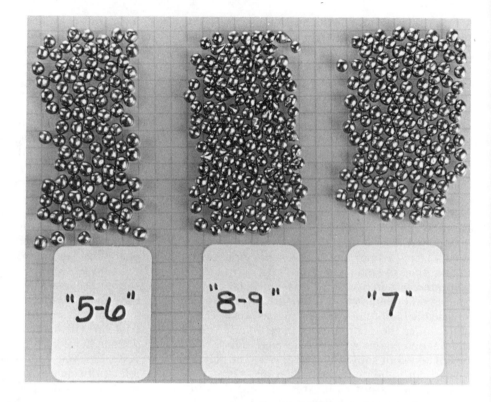

have been developed with No. 9 shot, as a skeet round. The nines work pretty well for early season quail and doves, too, but later in the year I'll switch to No. 7½ to 8½ (making no change in the tooling except to fill the shot hopper with pellets of a different size). Still later in the winter, I go to No. 6 (extra-hard shot) for decoying ducks, late-season pheasants, etc. Everything else remains unchanged—powder, powder charge, primer, all die and charge-bar adjustments. The loads pattern well in several different shotguns with different choke combinations, and the tool is always ready to go. Not a bad strategy!

The strategy is so good, in fact, that I have more than one loader, not only for different gauges but also for different standard loads. These are the ones I shoot enough of to make handloading them worthwhile.

STEEL SHOT

I come now to one of the touchiest parts of this entire book. In the late 1970s, I wrote that steel shot could not be safely handloaded, at least not until tested, compatible components and authoritative data became available. That was long ago. Now, good "steel" shot, special wads, and buffering materials are beginning to be distributed, and some reliable loading information has been published.

Moreover, the proponents of steel shot have made great strides in imposing their desires on the rest of us, to the degree that someday steel shot will be the only legal ammunition for waterfowling anywhere in the United States with any gauge or kind of gun, even muzzleloaders. Nor is it unthinkable that within the life of this book steel may be mandated for all mi-

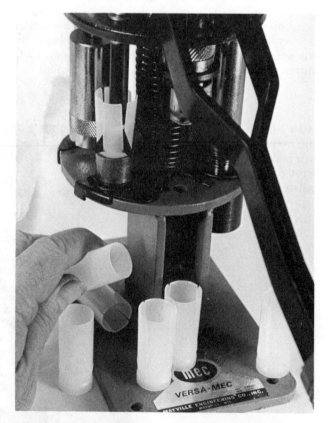

Polyethylene wads for use with steel shot are especially formulated and very thick, and come unslit, as shown by the specimen in hand. A tool for cutting the shotcup wads into petals is available (installed in press), or you can cut the wads with a razor blade. Take your pick.

gratory upland birds, as well. That would include mourning doves and woodcock, among other species. In view of the high price of factory-loaded steel ammo, reloading for many hunters could become the difference between continuing to hunt and taking up golf or mumblety-peg. Reloading can thus also become the means by which another generation is introduced to the shooting field sports.

It goes without saying that, with sport hunting under great and growing pressure from the antihunting, antigun fanatics, we cannot afford to lose any defectors from our ranks, much less a whole generation. Without the political clout we derive from sheer numbers, we shall lose our sport and our game altogether. I'm about convinced that this is exactly what a great many of the more fervent steel-shot supporters have in mind.

Handloading steel shot is, if anything, even more demanding than loading lead, especially in the need to follow loading formulas exactly. Corners cannot

be cut safely. With steel, you're working much closer to the edge, so to speak, without much margin for error. A 2¾-inch 12-gauge load of steel is short on internal space to begin with, because of the greater size and number of pellets required to equal a given weight of lead. There is, for example, no room for a collapsible cushioning section in the wad, and no need for one either, due to the hardness of the pellets. Because of the danger of bore damage from pellet-scrub, only special, thick, high-density polyethylene shotcup wads made especially for this purpose can be used, and a granular buffer is necessary. Only a few types of hulls are suitable for steel-shot loads, and only one or two of the standard canistered powders work well in these loads.

As with lead, the range of quality in steel-shot components available is quite wide. Some so-called steel shot is actually ball bearings that, although annealed somewhat, are still much harder than SAAMI (Sporting Arms and Ammunition Manufacturers In-

LEAD SHOT SIZE AND PELLET NUMBER PER CHARGE

Average Number Pellets per Charge (Nominal)

Oz.	½	¾	⅞	1	1⅛	1¼	1⅜	1½	1⅝	1⅞	2
9	292	439	512	585	658	731	804	877	951	1097	1170
8½	245	365	425	485	545	605	665	725	785	845	905
8	205	308	359	410	462	513	564	615	667	769	820
7½	175	262	307	350	393	437	481	525	568	656	700
6	112	169	197	225	253	309	281	337	396	423	450
5	85	128	149	170	192	213	234	255	277	319	340
4	67	101	118	135	152	169	185	202	221	253	270
2	45	68	79	90	102	113	124	135	146	169	180
BB	25	37	43	50	57	63	70	76	84	90	96

(Shot Size)

STEEL SHOT SIZE AND PELLET NUMBER PER CHARGE

Average Number Pellets per Charge (Nominal)

Oz.	⅝	¾	⅞	1	1⅛	1¼	1⅜
6	182	219	255	291	327	363	399
5	152	184	214	244	275	307	339
4	117	141	164	187	211	235	258
3	102	122	142	163	183	203	224
2	80	94	108	125	142	156	170
1	64	77	90	103	116	129	141
B	53	64	75	86	97	108	119
BB	46	54	62	70	78	87	96
BBB	38	46	53	61	69	76	84
T	36	42	48	54	60	67	74

(Shot Size)

stitute) specifications for true steel shot. The tip-off is that these pellets do not correlate in any way with standard lead-shot pellet sizes. I am informed that the shot sold by Non-Toxic Components, Inc. of Portland, Oregon, is purchased from the same company that makes the shot loaded into Winchester, Remington, and Federal factory loads, and that it meets the same specifications. This may be true of other handloading components suppliers, as well, and other prime sources may enter the picture as demand increases with the U.S. Fish & Wildlife changeover to all-steel waterfowl seasons nationwide.

Don't even think about using standard, conventional one-piece wads with steel shot. You will surely ruin your shotgun's barrel if you try it. I did not say that you *might* ruin it; I said you *will* ruin it, and I meant it. Use only the wads recommended, according to data published by a reputable wad maker, and use them only as recommended.

By the way, as far as I've been able to determine, proper (factory or equivalent) steel-shot loads will not harm a modern, high-quality gun's choke, contrary to protestations and lamentations. At least, the steel load is no more likely to do so than heavy, high-velocity lead-shot loads. In fact, there's little doubt that some of the choke expansion charged to steel in recent years had already been accomplished by premium lead waterfowl loads. The phenomenon was not noticed until firing of steel brought about a detailed examination of the choke. In any event, those changes are cosmetic only. There are some shotguns in which I wouldn't fire steel, and they include older, tightly choked, high-grade guns, mostly of European origin, especially those of very light weight for the gauge with thin barrel walls. The Belgian Browning doubles lead the list. But, then, I would not fire Winchester Super XX lead loads in such guns either.

I will add here too that I've shot quite a few ducks and geese with each of the several generations of factory steel-shot loads. I kill as many or more birds for the shells expended and seem to cripple no more, if as many, as with lead. However, I've never been much of a skybuster with any kind of ammunition and try

to hold all shots at geese to 50 yards or less, with 40 yards the outside limit for ducks.

Properly-loaded steel-shot shells usually produce beautiful, dense, uniform patterns and remarkably short shot strings. Most of them feature quite high velocity. These qualities offset to some extent the ballistic inferiority of soft steel *vs.* lead. A more open choke is required with steel than would be used with the same sizes of lead pellets, meaning an Improved-Cylinder-and-Modified may become the standard waterfowl double gun in place of the old-timey modified-and-full or full-and-full. An IC-&-M over/under 12-gauge Winchester Model 101 Pigeon Grade, in fact, has become my favorite steel-shot waterfowl weapon.

BUFFERING MATERIALS

A word about fillers or buffers for shotshells: almost everything from baking flour through ground-up horse manure to high-tech polymer products has been tried at one time or another to separate lead pellets from each other during the trip through the barrel. This practice definitely produces rounder pellets (at least in larger sizes) and better long-range patterns. With the advent of steel shot, buffering has proved necessary to protect the gun's bore from the shot, rather than the shot pellets from each other.

Nowadays, all commercially available buffering agents are, as far as I know, granulated polyethylene, but there are differences in density, weight, and granulation size. Winchester–Western "Super Grex" is perhaps the best-known example, and buffering products are also offered by Tru-Square, Ballistics Products, Supersonic, and Non-Toxic Components.

You cannot simply and safely add a buffering agent to a shotshell loading formula. The buffering effect with either lead or steel pellets is complex and not clearly understood, even by professional ballisticians. But they do know chamber pressures invariably rise sharply with a buffer. Best bet, as usual, is to employ a buffer only in load formulas from reliable sources that explicitly call for one.

28 Assembling Shotshells

I might as well begin this chapter with a repetition of the principal admonition of the previous chapter, it can't be said too often. Don't substitute components or alter recommended charge weights (either powder or shot) in either direction from those listed in reliable published loading data. Pick a load that sounds good to you and acquire enough components to load *lots* of rounds, or inventory your accumulation of components and pick a load that will use up your excess stocks. But either way, load components exactly as listed.

HULL INSPECTION

The first step in shotshell reloading is the same as in stuffing metallics: visually sort and inspect the fired cases. Never mix brands of tubes (or types within brands). Best of all, keep large lots of hulls segregated so that all cases in each lot have been fired the same number of times. Then, when a significant number of the lot begin to reveal serious wear or fatigue, deep-six the whole lot at once.

During inspection, look first at the mouth of the case to see that it's all there and not split or torn. Then check the head, especially the edge of the rim. High pressure often ruptures the brass head of a shotshell at that location. Also, the face of the case head should be neither bulged nor dished, and the primer should be normal in appearance.

If the hull is paper, check the body just ahead of the brass head for pinhole burn throughs.

A quick glance inside a casing that looks good externally completes the inspection. See that the basewad (if separate) is sound and in place. Make

certain there's nothing inside that you don't want in there when you fire this lot of reloads.

As to unwanted objects inside a hull, some years ago I suffered misfires in about half the rounds I tried to fire during a round of skeet. I (gun "expert," and reloading author) received looks ranging from politely sympathetic to quizzical to outright sneers as I lost bird after bird because the shotgun went click instead of bang. Back at home and still smarting with embarrassment, I did what I hadn't bothered to do when I loaded that batch of ammo; I looked inside the empties of the remainder of the lot from which I'd worked. Sure enough, about half the hulls had one or more mourning dove feathers inside, from having been dropped in with the doves in the game pocket of my shooting vest. The feathers often blocked the flash hole so the primer flash couldn't reach the powder. Both my ego and my local reputation suffered as a result of my carelessness.

As a sidelight, feathers are not as easy to get out of an empty 20-gauge hull as you might think. When I loaded the rest of that lot, I adopted the practice of removing the hull from the loader after depriming and puffing lustily into the flash hole. By the time I'd loaded a couple of hundred rounds, the room looked as though someone had broken a feather pillow in it. But all the cartridges fired routinely next time around.

The presence of any of these symptoms (except the presence of removable foreign objects) is reason enough to discard the hull. Worn, soft mouths pose no danger but do decrease the reliability of ignition and uniformity of powder combustion. There is always a temptation to try to get just one more firing out of a case. Sternly resist that.

On second thought, worn case mouths could, conceivably, contribute to a dangerous situation, in that they can be responsible for "blooper" loads. Blooper loads can leave a wad lodged in the barrel. The next shot fired, if the obstructing wad is not cleared, will quite probably damage the gun. In a worst-case scenario, it could be disastrous to both gun and shooter. Worn case mouths and the weak crimps they engender are not the only cause of blooper loads, by any means, but shouldn't be ignored as one of the prime causes. The moral is that a prudent shooter always ceases fire instantly and inspects his bore(s) after any shot, with any kind of ammunition, that either sounds or feels abnormal in any way.

ANALYZE YOUR OPERATIONS

With your loading tool set up and properly adjusted, it's worthwhile taking a few minutes to load a few rounds very slowly, analyzing the hand movements necessary with component stocks in various locations and trying different systems. Almost invariably, you'll find one sequence of movements that permits noticeably higher production rates with fewer errors and less fatigue over a long session. And, just as surely, this sequence *won't* follow the way you laid things out at the start. Different loaders work differently for different operators, and of course, left- and right-handedness must be taken into account. Once you discover the sequence that feels most natural and works best for you, you'll find that speed of production will just come along naturally with little effort on your part.

JUDGING HANDLOAD QUALITY

Speed is nice, but it's far less important than the uniformity and quality of your finished product. Firing the reloads in the gun for which they're intended is, of course, the acid test. Feeding (in a repeater), chambering, firing, extraction, and ejection should be considered unacceptable if less reliable than factory ammo. I have already covered pattern-testing.

However, just a quick glance at the crimp of each completed shell as it comes off the tool can tell you a lot about how good your gear is and how good you are at adjusting and operating that gear.

In general, the more closely the crimp resembles that of an unfired factory cartridge, the better. It should be neatly folded and perfectly flat, neither bulging nor dished inward. The rolled lips should be smooth and never larger in diameter than the body of the hull itself, preferably tapered inward slightly.

Crimp-starters come in six- or eight-point models. This is an eight-fold starter. The more sophisticated tools are self-indexing.

Crimp quality is a reliable indicator of shotshell reload quality. These crimps, in different kinds of plastic and paper 20- and 12-gauge hulls, closely approach the appearance of those in factory ammo. The second cartridge from left is waterproofed with candle wax.

A small hole at the center of the crimp on a plastic hull is acceptable. It is, in fact, inevitable with once-fired factory hulls of most brands. They are factory heat-sealed at the crimp's center with a small disk that is blown away upon firing. Since it cannot be replaced by the reloader, the small opening it once covered will occur. This is not a flaw unless it's large enough to allow shot pellets to escape.

If the hole is so large it would let shot pellets escape, you can close it in a couple of ways. A disk of light bond paper on top of the shot column works well. You will occasionally see some sort of overshot card wad mentioned for this purpose, which is okay for rolled crimps (one sees almost none of them these days), but the bond paper is better for folded crimps. The card wad is hard enough to prevent the folds of the crimp from digging down into the top of the shot charge, as they must, whereas the lighter paper keeps things soft and flexible yet still contains the pellets. It will also interfere less with the pattern after the payload leaves the muzzle.

The other technique for closing the crimp hole is a drop of molten candle wax. In some ways this is best of all, especially for steel-shot loads because it tends to make the shell a little more nearly waterproof, as well as holding stray pellets inside the case. Steel-shot loads, so far, are entirely for waterfowling, which is done in a damp environment. And low-carbon steel will rust! In fact, I've seen steel-shot charges that had rusted into a conglomerated mass; the thought of heaving such a glob of rusty iron firing down a fine shotgun barrel makes my skin crawl. Anticorrosive coatings for steel shot pellets are being considered, and the rust problem may be greatly reduced by the time you read these lines. In the meantime, I light the candle and start dripping.

After eyeballing the crimp, cast a quick glance at the midsection of the reloaded hull just ahead of the brass head, if any, or about where the brass head would stop if one were present. If there's a roll or wrinkle there, some adjustments are in order for that type of case in that machine.

Some factory-loaded shotgun shells today are closed with a six-fold pie crimp, some with an eight-fold crimp. Fired plastic hulls insist on having subsequent crimps folded along exactly the same lines as the original one. Unless you're certain you'll reload only one type of case, you'll probably save yourself a lot of time and trouble if you buy two crimp-starters—one for each type of crimp—when you purchase the loader. Some brands, by the way, have both six- and eight-point starters included with the equipment.

POWDER AND SHOT CHARGES

Powder and shot charges are controlled in all tools by means of cavities that meter out the materials by volume. In some tools these are in fixed bars, so that to change either charge one must change the entire bar (in a few cases, charge bars will have a fixed cavity for the powder and a hole accepting interchangeable

For small batches of experimental loads or when the correct powder bushing is not at hand, there's nothing wrong with using an ordinary powder measure to meter shotshell charges.

bushings for the shot). In others both powder and shot are measured through replaceable bushings. Bars with micrometer-adjustable cavities for both are also available, both as original equipment or aftermarket equipment. These are obviously the most flexible and precise of all.

As the handloader accumulates more bars and/or bushings, a potential hazard grows. Here the danger is that he will inadvertently install the wrong bushings for the load he intends to assemble. A larger powder bushing can dump a dangerous overload, while the wrong shot bushing can place too heavy a payload in front of a properly-metered powder charge. Sometimes, one of these mistakes will reveal itself by causing an abnormal crimp on the case, but, all too often, just a little extra force on the operating handle will crimp the load. (Perhaps "bomb" is a better word than "load.") A similar result can be obtained in some older tool designs by filling the powder hopper with shot and the shot hopper with powder and reversing the sequence of operation of the charge bar. Normally, powder and shot bushings have different outside diameters so that they cannot be accidentally interchanged in the bar itself. Always make certain you have the correct bar or bushing installed, the correct powder in the hopper, and the powder and shot in the correct hoppers.

Do not accept the markings of powder and shot bushings at face value. It is as necessary to check bushing results (and to set adjustable bars) against a good powder scale in shotshell loading as it is to verify the output of a powder measure in metallic reloading. It may be that no bushing available for your equipment throws the exact powder charge you want. If the load is one you'll load in large quantity, it's worth modifying a bushing permanently. Start with the next smaller cavity and enlarge it carefully, using

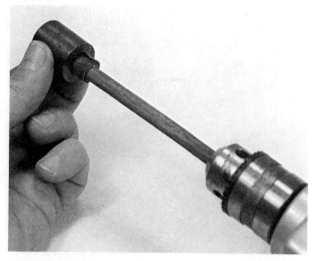

A powder, or shot, bushing can be reamed to drop precisely the correct charge by use of an emery cloth wrapped around a dowel in a drill or drill press.

a piece of coarse emery paper on a split wooden dowel, turned by an electric drill or drill press. Work cautiously and check results often, until the bushing delivers precisely the desired charge. Then mark it and keep it in the safety deposit box between uses!

A slightly oversized bushing cavity can be "bushed" with bits of electricians' tape. In testing your progress in adjusting a bushing, take sample charges for weighing only while going through a complete, normal operating cycle—while actually processing cases, that is. The reason is that the manner in which you operate a shotshell loader has everything to do with the powder charges it drops. The bumps and jars to which the loader is subjected during the loading cycle tend to settle the powder in the bushing or cavity in a certain way, and a deviation in the cycle can produce a significantly different charge weight.

When I sat down late one evening to load a couple of boxes of shells for a quail hunt early next morning, I found that I lacked the correct bushing for the load I wanted of the powder in question. I did have one that threw a few tenths of a grain lighter, however, and a little experimenting demonstrated that I could produce exactly the right charge merely by bumping the loader's handle against the stop *twice* on each downstroke instead of my customary single bump. That small alteration in technique changed the bushing's output with that particular powder by almost half a grain.

For the same reason, be aware that every different operator will deliver a slightly different charge weight of powder from the same tool and bushing, because of unconscious differences in operating technique. Once, after five friends had chipped in to purchase a shotshell loader, plus bulk quantities of such components as cases, powder, primers, and wads, I helped set up the machinery. The friends had agreed

on one load for everything, and I carefully modified a powder bushing, as described above, to drop precisely the correct charge. For me, that is! Every one of those five guys got a slightly different charge weight out of the same bushing, and I could've saved my patience and time in polishing that bushing out to the last, precise tenth of a grain.

The "operator factor" is not a major problem, but it's certainly worth remembering in the event you train your spouse, youngsters, or next-door neighbor to stuff shotshells for you.

WAD PRESSURE

The amount of pressure used to seat a wad column on the powder was of crucial importance to good ballistics in the days when built-up, multi-piece wad columns were the only kind we had. But, like most other things in this game today, the one-piece wad has changed things. With most loads, all that's necessary is to seat the wad with enough pressure to shorten the column to the correct point for a perfect crimp. Then set it and forget it. Somewhere around 40 to 50 pounds of seating pressure will be right for most loads.

However, an eye on the wad pressure scale on your reloader while working and regard any substantial variation in the present pressure as a sign of trouble. If the pressure is supposed to be 40 pounds, and a single round runs much higher or lower than that, the variation could indicate the accidental intrusion of a wad or hull of the wrong type or gauge, a dangerously heavy or light powder charge, a loose basewad, an obstruction, or any of several other problems. Including dove feathers.

PATTERN SPREADERS AND SQUEEZERS

As some of the photos in this chapter show, all sorts of ingenious gimmicks have been, and still may be, used to alter the patterning of a shotshell handload. In recent years, however, more devices for these purposes have been built into the wad itself or furnished as separate items for use with any conventional wad. There are "post" wads to spread patterns for short-range work through medium-range chokes, and there's a very similar-looking device called a "compressor," that is supposed to have exactly the opposite effect. The manufacturer of the compressor (Ferri & Associates of Trinidad, Colorado) also makes a "Spreader."

Granulated polyethylene buffering material is one of the most reliable pattern-squeezers, but there seems to be no really fast and convenient method of putting it into a shell. Believe me, all the methods that will occur to you have probably been tried, and each has its drawbacks.

The best way I've found is as follows: meter the shot charge into the shotcup, already seated in the hull normally. Use a rotary powder measure to drop the correct weight of Grex buffer (previously deter-

This is how a buffered steel-shot load looks after the buffering agent is vibrated in and before crimping.

mined by experiment) into any convenient receptacle. Hold the shell on or against a source of vibration, such as a vibratory case cleaner, and pour the buffer in slowly. It will settle to the bottom of the shot charge and fill the interstices between the pellets in about 15 to 30 seconds. The correct level is reached when the tops of the top layer of pellets are just peeking through the buffer. This is, obviously, a lot of trouble and a time-consuming extra step in reloading, but it *must* be done with steel shot, and the results with long-range lead loads make it worthwhile.

SLUGS AND BUCKSHOT

The granulated buffering material is highly effective with buckshot loads too, so much so that handloading of buckshot might be worthwhile if that were the only way to get buffered buckshot loads. However, most or all of the major manufacturers now routinely buffer their commercial buckshot loads. That leaves me with only two possible theories about why anybody would bother to handload the big pellets. The first is just to say you've done it, and the second, more logical, is so that you'll fully appreciate the contents of those neat little five-packs of buckshot loads you can buy at your ammunition store.

The same applies to slugs—almost. However, in the several states that permit only shotguns for hunting deer, the serious hunter/reloader may wish to experiment with some of the newer and more exotic types of projectiles in his particular gun. Examples are the Brenneke and Vitt-Boos ribbed slugs, with wads screw-attached to the base, the BRI Sabot/500, or even the spherical "pumpkin balls," which often produce surprising accuracy.

The first problem is reliable data. The suppliers of the fancy slugs provide some tested reloading data for their products. The Lyman shotshell handbook still includes data for loading buckshot and slugs cast in Lyman molds (12- and 20-gauge only).

Many of these slug loads require a rolled crimp, rather than the otherwise almost-universal folded crimp, which means you may need some accessory crimp tooling for such experimenting.

STEEL-SHOT AND LEAD-SHOT DIFFERENCES

Steel shot is an entirely different animal from lead shot, and the differences must be understood. Obviously, since steel shot is only about two-thirds as heavy as lead, the same shot bushings cannot be used for both. This means that most loaders who use fixed charge bars will require retrofitting with special steel-shot charge bars. If bushings are used, you must remember that a shot bushing marked "1⅛" for lead is useless with steel. Mayville Engineering Co. (MEC) single-stage loaders are the only ones at the moment that can be suitably retrofitted with steel-shot charge bars. If your single-stage loader is of another brand, you can probably load steel. But you will have to hand-weigh shot charges on a reloading scale, rather than dropping them from a hopper in the usual fashion. To the best of my knowledge, no current progressive press is entirely suitable for use with steel shot, even by hand-weighing shot.

Even with all the proper equipment, steel-shot sizes #1, B, and BB may give bridging trouble in the charge bar, requiring a sharp rap with the fist on the charge-bar assembly. With BBs it's probably best simply to build this act into the loading routine, doing it on every round. With BBB and T pellets, currently the largest real steel shot sold, shot charges will probably not be sufficiently accurate for safety through *any* current loading machine. Buffering agents are absolutely necessary with these sizes.

Shot harder than SAAMI specifications for steel shot, which is 90 DPH (Diamond Pyramid Hardness) maximum, may increase breech pressures and does increase strain on the gun's choke, and so should not be loaded under any circumstances.

In the past at least, some products that were advertised as "soft steel shot" still exceeded this limit. Likewise, pellets larger than "T" size (.200-inch diameter) dramatically increase stress on the gun's choke. Beware of so-called "steel shot" that fails to conform to standard American shot-pellet sizes. Muzzle velocities higher than 1,425 FPS also push choke-strain into the danger zone.

Only specially designed steel-shot wads of high-density polyethylene that contain the entire shot charge, to the last pellet, can safely be used with steel shot. These wads usually come with the shot cups whole, instead of being divided into petals by slits. The wads must be slit by hand, which can be done with a kitchen knife or razor blade, but I'll guarantee that doing 100 wads in this fashion will send you scrambling to the post office to order a wad-slitter (photo shown in previous chapter). Wad-slitters are cheap, fast, cut uniform petals, and are *THE* way to go. If you take my word for it and order one with your first order of steel-shot components or equipment, you'll later thank me.

Powder and shot measurement for steel must be somewhat more precise than for lead—although such metering *should* be very precise with any kind of shotshell reload. Steel is less forgiving than lead, however, and variations in powder charge weight greater than 0.5 grain, or in shot charge weight greater than 15 grains, are unacceptable.

Finally, I hope it's superfluous to say that, in loading steel shot above all, deviations from the exact load recommendations are for the foolhardy. Components and quantities may not be changed, substituted, increased, decreased, added, subtracted, or otherwise altered in any way. "That's close enough!" in steel-shot work is *never* close enough. Take loads from a good book and do it the way it says in the book.

RHYTHM AND BLUES

The subtitle of this section is derived from the fact that there is an unmistakable rhythm to proper shotshell-loader operation, and if you ignore it, you're sure to be singing the blues.

This is a classic example of an activity in which it pays to make haste slowly. Most of us are striving for maximum production, but not at the cost of inferior, unreliable ammo. Slap-dash, slam-bang operation of a loading tool is the wrong way to hurry. Smooth, unhurried, rhythmical operation produces better ammo faster in the long run, and wastes fewer components.

Just one example: the crimp folds of a once-fired plastic case have a persistent memory, and now and again one of them will force its way between the fingers of a wad guide, to nick the lip of the overpowder cup on a one-piece wad. That event will be signaled to a steady, experienced operator by an almost imperceptible catch on the downstroke of the wad-seating operation. The operator without an established rhythm will probably not even notice it. That round, however, will surely produce a blown pattern or other substandard ballistics. It could be the round in the chamber during the miss-and-out shootoff at a club's annual championship. Need I say more?

To sum it up, you should try to develop a subtle "feel" for the operation of the loader, based on uniformity of operating technique. That uniformity is as important to consistent quality in shotshell reloads as it is to operating a powder measure. Ideally, each movement is performed in exactly the same manner, with the same force, every time. Whenever you notice any small glitch or whenever an operation requires greater or less force than normal, stop and sort out the cause. It's easy to load excellent shotshells on the equipment now available, but it isn't automatic. The operator must still learn the feel of his equipment and devote his entire attention to the process at all times.

I suppose I was lucky with those dove feathers, at that. A little embarrassment is a minor penalty to pay for unwarranted haste and inattention in reloading. Even blown patterns are better than blown shotguns, and that can happen too, if you begin to measure success solely in terms of boxes per hour.

29 Shotshell Loading Tools

Consider production requirements as the basic factor when purchasing a shotshell loading tool. Will you be happy stuffing hulls at the rate of, say, 25 per hour, or do you really want to produce 500 or more an hour. Either the MRC (Mequon) Loader or Lee Load-All Junior will supply the first need at a retail price, as this is written, of about $20. Ponsness–Warren, MEC, Camdex, Hollywood, and Hornady all offer machines that will meet or even exceed the 500-shell-per-hour rate at prices ranging from a few hundred to nearly a thousand dollars. Hollywood Automatic costs over $2,000. The faster machines are so fast that maximum production can only be sustained with a two-man crew, one to yank the handle and the other to keep the components moving and hoppers filled.

THE HAPPY MEDIUM

Between the two cost extremes lie most of the shotshell loading tools on the market today. Production rates average between 100 and about 250 rounds per hour, and prices run from one hundred to a few hundred dollars. The Lee Load-All fits into this production-rate niche, but at a price under $50. The rest are offered by MEC, Texan, Hornady, and Ponsness–Warren. The needs of the vast majority of handloaders are easily satisfied by equipment in this happy-medium category.

The tools in this grouping are for the most part "single-stage" loaders, meaning that each pull of the handle performs one operation on one shell, instead of multiple operations on several shells at once, as in the progressive machines. One other manual operation (besides pulling the handle) is usually re-

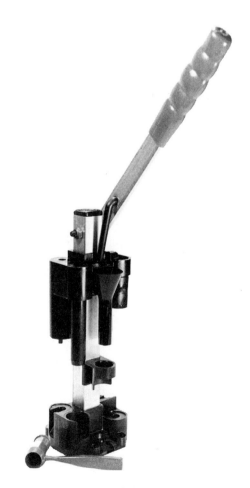

At about $20, the Lee Load-All Junior is about the least-expensive bench-mounted shotshell tool available. Powder and shot dippers are included, the adjustable shot dipper here near the base of the tool.

Left: The Lee Load-All Senior is next up the price-and-features scale from the Load-All Junior shown on the previous page. It produces good ammo somewhat faster than the Junior. *Right:* The Mayville Engineering Co. "Versa MEC" is probably the best-selling shotshell tool in history.

quired for each handle-cycle. This will consist of moving a hull from one station to another, operating a charge bar, positioning a primer or wad, or other similar task.

Somewhere in all this activity, the case will be re-sized. In some systems, this occurs at the decapping station, and in others it's integral with the crimping operation.

All loaders have powder and shot hoppers or bottles built-in. Some have automatic primer feeds, while others store primers in a magazine but move them into position for seating, one by one, by a manual operation. On the high-production presses, all the operator has to do is insert empty hulls at one end, position wads for seating, pull the lever, and take completed rounds from the other end. He gets one fully loaded cartridge for every pull of the handle. Some of the big loaders even eliminate all that tiresome handle-pulling. They are actuated by a hydraulic system; the operator needs only to touch a foot pedal for each cycle.

In general, the higher the production capacity of a loading machine, the less flexible it is, especially for loading small batches of shells for experimental shooting. Therefore, the gunner who intends to assemble only a single load and who fires large quantities of that loading is best served by one of the big, fast, mass-production tools (if he can afford one). On the other hand, the hunter who likes to play around with loads to optimize the performance of his guns, who hunts many different kinds of game, who wants to put together an occasional batch of target ammo, or who owns guns in more than one gauge is probably better off with one of the simpler, single-stage tools. He'll find it much easier to adjust when changing loads, and it should still produce at least four or five boxes of ammunition per hour. In the case of at least one model under $200, changing gauges requires only 5 minutes; changing to a different load (different hull, wad, and powder charge) within a gauge may, however, take much longer, as all the individual dies may need readjustment.

All the shotshell loaders on the market I'm familiar with will reload good ammunition, usable in any kind of gun, provided they're competently adjusted and operated. I haven't worked with every model, but I have used at least one tool manufactured by each of the companies represented by the current crop of loading machines.

GAUGE CHANGES

Loading dies are available in all viable gauges—10, 12, 16, 20, 28, and .410—and all but the simplest tools can be converted between gauges, as well as between standard and magnum case lengths within a gauge. Depending upon the brand and type of tooling, a complete conversion die-set runs from about $35 up to well over $100. Conversion between standard and magnum lengths is cheaper, usually requiring only two new dies plus readjustment of the rest.

ACCESSORY TOOLING

Shotshell loading machines are much more self-contained than most of those for metallic cartridges, incorporating as they do powder and shot measures. As a result, the scattergun reloader needs fewer accessories on his bench than the metallic reloader.

The most important item is a high-capacity hand-loading scale for verifying both powder and shot charges. A scale with 1,000-grain capacity is desirable for weighing shot charges—a 2-ounce charge being the equivalent of 875 grains.

RCBS, a major force in metallic-cartridge reloading equipment for a generation, makes no shotshell press as such, but has introduced a die kit with which to convert a metallic press into a single-stage shotshell loader.

For the shooter who enjoys playing with different

I have had many years of satisfactory service from several single-stage reloaders from Texan.

Micrometer-adjustable powder-and-shot measuring bars are available as aftermarket items for most popular tools that do not come factory-equipped with them.

Storage of shotshell reloads is always a problem. One solution is this MTM ammo carrier. It has inserts that can serve as loading blocks as well.

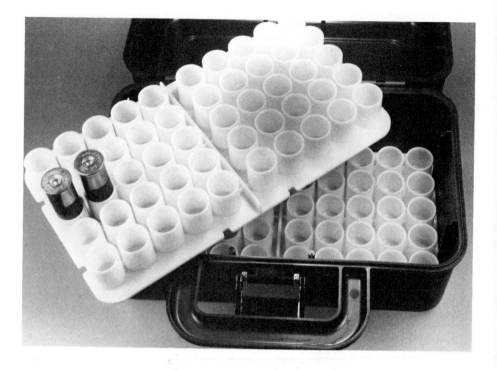

loads, an adjustable powder measure like those used by metallic handloaders comes in handy, since no man alive ever had every single powder bushing he needed for any conceivable load. The measure is optional, of course; the scale remains mandatory. The scale will be required for, among other things, making up steel-shot charges for use in loading machines other than the single-stage MECs, at least for a while.

Among specialized tools for steel-shot loading, you'll need wad-slitter. And some means of vibrating a case for sifting buffering material down through a shot charge may come in handy, either for steel or lead loading.

Separate shotshell conditioners are offered by MEC and Texan in the $50 to $70 range. These do not merely resize hulls. They also recondition both the body and head of the case, doing a more thorough and precise job than any loading machine itself can hope to do.

Then there are loading blocks for shotshells, primer-tube fillers, and a few other minor items borrowed from the metallics-loader's arsenal, such as funnels and calipers. One of the most useful is the MEC E-Z Pak, an ingenious little sheet-metal gimmick; available for all gauges, it makes packaging shotshell handloads in their original boxes fast and easy.

SHOTSHELL RELOADING RECORDS

Finally, a record-keeping system. Keeping good records is as important in shotshell reloading as for the metallics, although for somewhat different reasons. Every load tried should have its recipe written down—at a minimum, complete identification of hull; brand, type, size, and weight of shot; brand and type

of wad; powder type and charge; brand and kind of primer; and other pertinent data. Bushing numbers and wad-pressure settings should be included. Results of chronographing, pattern-testing, and so forth for each barrel, gun, or choke-tube or setting should be recorded, along with such subjective observations as recoil sensation. Why go to all the trouble to shoot and count patterns unless you keep the results on file so you'll always have access to the information? If the load was either adopted as one of your standards or rejected, note that information along with the reasons. Among other benefits, this habit will help you avoid repeating your mistakes.

Records will also help you track various lots of shotshell hulls through their reloading lifetimes. It's worth knowing whether one type of hull gives twice the number of loadings yielded by another, for example, or double the number of shots with one powder and wad than with a different combination. Furthermore, if you note that casings in a certain lot seem to be getting pretty ragged, you'll find it useful to refer to a notebook and confirm that the lot has undergone eight or nine firings, or only three if that is the case.

Requirements for shotshell data differ from those for metallic–cartridge reloading; so my "Ditto Data Form," that I use for metallics, cannot easily be adapted for shotshells. The principle remains sound, however, and it shouldn't be difficult to design a labor-saving version for shotshells. For one reason or another, I myself have never gotten around to it and keep my own shotshell records in a small, loose-leaf notebook, one load to the page. It's adequate, but might not be if I experimented as extensively in shotshells as I do in rifle and pistol rounds. If a commercially-printed shotshell reloading record book is available, it has not come to my attention.

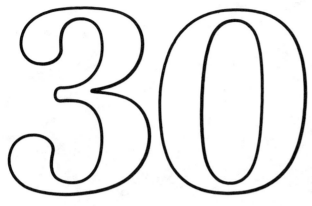

A Roundup of Reloading Safety

Throughout this book I have attempted to note essential safety considerations for every reloading operation. Even so, it's worthwhile to condense for easy reference a review of the general safety principles. Almost decades ago, I wrote a humorous article on reloading safety for a firearms magazine. Since then, I have noted that most of the ideas I set forth in that article have appeared on various lists of safety rules for handloaders, although I do not remember having seen such a list before that writing. This, of course, is not to be taken as a claim that I invented the rules. They are nothing more than plain old common sense, bolstered by experience. In fact, the first rule on the list is just that:

Exercise care and common sense at all times while reloading. Another way to put it would be: THINK! Think of what you're doing, and think of the possible consequences of your actions at each step of the process.

The second general rule is really a restatement of this one. *Pay attention to the business at hand while at the loading bench.* Don't try to load while watching a TV football game. Don't invite a bunch of your buddies over and attempt to carry your end of a general bull session while stuffing ammo. Reloading is a fairly technical activity and mistakes can be serious. Don't permit distractions in the same room with your loading tools.

I said it in the last chapter about shotshells, but NEVER RELOAD IN HASTE applies just as fully to every other aspect of handloading. Loading in a hurry can mean an unnoticed wrong setting on a powder scale or even the wrong powder in the measure. At best, haste defeats the whole purpose of reloading, which is superior ammunition for your guns. At worst, haste can result in disaster.

Use equipment as the manufacturer intended and do not take shortcuts. Self-explanatory; jury-rigging is usually bad news.

Store powder in a cool dry place. Along with this, one should do the following: Store powder in small quantities in approved containers, away from such combustibles as solvents, inflammable gases, and of course, open flame. Furthermore, keep gunpowder away from children and vice versa.

Never use a powder unless you're positive of its identity. Repeat: *never!* Don't guess, and don't try to identify gunpowder by its physical appearance. Not even an expert can do it. The one and only acceptable identification of a powder is the label on its can, provided it is still in the factory container in which it was originally packaged.

Never smoke while handling powder. Surely this is too obvious to need comment, especially to anyone intelligent enough to read this book.

Never mix gunpowders. Not in a cartridge case and not in a canister. If the latter happens as a result of violations of other safety rules, destroy the resultant mixture. Do *not* attempt to extrapolate a new burning rate for the mix and use it; relative quickness is not all that simple.

Never store small-arms primers in any kind of container except the factory packaging. Period. End of paragraph.

Observe all maximum load warnings in reloading manuals. See my discussion of this in the chapters on powder charging and load development, chapters 8 and 10. A corollary is: *Approach those maximums only from 10 percent below.*

Inspect all cases—rifle, pistol, or shotgun—for condition before loading, and discard any that are less than perfect. Trying to squeeze just one more shot

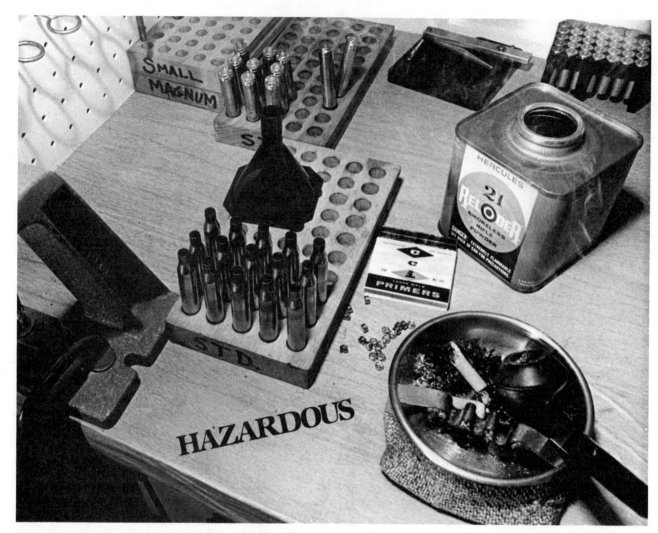

This is a photograph of an accident waiting to happen: loose primers, open powder canisters, and burning tobacco do not mix—a rule so obvious it shouldn't require restatement.

out of weakened brass has spelled catastrophe for more than one reloader. It ain't worth it.

Watch for signs of high pressure while working up a handload. This means extraction difficulty (however slight), flattened primers, cratered primers, ironed-out headstamps, polished headstamps, ejector marks, case-head expansion, and excessive recoil and muzzle blast. And anything else whatever that strikes you as abnormal about the load.

Develop a routine in reloading to guard against mistakes, just in case your attention does occasionally wander. You'll form habits at the loading bench anyway; it's just as easy to establish well-thought-out habits for safety as slipshod ones that may permit you to slip into dangerous practices without realizing it. This rule really applies as much to shooting your handloads as to making them up. For example, a personal rule of never having more than one ammunition box open on the shooting bench at one time may prevent your trying to fire the wrong cartridge in a rifle.

Safety in handloading goes, of course, further than just common sense, even though most of us are sen-

sible enough to figure out what we should and should not be doing. Still, sometimes it's helpful to tune into the suggestions of those who serve as watchdogs of handloading, the Sporting Arms and Ammunition Manufacturers' Institute, or SAAMI. They have compiled the following list of do's and don'ts for the handloader. Some of their rules more or less repeat some I have just given, but information of this sort can certainly bear repeating. After all, we're talking about avoiding some potentially serious accidents.

SAAMI DO'S AND DON'TS FOR HANDLOADERS
GENERAL
- Follow *only* loading recommendations of a recognized current handloading guide. Better still, check two guides. Components and propellants change and old recommendations may be dangerous.
- Don't use word-of-mouth loading data without

checking a recognized current handloading guide.

- Have the headspace of your firearm checked by a competent gunsmith at regular intervals, preferably by a factory-authorized repair station.
- Examine fired cases for signs of excessive pressure, such as primer gas leaks, excessive primer flattening, loose primers, expanded heads or bodies, and side-wall stretching.
- Investigate and determine the cause of any unusual or abnormal condition or appearance before continuing any operation.
- Keep all components and loaded rounds positively identified.
- Keep your work area and handloading bench scrupulously clean at all times. Immediately clean up any spillage of powder, primers, etc.
- *Do not* chamber a round that resists easy closing of the bolt or action. The cartridge is too long or large in diameter and high pressure may develop.
- *Do not* forget that a maximum load in your rifle may be dangerous in another one of your rifles or in a friend's rifle even if it is the same make, model, caliber, etc.
- Components suitable for lead-shot loads are *not* adaptable to steel-shot loads.
- The interchange of steel shot for lead results in dangerously high pressures that may damage shotguns. Ball bearings or steel air rifle shot are not suitable for shotshell loads. They are much harder than steel shot.
- Keep all components out of the reach of children.
- Keep accurate, detailed records of all loads.
- Do not load with charges that measure out to more than 10 percent below minimum recommendations.
- Cartridge cases should be clean and dry before reloading and before firing. Oily cases greatly increase thrust against the bolt face.
- *Do not* fire form factory cartridges in lengthened chambers. The excessive headspace is likely to be dangerous.
- Be extremely careful to identify properly wildcat cases since the headstamp does not identify the new cartridge, which may have a larger diameter bullet than the original cartridge.
- Do not use too much heat to dry cases to avoid softening the brass.
- Do not use brass cases that have been in or near a fire.

COMPONENTS

Bullets. Be sure that they are the recommended diameter and weight. Keep bullet calibers and weights in separate and accurately marked containers.

Do not mix or interchange bullets from various manufacturers in the same reloading formula.

Don't substitute calibers, use only that which your gun is chambered for exactly, e.g., .300 Winchester Magnum is not a .300 Savage.

Primers. Inspect for presence of anvils before seating. Store only in original manufacturers' package. Keep a minimum amount on your loading bench. Remove unused primers from your loading tool after each session and return to the original package for storage.

Keep out of reach of children.

Store in a cool dry place.

Do not store primers in bulk. Mass detonation may occur. Use only the brand of primers specified in the loading recommendations.

Cases. Do not mix brands—case volume may be different affecting loading density and pressure. Inspect for cracks, splits, stretch marks, separations, etc. after firing and before reloading. Do not load damaged or defective cases. Do not ream or enlarge primer flash holes.

Examine fired shotshells for head damage, tube splits, pinholes, and location of basewad before reloading. Discard defective cases. Discard cases that show leakage around the primer or battery cup.

Do not mix shells with high and low basewads.

Do not mix brands of cases—volumes may be different.

Powder. Store in a cool, dry place in the original container in an approved storage cabinet. Keep container closed except when pouring.

Keep powder out of reach of children.

Have only one type and speed on your bench at one time to avoid mixing types.

Keep a minimum amount of powder in the loading area.

Never mix powders.

Don't use any powder when you are unsure of its identity. Do not use any powder that appears discolored or is giving off fumes.

Wads. Use only the specific type listed in the recommendations.

Do not mix or interchange types as pressure levels can be affected.

Don't mix powders of the same type designation made by different companies. DuPont IMR 4350 is not the same as Hodgdon's H 4350.

Shot. Check weight of charge thrown by your measure or bar to be sure it conforms to the recommendations.

LOADING OPERATIONS

Avoid distractions while performing any of the loading operations.

Keep all matches and smoking materials out of the loading area.

Do not smoke in the loading area because of primer residue or powder that might ignite.

Decapping. Use proper decapping pin to avoid distorting or enlarging the flash hole. Examine flash holes for roundness, burrs and enlargement before repriming. Do not remove live primers by driving out of the case with a sharp hammer blow. Decap in a press slowly.

Resizing. Lubricate sparingly to avoid oil dents in the shoulder area of the case. Some lubricant must be used to prevent scratches from dirt on the cases and in the dies.

Check overall case length and trim the mouth when case elongates beyond recommended length. Check neck wall thickness and ream or turn to original thickness to assure adequate clearance between case neck and chamber.

Be sure that the resizing die is properly adjusted so that the shoulder of the case is not set back too far producing excessive clearance between the shoulder of the case and the chamber.

Priming. Inspect pockets and clean before inserting new primers.

Seat primers slowly with a punch that conforms to the profile of the primer to flush or slightly below the case head. Do not prime cases with a hammer or mallet. It is a dangerous practice. The object is to seat the legs of the primer anvil on the bottom of the primer pocket. Case should be held by the rim or on a vented punch because a primer may fire accidentally.

Discard cases in which the primer is loose in the pocket.

After each loading session wipe base of the tool with a slightly oily rag to pick up any primer mixture dust.

Do not use pistol primers for rifle cartridges or rifle primers in pistol or revolver cartridges. The thicker primer cup of rifle primers may cause misfires in pistols, while the thinner cup of pistol primers may pierce or blank at the higher pressure levels of rifle cartridges.

Do not use pistol or revolver or rifle primers in shotshells. The priming charge is inadequate for proper ignition of the powder. A transparent shield of lucite or equivalent is recommended between the loading machine and the operator.

Use only a well-designed and constructed tool.

Seating of primers with a hammer and punch is dangerous.

Powder Charging. Inspect the inside of all cases for foreign objects before dropping a charge into the case.

If a powder measure is used, the first five charges thrown by the measure should be weighed on a reliable scale and checked against the recommendations. Periodic checks for weight should be made to be sure that uniform weights are being thrown.

Examine charged cases to be sure that no gross errors in charging have been made, i.e., double charges or empties. A simple powder height gauge is recommended.

Start with the minimum charge recommended and watch for pressure signs on the fired cases from your firearm before increasing.

Do not load more than one charge per case.

Bullet Seating. Seat bullets to the length recommendations only. Pressures are affected by cartridges that are either too long or too short.

If cartridges are to be used in either box or tubular magazines, a mouth crimp is recommended to prevent lengthening or shortening due to recoil.

Be sure bullets are tight in the neck to be sure that the bullet will not pull out if a loaded round is extracted.

Do not load by changing bullets in loaded rounds even if the weights are the same.

After loading shotshells, the crimps should be inspected for uniform depth. Excessive length variation may indicate a loading error that could be dangerous.

Do not seal the crimp with tape.

IN CLOSING

Reloading centerfire ammunition ranks far below children's toys as a source of accidental injury. Overall, it's a remarkably safe pastime, especially considering the volatile nature of some of the components being handled. The potential for accidents is inherent in the man and not in the hobby, equipment, or materials. By the same token, *you* are your own margin of safety—and mine, if I happen to be shooting on the next bench at the rifle range. And, since I happen to value both readers and my scalp very dearly, I trust you'll heed these safety rules.

See you at the range.

Appendix: Sources of Supplies

Below are addresses of sources of handloading tools and components mentioned in this book. Some may supply you directly by mail. Others may instead offer names of dealers near you. Since phone numbers change more frequently than addresses, we've omitted phone numbers. If you prefer to phone, either consult your information operator or the annually updated "Directory of the Arms Trade" in *Gun Digest*. (Addresses of ballistic computer software suppliers begin on page 97.)

Accurate Arms Co., Inc., (Propellents Div.), Rt. 1, Box 167, McEwen, TN 37101

Alox Corp., P.O. Box 517, Niagara Falls, NY 14302

Ballistic Products, Inc., 2105 Daniels St., Long Lake, MN 55356

Barnes Bullets, Inc., P.O. Box 215, American Fork, UT 84003

Belding & Mull, Inc., 100 N. 4th St., Philipsburg, PA 16866

B.E.L.L., Brass Extrusion Laboratories, Ltd., 800 W. Maple Lane, Bensenville, IL 60106

Bitterroot Bullet Co., Box 412, Lewiston, ID 83501

Bofors (See Hercules)

Bonanza (See Forster Products)

Browning (General Offices), Rt. 1, Morgan, UT 84050

Brown Precision Co., 7786 Molinos Ave., Los Molinos, CA 96055

Camdex, Inc., 2330 Alger, Troy, MI 48083

CCI (See Omark Industries)

C-H Tool & Die Corp., 106 N. Harding St., Owen, WI 54460

J. Dewey Mfg. Co., 186 Skyview Dr., Southbury, CT 06488

Dillon Precision Products, Inc., 7442 E. Butherus Dr., Scottsdale, AZ 85260

Division Lead Co., 7742 W. 61st Pl., Summit, IL 60502

Dixie Gun Works, Union City, TN 38261

Dynamit Nobel of America, Inc., 105 Stonehurst Court, Northvale, NJ 07647

Eley-Kynoch, ICI-America, Wilmington, DE 19897

English PAK Tool, 25238, S.E. 32d St., Issaquah, WA 98027

Federal Cartridge Co., 900 Ehlen Dr., Anoka, MN 55303

Forster Products Inc., 82 E. Lanark Ave., Lanark IL 61046

Golden Powder Int'l, 860 S. Los Angeles St., Suite 220, Los Angeles, CA 90014

Hanned Precision, P.O. Box, 2888, Sacramento, CA 95812

Robert W. Hart & Son, Inc., 401 Montgomery St., Nescopeck, PA 18635

Hensley & Gibbs, Box 10, Murphy, OR 97533

Hercules Inc., Hercules Plaza, Wilmington, DE 19894

Hoch, P.O. Box 132, Fruita, CO 81521

Hodgdon Powder Co., Inc., P.O. Box 2932, Shawnee Mission, KS 66201

Hollywood, 10642 Arminta St., Sun Valley, CA 91352

Hornady Mfg. Co., P.O. Drawer 1848, Grand Island, NE 68802

Huntington's, 601 Oro Dam Blvd., Oroville, CA 95965

IMR Powder Co., 122 Lakeside Dr., Glassboro, NJ 08028

J&J Custom Bullet, 1210 El Rey Ave., El Cajon, CA 92021

Lead Bullets Technology (LBT), Box 357, Cornville, AZ 86325

Lee Precision Inc., 4275 Hwy. U, Hartford, WI 53027

Lyman Products Corp., Rte. 147, Middlefield, CT 06455

Marian Powley, Petra Lane, R.R.1, Eldridge, IA 52748

Marquart Precision Co., P.O. Box 1740, Prescott, AZ 86302

Mayville Eng. Co., 715 South St., Mayville, WI 53050

MEC, Inc. (See Mayville Eng. Co.)

Mequon Reloading Corp., P.O. Box 253, Mequon, WI 53092

Miniature Machine Co., 210 East Poplar, Deming, NM 88030

MMC (See Miniature Machine Co.)

MTM Moulded Prods. Co., 3370 Obco Ct., Dayton, OH 45414

N.E.I. (See Northeast Industrial Inc.)

Non-Toxic Components, Inc., P.O. Box 4202, Portland, OR 97208

NORMA (See Federal Cartridge Co.)

Northeast Industrial Inc. (N.E.I.), 405 N. Canyon Blvd., Canyon City, OR 97820

Nosler Bullets Inc., 107 S.W. Columbia, Bend, OR 97702

Oehler Research, Inc., P.O. Box 9135, Austin, TX 78766

Ohaus scale (See RCBS)

Omark Industries, P.O. Box 856, Lewiston, ID 83501

Pacific Intl. Merchandising Corp., 2215 "J" St., Sacramento, CA 95818

Pacific Tool Co., Ordnance Plant Rd., Grand Island, NE 68801

Ponsness-Warren, P.O. Box 8, Rathdrum, ID 83858

Pyrodex (See Hodgdon Powder Co. Inc.)

Quartz-Lok, 13137 N. 21st Lane, Phoenix, AZ 85029

Ransom Handgun Rests, Ransom Intl. Corp., P.O. Box 3845, Prescott, AZ 86302

RCBS, Inc., Box 1919, Oroville, CA 95965

R.D.P. Tool Co. Inc., 49162 McCoy Ave., East Liverpool, OH 49174

Redding Inc., 1089 Starr Rd., Cortland, NY 13045

Remco, 1404 Whitesboro St., Utica, NY 13502

Remington-Peters, 1007 Market St., Wilmington, DE 19898

Rooster Laboratories, P.O. Box 412514, Kansas City, MO 64141

RWS (See Dynamit Nobel)

SAECO (See Redding)

Shiloh Products, 37 Potter St., Farmingdale, NY 11735

Sierra Bullets Inc., 10532 So. Painter Ave., Santa Fe Springs, CA 90670

Speer Products, Box 856, Lewiston, ID 83501

Sportsman Supply Co., Marshall, MO 65340

SSK Industries, Rt. 1, Della Drive, Bloomingdale, OH 43910

Star Machine Works, 418 10th Ave., San Diego, CA 92101

Taracorp Industries, 16th & Cleveland Blvd., Granite City, IL 62040

Texan Reloaders, Inc., 444 So. Cips St., Watseka, IL 60970

Thompson-Center Arms, P.O. Box 2426, Rochester, NH 03867

Tru Square Metal Products, P.O. Box 585, Auburn, WA 98002

Weatherby, Inc., 2781 Firestone Blvd., South Gate, CA 90280

L.E. Wilson, Inc., 404 Pioneer Ave., Cashmere, WA 98815

Winchester/Olin, 427 N. Shamrock St., East Alton, IL 62024

J.C.L. Zigor Corp., P.O. Box 238, Kearneysville, WV 25430

Index